ADOLESCENT DEVELOPMENT

A PSYCHOLOGICAL INTERPRETATION

Guy J. Manaster

THE UNIVERSITY OF TEXAS AT AUSTIN

F. E. PEACOCK PUBLISHERS, INC.

ITASCA, ILLINOIS

ILLUSTRATIONS BY MICHAEL CRAWFORD
with additional drawings for
openings of chapters 6, 7 and 14 by
Shari Margolis

ook is to be returned on or before
last date stamped below.

CONTENTS

INTRODUCTION

The generation and flow of scientific information in contemporary America is so great and fast that an author of a text has in hand, at the time a book is published, studies and data that were not out when the final manuscript was submitted to the publisher. Data related to adolescence are produced at such an enormous pace that keeping up with them is a full-time job. Fortunately or unfortunately, keeping up with significant data and findings is not as taxing. A tremendous portion of new information supports the old information. New data support existing theories. New ideas do arise from year to year, but ideas and findings that force major changes in our understandings are not frequent.

This book comes out about 10 years after my previous book on this topic. This book, *Adolescent Development*, is built on the previous book, *Adolescent Development and the Life Tasks*, for the reasons just given: there is new information about adolescence and adolescents and some of this information alters the understanding we had. Moreover, my understanding of the field has, I hope and feel, developed, and therefore this book is my attempt to update understanding of the period called adolescence and the people who are adolescent.

This text is not just a review of "facts," findings, and theories about adolescents. I have tried to integrate what is known and conjectured about adolescents into a working, practical framework, so that the text moves from facts and findings through theories to a variety of possibilities about adolescence as a time of life and adolescents as individual persons living through that time.

Throughout the text are diagrams that attempt to visually portray the relationships, corelationships, and influences discussed. I had thought that if we could publish these diagrams as transparencies, they could be used for discussing each contribution. Then, as each topic was read and discussed, one transparency could be placed over the other to illustrate our growing under-standings and the complexity of the field. Unfortunately, by the time we put the final transparency over all the others, we would have so many lines and arrows overlapping and intersecting that we could no longer make sense of any of them. Nonetheless, such an outcome would not just be the result of a silly idea, but would represent the state of the field of psychology.

On the one hand, psychological research has made extraordinary strides in explaining particular aspects of human thought and behavior, but when you put all of these parts together (as in laying the transparencies on top of each other) you do not get a person, you cannot explain the individual. You can better explain people in general and you can better explain each facet, depending on how you break people into parts. But to understand people, you need another view. Therefore, on the other hand, some psychological theory views individuals holistically — not in parts or as the sum of the parts, but in their individual entirety. Then the trick, or the task, for psychologists, or anyone trying to understand people, is to hold both views in mind so that each informs the other. I try to do this in this text. I attempt to provide some balance by adhering to a holistic view in the face of discrete empirical data, and vice versa. In that respect, I try to tell a story in this book, while including the scientific basis for the "facts" of the story. The story may be applicable to any life and generally to all lives at the time called adolescence for the peo-ple called adolescents.

The organization of this text is designed to promote the understanding I hope the story conveys. The chapters in the first section present the develop-mental facts and theories about what goes on within people during the period called adolescence. These chapters tell how people change physically, cognitively, and in their thinking about the world during these years. The second section talks about the changes and consistencies during adolescence in the way people see and feel themselves — their personality, their self, and their identity. The third section deals with the life tasks of adolescence — in effect, where the adolescent lives — and thereby the adolescent at home, with friends, in school, in work, and in love. Whereas the first sections discuss "normal" adolescence and adolescents, the last section, one long chapter, is devoted to what I call the 3 Ds — the three major deviancies of delinquency, drugs, and disturbances (pathology or psychopathology). In the chapter on the deviancies I try to explain the basic "facts" and theories about why some adolescents become other than "normal" in these ways. I also posit possibili-ties, this time in relating the notions raised about normal youngsters to these deviancies. The purpose in this chapter, as in the rest of the book, is to help the reader understand adolescents in general, and maybe a specific adolescent.

The plot of the story then appears relatively simple. Each person grows to a time of life, adolescence, in which certain changes occur for everybody and some changes occur for some. And during that period of life, each person fulfills the role of adolescent as part of his or her other roles. So one goes from being just a son or daughter to being an adolescent son or adolescent daughter. And in our society, at least, one plays the role of adolescent as one understands it and uses the role for his or her own interests as he or she understands those also. The outcomes of the story are extremely varied. The changes that occur in adolescence are positive for some and negative for others, more beneficial for some than for others, and of little or no personal consequence for some. The role of being an adolescent is easy for some, hard for others, devastating for some, and of little or no consequence for others. The story, then, is unique for each person who lives it. The commonalities, developmental and social, influence each person in a unique way. The purpose of this story is to tell what we know may influence people at this time of life so that we can understand the ways in which they are similar while seeing how the range of influences promote their differences.

My own education in the field has been dramatically extended during the 25 years since I started studying adolescence and 10 years since writing the first text. As I wrote the first book, our oldest child was coming into adolescence. As I write this book, she has left her teenage years behind and, regardless of the definitional issues discussed in Chapter 1, as a married woman and teacher no longer considers herself an adolescent. However, we now still have two other late teenagers. Our three teenagers have taught me two basic facts:

1. The developments in adolescence that have been identified are crucial, yet may be easily seen in individual adolescents and are helpful to know both for the adolescent and the adult dealing with the adolescent.
2. The problems identified as part of adolescence are merely potential problems related to the physical and cognitive developments and the adolescent's social situation, but with knowledge, understanding, common sense, and love, the problems need be no more than everyday concerns, as everyday as those we all meet as normal challenges of living each stage of life.

Thus, for all they have taught me, for the joy of their being, with my wishes for them always, I dedicate this book to our kids—Kim, Rex, and Dawn.

Adolescence— What It Is

CHAPTER 1

THE FIELD: AN APPROACH

To begin a serious text on a humorous note may be unusual, but will, I hope, set a healthy tone. As Nicholas Murray Butler, the revered former president of Columbia University, said, "The one serious conviction that a man should have is that nothing is to be taken too seriously."

So to begin, it is said, "Chivalry is not dead. Only the people who practice it are." So too, adolescence is not new — only the people who recognize it are. And at that, they are not that new.

Aries (1962) notes that adolescence is mentioned in a 13th-century translation from Latin of ancient Byzantine writers. Jean Jacques Rousseau, in 1762, formally proposed the idea of adolescence as we now generally understand it. G. Stanley Hall's *Adolescence* (1904) really signified the beginning of a new scientific field — adolescent psychology.

So, although there have been, through history, people of the age, stage, attitude, aptitude, size, shape, or place we call adolescence, this has not been formally and generally recognized and studied until this century. This makes sense, and is explained, if we substitute the word *adolescent* for *child* in the following quote by William Kessen, an important child psychologist at Yale. He wrote: "Not only are American [adolescents] shaped and marked by the larger cultural forces of political maneuverings, practical economics, and implicit ideological commitments (a new enough recognition), [adolescent] psychology is itself a peculiar cultural invention that moves with the tidal sweeps of the larger culture in ways that we understand at best dimly and often ignore" (1979, p. 815).

We study adolescence today because adolescence as a distinct period of life has become a social fact in developed nations over the course of the last

150 years. Compulsory education, child labor laws and organized labor, and the separate development of the juvenile legal system established adolescence as a social fact in America (Bakan, 1975). Prior to adolescence as a social fact, the developments, physiological and cognitive, no doubt still occurred, but the social setting that created the distinctiveness of the period did not.

> The important point to be remembered is that the developmental period of adolescence does not exist outside of the social factors which caused its emergence. Psychological researchers not cognizant of the relationship between those factors and the concepts they are developing are in danger of making attributions to the adolescent which exist because of societal conditions. These attributions are, of course, important. As long as societal conditions remain relatively static, they are valid and useful. They are not, however, intrinsic to the persons themselves. They are intrinsic to the person living under a particular set of societal constraints and dictates. (Proefrock, 1981, pp. 857–58)

Adolescence, and the psychology of adolescence, can, then, only be fully understood using an approach that takes notice of the social context in which changing people, adolescents, live. This demands that a broader view must be taken. This view, which incorporates the psychological, sees each part of life as part of a whole, the person continually developing throughout life. Aptly, this view is known as the life span human development approach, or perspective. Richard Lerner summarizes how the life span human development perspective influences the way in which adolescent development is understood:

> First, developmental change is a potentially life-span phenomenon. Second, such change involves a contextual view of the person, that is, that the person is reciprocally embedded in his or her world. Third, such change therefore involves adaptations of changing people to their changing world. Fourth, adolescence, . . . especially involves changes within the person, in the person's social context, and therefore between the person and the context. Thus, fifth, not only is adolescence a key time within which to focus research in order to substantiate this view of development, but in turn, in order to understand adolescence one must appreciate the multiple changes involved in development at this time of life, and the integrative pressures on the person in order for adaptation to occur. (1981, p. 259)

The life span human developmental perspective will be used in this book. This will next be seen in the definitions presented below, which cover the full range of behavioral science views of adolescence, including those of sociologists, educators, and psychologists of varying stripes. But before asking what adolescence is, the next few lines by a historian might be mulled.

They apply to adolescence as well as adulthood and reinforce the recency of our science and viewpoint:

> It is an interesting commentary on our culture that we find ourselves asking: What does adulthood mean? From an historian's vantage point, what is arresting is that we should be asking a question that would have made so little sense to our forebears. (Jordan, 1978, p. 189)

WHAT IS ADOLESCENCE?

Hall (1904) described adolescence as a period of "storm and stress," beginning at puberty, around age 12 or 13, and ending when full adult status has been attained, by ages 22 to 25. Hall defines the beginning of adolescence by a physiological change and the end by psychosocial change.

Since Hall's initial efforts, a multitude of definitions of adolescence have been presented. Dorothy Rogers traces the term *adolescence* to its Latin root, *adolescere*, which means "to grow to maturity." She defines adolescence as "a process rather than a period, a process of achieving the attitudes and beliefs needed for effective participation in society" (1972b, p. 9). She points out that these definitions fall into categories: adolescence as a period of physical development, as an age span, as a discrete developmental stage, as a sociocultural phenomenon, and as a way of life or a state of mind.

Looking at a selection of definitions of adolescence, we see that few, if any, rely solely on physical change, although many definitions begin with a physical base and then expand to more general concepts. For instance, Anderson says that adolescence "is divided into an early and late period, extends from puberty to the attainment of full height and weight and the cessation of growth. It is the period in which the person moves out of the home circle and becomes physically and mentally independent" (1949, p. 64).

Two good catchall definitions that push the limits of the psychological definition are:

> Adolescence is the bridge between childhood and adulthood. It is a time of rapid development: of growing to sexual maturity, discovering one's real self, defining personal values, and finding one's vocational and social directions. It is also a time of testing: of pushing against one's capabilities and the limitations as posed by adults. (Ambron, 1975, p. 393)

> The adolescent phase is heralded by the development of secondary sexual characteristics, which first lead to mastery experiences and then eventually create the mature adult. We regard adolescence as a period in which mood swing occurs, peer group acceptance is critical, and turmoil is expected. Out

of all this the ego solidifies and the young adult emerges. (Gilberg, 1978, p. 89)

Erik Erikson similarly notes that "adolescence is a period of rapid change — physical, physiological, psychological, and social; a time when all sameness and continuities relied on earlier are more or less questioned again" (1963, p. 261). Erikson points to both social and cognitive change aspects, as does Piaget: "The adolescent, unlike the child, is an individual who thinks beyond the present and forms theories about everything, delighting especially in considerations of that which is not" (1947, p. 148). Piaget and Inhelder note that adolescence is "the age of great ideals and the beginning of theories, as well as the time of simple present adaptation to reality" (1969, p. 130).

In this same tradition, Elkind describes early adolescence, "roughly the years from 12 to 16", as

> an allegro of rapid growth that transforms the child into an adult. It is the period in which the young person attains adult stature and appearance. By the time the adolescent is 16, he has attained sexual maturity, in the physical sense, at any rate, and is capable of procreation. Finally, during the years from 12 to 16, the adolescent develops formal or abstract thinking abilities that permit him to engage in scientific and philosophical thinking, to plan realistically for the future, and to understand the historical past. (1971, p. 93)

These general and more cognitive definitions of adolescence illustrate the extent, maybe the extreme, development that is thought to describe and define adolescents. Defining adolescence as an age span, a review of over 100 definitions found the earliest age for onset of adolescence as 8 and the latest age for the end of adolescence to be around 25. A more conservative estimate is given by Kennedy: "Adolescence: the transitional years between puberty and adulthood in human development; usually covers the teens" (1975, p. 489).

It is relatively easy to associate ages with the beginning of adolescence if we use physical change as the indicator. However, because there is no physical event marking the end of adolescence, the legal demarcation of adulthood has been used to signify the end of adolescence. This approach has problems, as can be seen in two definitions, at two different times, by Hurlock:

> Adolescence can be described as the years extended from the time the child becomes sexually mature, about age 13 and 14 for boys, to legal maturity, at 21 years of age. (1964, 28)

As it is used today, the term adolescence has a broader meaning and includes mental, emotional, and social as well as physical maturity. Legally, in the United States, the individual is mature at age 18. (1975, p. 173)

It would be hard to conclude that legislation lowering the age of maturity would effectively decrease the time it takes people to go through all of the changes attributed to adolescence. Laws do not arbitrarily end adolescence.

"One can view adolescence as a change in group belongingness. The individual has been considered by himself and by others as a child. Now he does not wish to be treated as such" (Seidman, 1953, p. 33). Hollingshead calls the adolescent years a period in life "when the society in which he functions ceases to regard him . . . as a child and does not accord him full adult status, roles and functions" (1949, pp. 6–7). Landis states that "viewed from a sociological perspective, adolescence comprises that period in life when the individual is in the process of transfer from the dependent, irresponsible age of childhood to the self-reliant, responsible age of adulthood. The maturing child seeks freedom, and in finding it, becomes accountable to society" (1945, p. 23). "Adolescence can be viewed as a paradoxical period. On one hand, it is a preparatory stage for entrance into the mainstream of society. At the same time, there are no clear-cut rules on *how* to make the transition from adolescence to adulthood, nor are there rules specifying *when* the transition is complete" (Hotaling et al., 1978, p. 401).

These same definitions are put in the distinct stage and sociocultural phenomenon categories by Schulz, who says that adolescence is a "normative crisis when the young adult is permitted to experiment with various adult roles without having to pay the consequences of full public responsibility" (1972, p. 323). A general, but distinct, stage definition by Eisenberg states: "Adolescence may be defined as a critical period of human development manifested at the biological, psychological, and social levels of interaction, of variable onset and duration, but marking the end of childhood and setting the foundation for maturity" (1969, p. 21).

A distinct stage definition in the psychoanalytic tradition by Blos (1962) recognizes "adolescence as the terminal stage of the fourth phase of psychosexual development, the genital phase, which had been interrupted by the latency period" (p. 1). "The term adolescence is used to denote the psychological processes of adaptation to the condition of pubescence" (p. 2), "the sum total of all attempts at adjustment to the stage of puberty" (p. 11). This psychoanalytic interpretation of adolescence is particularly interesting in that there are no upper-age bounds on the distinct stage. In a sense, this definition could accommodate the behavior, often called adolescent, if not childish, of the 40- or 50-year-old who divorces and appears less responsible, possibly promiscuous, as he "plays around." If you are reading this during the fall semester, you may wish to use this definition to characterize the behavior of some alumni at Saturday's football game, wondering if their behaviors are "attempts at adjustment to the stage of puberty." And then again, you may not.

UNIVERSALITY OF ADOLESCENCE

When a definition relies on physical development, i.e., puberty, as the onset or indicator of adolescence, a universality is implied — everyone, everywhere goes through it. When a definition relies on or includes theoretically related psychological correlates or manifestations, such as storm and stress, universality may be implied by the theory but extensive empirical testing is necessary for validation. When a definition refers to age span and/or sociocultural phenomena, universality is not implied, because the meanings of the age period and/or sociocultural phenomena are particular to each society and culture and vary among societies and cultures. When definitions are general and, therefore, include physical, psychological, age, and sociocultural phenomena, they may have universal applicability as they describe presence or absence and extent of the various phenomena in each culture, but they do not necessarily speak to the universality of adolescence itself, as described.

Kiell agrees with Benedict (1934) that "adolescence is a physiological state 'as definitely characterized by domestic explosions and rebellion as typhoid is marked by fever' " (1964), p. 12). Bloch and Niederhoffer indicate the universality of adolescence, saying that a period of striving for adult status occurs in all cultures, producing similar experiences and reactions. Just how intense and vehement the expression of the adolescent experience is in each culture depends on factors such as "the general societal attitudes toward adolescence, the duration of the adolescent period itself, and the degree with which the society tends to facilitate patterns, ceremonials, rites, and rituals, and socially support emotional and intellectual preparation" (1958, p. 17). They go on to say that if a society does not provide for the transition to adulthood, the adolescent group itself will generate forms of behavior and rituals to serve the same function.

Overall our society has provided little emotional, intellectual, and ceremonial support during the long period of adolescence to lessen the intensity of the adolescent experience. Among some subgroups, however, ceremonies and structures have been developed that give adolescents a secure status and a set of responsibilities that appear adultlike. The rituals and structures of some of these subgroups may appear negative, as in initiation and organization of gangs, or childish, as in pledging and initiation into fraternities and sororities, but they do serve the purpose of securing status and defining cooperative responsibilities.

Ceremonies and structures have been developed within some religious denominations that serve, it may be said — positively, the same purposes. Often the adolescents who participate in the activities of their religion seem different, or "straight," to their nonactive peers. The nonactive peers, not having a subgroup support system, are at the mercy of the prevailing societal attitudes. They are the ones who delve into the behaviors and rituals of adolescence that are developed by the adolescent group itself. As part of no other group, and with questions of where they belong, they do what their peers do.

Without a clear feeling of belonging, and indicators and behavior that reinforce that feeling, adolescents grasp at symbols. Clothes have long been such a symbol for adolescents (as well as for adults, but they are a more important symbol for many adolescents). To these adolescents, if you wear the "in" clothes you feel that you fit in, or at least that there is a chance that you might be able to get in. It is a painful experience for these adolescents when they do not have the kind of clothes their friends consider right. They have the feeling, or at least communicate this position to their parents, that what they wear, or don't wear, is what separates them from the others.

Bloch and Niederhoffer seem to be saying that if the society does not consider adolescence important, major, or lengthy, while clearly marking the entrance into adulthood of emotionally and intellectually prepared individuals, the intensity of the adolescent experience may be greatly lessened but the experience will still occur. In American society, where the opposite conditions exist, the adolescent experience occurs with a vengeance for many.

INSTANCES OF NO ADOLESCENCE

There are examples in the anthropological or cross-cultural literature of societies in which there is either no adolescent period or no "turbulent" adolescent period. An example is the Arapesh society in New Guinea, where there was an initiation rite for boys at age 13. They were prepared for the initiation, did not become upset or ashamed or self-conscious, and proceeded directly into adulthood (Mead, 1935). Adult status and puberty coincided, and there was no adolescent period in the Arapesh culture.

In a case study of the Cheyenne Indians, Hoebel (1960) points out that "Cheyenne youth have little reason to be rebels-without-a-cause. They slip early into manhood, knowing their contributions are immediately wanted, valued, and ostentatiously rewarded" (p. 93). He attributes this to the basic postulates underlying Cheyenne culture, which are dominant in controlling Cheyenne behavior: "Children (excluding infants) have the same qualities as adults; they lack only experience. . . . Children should, on their level, engage in adult activities. . . . Children become adults as soon as they are physically able to perform adult roles" (p. 99).

Sieg (1971) presents this notion most strongly when she suggests "that the stage of adolescence is not a stage necessary to human development, but is merely a cultural phenomenon — necessary, perhaps, to our culture, but not present in all cultures" (p. 337). She then defines adolescence as "the period of development in human beings that begins when the individual feels that adult privileges are due him which are not being accorded him, and that ends when the full power and social status of the adult are accorded to the individual by his society" (p. 338).

COMPREHENSIVE DEFINITION

Clearly there is some truth to all of the definitions of adolescence given so far. What we are looking for here is a comprehensive definition, one which includes all that is factual and leads us to consider all that might be relevant. Although it is difficult in the social and behavioral sciences to reach agreement and consensus on almost any point, virtually everyone agrees that in America today there is a period of time during which young people are adolescents. That much is fact for a definition of adolescence in America.

Puberty, except precocious puberty, i.e., under age 8, signifies the onset of adolescence. However, for some individuals, the onset of adolescence may occur prior to puberty if a change in group belongingness is forced by the immediate environment and the greater society. That is, a girl, for example, who has not reached puberty but who attends a junior or senior high school where the majority of students are pubescent or postpubescent may (1) think of herself as adolescent, as part of the adolescent group; (2) be thought of by her peers, her teachers, and possibly also her parents as adolescent; (3) begin to take on the attitudes and behaviors she thinks appropriate to this stage; and (4) begin to think about and plan for the future. For prepubescent girls, taking on the "in" clothes, fads, and fashions may be an indicator of the process of identifying with the adolescent group. An intriguing indicator of the pressure to belong and conform, as well as the child-adolescent's wish to belong and conform, is the optimistic use of a bra before it is necessary — what is sometimes referred to as a training bra.

Boys in the same position, prepubescent and not as physically mature as their peers, may also take on the attitudes and style they feel are appropriate to being, or pretending to be, adolescent. These boys not only may try to look like older, more mature adolescents through dress and hairstyle, but may also attempt to prove that they are adolescent, worthy participant members of the adolescent group. Proving oneself may, and unfortunately sometimes does, lead the young adolescent boy to reckless, irresponsible, and/or unlawful behavior. Moreover, the less mature boy may be used by the more mature adolescents he emulates and with whom he aspires to associate. "The guys told me to say that to her, . . ." or "to break that window, . . ." or "to smoke that joint," are the kinds of quotes that teachers, principals, and juvenile officers frequently hear from these boys.

The onset of adolescence (see Figure 1.1), then, in an inclusive definition, (1) is based on a physical change, i.e., puberty; (2) may be facilitated by social factors, i.e., change in group belongingness that is perceived or desired; or (3) is defined by age and related social situations, i.e., if you're in eighth grade and 13, you must be an adolescent.

The adolescent period extends (see Figure 1.1) until the individual reaches adult maturity; until he or she is accorded the full power, social status, and responsibilities of the adult; and until he or she becomes physically, mentally, emotionally, socially, and legally independent from the perspective of adult maturity. If we consider adult maturity at a minimal or threshold level, in effect a beginning level, we recognize and allow by definition considerable and continuous growth and development in adulthood. If we consider adult maturity at a high, final level, at some standard of absolute maturity, we not only deny that growth and development will occur in adulthood, but we also seem to eliminate any prospect of anyone's becoming fully mature. That is to say, if we only consider a 20-year-old mature if he or she behaves with the wisdom, calm, and tact of a 60-year-old, we are denying the continual development from 20 to 60 while being disrespectful of the degree of maturity held by the 20-year-old.

The age span implicit in this definition of the onset and end of adolescence obviously varies. In America at this time adolescence usually begins at or after age 10 but not later than 13, and ends by age 18 for some and by the early-to-mid twenties by almost all.

During the period of adolescence, then, the individual is in the process, through learning and testing himself and society, of achieving the attitudes, beliefs, and skills needed to be an effective participating adult in the society. During this same period, it should be noted, the individual is also in the process of living as an adolescent and trying to be, or learn to be, equally effective and as much of a participant in the adolescent peer group as one

PSYCHOLOGICAL CHANGE AND DEVELOPMENT

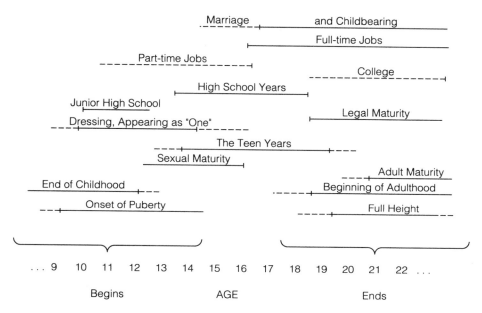

Figure 1.1. Onset and end of adolescence based on the various definitions and descriptions of physical, developmental, social, and psychological changes that mark the start and finish of adolescence

would hope he or she will eventually be in the adult world. In the next section of this chapter, the attitudes, beliefs, and skills that need to be learned — the tasks of adolescence — will be presented and discussed.

But what about the terms that have been used in the definitions of adolescence that have not been included in this "comprehensive definition," such as "storm and stress," "peak in human growth and change," "a time when all is questioned again," "the age of great ideals," "a normative crisis," and so on? Are these terms applicable to adolescence as a stage? Are they applicable to all adolescents? That, in effect, is what the rest of this book is about — to investigate the process of adolescence and the generalizability of the huge array of terms that have been used to describe adolescence and adolescents.

GENERALIZING ABOUT OLDER ADOLESCENTS

The period of adolescence that ends with leaving high school will be the primary focus in this text. In general, reaching legal adulthood at the age of 18 coincides with finishing high school. After high school the qualitative differences in the social situation of adolescents are so dramatic and extensive that consideration of a single group called adolescents after that point is probably not valid or valuable.

Most adolescents live very similarly as they proceed through late high school or finish high school. They attend school, live at home as members of a family, and are dependent on a parent or parents for most or all financial support. On leaving high school, however, a great variety of life-styles are available to the late adolescent. Some adolescents, on finishing high school, by virtue of their age and adult legal status, and also possibly their occupational and marital status, consider themselves and are considered adults. Other adolescents, on finishing high school, look ahead to a long period as official students in college and postgraduate school. They may not wish to, but they may also not be able to, take on many of the responsibilities of adulthood for some time. Yet other adolescents leave high school before finishing and spend a long time without any of the symbols of adulthood — occupation, family, independence, and so on — except age.

The period of late adolescence is sometimes referred to as a separate time called "youth," which would seem to apply only to those post–high school adolescents who have not taken on the responsibilities of adulthood. Keniston (1975) proposes themes that characterize the "youth" stage which are the same as themes used earlier in the definitions of adolescence — themes such as tension between self and society, alternating feelings of isolation and idealism, youth-specific identities, and youthful countercultures. Are these the same for high school adolescents and post–high school youth? Are they of equal import? Are these themes of importance only to high school students who will become "youth," i.e., who will not immediately take on adult responsibilities? How does the future, in the sense of late adolescence, affect the themes of the early adolescent? These, and other questions of this type, will be investigated in this attempt to understand adolescence through high school.

DEMANDS OF ADOLESCENCE

It can be said that two broad demands are made on the individual during the period of adolescence. First, in keeping with the thrust of the definitions that stressed socialization into adulthood, the adolescent must make the transition from child to adult — he or she must come out at the end of adolescence prepared to be an adult. Second, and probably more pressing on a day-to-day basis for the individual adolescent, he or she must "make it," succeed, as an adolescent.

The conflict between these two demands presents itself to college students frequently enough. For instance, consider the hurdles of college and the reward for completion of these hurdles. You have to put up with the requirements and the basics in order to get into the courses and programs you feel you need to end up doing what you want. You have to, as the psychologists say, delay gratification, weighing and balancing immediate reward with future gratification. And you must analyze the present presses and meanings of your behavior in terms of the long-term, future presses.

The adolescent through high school must also make these kinds of evaluations. Yet the younger adolescent probably does not know it. The younger adolescent has little or no experience planning and thinking for a long-term future. Therefore the dual demands, to *be* an adolescent and to *become* an adult, are problematic.

In order to deal with the present and future natures of the demands of adolescence, two conceptions of these demands will be merged throughout this book. The *developmental tasks*—those demands placed on persons in one stage to foster satisfaction and accomplishment at the next stage—and the *life tasks*—those areas of life that demand attention and effective coping at all times of life—will be looked at together in order to understand the process and presses of adolescence.

LIFE TASKS AND DEVELOPMENTAL TASKS

"Is a human like a flower or like an automobile? Are we essentially unitary or are we made up of parts? Are we body/mind or are we body *and* mind? . . . [This text] firmly takes the position that we are indivisible units. Like the flower which came from a single fertilized cell, we are a unity; we are not an assemblage of parts like a machine" (Manaster and Corsini, 1982, p. 2). The position taken herein is that the individual person is, by definition, indivisible—not divisible—of one essence. Nonetheless, for heuristic purposes, in order to further investigation, certain divisions will be used—we will look at parts and divide the indivisible.

The life tasks notion originated by the famous Viennese psychiatrist Alfred Adler and the framework of developmental tasks by the important social scientist and educator Robert J. Havighurst are the heuristics on which this text bases the organization of adolescents' lives and their purposes during the adolescent years.

" 'For the sake of clarity,' Adler divided all the problems of life into three parts: 'problems of behavior towards others, problems of occupation, and problems of love' " (Ansbacher and Ansbacher, 1964, p. 429). These three major problems he termed the life tasks. "Work, society, and sex, Adler and subsequent Adlerians wrote, comprise the three life tasks with which each person must cope and attempt to find solutions" (Dreikurs and Mosak, 1966, p. 18). Put another way, "The human community sets three tasks for every individual. They are: work, which means contributing to the welfare of others, friendship, which embraces social relationships with comrades and relatives, and love, which is the most intimate union" (Dreikurs, 1953, p. 4–5).

Additional life tasks have been suggested. Neufeld (1955) suggested "Four 'S' Problems — Subsistence, Society, Sex and Self." Dreikurs and Mosak (1967) agreed that Adler implied a fourth life task, "getting along with oneself." Moreover, they said that Adler's writings justified a fifth life task, the existential task, which defines "the need to adjust to the problems beyond the mere existence on this earth and to find meaning to our lives, to realize the significance of human existence through transcendental and spiritual involvement" (1966, p 22).

The three basic life tasks as described by Alfred Adler and other Adlerians will often be referred to in this text, while the two proposed additional tasks will be covered obliquely. In order to understand human beings one needs a framework, and Adlerian theory is very useful. A concise statement of the Adlerian position, written by Heinz Ansbacher, was long published (1958–1981) on the inside front cover of the *Journal of Individual Psychology* (now *Individual Psychology*). Alfred Adler's Individual Psychology

> is devoted to a holistic, phenomenological, teleological, field-theoretical, and socially oriented approach. . . . This approach is based on the assumption of the uniqueness, self-consistency, activity, and creativity of the human individual (style of life); an open dynamic system of motivation (striving for a subjectively conceived goal of success); and an innate potentiality for social living (social interest).

In our attempt to understand adolescents, they will, as far as possible with existing theory and data, be viewed as total, complete individuals (holistic), whose own feelings and perspectives (phenomenological) influence their own personal goals (teleological) within their own environments (field-theoretical) as each lives as a member of society, as they must (socially oriented approach).

From this holistic approach, we must grant the interrelatedness of the life tasks. "These three problems are never found apart; they all throw crosslights on the others; and indeed, we can say that they are all aspects of the same situation and the same problem — the necessity for a human being to preserve life and to further life in the environment in which he finds himself" (Adler, 1932, p. 241).

All of the problems, central issues, of life can be included within the three basic and two additional life task headings: love and sex, work and school, friends and community (society), self, and the meaning of life (the existential task). Although the tasks differ in importance for different individuals, from early adolescence to death, all of their problems and all of their efforts are inevitably related to these life tasks. The value of the life task approach rests in allowing us to maintain a holistic view of people while categorizing the goals of their efforts within five distinct but related areas.

The developmental tasks (Havighurst, 1972) provide the specific tasks that must be learned at each age stage in order to cope successfully with the life tasks. Havighurst presents developmental tasks appropriate at each stage, describes the nature of the task, and its biological, psychological, and cultural basis. Havighurst's developmental tasks may be seen, then, as the specific tasks at each age stage which aim at solving the life tasks.

A developmental task is defined as a task that arises at or about a certain period in the life of the individual, the successful achievement of which leads to happiness and success with later tasks, and the failed achievement of which leads to unhappiness in the individual, disapproval by the society, and difficulty with later tasks (Havighurst, 1972, p. 2).

Figure 1.2 illustrates, and the following paragraphs discuss, the relationships among the specific developmental tasks and the general life tasks. As can be seen, most of the developmental tasks are associated with more than one life task. As Adler showed the life tasks to be interrelated, so too the developmental tasks are related to more than one life task. For example, developmental task 1, achieving new and more mature relations with agemates of both sexes, obviously and directly relates to the general life task of friends and community, and somewhat less directly relates to an adolescent's ability in the area of love and sex. But stretching the notion just a bit, one can see how success in this developmental task would affect the adolescent's sense of self and ability to get along in work and school settings. The discussion that follows will speak to the principal associations among the developmental tasks and the life tasks.

Developmental task 1: Achieving new and more mature relations with agemates of both sexes. **Life tasks:** Friends and community (love and sex).

Interacting with peers as equals, rather than as one of a group established from without, and unequal at that, is a new development at adolescence. So-

Developmental Tasks	Life Tasks
1. Achieving new and more mature relations with agemates of both sexes	Friends and community (love and sex)
2. Achieving a masculine or feminine social role	Self, friends and community, love and sex
3. Accepting one's physique and using the body effectively	Self, love and sex
4. Achieving emotional independence of parents and other adults	Self, friends and community (love and sex)
5. Preparing for marriage and family life	Love and sex
6. Preparing for an economic career	Work and school, self
7. Acquiring a set of values and an ethical system as guides to behavior—developing an ideology	Existential (friends and community)
8. Desiring and achieving socially responsible behavior	Friends and community, work and school, existential

Figure 1.2. Developmental tasks and the life tasks with which they are associated

ciety expects, and certainly middle-class parents expect, social development and social success. Middle-class parents and subculture present adolescents with more formal, organized social group opportunities. Nonetheless, through friendships and group belongingness of choice rather than convenience, the adolescent develops in the life task of friends and community. The adolescent keenly feels his or her degree of social success. In the long term the adolescent's success with this developmental task may influence mate selection, occupational choice, sense of self, and the quality of adult social life.

Developmental task 2: Achieving a masculine or feminine social role. **Life tasks:** Self, friends and community, love and sex.

The all-pervasive and rigid sex roles of the past are ebbing and evolving. During this transitional period, the development of a viable conception of oneself as a man or a woman will be more difficult. When there was no choice to be made, the vast majority of people recognized no problem. During this period of change, each adolescent will have to develop for him- or herself a workable notion of sex role. A significant portion of this issue rests within the life task self, but, too, the nature of love and sex relationships, friendships and community roles, and occupational choice will be influenced by one's decisions and effectiveness in this developmental task.

Developmental task 3: Accepting one's physique and using the body effectively. **Life tasks:** Self, love and sex.

The physical changes at adolescence make adolescents reevaluate, rethink, their physique and stature in relation to their peers. The physical changes that occur may not be for the better. In relation to their peers, and their previous sense of their body, their "new" body may not fit. Regardless of how they feel about their changing or new body and physique, within the limits of what physical fitness procedures and beauty aids can do, they are stuck with it. Adjusting to and accepting one's new physical appearance falls primarily within the life task self. Rejecting one's body and not learning how to use it effectively may prohibit, or severely limit, the adolescent's ability to be physically close to another person and thus satisfied in the life task love and sex.

Developmental task 4: Achieving emotional independence of parents and other adults. **Life tasks:** Self, friends and community (love and sex).

Ambivalence marks both parental and adolescent attitudes toward this developmental task. Parents want their children to feel affection for them while becoming independent adults, and their adolescent children want the same for themselves. At the same time, the parents are only too aware of the difficulties and pitfalls that confront the developing adolescent. They lack confidence that their adolescent can succeed without parental help. The adolescent, too, is unsure that he or she can make it alone, but wants to be able to do so.

At best there is give-and-take, at worst rebellion and rejection, in the process of gaining and giving independence. The conflict over independence with continued affection goes on within the self of the adolescent. The more active life task areas of working out this developmental task are with friends and love objects. In cases of excessive or continuing childish dependence, the work and school life task is affected. For whom, self or parents, does the adolescent achieve or choose a career?

Developmental task 5: Preparing for marriage and family life. **Life task:** Love and sex.

Preparing for marriage and family life involves education in the meaning and operation of marriage and long-term relationships, but assumes, for success, the satisfactory solution of two other developmental tasks — satisfactory relations with persons of the opposite sex and emotional independence of parents. As difficult as this love and sex task can be for adolescents who are successfully dealing with the other two developmental tasks, if they are not successful in these other tasks, this one will be even more difficult and painful. Whatever one's definition of marriage and whatever marriage may be in the future, the need for a close sustained relationship with another will maintain. Adolescence is the period in which the initial attempts and learnings to establish this kind of relationship are experienced and practiced.

Developmental task 6: Preparing for an economic career. **Life tasks:** Work and school, self.

The two goals of this task according to Havighurst involve organizing and planning so that one can enter a career and feeling that one can do so. In school, adolescents are in the process of developing their sense of what they can do well and determining what they want to do. For adolescents in high school, although many of them do work for money, school achievement itself is their work. Their habits, attitudes, and successes in school form a basis for their progress into the adult working world. To enthusiastically take a job at any level demands preparation and the feeling that the choice was made on the basis of one's own wishes and perception of abilities.

Developmental task 7: Acquiring a set of values and an ethical system as a guide to behavior—developing an ideology. **Life tasks:** Existential (friends and community).

The seeds of the values and ethical system that one will eventually adopt are presented through all the influences that act on individuals in a society. Parents' values, peer and community values, and the values and ethical system of one's church are most readily available to the developing person. The conclusions one makes about his or her own values include a strong element of self. That is, whether one accepts an existing system (as in believing and living by the absolute tenets of an organized religion) or develops a unique personal system, in the end the choice is one's own. This developmental task for most adolescents may be seen in their coping with the existential life task and religion. When they develop their own creed, or when their developing values are, say, more similar to their friends' and less similar to their parents', the potential for conflict grows in the other life task areas. While adolescents experiment and fluctuate with ideologies they run into conflicts between their behavior and the expectations of others in all life tasks.

Developmental task 8: Desiring and achieving socially responsible behavior. **Life tasks:** Friends and community, work and school, existential.

The goals of this developmental task include the development of a social ideology that allows the adolescent, when an adult, to be a responsible participant in his or her community and country. To be a responsible adult and citizen demands that one "take account of the values of society in one's personal behavior" (Havighurst, 1972, p. 75). Where in the life tasks does "desiring and achieving socially responsible behavior" come in? Everywhere! This means that, as an adolescent, one learns, tries, and experiments with what he or she thinks and feels to be the "right," "good," and "responsible" way to behave for the self, loved ones, friends, and, if you will, God and country.

The developmental tasks of adolescence are clear descriptions of abilities and attitudes that the adolescent must have to move successfully into adulthood. They are described in such a way that students of adolescence and those who are working or will work with adolescents can understand them. The life tasks are more general and not as neat. They are "where they live" descriptors. Merging the developmental tasks and the life tasks is intended to help us understand adolescent development by clarifying "where" the adolescent is and how the adolescent feels.

CHAPTER 2
Physiological Development

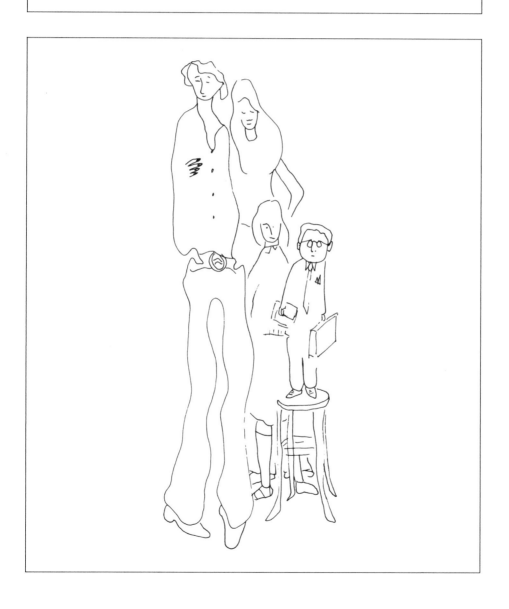

CHAPTER 2

The purpose of this chapter is to present the relevant facts about the order and ages of physiological changes for boys and girls into and through adolescence, and the meaning of these changes to the adolescent. The chapter does not detail the biological, chemical, and hormonal bases for the physiological changes under discussion. The assumption made throughout this book is that all behavior is social in nature. All events and behaviors are of relevance and understood by individuals as they see themselves in relation to the individuals and groups with which they interact and identify. In this regard, physiological developments have social meaning to the individual and others.

This chapter will describe the physiological changes and the order and ages of these changes for adolescent boys and girls. These changes will then be considered as they psychologically and socially affect those adolescents who are early and late in coming to them. The second major portion of the chapter will deal with the trend over time, called the secular trend, for adolescents to mature earlier.

PHYSIOLOGICAL CHANGES

The physiological changes at adolescence that carry social significance for the adolescent and for those who see and deal with him are most easily categorized as those having to do with the growth spurt in height, weight, and muscle, and those having to do with development of both primary and secondary sexual characteristics.

Adolescent Growth Spurt

After the extraordinary initial growth spurt from birth to age 2, growth in height is very constant over the remaining 18 or so years, with the exception of a second growth spurt, called the adolescent growth spurt, which occurs in early adolescence (Krogman, 1943; Watson and Lowrey, 1951; Tanner, 1961). The velocity of height gain per year, showing clearly the adolescent growth spurt for girls and boys, is given in Figure 2.1.

The growth spurt for girls occurs approximately two years earlier than the growth spurt for boys. In the data in Figure 2.1, first published in 1939, the spurt for boys occurred on the average between 13 and 15.5 years of age. On average the peak velocity, the highest rate of height gain, for boys is about 10 centimeters a year, while the average peak velocity is somewhat less for girls. Prior to the growth spurt there is little difference in height between girls and boys (about a 2 percent difference), whereas after the growth spurt the difference in height between boys and girls is about 8 percent (Tanner, 1964).

In terms of height, then, the adolescent growth spurt, because it comes later, giving boys more time to grow before the spurt begins, and because it is of greater intensity in males, has the effect of producing males taller than females. With individual differences and differences in timing and intensity, it may be said that almost all parts of the body participate in the growth spurt such that the adolescent at the end of the growth spurt has the size, shape, and strength characteristics of an adult male or female.

Development of Primary and Secondary Sex Characteristics

Figure 2.2 shows the sequence of events in physical development in adolescence, including the height spurt and the primary and secondary sex characteristics for boys and girls. Primary sex characteristics refer to sex organs, whereas secondary characteristics refer to developments such as axillary hair, voice change, and the other physical features that distinguish men and women.

"There is general agreement among endocrinologists that the events of the adolescent growth spurt take place under hormonal control" (Committee on Adolescence, 1968, p. 105). The rapid development of the reproductive system and the secondary sex characteristics are related physiologically and thereby chronologically to the spurt in height and muscle at adolescence. This is obvious in Figure 2.2.

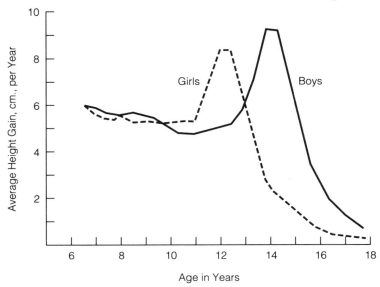

Figure 2.1. Adolescent increment growth curves in height for boys and girls who reached puberty at the average times (Reprinted by permission from J. M. Tanner, *Growth at Adolescence,* 2d ed. Oxford: Blackwell Scientific Publications, Ltd., 1962.)

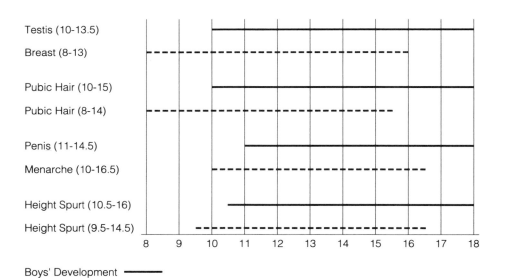

Figure 2.2. Usual sequence and range of ages of physical changes in development for boys and girls (Adapted from Committee on Adolescence, 1968, and Tanner, 1962.)

As these diagrams indicate, the normal age range for the onset and termination of the physiological developments is great. Using the example of menarche, MIT biologist Leona Zacharias noted: "The most striking thing we found is the great variability of the onset of menstruation. It's really wrong to talk about an average age and to think that there's some 'normal' age. 'Normal' is any time between 9 and 18" (Knox, 1976). However, the sequence of events occurs within approximately the same amount of time for each individual, although children who begin to mature earlier move through the sequence of development at a somewhat faster rate than do those who begin to mature later. Even though the order of these developments may differ slightly from individual to individual, may be completed within somewhat longer or shorter periods of time, and may begin over a fairly long age range, the sequence normally is a cohesive, clear growth period for each adolescent.

Part of this physical development is growth in strength, speed, stamina, and coordination. The increase in these abilities is, overall, greater and continues longer in American boys than in girls. There has been a very strong social element in athletics in America, both in the sex-appropriateness of sports and in the need to excel. The growth potential is there for boys more than for girls but it is there for both sexes, while there appears to be no physiological reason for greater awkwardness in adolescence for either sex.

> Sex differences in performance are considerable during adolescence. The slopes of the performance curves are steep for boys, while those for girls are rather flat. In all performance tasks, except throwing, the average performances of girls fall within one standard deviation of the boys' means during early adolescence. From 14 years of age on, the average performance of girls is consistently outside the limits encompassed by one standard deviation below the boys' mean performance. . . . It is interesting to note that recent cross-sectional studies, using physical fitness tests incorporating similar skill items, indicate a slight, but continued improvement in the running and jumping performance of girls through 17 years of age. This would seem to emphasize the importance of cultural factors in determining the motor performance of adolescent girls. (Malina, 1974, p. 128)

EARLY AND LATE MATURING

The normal range of ages of onset and completion of puberty is so broad that perfectly healthy, normally developing youngsters of the same age can be at very different levels of physical development, and these differences can have social and personal implications for them. A few weeks or months between emerging signs of maturation in one child and their onset in the child's friends can be a time of considerable worry and concern—whether the child is earlier or later than the friends. In these next pages studies that have looked at the effects of these differences between early and late maturers will be discussed.

It is possible within the normal time of development that some boys in a class may have finished their growth spurt, have fully developed reproductive organs, have deep voices and be shaving, while other boys in the class have not begun or are just beginning the sequence of adolescent physical development. For girls the same variance applies. Some girls will be almost their adult height, with full breast and reproductive development, while other girls in their class are only beginning or have not begun the process of puberty.

The divergence in levels of physical maturity seen within each sex group is magnified among adolescents regardless of sex, that is, as a single group. One can see that *some* girls have begun to mature, are growing more quickly, and have begun to menstruate and develop breasts before *any* boys of the same age in their class are in pubescence. At the other end of this developmental sequence, almost all, if not all, girls in a class, of an age cohort, will have completed their growth spurt and be almost fully developed in primary and secondary sex characteristics, whereas a number of boys in the class will only be entering the sequence of pubertal developments.

It is interesting that, except in very early childhood, at no time prior to adolescence is there the divergence in physical development among agemates that there is at adolescence. Until adolescence, children of the same age show only slight differences in developmental level and primarily individual differences due to other factors. Adolescents have to cope with the varied times of physical maturation within their group. And interesting also, after adolescence, with wider age ranges comprising peer or social groups—i.e., twenties, thirties, middle age—there is no period, until old age, when there is again such variance in physical development within social or peer groupings.

PSYCHOSOCIAL EFFECTS OF EARLY AND LATE MATURATION

Studies relating early and late maturation to personality development, attitudes, and behavior treat boys and girls separately. Jones found, overall, that early maturing boys showed a number of advantages over late-maturing boys, including higher ratings from peers and adults on variables such as physical attractiveness, athletic prowess, heterosexual status, self-confidence, and independence (Jones and Beylet, 1950; Jones, 1957; Mussen and Jones, 1957; Mussen and Jones, 1958; Jones, 1965). Late maturers were seen as less attractive but were rated higher in sociability, social initiative, and eagerness. The hypothesis "that the late-maturers' emphasis on social activity and their social initiative and participation are largely of an attention-getting, compensatory nature" was supported by Mussen and Jones (1958, p. 451). In a follow-up study in adulthood, Jones (1965) found that the early maturers continued to be socially successful, although they tend to be more conventional in their cognitive and coping skills (Livson and Peskin, 1980). While the late maturers in adulthood could not be said to be unsuccessful, they appeared to have compensated and were described as insightful, exploring, independent, and impulsive, which, interpreted positively, shows the late-maturing boys in adulthood as having greater curiosity, more social initiative, and greater creativity in solving problems (Livson and Peskin, 1980).

Frisk et al. detailed a number of ways in which "delayed development constituted a problem for both girls and boys, but particularly the latter" (1966, p. 139), as in poor physical performance, sex-role doubts, and feelings of failure. Jones and Mussen did not expect to find the same pattern for girls as for boys, but did, and concluded "that the late-maturing adolescents of both sexes are characterized by less adequate self-concepts, slightly poorer parent-child relationships, and some tendency for stronger dependency needs" (1958, p. 500).

Jones and Mussen (1958) had predicted that early maturing girls would have more negative self-feelings and interpersonal attitudes. Faust tried to discern "for girls whether level of physical maturity is a determinant in prestige during adolescence," and found that "precocious physical development tends to be a detriment in prestige status during sixth grade, while it tends to become a decided asset during the three succeeding years" (1960, p. 182). Petersen (1987), on the other hand, found that "being an early or late maturer (one year earlier or later than average), affected adolescents' satisfaction with their appearance and their body image — but only among seventh and eighth graders, not sixth graders" (p. 30). She found the early maturing girls in the higher grades to be "generally less satisfied with their weight and appearance than their less mature classmates" (p. 30). Frisk et al. found in a group of adolescents with "psychic problems" particularly high proportions of early maturing girls and concluded that, among the girls, "early maturation often led to a crisis in connection with the development of womanhood" (1966, p. 137).

How can these data be interpreted? First, the studies cited are on white American youth in general. When Mussen and Bouterline-Young (1964) investigated this issue with Italian-American boys, they did not find the same pattern of differences between early and late maturers, suggesting that body

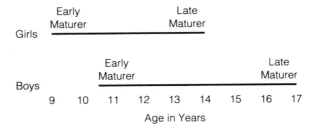

Figure 2.3. Age relationships among early- and late-maturing girls and boys

build may be of differing social value and related personal gain to earlier maturers in various subcultures.

The diagram in Figure 2.3 should be borne in mind in interpreting these data, as well as the simple social fact that basically everyone wants to belong. The earliest maturing girls and the latest maturing boys are clearly, for a period of time, odd — they are different from their friends. The difference is generally positive for early maturers in that they are admired and valued, even if envied.

The difference generally has negative social value for later maturers. Looking at Figure 2.3 in light of these observations and the studies cited, it can be seen that early maturing girls who gain points by being more "adult" physically also lose social points by being different from peers and having to be the first to learn the burdens and hazards of adult sexuality. Early maturing boys gain much socially and personally from their maturation and do not stand out from the total group because some girls have already begun to mature. In the same way, the late-maturing girl, although behind her female agemates in physical development, is still ahead of the late-maturing boys. The late-maturing girl suffers and bears some scars because of the social effects of her late maturation but not as severely as might the late-maturing boy who is also the odd man out.

> It is plausible to suppose that the early maturer engages in a socially sanctioned "flight" into adulthood from his less tolerable puberty; the late maturer, whose tolerance for puberty lessens the need for external supports and rewards, continues to regulate impulses by active cognitive and affective experimentation. The early maturer may be said to move more rapidly toward the perceptible rewards, serious responsibilities, and firm images readily offered him by the external world and to make important life commitments at an earlier time. . . . Early maturers, writes Jones (1965), appear to "escape prematurely into adulthood, while the late maturers take more

time in which to integrate their impulses and capacities" (p. 907). . . . It is perhaps fair to conclude that early and late maturers, considered collectively, eventually come to differ less in degree of psychological "health" than in these types of character structure. (Peskin, 1967, p. 13)

In the process of adolescence, early and late maturation can affect the individual's sense of belonging, and, as Peskin (1967) described, affect the manner in which he deals with his transition from, as well as his presence in, adolescence. The long-term effects of early and late maturation are not as dramatic as the feelings of those adolescents who are, for a time, far ahead or far behind their peers in physical development.

THE SECULAR TREND

Grandparents, parents, teachers, and academics who study adolescence shake their heads and wonder why kids are doing things younger than in previous generations. There are many reasons, but one of them may be the effects of the secular trend. The principal author on the subject, James Tanner, explains the secular trend:

> During the last hundred years there has been a very striking tendency for the time of adolescence to become earlier, and for the whole process of growth to speed up. Thus, children born in the 1930s, for example, were considerably larger at all ages than those born in the 1900s. The change seems chiefly or entirely to be one of body size rather than proportion or build. (1961, p. 113)

Utilizing data on (1) heights and weights of children at each age, (2) longitudinal growth curves with emphasis on the peak, and (3) age at menarche, collected by a great variety of researchers over a three-hundred-year period, Tanner (1965) came to a number of conclusions about the extent of the secular trend.

Referring to British, Scandinavian, and North American data, Tanner (1961) concluded that between 1880 and 1950 average increases of about 1 pound and 1/2 inch per decade were found for ages 5 to 7, 4 pounds and 1 inch per decade for adolescence, and about 1/2 inch per decade for adults.

Roche (1979) points to some of the discrepancies between age groups and geographic areas in the prominence of the secular trend. Rates of growth during childhood have increased considerably during the past 50 to 100 years. Because they are associated with increased rates of maturation, these size increases are maximal at ages when recently measured groups are pubescent but those measured in the past had not reached pubescence. Large secular increases in rates of growth and maturation have occurred in all developed countries but not in many other countries.

All the data from Europe and America are in good agreement, showing that menarche has been getting earlier for the last one hundred years at a rate of as much as three or four months per decade. The differences in age of menarche between generations are illustrated in a study by Damon et al. (1969), which showed the mean age for menarche for mothers in the sample of American whites as 14.38 and the mean age of their daughters as 12.88.

There are a number of reasons posed for the decrease in age of the growth spurt and menarche. Three of the most frequent reasons given are health, nutrition, and what is often referred to as "hybrid vigor"—marrying and breeding from outside the traditional breeding group, as has occurred increasingly with greater migration nationally and internationally. Controversy continues over which cause is more important, and all arguments seem confounded and interrelated.

The hybrid vigor factor, scientific name—heterosis, may have been of importance in producing the secular trend. However, the intention of the geographic mobility necessary for heterosis to occur was not, presumably, just new mates. People were mobile in order to take advantage of the opportunities of the industrial revolution. As, by and large over time, they were successful in finding better living conditions, health care, and nutrition in more developed areas, the secular trend that followed cannot be attributed only to mating practices, but also to the improvements in living standards.

Although we might want to suggest better nutrition as the reason for the secular trend, "in the United States, there have been per capita increases in the intake of protein and fat from animal sources, decreases in carbohydrates and fat from vegetable sources, and little change in caloric intake. It is not clear that these changes constitute better nutrition" (Roche, 1979).

Robert M. Malina suggests "that the most important cause, or at least a very important one, is the improved health status reflected in the marked reduction in infant and childhood mortality and morbidity during the nineteenth and twentieth centuries. . . . With lesser morbidity from . . . diseases, developing children are more capable of normal growth and development" (1979, pp. 88–89).

"If improved nutrition and the corresponding decreases in illness and disease are responsible for the trend toward earlier puberty in the past century, the trend should level off when people are nourished at an optimal level. There is some evidence that this is occurring in industrialized countries" (Petersen, 1979, p. 45). Evidence suggests "that the downward trend has now stopped. Some scientists suggest that the average age of 12 1/2 (where the downward curve has leveled off) may represent the 'physiological limit' for early onset of menses" (Jennings, 1975, p. 1979).

Whatever the reason, or reasons, for the secular trend, it has profoundly changed the age of onset of pubescence, thereby the nature of adolescence and the process through and relations within the life cycle. As the secular trend has gone on it has had implications for adolescents and all around them. As it ends, in the countries where it is ending, this too will have implications for adolescents and these societies. These implications will be explored in the next section.

IMPLICATIONS OF THE SECULAR TREND

As clearly as can be determined, the physical changes at adolescence are timeless. They have for centuries occurred in the same pattern for all growing humans and there have been no recent evolutionary developments. It may be said that, with the exception of the age at which it happens, youngsters today are physically passing through puberty as did you and your peers and your grandparents and so on.

In speaking about the implications of the secular trend for the contemporary adolescent and society, it is important to mention that societal events and changes affect the adolescent at least as much as they do adults. Whether adolescents are more amazed, cynical, optimistic, or frightened about the state of the world than adults, whether the adolescent generation came to a general consensual position on issues on their own before adults, or whether they are vocal and active or not are questions that may only tangentially implicate earlier maturity in their answers. The effect of world, national, and local events and beliefs on adolescents may vary with the times. Nonetheless, a number of possible social significances for adolescents and those who deal with them would seem to be related to the secular trend phenomena. For example:

1. Changes in sexual mores, early dating and marriage, and increases in early teenage unwed mothers would not have been considered, or feasible, when puberty occurred at a later age.
2. If, and as, intellectual development is related to physical development, changes in school curricula may have been forced, and may still be demanded, by earlier cognitive development, greater early abilities, and broader and/or different interests.
3. School dropouts and runaways may indicate unrealistic societal expectations for fully (physically) mature youths to sit in schools designed, environmentally and organizationally, for children, and for parents

to relate to their adolescent children without regard for their physical maturity.

4. The battles over efforts to legislate alterations in legal majority, laws on censorship, availability of birth control devices, and the like have and will be affected by the status of the secular trend.

Society and culture are based on law and tradition. Many traditions and laws have had to, and will have to, be changed as they pertain to an age group that is notably more mature than parallel age groups were when the traditions and laws were established.

The extent and importance of a "generation gap" have been exaggerated in the last two decades, largely due to the publicity given to student activists and student opinion during the Vietnam War protests and the Watergate era and overgeneralizations drawn therefrom (Petroni, 1972; Adelson, 1979). In a fast-changing world, where individuals are deluged with news and information, younger and older people may naturally have differences of opinion, especially on issues that affect them differently. And there may always be issues on which younger and older people disagree, particularly parents and their children, but a massive polarization between youth and their elders is neither necessary nor implied by the term "generation gap."

The potential for differences between the generations is always there. On average, parents are over 25 years older than their children. Parents, like everyone, relate to other persons by referring to their own experience. Our empathy for and understanding of others is in part built on our ability to infer from our feelings about situations to others' feelings about similar situations. Parents refer to their own adolescent experiences when trying to understand the experiences and feelings of their own adolescent. As trite as this may seem, with the recent rate of change in the world, and particularly in America, the values and goals to which an adolescent was exposed 25 years ago were vastly different from those to which her child is exposed today. Thus the attitudes of parents differ from the attitudes of their adolescents, both as adult attitudes differ from adolescent attitudes at any one time and as adolescent attitudes and values today differ from those of adolescents approximately 25 years ago.

The potential for differences between the generations may have been, and may still be, exacerbated by the secular trend, as seen in Figure 2.4. The secular trend data show that there is considerable difference in age of maturation over the course of a 25-year generation—e.g., there would be approximately a 1.4-year difference between mother and daughter in age at menarche. As attitudes, interests, and behaviors are related to developmental age—i.e., as a girl past menarche differs from a girl before menarche, the

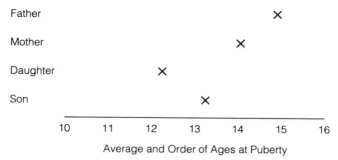

Figure 2.4. Model of family order of age at puberty showing effects of secular trend and sex differences. These could well affect parents' understanding of their children, who are physically maturing earlier than they did.

question of parental understanding and empathy for an adolescent who is much more developed than the parent was at the same age arises. If the mother draws parallels between herself and her daughter in light of menarche, if she looks at the child's developmental age instead of the child's chronological age, their "generation gap" should not be as large. In fact, in this century, the age at which mothers developed is closer to the age at which their sons began puberty than it is to the age at which their daughters developed. Fathers have been the furthest out of line. Using the decrease of four months per decade as a general rule, sons probably matured ten months earlier than their fathers. Daughters matured approximately three years earlier than fathers (the two-year average difference in age of maturation between the sexes plus the effect of the secular trend over twenty-five years). Put in this way, the difficulties parents, notably fathers, have had in empathizing with the changes in their adolescents become clearer. And vice versa — the difficulties that adolescents, especially early adolescents, have with their parents become clearer. As Petersen concluded from her data: "It's clear that puberty alone does not have the overwhelming psychological impact that earlier clinicians and researchers assumed it did. But it does have many effects on body image, moods and relationships with parents and members of the opposite sex" (1987, p. 30).

Of course, the significant question now is whether, with the cessation or diminution of the secular trend, parents will better understand and empathize with their adolescents, whether the perception of the "gap" will diminish and parent-adolescent relations will improve. Of interest too, in the United States, will be the degree to which the hypothesized social effects of the secular trend will continue among those new citizens who have immigrated from less developed countries. As their new life-style and nutrition affect the rate of development of their children, one can imagine that the secular trend will operate and exacerbate the difficulties of understanding their children's assimilation into the new culture.

CONCLUSION

The major effects of physiological development in adolescence discussed in this chapter may have important consequences for individual adolescents and for society. However, the normal changes that occur in the body of the adolescent probably provoke the greatest amount of anxiety, concern, and consideration among the greatest number of adolescents.

The changes in size, build, and composition from preadolescence to adolescence result in an altered bodily configuration. The developing adolescent must adjust to his or her "new" body. The manner in which an adolescent boy or girl comes to terms with his or her altered morphology has significant behavioral correlates. The adolescent's body image is, to a large extent, revised, especially in terms of appearance, limits of strength, and coordination (Malina, 1974, p. 128).

The first part of us others see is our body, our physical appearance. Adolescents, who put so much of themselves into question, stress that portion of themselves that they can concretely notice and that they think others see, even if the others are unaware. This seems to be the case for 15-year-old Josh, the hero of *There Must Be a Pony*:

> I got this gigantic complex people were only talking about the way I looked because they couldn't come up with anything else to say about me. Like how bright I was, or what a smashing sense of humor I had, or about my personality. Mainly, I guess you couldn't tell if I was smart or funny or even HAD a personality — because I couldn't communicate with people I felt because I couldn't do anything brilliant, people could only comment about me like they would about a piece of French pastry or something. (Kirkwood, 1960, p. 18)

The worry and embarrassment associated with physiological changes at puberty and through adolescence are recognized in a self-help book that advises adolescents not to be ashamed or afraid because the changes are normal. They are told to remember "that you're not the only one who has ever gone through this difficult time. It happened to your parents. It happened to your heroes. . . . They all came through it pretty well. So will you" (Mayle, 1975, p. 5).

CHAPTER 3
Cognitive Development

CHAPTER 3

The order of chapters in a book is certainly not random. In books of fiction the order tells the story as the author thinks it most effective, but primarily it tells the story. In a text such as this the order also reflects the story the author wants to tell. To this point the story of adolescence has been about the nature of the characters, who they are generally and physically.

This chapter is about cognitive development, the orderly way in which people come to think and know about the world and themselves. The chapter on cognitive development comes at this point because, in this author's view, all that makes human beings uniquely human has to do with their ability to think, the development of this ability, and the ramifications and relationships of this ability to their knowing, feeling, and behaving, both individually and together. The different stages of life have to do with how humans think at each stage, what they know, and what they then can do, within the roles and demands of their society and time.

There is a point when your pet puppy becomes less puppyish and more doglike, and a time when it becomes an old dog. These changes and differences have little or nothing to do with what your dog knows, only with what it physically can do in a situation with which it is familiar. Physical ability and response to immediate situations are definitely implicated in human stages of life, but more importantly, the nature of life around each person, how the person understands life, the environment, and herself, and how she acts on these understandings dictates human life stages. Thus, in the story of adolescence, the chapter on cognitive development comes early because how adolescents think, and what they know, underlie so much of what they do in, and after, adolescence.

In this chapter, cognitive development in adolescence will be defined and described within the context of the theory originated by Piaget. The final stage of cognitive development, called formal operations, begins to, and may, develop in adolescence, according to Piaget. Formal operations—its nature, onset, and attainment—will be looked at in itself and in relation to other emotional, developmental, and cultural phenomena. The chapter closes with a summary framework that is intended to be helpful and applicable to understanding the other developmental changes, as well as the life tasks, in adolescence.

PIAGET'S THEORY OF COGNITIVE DEVELOPMENT

Stage theories presume a series of identifiably different stages, or levels, through which individuals pass in a specific, invariant (constant) order. The stages in Piaget's cognitive-developmental stage theory represent an ordered set of differences in the way people think. Infants, young children, and grade school children proceed through different thinking modes, different stages. The final stage in childhood cognitive development is the concrete operations stage, to which all normal children are presumed to develop.

In order to understand cognitive development in adolescence, one must understand the final stage of cognitive development to which adolescents presumably move, the formal operations stage, as well as the childhood stage from which they move, the concrete operations stage. The next section describes and compares, in brief, the concrete and formal operational levels of thought.

CONCRETE AND FORMAL OPERATIONS

In concrete operations the child is concerned with, or focuses on, relations between objects, which the child classifies, categorizes, and orders. In formal operations the adolescent, or adult, has the ability to think about the possible as well as the real. Instead of having to deal with things as they *are*, with hypotheses about how things are, the formal operational person may deal with how things *might be*, with hypotheses about how they might be. This allows the person with formal operational ability to consider relations between relations, to work with propositions, correlations, and probability. "The term *formal* is used because a person at this level of thinking possesses the ability to consider the possible and, therefore, is able to reason about the form of an argument apart from its content" (Peel, 1960, p. 115).

The most salient characteristic of formal operations, differentiating it from concrete operations, is that thought becomes oriented toward possibility and is no longer completely dependent on reality, no longer dependent on concrete content. Thought becomes abstract in that it can proceed in the absence of the data of reality. All differences between concrete and formal operations can be seen as reducible to "the subordination of reality to possibility" (Inhelder and Piaget, 1958, p. 255).

A second characteristic of formal operations is the use of the hypothetico-deductive method. The concrete operational child initiates his thought processes with a set of hypotheses that are successively confirmed or denied as the empirical data of reality dictate. However, the formal operational person can proceed in the absence of any empirical data, "can consider hypotheses which may or may not be true, and consider what would follow if they were true" (Hunt, 1961, p. 230).

The third characteristic is that formal operations are second-order operations because they are performed on the results of first-order operations, concrete operations. The person with formal operations has the "ability verbally to manipulate relationships between ideas (second-order relations) in the absence of recently prior or concurrently available concrete-empirical props (first-order operations)" (Ausubel and Ausubel, 1966, p. 405). The logic used under the aegis of formal operations is termed *propositional logic*.

In sum, the three characteristics differentiating formal operations from concrete operations are reality's becoming subordinate to possibility, the hypothetico-deductive method, and propositional logic based on second-order operations.

Abstraction. Another approach to viewing and understanding the changes in cognition and reasoning that are said to occur during adolescence focuses on the degree of abstractness in adolescent thought. Although a conception of formally operational thought as abstract thought is not completely equivalent to Piaget's conception, it may help in understanding these cognitive phenomena. Hayakawa (1964) presented the term *abstraction ladder* to describe the changes, from a linguistic point of view, that take place in the process of learning through adolescence to adulthood. He posited that a consciousness of abstracting is indicative of adulthood.

Peel looked at the changes that occur in adolescence in preference for and use of abstraction by using a sentence-preference test that he devised. He made a "distinction between two aspects of forming a concept, by which extending the array of exemplars might be called generalizing, and formulating the rule for including instances would require an act of abstracting" (1975, p. 177). Each item in Peel's test contains four sentences with the same key word, and the subject is asked to check the sentence that he prefers as most significant for him. The sentences are keyed as abstraction (A), generalization (G), and membership (M). Membership may be likened to categorization, a concrete operation. The fourth sentence in each item is not relevant to our discussion here. Some examples of test items are:

A   The city is an administrative concept going back to Roman times.
M   Liverpool is a city.
G   A city is a unit of local government.

G   Playing is a universal activity among higher animals.
A   Playing is frequently discussed in studies of children.
M   Playing is tennis and football.

M   Mars is a planet.
A   The planet is an astronomical class.
G   A planet is a heavenly body.

Peel found an increase in generalizing and an even more marked increase in abstracting during the adolescent years 12 to 16, as shown in Figure 3.1. The preference for M, membership, decreased during these years. These results show the increase with age in adolescence of the preference to abstract. It should also be noted that although the preference for abstracting increased, at age 16 it only accounted for approximately 20 percent of the fre-

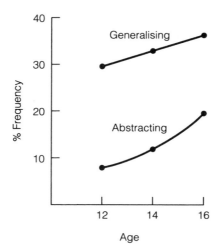

Figure 3.1. Age trends in the tendencies to abstract and generalize (From E. A. Peel, "Predilection for generalising and abstracting," *British Journal of Educational Psychology* 45 [1975], 1977–88. Reprinted by permission of the author and Scottish Academic Press.)

quency of preferences. The wish to venture into the world of abstraction appears to be a part of moving into formal operations, at least for some adolescents.

It may be worth playing with notions that you consider abstract to see whether you are thinking about them abstractly, without regard to concrete referents, or whether you are generalizing from concrete referents in order to establish a total, albeit concrete, picture that approximates the abstraction as you understand it. You may recognize the difference in the midst of discussions or lectures in which you have felt comfortable with the use of abstract terms and then have become confused. At that point you may mentally search for a definition or you may reconstruct the term or concept from particular events, objects, numbers, etc. In one approach you are dealing with abstractions and in the other you are generalizing. As will become clear in the next sections, much of the thought of adolescents which we, and teachers and counselors, think is abstract or formal is probably concrete generalizing. There is nothing wrong with this manner of thought, but it has the limits of concrete thought—that is, it does not have the properties of formal thought.

PROCESSES AND INFLUENCES IN COGNITIVE DEVELOPMENT

Ginsburg and Opper (1969) note four influences, or factors, in cognitive development: (1) maturation of the nervous system, (2) active personal physical experiences, (3) environmental effects (including culture, language, and education), and (4) equilibration. The importance of the first three of these four factors will be examined in the succeeding pages. The fourth factor, equilibration, although exceedingly important in cognitive development, differs from the others in that it is conceptually a part of the functioning of cognition and cognitive development as well as an influence.

We need to have a sense of how the intellect grows and changes, and thus need to know how the intellect functions. Simply and loosely, but accurately, there are two important structures in Piagetian theory and three functions that together will give us a sense of cognitive functioning and development.

The basic unit of knowledge, the basic underlying cognitive structure, although it may not be something that we can clearly see and speak about in ourselves, is called a *scheme*, or *schema*. The scheme is a result of, and a part of, acting on the environment and forms a central unit of some behaviors that seem to go together. The scheme is seen as the child acts as if he or she had a notion, an idea, about how something is, its cause and effect, and generally acts in relevant situations as if the idea were true. Schemata may be more physical when children are younger and more mental when they are older, but they are these inferred units of knowing.

Schemata develop from the individual's acting on the environment. Individuals also internally, mentally, act on what they "know," act on their schemata. The process of mentally acting on schemata—building, rebuilding, and unbuilding—what Piaget calls reversibility, is termed *operations*—mentally operating on cognitive structures, schemes. Operations allow schemes to be put together with other schemes in ways that make sense according to the schemes, thereby building structures. The structure of intellect in this theory is then schemes that may be operated on and thus manipulated into structures. The changes in the schemes, operations, and structures as they are orderly, invariant, etc., constitute the changes from stage to stage.

The three functions are assimilation, accommodation, and equilibration. "Assimilation is the process of incorporating new pieces of information into old ways of thinking or behaving. . . . Accommodation involves modifying some elements of the old ways of thinking and behaving" (Ault, 1983, pp. 15–16). When information, or an experience, is not understood and is rejected or forgotten, there is no assimilation or accommodation and cognitive structure remains as it was. However, the usual process of ingesting experiences demands a continuous effort to balance what one experiences so it is known and understood. This total process is called *equilibration*.

"Equilibration is defined as compensation for an external disturbance" (Muuss, 1968, p. 153). In effect, when an experience, information, is noted and generally fits what is known, it is assimilated into the old scheme. When information is noted and does not fit what is known, the old scheme is changed to accommodate the new information. "External disturbance" in Muuss' definition means information that is seen as relating to existing structures and can be acted on through accommodation or assimilation, or information that is noticed and demands a new, fuller, or different scheme. There is much out there in the environment, in the world, that we do not notice, don't see and don't understand that does not relate to our schemes and structures. It is all there, but it does not constitute an external disturbance for us. Some people are so constituted that their cognitive equilibriums are disturbed by many more objects, experiences, and pieces of information than are other people's cognitive equilibriums. They would, it would seem, be building and refining more schemata and structures than others. As Figure 3.2 attempts to show, we might say that they are more intelligent, and Piaget defines intelligence as a "form of equilibration . . . toward which all cogni-

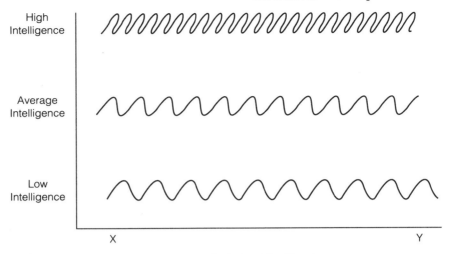

Figure 3.2. Equilibration and intelligence. This figure attempts to show how and why greater equilibration—more frequent compensation of external disturbances (noticing more and assimilating and accommodating more)—is related to higher intelligence.

tive functions lead" (1962, p. 120). This process, which has an important motivation function, is crucial in understanding adolescence.

VALIDITY OF PIAGET'S STAGES

Fairly constant discussion and argument continue in the field of development over the validity of Piaget's stages. In a 1966 paper Ausubel and Ausubel termed irrelevant the various arguments that disputed the legitimacy of Piaget's stages of intellectual development. The facts they considered irrelevant are that the transition between stages is not abrupt but occurs gradually, that age variability in the transition between stages exists between and within cultures, that children fluctuate in the level of cognitive functioning they manifest over time, that children may move to formal operations in some subject fields and subfields while not having yet done so in others, and that environmental factors influence the rate of cognitive development.

These facts do not jeopardize the validity of the stage notion of the changes in intellect described by Piaget, although they may disagree with some of what he said about the stages and his theory. The facts themselves, however, are very important for understanding the nature, rate, and frequency of development to formal operations in adolescence. For example, put very simply, children need to be able to notice aspects of their environment in order to act on them, physically and mentally, in the development of schemes and structures and in movement through stages. If adolescents (1) do not have the ability to notice, to discriminate, many and various aspects, or (2) have not been exposed, formally or informally, to certain aspects, they cannot have the schemes and structures on which to reflect. These adolescents could not develop formal operations either at all or in certain areas where the necessary aspects are missing. Children from particular environments, cultures, or subcultures, for genetic reasons and/or due to the absence of certain objects, experiences, or ideas in their group, may not develop formal operations in all or some areas. When first inklings of formal operations emerge in certain areas, they may not be firmly held, they may seem to come and go, which is seen by researchers as a question of competence and performance (Flavell, 1982; Shayer, 1979; Stone and Day, 1980).

Rather than putting Piaget's stages into question, these facts make various characteristics of adolescents more understandable and are very relevant to the issues of intelligence, age, cultural, and individual differences in cognitive development. Although there are difficult problems of measurement, Piaget's formulations, particularly as they apply in general and to formal operations, have been validated (Gallagher, 1973; Elkind, 1963; Wallach, 1963). Lovell, after extensive research, concluded that "the main stages in the development of logical thinking proposed by Inhelder and Piaget have been confirmed" (1961, p. 149).

RELATION BETWEEN FORMAL OPERATIONS AND OTHER ASPECTS OF DEVELOPMENT

FORMAL OPERATIONS AND MEASURED INTELLIGENCE

> By intelligence we simply mean a measurement construct designating level of ability in performing a graded series of tasks implicating the component aspects of cognitive functioning at any given stage of intellectual development. (Ausubel and Ausubel, 1966, pp. 411–12)

This definition of measured intelligence points to a basic characteristic in the construction of intelligence tests—that the tasks be appropriate to the general age-stage group for which they are designed. Questions at an abstract, formal operational level are either not presented to or not answered appropriately by persons who have not reached this stage. Formal operational tasks are more prevalent and successfully passed in tests designed for persons approaching and in the formal operations stage. To the extent that the intel-

ligence tests given to preadolescents and adolescents implicate the component aspects of cognitive functioning at the formal operations stage of intellectual development, a relationship should be found between intelligence
test scores and level of cognitive development in adolescence.

Studies of cognitive development have long included IQ as a variable.
Case and Collinson (1962) and Lovell and Shields (1967) found a positive
relationship between IQ (or mental age) and incidence of formal operations.
Studies comparing groups of children varying in intelligence levels support
the same contention (Jackson, 1965; Stephens and McLaughlin, 1971;
Yudin, 1970). Dudek et al. (1969) found significant correlations between the
Wechsler Intelligence Scale for Children (WISC) and several of Piaget's measures, concluding that although the purposes and theory underlying the construction of the two measures of intelligence are different, they are highly
correlated and seem to be sampling the same cognitive processes to the degree that they are correlated. "The significant correlations obtained between
scores on the proportion test and nonverbal intellectual capacity, as measured
by the Raven matrices, support the finding . . . that Piagetian tasks are
positively correlated with IQ measures (Cloutier and Goldschmid, 1976, p.
1101).

IQ AND AGE, MATURATION, SIZE, AND SOCIAL CLASS

Some change in IQ scores from testing at one age to another is usual and expected due to statistical, test construction, and test administration inconsistencies and intraindividual variations. Nonetheless, highly significant
correlations of about .60 between IQ scores in childhood and adolescence
and correlations of about .80 between IQ scores in adolescence and adulthood are found (Bradway and Thompson, 1962).

> The greatest changes in IQ occur among those who score in the average
> range between 90 and 110, but even though there is an absolute change in
> score, the chances are that the person will remain in the average category.
> Put differently, if we think of IQ standing in terms of gross categories such
> as above average, average and below average, rather than in terms of abso-
> lute scores, then the IQ does remain relatively stable from childhood
> through adolescence. (Elkind, 1968, pp. 136–137)

The dispute over the relative power of heredity and environment in determining or affecting intelligence continues unabated. Heredity, as it relates
to size, maturation, and environment as evidenced in social class and cultural
differences, will be looked at in relation to measured intelligence, while always keeping in mind that the greatest differences in measured intelligence

are individual. In the following section this same view will be used with cognitive development through formal operations.

The following conclusions, though based on ample evidence, refer to group differences, which means there is room for considerable overlap between groups and enormous room for individual exceptions. "Children who are physically advanced for their age do in fact score higher in mental ability tests than those who are less mature, but of the same chronological age" (Tanner, 1961, p. 44). "One consequence of the relation of test scores to physical maturity is that large children, who on average are more advanced, score higher than small children of the same age" (Tanner, 1961, p. 46). These differences are presumed to diminish, although not necessarily vanish, in adulthood.

The findings by Terman et al. in the *Genetic Study of Genius I* (1925), which started with 1,500 young people with very high IQs averaging about 150, emphasized these points. The children in the study were "nonrepresentative physically as well as intellectually" (Herrnstein, 1971, p. 52). Overall they tended to be greater in height and weight, stronger, and of earlier sexual maturity than average IQ children. They were also nonrepresentative of the general population by ethnic group and social class, with a large percentage having parents in professional jobs.

"Children from different socioeconomic levels differ in average body size at all ages, the upper groups being always larger" (Tanner, 1961, p. 109). "The correlation between IQ and social class is undeniable, substantial, and worth noting. A cautious conclusion, based on a survey of the scientific literature, is that the upper class scores thirty IQ points above the lower class" (Herrnstein, 1971, p. 50). Both sides to the issue of whether these differences are based on heredity or environment are presented by Scarr and Weinberg with their position strongly stated:

> The persistent finding that differences in class background bias adult achievements has been interpreted to mean that differences in family environments during the child-rearing period enhance or impede the intellectual, educational, and occupational achievements of the offspring for a lifetime. From our data, it appears to us that these linkages should be reinterpreted to mean that differences in family background that affect IQ are largely the result of genetic differences among parents, which affect their own status attainments and which are passed on genetically to their offspring, whose status attainments are subsequently affected. (1978, p. 691)

Regardless of the relative importance of heredity and environment in causing these findings, it is clear that age at maturation and size are related to intelligence in adolescence in the same way that social class is related to the physical and mental measures.

In the chapters to come it should be remembered, and will be noted, that group differences in attitudes, behaviors, and the whole emotional world of adolescence may be analyzed with these relationships in mind. The tremendous variance in size, age of maturation, and particularly intelligence within, and also between, socioeconomic groups must be remembered. The Scottish Council concluded, "The difference between the groups is not that the 'upper' social classes contribute more intelligent children to the total population; it is that a higher percentage of their children are intelligent" (Scottish Council for Research in Education, 1953, p. 45). Put another way, "only about 10 percent of our people meet the criteria for the upper and upper-middle classes, while about 65 percent are in the working classes, . . . But only about 50 percent of the people have subnormal (below 100) IQ's. And so, there must be at least 15 percent of our population in the bottom classes with supranormal (above 100) IQ's" (Herrnstein, 1971, p. 50).

ATTAINMENT OF FORMAL OPERATIONS AND AGE, SOCIAL CLASS, AND CULTURE

Piaget originally hypothesized that the onset of formal operations occurred at approximately age 11 or 12 and stabilized around the age of 14 or 15 (Inhelder and Piaget, 1958). Subsequent research has shown the situation to be more complicated, with such variables as intelligence, socioeconomic status, cultural background, and amount of schooling affecting age of attainment of formal operations.

Goodnow (1962) administered several tasks and a reasoning test to European and Chinese middle- and lower-class adolescents and found minor differences on some tasks but major differences on the test of reasoning, which required formal operations ability. Middle-class subjects performed better than lower-class subjects regardless of ethnicity.

Feldman and Markwalder (1971) studied black, white, and Chinese children of various ages and levels of social class. They found that blacks made more concrete operational responses and fewer formal operational responses than did whites or Chinese. They attributed this to disparities in the ages at which formal operations are attained across the groups. Vernon (1965) found English children performed at higher levels on various tasks than did West Indian children, but he did not have social class controlled.

Greenfield studied rural and urban, schooled and unschooled children in the Wolof tribe in Senegal. She found that performance on concept formation problems was dependent on schooling. Unschooled rural and urban children failed to improve their performance after the age of 8 or 9. In contrast, the "Wolof schoolchildren . . . did not differ essentially from Western children in this respect" (1969, p. 7).

Buck-Morss reviewed socioeconomic and social structure effects in relation to cognitive development, showing that "it is well documented by Western studies that lower-class children lag in Piaget-test performance even though they live in industrialized societies. . . . What the lower classes in industrialized countries have in common with the 'face-to-face' societies of third-world rural villagers is that their experience is limited to a realm of concrete immediacy. Meanwhile the workings of the larger social whole take place literally 'over their heads' " (1979, p. 359).

A number of other studies have shown variability not only in the age at which formal operations is attained, but also in the areas of experience for which formal thought is available (Case and Collinson, 1962; Lovell, 1971; Lovell and Butterworth, 1966; Stephens, Piaget, and Inhelder, 1966).

Higgins-Trenk and Gaite provide evidence that many adolescents may not attain the stage of formal operations until the late teens or early twenties, if at all. Even in their oldest group, mean age 17.7 years, "over 50% of the [subjects] were not responding at the level of formal operational thought" (1971, p. 202). Shayer pointed out that "by 1974, 19 years after the initial publication of 'The Growth of Logical Thinking,' no one had produced work which would decide between the original assumption that all adolescents develop formal operational thinking, that between a quarter and a third do, or even that maybe only 5 percent of 14-year-olds do" (1979, p. 272). Piaget (1972b) came to recognize this problem and suggested that the attainment of formal operations may occur later than he originally thought, possibly from 15 to 20 years of age, and then, possibly, only in specific areas according to aptitudes and areas of greater experience.

Research continues on cognitive development at all levels and, for our interests here, on these developments beyond adolescence and formal operations. An example of this work is the study by Arlin (1975) suggesting that a fifth stage in cognitive development may occur either after formal operations or as a second part of the formal operations stage. Arlin renamed the formal operations stage the "problem-solving stage," and called the proposed new stage the "problem-finding stage." Whether this is an additional stage or not is questioned (Fakouri, 1976; Cropper, Meck, and Ash, 1977), but the entire area remains of great interest and importance.

The studies cited in this section show that cognitive development in adolescence is influenced by maturation of the nervous system (age differences in formal operations attainment) and personal and environmental experiences and effects (as in class, educational, and subcultural differences) and that it is not universally equal. Not all adolescents reach formal operations or reach it to the same level and across all tasks. The conclusion must be that for a variety of reasons and influences, differences exist among individuals and groups in measured intelligence as well as attainment of formal operations.

The implications of these facts for education in general and classroom teachers in particular are great. In a workshop of high school language arts teachers working with the gifted, the topic became whether differences among students on synthesizing and integrating tasks might sometimes reflect differences in cognitive development. In this case should a teacher reward formal operational performance? If she does, is she punishing other students for not producing beyond their ability and, in fact, possibly beyond their physical maturity level? A sticky problem. In any event, it obviously behooves teachers to become sensitive to the changing nature of the thought processes of at least some of their pupils during these years and to recognize the factors that may be influencing individual differences in these changes.

AFFECT AND FORMAL OPERATIONAL THOUGHT

Formal thought, to the degree that it develops in any one individual, develops differentially. With age, abilities become more specialized according to practice and need. An individual may be able to operate at the formal level in some tasks and not in others. So too, all of one's thought, not only task-specific thought, may be able to be or not be at the formal stage. One's thoughts about oneself, others, right and wrong, family, society, and the world may be affected by the development of formal operations. And many aspects of life may be amenable to formal operations for those who are able, but for whom it would seldom or never be required or make sense to think of these aspects in terms of formal operations. For instance, a fully formal operational person might be able to think about movement of objects in multidimensions but have little reason to, especially when waiting for a bus.

The adolescent finds herself in many of the same situations (family, home, neighborhood) and many new situations (new school, new friends, new responsibilities). New situations open new possibilities and demands for acting, feeling, and thinking for all youth. But formal operational youth begin to see all aspects of life as they have been known to be, as they actually are, and also as they possibly could be.

These new thoughts about what the world might be present the challenge of adolescence to the formal operational adolescent. Responses may range from new highs about the individual's strengths and the beauty of the possibilities for the self and the world to deep depressions about personal weaknesses and faults and the impossibility of breaching the gap between what is and what might be. Responses of one kind or another may persist for an adolescent as they are in concert with his or her own personality, or they may vary appropriately from that personality. That is, one effect of the new thoughts is to give the adolescent a broader perspective for reinforcing his or her view of the self and the world. The new possibilities require testing the accuracy of conclusions. Equilibration is, in this case, the adolescent's bringing the new possibilities into his or her system and accommodating them — i.e., compensating for an external disturbance. As Peel states that "the urge to come to intellectual terms with one's world provides the mainspring of intellectual development" (1963, p. 494), we may say that coming to intellectual terms with one's world — for the adolescent, developing formal operations — is also coming to personal and affective terms with oneself and one's world.

From this perspective, the degree of personal upset an adolescent encounters in coming to formal operations is a function of the ease with which his or her existent cognitive structures of self, world, and tasks can accommodate the new thoughts the formal operations stage elicits. Put another way, the new thoughts of formal operations will be more upsetting to a youngster who comes to formal operations with cognitive structures, and the related personality and life-style, that are inappropriate for dealing with the reality of life and the possibilities for development.

A first effect of the personal challenge of formal operations is to force the adolescent to establish a new equilibrium, accommodating his new thoughts to reestablish his personality with this new data. The assimilation and accommodation process that makes up equilibration is set off by external disturbances that may be thought of here as new information and new ideas. In a sense, the adolescent feeds on herself, feeds on the new ideas she herself has created. Yet the changes that are disturbing to her equilibrium are accommodated to an existing self and assimilated by an existing self, which in the normal adolescent results in self-growth but does not grossly affect self-consistency. The adolescent coming into formal operations has not spent much time or effort on the kind of person she might be, could be, or should be in light of the full range of possible selves. Much of the identity issue for adolescents is a question of establishing equilibrium between the existing self and the disturbances that the use of propositional logic aimed at oneself brings.

This questioning produces a second behavioral effect of formal operational thought in adolescence, an experimenting effect. Adolescents to this point have had a concrete conception, however erroneous, of what they are and can do and what their personal world is like. With formal operations, they attempt to find out what they might be and the potential of their ability, thoughts, and feelings. The "extreme" behaviors of adolescence and the wide swings in behavior and mood are examples of experimenting. How far can I go in love, friendship, achievement? How good can it be? How bad can it get? There must be an infinity of possibilities and contradictions that a formal operational adolescent can construe and test in the process of coming to grips with the realistic possibilities for himself and the world.

As the formal operational adolescent considers these potentials and thinks about his own thinking and thoughts, there are social, affective, and behavioral effects (Elkind, 1968, 1969, 1978). "Much of what is considered typically adolescent in the way of emotionality can only be fully understood in the context of formal operational thought" (Elkind, 1968, p. 152). The adolescent's preoccupation with his thoughts result in his being preoccupied with himself AND his thoughts, what Elkind calls the egocentrism of adolescence. According to Elkind (1978), some of the effects of adolescent egocentrism are the adolescent's pseudostupidity (approaching tasks at a more complex level than the task demands and thus failing to see the obvious), the imaginary audience (when the adolescent thinks others are as intensely interested in the minutiae of his appearance and behavior as he is), the personal fable (a story he tells himself that accentuates his uniqueness, greatness, supranormal worth, and the reactions of others to his fantastic victories, crushing defeats, and untimely death), and apparent hypocrisy ("often a failure to distinguish between the expression of an ideal and its pragmatic realization" [p. 134]).

Adolescent egocentrism is said by Elkind to decrease by age 15 or 16, which overall may be true, "but adolescent egocentrism, however, may not be a unidimensional construct which steadily decreases throughout the adolescent years. Instead, certain aspects of egocentrism may unfold at different times during the adolescent period" (Enright, Lapsley, and Shukla, 1979, p. 695). And, I think it must be cautioned, although the effects of adolescent egocentrism, such as the imaginary audience and the personal fable, make sense as effects of adolescent egocentrism, they may make equally good sense as effects of adolescence itself — i.e., as props and mechanisms for putting up with the excessive demands adolescents feel.

The purpose of this section has been to introduce the manner in which formal operations development affects the social and affective sides of adolescent behavior. In addition, this section has illustrated the extent to which the development of formal operations and its social and affective correlates are generalized to all adolescents. The extent of these generalizations is questioned in the next section.

ADOLESCENCE AS FORMAL OPERATIONS?

It has been shown to this point that measured intelligence is related to cognitive development as defined by Piaget and that both forms of intellectual development and ability are related to other variables. Inhelder and Piaget acknowledge these factors: "The appearance of formal thought . . . is a manifestation of cerebral transformation due to the maturation of the nervous system." The studies citing relationships with physical maturation and early maturation pertain here. "[But] the maturation of the nervous system can do no more than determine the totality of possibilities and impossibilities at a given stage." These words parallel statements about heritability or the genetic portion of measured intelligence. "A particular social environment remains indispensable for the realization of the possibilities," as can be seen in the social-class differences in IQ and attainment of formal operations. "It follows that their realization can be accelerated or retarded as a function of cultural and educational conditions" (1958, p. 336).

The logic and data in this chapter do not allow the characterization that adolescence is the stage of formal operations. Formal operations may develop during adolescence, but not all adolescents attain formal operations. Of those who do, there are differences in level of attainment, patterns of areas, and tasks in which formal operations are attained. And development of formal operations may continue through, at least, young adulthood.

Many of the problems and tasks associated with adolescence are related to changes in the social situation in which adolescents find themselves. But as the material in this chapter indicates, many of the same, and other, tasks and problems associated with adolescence are related to cognitive development as it occurs in adolescence. Therefore, as a working hypothesis, much of what is said about adolescence as a period and adolescents as persons relates to all adolescents, while some of what is said about adolescents only relates, or relates in the extreme, to those adolescents in whom formal operational development is implicated in their thoughts, behavior, and emotions.

In order to pursue this hypothesis in succeeding portions of this book, a set of probabilities will be presented, and the hypothesis will be expanded in light of these probabilities. We will posit that higher IQ and earlier and eventually greater attainment of formal operations are related, singly or in combinations, to early maturation, bigger size, higher socioeconomic status (SES), better education, and particular cultural backgrounds. Excepting many individual differences, and mentioning that these are characterizations or generalizations, we might, on the other hand, posit that lower IQ plus later and little or no attainment of formal operations are related, singly or in combination, to late maturation, smaller size, lower SES, poor education, and particular cultural backgrounds.

Five general types of cognitive development in adolescence, expressed in terms of timing and degree of development of formal operations, are presented in Figure 3.3. The types are constructed from the statement of tentative conclusions earlier in this section. These types are rank ordered in terms of the theoretical probabilities that persons of these developmental types would attend college. And lastly, the developmental types are labeled to indicate whether or how the fullest descriptions of adolescents in the psychological research and theoretical literature apply to each type.

Two assumptions underlie the probability columns in Figure 3.3. The college attendance probability rank ordering is based on the known relationships among IQ, school achievement, social class, particular cultural backgrounds, and attendance at college. As we have also presupposed positive relationships between these variables and attainment of formal operations, the rank ordering posits the same manner of relationship between formal operations and college attendance.

The column referring to the probable applicability of the general descriptions of adolescence in the literature is based on a separate premise. It is often stated that what psychologists know about people is based primarily on university undergraduates because so much psychological research is carried out with this group as subjects. This is not altogether true, nor is it altogether false. Much research has been done in high schools and junior high schools, but here too there has been more research in schools in or near universities or in more progressive schools, which are more open to research. Very little research, comparatively, has been done on out-of-school youth, either high school dropouts or graduates. Cumulatively, psychological research on adolescents overrepresents in-school youth, particularly in better schools, and in-college youth.

Moreover, most of the psychological theorists who have dealt with adolescence have been prominent practitioners and/or professors in highly selective institutions. They have experienced primarily patients and students apt to be of higher SES, of higher IQ, and well into or having attained formal operations. In addition, their own "super" intellects may well have affected their own adolescent experiences and their views on adolescence in general.

College Probabilities Rank Ordered	Developmental Types	Probable Applicability of General Descriptions Descriptions Should:
1	Develop formal operations on time	Apply
2	Develop some formal operations over time	Apply in part
3	Develop formal operations late	Apply with age differences
4	Develop some formal operations late	Apply in part with age differences
5	Develop no formal operations	Not apply

Figure 3.3. Cognitive-developmental types in adolescence, probabilities for college attendance, and application of general descriptions of adolescents

The column labeled "Probable Applicability of General Descriptions" is based on the premise that, in the main, the study of nonrepresentative, higher intelligence youth is fully descriptive of them alone and is not as applicable to other youth.

These hypotheses will be considered through the psychological theories of adolescence and research on the life tasks. At this point, a few words about each of the hypothesized cognitive development types in adolescence is needed.

The "Develop Formal Operations on Time" type refers to those adolescents who are able to use formal thought in a variety of areas within the general age limits proposed by Piaget. It is presumed that they most probably are of above-average intelligence, SES, and maturity and of cultural and/or familial backgrounds conducive to growth of the intellect. They will most probably attend college. The personal and social trials, travails, and tasks usually ascribed to adolescents most probably apply to them.

The "Develop Some Formal Operations over Time" type does not develop formal operations as quickly or over as broad a range of areas as the previous type. They may be lower on the associated variables than the previous type. And the confusions and difficulties generally associated with adolescence will pertain to them, though possibly not as strongly as to the previous group.

The "Develop Formal Operations Late" type will develop formal operations but not begin development as early as the "on time" type. This may be because of later maturation and/or deficiencies in experiences due to sociocultural factors. The qualities of adolescence will apply to them but appear later than in the first type. They may be thought of as late bloomers.

The "Develop Some Formal Operations Late" type will experience the so-called storms and stresses of adolescence to a lesser degree early on but continue later than the literature would predict.

The "Develop No Formal Operations" type will have the problems of adolescence that come from changing social groups, roles, and settings, but will not have the personal emotional problems said to be part of adolescence that, we posit, are associated with developing formal operations. They are least likely to attend a university and least likely to be geographically or socially mobile.

The development of formal operations in adolescence is of great importance, particularly in its relation to further education and its personal and emotional effects. The hypothesized clusters of variables related to attainment of formal operations all influence the probability of college attendance. But the related variables are by no means causative. Rather, here as always, it is the individual who ultimately determines a destiny such as college attendance. In attempting to understand adolescents, change and new experiences produce upsets and crises. The social, physical, and situational changes that are necessarily a part of growing up, of adolescence, produce situations ripe for storm, stress, and crises. The cognitive changes, when and if they occur, produce intrapersonal notions and feelings that make the changing individual even more ripe for storm, stress, and crises. And it is a tribute to adolescents, to humankind at that age, that the potentials for storm, stress, and crises are so often met and adequately coped with by so many.

CHAPTER 4
Moral and Social Development

CHAPTER 4

During the years of adolescence problems arise as adolescents are faced with new situations, ambiguous and contradictory messages from an expanded number of persons and groups, and demands to make decisions at a level of import and complexity previously unknown to them. Adolescents face these problems in each of the life tasks. As they face these problems they bring to bear their full complement of knowledge and ability. The nature, and possibly the success, of their resolutions of the problems may well depend on what they know and how they know it. Thus adolescents' cognitive development in areas of social knowledge will influence the process and outcome of their living in adolescence.

In this chapter some of the social areas in which cognitive development in adolescence is seen will be discussed. More of the chapter will be devoted to moral development because this area has been most extensively researched and considered.

Many common adolescent problems have to do with conceptions of right and wrong—what should or should not be done. The Watergate and Iran-Contra hearings made it clear that such problems are not unique to adolescents. In order to understand the magnitude and quality of these dilemmas for adolescents, we will look at psychological literature on the development of moral judgment and moral behavior, and examine moral development and cognitive development as they interrelate and develop differentially among the various subgroups of adolescents.

The moral-developmental theories and research of Piaget and Kohlberg that follow are based on the assumptions characteristic of cognitive-developmental theories. In speaking about social-emotional development, which includes moral development, Kohlberg presents four additional related assumptions:

(1) Affective development and functioning, and cognitive development and functioning are not distinct realms. "Affective" and "cognitive" development are parallel; . . . (2) There is a fundamental unity of personality organization and development termed the ego, or the self. . . . Social development is, in essence, the restructuring of the (a) concept of self, (b) in its relationship to concepts of other people, (c) conceived as being in a common social world with social standards. . . . (3) All of the basic processes involved in "physical" cognitions, and in stimulating developmental changes in these cognitions, are also basic to social development. In addition, however, social cognition always involves role-taking. . . . (4) The direction of social or ego development is also toward an equilibrium or reciprocity between the self's actions and those of others toward the self. . . . The social analogy to logical and physical conservations is the maintenance of an ego-identity throughout the transformation of various role relationships. (1969, p. 349)

These assumptions will become evident in the discussions that follow. Piaget, in his studies of moral development, looked at the judgments that children made while playing games and in answering questions about stories and moral dilemmas. These strategies have continued to be used by Kohlberg and his followers, who greatly improved on the techniques and theory of Piaget, the pioneer in this area. Piaget's position is presented here both for its historical significance and because its relative simplicity may help us understand the gross differences between the way in which children usually define right and wrong and the way in which adolescents and persons at higher cognitive levels do.

According to Piaget (1948) and illustrated in Figure 4.1, two sets of attitudes, or cognitive orientations, the heteronomous and the autonomous, characterize and differentiate between young children's and older persons' definitions of right and wrong and senses of justice.

The young child's egocentrism does not allow him a relativistic perspective. This, added to the confusion or inability to distinguish his subjective stance from the objective world about him, leads him to attribute moral rules with fixed eternal characteristics. Piaget calls this moral ideology "moral realism."

Older persons come to see rules as a result of group efforts and cooperation. The individual is not subjugated to predetermined rules but rather has an "autonomous" relation to others and rules that he can differentiate. Piaget calls this the moral ideology of "mutual respect."

Kohlberg differs with Piaget on the relevance of form and structure of cognitions in moral judgment. He shows that the dimensions that are a matter of content rather than form do not prove through research to adhere to

Younger Children's Moral Realism Ideology	Older Children's Mutual Respect Ideology
1. Objective responsibility	Intentionalism
2. Rules unchangeable	Rules flexible
3. Absolutism of value (judgment universal)	Relativism—many points of view
4. Moral wrongness defined by sanctions	Moral judgments independent of sanctions
5. Duty defined as obedience to authority	Duty defined as conformity to peer expectations
6. Defines obligations ignoring reciprocity	Defines obligations in terms of rights of contract and exchange
7. Expiative justice—punishment for transgressor	Restitutive justice—restoration to the victim
8. Immanent justice—culprit will be struck down	Naturalistic causality—logic of the social order brings justice
9. Belief in collective responsibility	Belief in individual responsibility
10. Punishment by authority	Retaliative reciprocity by victim
11. Favoritism by authority in distributing goods	Impartiality, equality, distributive justice

Figure 4.1. Right and wrong, sense of justice, from moral realism and mutual respect ideologies as developed by Piaget (Put in tabular form and abstracted with permission from L. Kohlberg, "Moral development and identification," in H. W. Stevenson (ed.), *Child Psychology*. Chicago: National Society for the Study of Education, 1963, 314–15.)

regular and universal age trends of development. Kohlberg concludes, "While Piaget attempted to define two stages of moral judgment (the heteronomous and the autonomous), extensive empirical study and logical analysis indicate that his moral stages have not met the criteria of stage he proposes, as his cognitive stages do" (1969, p. 375).

KOHLBERG'S THEORY OF MORAL DEVELOPMENT

To correct the deficiencies he noted in Piaget's conceptualizations in the area of moral development, Kohlberg worked for many years to develop a more specific typology that met the criteria for regular, universal stages. His phenomenal dissertation (1958) and his subsequent efforts, with his colleagues, have shown his success.

Kohlberg developed 10 hypothetical moral dilemmas that he presented to the subject individually in a one-to-one interview (although they have since been given to groups in written form). As the subject responds to the probing questions of the interviewer, the full nature of his or her thinking about each dilemma is elicited. For example:

In Europe, a woman was near death from cancer. One drug might save her, a form of radium that a druggist in the same town had recently discovered. The druggist was charging $2,000, ten times what the drug cost him to make. The sick woman's husband, Heinz, went to everyone he knew to borrow the money, but he could only get together about half of what it cost. He told the druggist that his wife was dying and asked him to sell it cheaper or let him pay later. But the druggist said, "No." The husband got desperate and broke into the man's store to steal the drug for his wife. Should the husband have done that? Why? (1969, p. 379)

The subjects' responses are judged and coded according to one or more of 25 aspects of moral judgment. The ratings for each dilemma on the aspects of moral judgment combine to give an overall rating on the "Classification of Moral Judgment into Levels and Stages of Development." The aspects of moral judgment refer to concepts that are crucial to moral issues, such as punishment, revenge, and rights of property, which are thought to be present in all societies. For our purposes, the levels and stages themselves are sufficiently informative and are applicable to the aspects, so we will dwell on their validity and relationships.

Kohlberg's levels and stages form a typological scheme that describes the specific content, thereby overcoming Kohlberg's objection to Piaget's scheme. The typology is composed of three distinct levels of moral thinking, within each of which are two related stages. The levels and stages are considered as separate moral philosophies and views of the social-moral world. In general the three levels are characterized as:

1. The preconventional level, in which children define good and bad in terms of physical consequences (punishment, reward, favors)
2. The conventional level, where the emphasis is on conforming, as in the preconventional level, but also with maintaining, supporting, and justifying the social order
3. The postconventional level, in which the adolescent or adult develops his own autonomous, moral principles that have validity and applicability separate from his identification with other persons and groups

These levels and stages are presumed and, as we shall see, appear to meet the criteria for a stage theory. They represent an invariant developmental sequence — a person moves forward through the stages (although not necessarily to the highest stage) without skipping a stage as he develops.

RELATION OF MORAL DEVELOPMENT TO OTHER VARIABLES

Before the levels and stages are reviewed in greater detail and related to sociocultural factors, some general points should be made about Kohlberg's view of structure and content in moral development.

Stage structure is not determined by the content of an individual's values or choices, nor does it determine those choices. The structure of moral thought reflects the basic and central theory or frame of reference through which the individual thinks and builds his thoughts.

Content may reflect structure or it may not. It may do so in two specific ways. The stage a person is at may influence the person's value hierarchy. Prediction of moral values and moral action requires that alternatives be ordered by a hierarchy related to the individual's basic structure (Kohlberg and Turiel, 1971). As an example, the highest value of Stage 2 is individual need, whereas Stage 4 places social order over individual need but questions whether property or human life is primary. Stage 6 unquestionably places human life as the highest value. In this way the stage a person is at (structure) influences the values he holds (content) and has available in decision making. Stage also is seen in content as the person is sensitive to aspects of situations to which persons at other stages are not yet, or no longer are, sensitive. As an example, principled subjects, at Level III in Figure 4.2, would be sensitive to issues of justice in a cheating situation while subjects at the conventional level would not be.

A difficult issue, to be discussed at greater length further on, has to do with moral behavior and age-developmental analysis (Kohlberg, 1964). A young child, an older child, or an older adult, for that matter, may all resist temptation. They may all behave in manners that appear to be equally moral. However, they may all behave in these manners for different reasons, i.e., according to their different stages. It is therefore difficult to show a consistent age by developmental-level relationship. Content may reflect structure, but behavior will not necessarily reflect stage. Moral behavior ratings show only a low correlation to later ratings, whereas longitudinal predictability is higher for moral judgments (Kramer, 1968).

Is moral development correlated with cognitive development? From various studies, correlations from .30 to .50 have been found for 12-year-olds between group IQ scores and moral judgment level, showing that there is a cognitive base to moral maturity. "The relation of moral judgment to intellective development is suggested by the fact that our stage definitions assume that Piagetian concrete operations are necessary for conventional (Stages 3 and 4) morality and that formal operations are necessary for princi-

Levels	Basis of Moral Judgment	Stages of Development
I.	Moral value resides in external, quasi-physical happenings, in bad acts, or in quasi-physical needs rather than in persons and standards.	Stage 1: Obedience and punishment orientation. Egocentric deference to superior power or prestige, or a trouble-avoiding set. Objective responsibility. Stage 2: Naively egoistic orientation. Right action is that instrumentally satisfying the self's needs and occasionally others'. Awareness of relativism of value to each actor's needs and perspective. Naive egalitarianism and orientation to exchange and reciprocity.
II.	Moral value resides in performing good or right roles, in maintaining the conventional order and the expectancies of others.	Stage 3: Good-boy orientation. Orientation to approval and to pleasing and helping others. Conformity to stereotypical images of majority or natural role behavior, and judgment by intentions. Stage 4: Authority and social-order maintaining orientation. Orientation to "doing duty" and to showing respect for authority and maintaining the given social order for its own sake. Regard for earned expectations of others.
III.	Moral value resides in conformity by the self to shared or shareable standards, rights, or duties.	Stage 5: Contractual legalistic orientation. Recognition of an arbitrary element or starting point in rules or expectations for the sake of agreement. Duty defined in terms of contract, general avoidance of violation of the will or rights of others, and majority will and welfare. Stage 6: Conscience or principle orientation. Orientation not only to actually ordained social rules but to principles of choice involving appeal to logical universality and consistency. Orientation to conscience as a directing agent and to mutual respect and trust.

Figure 4.2. Classification of moral judgment into levels and stages of development (From L. Kohlberg, "Moral and religious education and the public schools." In T. R. Sizer, *Religion and Public Education.* Copyright © 1967 by Houghton Mifflin Co. Used by permission of the publisher.)

pled (Stages 5 and 6) morality. . . . The Piagetian rationale just advanced, as well as other considerations, suggests that cognitive maturity is a necessary, but not a sufficient, condition for moral judgment maturity" (Kohlberg, 1969, p. 391). In a large study of adolescents and adults, Kuhn et al. (1977) found that only 30 percent of adults had consolidated formal operations, 15 percent had no formal thought, and the rest were transitional between concrete and formal operations. They found the logical and moral levels related and "that the emergence of formal operations is a prerequisite to the emergence of principled moral judgment. . . . Though most Ss had developed the prerequisite of at least some formal operational thought, less than one quarter showed any emergence of principled moral reasoning (p. 99).

If a particular cognitive-developmental level is necessary for the attainment of a particular moral-developmental level, but is not sufficient for it, then research should show that persons with that cognitive level will not necessarily have reached the moral level, but all persons at that moral level should have reached that cognitive level. This is exactly what Tomlinson-Keasey and Keasey (1974) found in a study of college women. "In no instance is there a principled moral thinker who does not evidence a substantial amount of formal operational thought" (Keasey, 1975, pp. 43–45). However, there were subjects at the formal operational level who did not evidence principled moral thinking. In reviewing this literature Keasey concluded "that cognitive development facilitates moral development" (1975, p. 54).

Kohlberg labeled the levels and stages he defined somewhat differently in 1964 than in 1969, and this continued through to the final published description of the stages by Colby et al. (1983). For the sake of better understanding, the earlier labels, which make his points clearly and form the basis for the greatest amount of research on this topic, are used and follow this guide:

Level I	Premoral (preconventional)
Stage 1	Punishment and obedience orientation
Stage 2	Naive instrumental hedonism
Level II	Morality of conventional role conformity (conventional)
Stage 3	Good-boy morality of maintaining good relations, approval of others
Stage 4	Authority maintaining morality
Level III	Morality of self-accepted moral principles
Stage 5	Morality of contract, of individual rights, and of democratically accepted law
Stage 6	Morality of individual principles of conscience

Kohlberg and Gilligan (1971) noted the relationship between development through the cognitive stages of Piaget and development through the moral stages of Kohlberg. Although growth to a new, higher cognitive stage is not enough to bring one to a new, higher moral stage, it is necessary before moral maturation can occur. The earliest cognitive-development stage, which Piaget called the sensorimotor period, is typified by the symbolic, intuitive thought of the infant. It does not relate to Kohlberg's six stages — but rather to an earlier "I want what I want" period. Concrete operational thought is necessary for attainment of Level I morality. Concrete operational thought is characterized by "inferences carried on through system of classes, reactions, and quantities maintaining logically invariant properties and which refer to concrete objects" (Kohlberg and Gilligan, 1971, p. 1063). As a child, at ages 6 to 10, develops, first, the ability to form conceptions of stable categorical classes and, second, conceptions of quantitative and numerical relations of variance, he has the basic, though insufficient, cognitive abilities for the first two moral stages.

Kohlberg goes on to describe three substages of formal operational thought. In a sense the first two substages describe more complex logical operations that are a step removed from the clear references to concrete objects of the earlier stage. But the first two substages of formal operations are not described, as the third substage is, as "true formal thought," including "construction of all possible combinations of relations, systematic isolation of variables, and deductive hypothesis-testing" (Kohlberg and Gilligan, 1971, p. 1063). The first two substages of formal operations are seen as necessary conditions for the development of the Stages 3 and 4 of the conventional level. "True formal operations" are necessary in order to develop postconventional moral judgments, Level III.

In sum, children at the concrete operations cognitive or logical stage have the necessary thinking ability to make Level I moral judgments, and in later childhood and early adolescence they may make Level II moral judgments. Early adolescents, adolescents, and adults who function at the early formal operations substages may make Level II judgments and broach Level III judgments. Lastly, adolescents and adults who have developed true formal operations may also, if environmental and experiential conditions warrant, make Level III judgments. It should be noted that, whereas substages of the logical stages relate directly to specific moral stages through Level II, true formal operations is seen as a necessary but not sufficient condition for Stages 5 and 6. It appears that it is not the cognitive stage, once formal operations are attained, that determines whether a person makes moral judgments from a perspective of social contract and high law (Stage 5) or a perspective of universal ethical principles individually held. Rather, it must be personal differences in motivation, background, and experience that allow formally operational persons to reach either Stage 5 or, in the rarest of persons, Stage 6 morality.

VALIDITY OF KOHLBERG'S THEORY

The reader should be reminded that Kohlberg continued to revise his scoring manual and particulars about the stages through four revisions, until his untimely death in 1987. His attempts were aimed at making both the scoring and the stages ever more valid. The bulk of the research on his theory has therefore been conducted using earlier manuals and definitions and, therefore, it is primarily that research which is referred to in this chapter.

From a variety of research approaches, Kohlberg's moral stages have been shown to be valid, i.e., to adhere to the criteria for a stage theory. Longitudinal evidence (Kohlberg and Kramer, 1969; Kramer, 1968) has demonstrated a definite increase in moral stage level with age as opposed to the inconsistency of results with moral character and moral conduct measurements (Kohlberg, 1964; Page, 1981). The stages show a predictable age-related patterning within individuals through adolescence (Rest, Turiel, and Kohlberg, 1969), although Rest, Davison, and Robbins found that "adults show stronger positive relationships with years of education than with chronological age" (1978, p. 263). Laboratory experiments have also borne out the invariant-sequence concept applied to these stages (Turiel, 1969). And it is clear that a person at a given stage understands the next higher stage better than the succeeding stages, showing the invariant direction of development. Shown in another way, Rest (1968) found that, under normal conditions, a person will not revert to a preceding stage—in fact he may reject the lower stage as inadequate. The consistency of an individual's judgments are indicated by the fact that, on average, 50 percent of an individual's moral judgments fit a single stage. Finally, the concept of equilibrium suggests that age should lead to increasing consolidation (equilibrium) and that the higher stages reflect more equilibrated stages (Turiel, 1969), which has in fact been proven (Turiel, 1969; Kramer, 1968).

One of the most crucial and interesting criteria for the validity of a stage theory is its universality. In order to determine the universality of a theory, attitude, behavior, or whatever, it must be studied among diverse groups. To establish beyond a shadow of a doubt the universality of a phenomenon, one would be required presumably to sample from all existent identifiable groups. Scientists are satisfied that by sampling from groups that differ culturally or socially in particular and known ways conclusions about universality may be drawn. "The point . . . is simply that the type and the number of cultures chosen dictate the limits of analysis and interpretation. For the broadest predictability and inferential analysis, relationships between at least three cultures must be studied" (Manaster and Havighurst, 1972, p. 159). Although it may be possible to test people around the world for moral judgment level using a Kohlbergian approach, it may be, as some attest, that the philosophical undergirding of this approach is not relevant universally and solely representative of the middle-class ideology of Western capitalism (Sullivan, 1977).

Kohlberg (1969) presents evidence from studies of middle- and lower-class urban boys in Taiwan, Great Britain, Mexico, Turkey, and the United States. At age 10 in all three countries, the most prevalent stage is the lowest stage of moral development, Stage 1, with decreasing percentages of each succeeding stage in order of increasing difficulty or maturity. At age 13, Stage 3 statements are most prevalent in all countries, with Stage 5 and Stage 6 little used. By age 16 the order in the United States is Stage 5 highest, then Level II stages, then Level I stages, with Stage 6 least frequently used. At age 16 in Taiwan and Mexico the order by level most to least frequent is II, I, and III. Although the orders are not exactly the same, particularly Stage 5 for 16-year-olds in the United States, and although it is clear that the rates of development are slower in Taiwan and Mexico than in the United States, the stages are evident and orderly in all cultures.

In comparing preliterate villagers in Mexico and Turkey, Kohlberg found a striking similarity between the patterns of moral development from ages 10 to 16 in the two villages. "While conventional moral thought (Stages 3 and 4) increases steadily from age 10 to 16, at 16 it still has not achieved a clear ascendancy over premoral thought (Stages 1 and 2). Stages 5 and 6 are totally absent in this group. Trends for lower-class urban groups are intermediate in rate of development between those for the middle-class and the village boys" (Kohlberg, 1969, pp. 382–383). The case for the universality of the moral judgment stages is strongly made.

MORAL JUDGMENTS, BEHAVIOR, AND STAGE TRANSITIONS

At each stage of moral development, as at each stage of cognitive development, the individual's thinking forms an organized system of interacting parts and processes. Logically, we would expect that, at any stage, individuals would need to have an organized perspective. Equilibrium leads to an understanding of the developmental process as the reorganizing of thoughts leads to equilibrium and as new inputs lead to disequilibrium. The need for a coherent, organized thinking process at each stage is evident in the individual's need to act. Regardless of the direction of behavior, the individual needs to feel that reasons exist for his behavior. Without an organized judgmental base, there would not be coherent action, behavior that the investigator or the actor might understand.

However, a difficulty in the moral-developmental stages is that, as has been mentioned, the emphasis is on structure of thought and not on content. Yet the structure of thought at the various stages indicates predispositions to particular contents. That is, reliance on authority may determine the nature of a judgment — and the choice of authority may then determine action. Or at a higher stage, property or human life may take precedence and determine judgment and, presumably, related behavior. As Kohlberg has developed the moral dilemma stories, responses may vary in content, but the judgmental level may be the same for quite different contents.

Nonetheless, Kohlberg's moral-judgmental measures show considerable predictive validity, whereas measures of moral attitudes and opinions have been notoriously unsuccessful as predictors of moral behavior in the past. As an example of the role of moral reasoning ability in behavior at the low end of Kohlberg's scale, Freundlich and Kohlberg (1971) showed in a sample of low-SES adolescents that 83 percent of delinquents were at the preconventional Level I, while only 27 percent of nondelinquent adolescents were at Level I. Krebs (1971) tested cheating behavior using four experimental tasks and determined moral-developmental level using Kohlberg's stories. Subjects at the preconventional level cheated more (73 percent) than did subjects at the conventional level (66 percent), whereas only 20 percent of the subjects at the principled level cheated. Kohlberg (1969) found 11 percent of principled-level college students cheated, while 42 percent of the same college group who were at the conventional level cheated. In a study of the participants in the Berkeley free-speech movement sit-ins, Haan, Smith, and Block (1968) randomly sampled the university student population and found that 80 percent of the Stage 6 students had sat in, 50 percent of the Stage 5 students had, and only 10 percent of the students tested who were at Level II, Stages 3 and 4, had participated in the sit-ins.

While maturity of moral judgment "is only one of many predictors of action in moral conflict situations, it appears to be a quite powerful and meaningful predictor of action where it gives rise to distinctive ways of defining concrete situational rights and duties in socially ambiguous situations" (Ernsberger, 1975). Nonetheless, there are many reasons why moral behavior will not be directly and strongly related to moral judgment in group data and in predicting individuals' moral behavior. Rest's (1983) proposed model for moral behavior in particular situations points to some of these reasons. Rest's model, which serves as the basis for a similar one by Kohlberg (1984), has four components and only the second one is heavily based on moral judgment. The components are (1) interpreting the situation, (2) figuring out the ideal moral course of action, (3) selecting among valued outcomes and determining the moral course of action, and (4) executing and implementing that intended course.

The exact timing of transitions to new moral stages is no more clearly determined than the ages of transition to new cognitive-developmental stages. Inasmuch as they are related, this makes sense. It seems as if there is a parallel in the research and conclusions at this date for both cognitive and moral development. In the previous chapter it was seen that current thinking shows cognitive development continuing into adulthood and proceeding at different rates for different people. These rates were dependent on maturational, personal, and social experiences. The notions of cognitive development extended into adulthood have not yet been researched to any degree and, as we see, this lack somewhat clouds the kind of definitive conclusions it would be nice to be able to make. So, too, research and thinking in the area of moral development are progressing in the same direction, and too little has been done to date to present definitive conclusions.

Although relationships between moral-judgmental level and moral behavior have been shown, until recently Kohlberg felt that adolescents regressed in moral stage during the course of transitions to new stages and that moral development was pretty well completed in adolescence. However, he more recently maintained that moral development goes on into adulthood and that, although adolescents may develop an awareness of principled moral reasoning, an actual commitment to its ethical employment does not develop until adulthood (Kohlberg, 1973). Moreover, reanalysis of moral judgments made during transitions to Level III are seen not to regress to earlier stages, but are more sophisticated forms of the same stage, possibly leading to a new stage.

What Kohlberg saw as regression may, in fact, be progression (Murphy and Gilligan, 1980). The more relativistic judgments that later adolescents (Guttmann, Ziv, and Green, 1978) make in new groups and roles lead to alternative notions of postconventional moral judgment, progressors rather than regressors, and alternative ways of understanding moral judgments (Dickstein, 1979; Murphy and Gilligan, 1980).

Particularly as this pertains to high school youth, Level III thought and judgment, as previously thought, may in fact be appeals to new higher authority, "conscience" and "moral law," but not principled judgments in the fullest committed meaning. In a sense, this is progress — this is the beginning of the transformation of Stage 4 thinking, as new elements are assimilated, and the beginning of the transition to Stage 5 thought. Turiel (1974) investigated the transition to Stage 5 and found support for the hypothesis that in moving from one stage to another, an awareness of the inadequacies and contradictions of the existing stage promotes rejection of the logic of that stage and the creation and construction of the new stage.

Turiel points out that the transition from Stage 4 to Stage 5 does not generally occur until late adolescence or young adulthood. It appears that the autonomy characteristic of post–high school living, a new and wider set of experiences, and, most notably, college attendance provide the impetus to question the Stage 4 orientation and begin the transition to Stage 5 (Kohlberg, 1973; Turiel, 1974).

Therefore, the judgments of high school–age adolescents that appeared to be principled are more probably a sophisticated Stage 4. Turiel studied high school students and college undergraduates using the moral dilemma stories and found, as expected, conflict and disequilibrium in the beginnings of the transition to Level III judgments:

> The first striking feature of their judgments was the forceful denial of morality. Typically it was stated that: (a) all values are relative and arbitrary, (b) one should not judge what another person should do, (c) it is up to every individual to make his own decisions, and (d) terms like "duty," "good," "should," or "moral" have no meaning. The second striking feature was the inconsistent way in which this relativism was applied. In addition to viewing moral values as arbitrary, there was a strong commitment to moral positions on specific issues. The simultaneous denial of morality and presence of moral assertions reflects the transitional process itself. (1974, p. 19)

The reader may be reminded of the reference to adolescent egocentrism and hypocrisy in the previous chapter.

The adolescents who come to this point of transition must feel the conflict. The live-and-let-live philosophy that obtains in the morning conflicts dramatically with the angry reaction to a classmate who did not do what he "should," a friend who acted "bad," or a parent who did not do his or her "duty." The conflict and inconsistency may not be as apparent to the adolescent as it is to the parent, teacher, or friend. But it can be quite surprising. In the effort to maintain equilibrium, the adolescent will attempt to make it seem coherent and organized but may experience difficulty in making it seem so.

Not all adolescents experience this transition, as most adults develop only to the level of conventional moral judgment, Stages 3 and 4. Remembering that formal operations is a necessary, but not sufficient, requirement for the attainment of Level III moral judgments, Kuhn et al. (1971) found in a study of adolescents and adults that 60 percent of their subjects over age 16 had reached formal operations but only 10 percent definitely showed principled moral thinking.

Affective, cognitive, and moral development parallel each other. In adolescence, those who are developing more, or more quickly, may experience greater conflict and tumult. In a world that itself is tumultuous, maintenance of a consistently clear moral judgment level must facilitate a greater feeling of security. Adolescents in transition probably feel the tumult doubly, both within and without.

I sometimes wonder whether every adolescent has not been confronted by a parent asking, "How are you going to act?" This section, and this chapter, have alluded to one reason why that is such a hard question for adolescents to answer.

SEX DIFFERENCES IN MORAL JUDGMENTS

Kohlberg stated "that the primary concern" of his theory "is with justice reasoning per se, and it is argued that there is no sexual, cross-cultural, or ideological bias to the theory in any strong sense of the term" (Levine, Kohlberg, and Hewer, 1985, p. 94). Nonetheless, he made this late statement as a rejoinder to critics who have noted these biases in his theory. Some studies have shown boys scoring higher than girls on Piagetian tasks (Pesch, 1984) and similar findings on moral judgment led Gilligan (1982) to protest the finding that women's performances on the Kohlberg scale were inferior and to suggest that women's judgments were different from men's in understandable ways.

Gilligan said that women see moral problems in terms of responsibilities rather than rights. Women emphasize responsibility to others, avoiding hurting others, and maintaining relationships—the context of the moral dilemma rather than the abstract notions emanating from the dilemma. Gilligan noted that these different ways of analyzing moral issues make clear "why a morality of rights and noninterference may appear frightening to women in its potential justification of indifference and unconcern. At the same time, it becomes clear why, from a male perspective, a morality of responsibility appears inconclusive and diffuse, given its insistent contextual relativism" (1982, p. 22).

Gilligan's analysis has not been universally accepted, and findings to support it have been inconsistent. Sometimes a sex difference is found in moral judgment studies and sometimes one is not. "But the vast majority of the cross-cultural studies I reviewed showed no significant sex differences favoring men" (Snarey, 1987, p. 5).

The point of Gilligan's argument is very important, however, both for understanding moral judgments and moral behavior and for understanding other sex differences in adolescence and through adulthood. Her analysis of the difference in viewpoint between men and women appears entirely consistent with the analysis of social-familial roles presented by Parsons and Bales (1955). They showed that males and females have different functions within the family, males having an "instrumental" function and females an "expressive" function. Note the similarity between Parsons and Bales' descriptions of these functions and Gilligan's. "Instrumental function concerns relations of the system to its situation outside the system, to meeting the adaptive conditions of its maintenance. . . . The expressive area concerns the 'internal' affairs of the system, the maintenance of integrative relations between the members, and regulation of the patterns and tension levels (Parsons and Bales, 1955, p. 47).

SOCIAL COGNITION

> The development of social conceptions, reasoning, thought — social cognition — is distinct from, though not unrelated to, the development of nonsocial cognition. (Selman, 1980, p. 14)

How many ways are there to categorize life, the world, the universe? Probably an infinite number. Anyone can think about any way, any aspect or category of life, people, and things. Some categorizations are more obvious. They seem more usual and commonsensical. Most of the tests that Piaget developed for determining stage of cognitive development have to do with mechanical and physical properties of objects. Kohlberg's procedures have to do with thinking and making judgments about important or grave moral issues. In this section we are looking at another fairly obvious category of cognition having to do with social cognition or interpersonal cognition, having to do with thinking about specific individuals, people in general, and groups of people — who they are, what they are, what they do and should do — and what we are and what we can and should do.

Clearly we all come to recognize that we have feelings, perceptions, thoughts, and intentions and that others do too. We come to know that the others' feelings, views, and motives are not identical to ours, though some people are more similar to us than others and some are very different. We come to realize that some people's reactions to us are more satisfying to us and vice versa. Psychologists and developmentalists have been constructing ways of understanding how we come to these recognitions and how we understand them differently as we develop. Muuss defined social cognition "as 'how people think about other people and about themselves,' or how people come to know their social world" (1982, pp. 503–4).

The structural-developmental model of social cognition by Robert L. Selman (1976, 1977, 1980) most closely approximates the positions regarding cognitive development and moral development that have been discussed so far and therefore will be used here to expand on the notions of how people think about different things as they come into and go through adolescence. Selman's "approach is primarily concerned with social reasoning and judgment; with *how* children reason about social phenomena, not just *what* they reason. The how of social reasoning is called *structure*, what is reasoned about, *content* — thus, the term structural-developmental stresses the how, i.e., stresses the developing process of social reasoning" (1977, p. 3).

The "developing process" can be seen in the five stages of interpersonal understanding delineated by Selman. The stages are:

Stage 0: Egocentric undifferentiated (approximately ages 3 to 6)
Stage 1: Differentiated and subjective perspective taking (ages 5 to 9)
Stage 2: Self-reflective thinking/ Reciprocal perspective taking (ages 7 to 12)
Stage 3: Third person/ Mutual perspective taking (ages 10 to 15)
Stage 4: In-depth, societal perspective taking (age 12 to adulthood) (Adapted from Muuss, 1982, p. 507).

These stage structures have been investigated in four content areas, called social domains: individual concepts, friendship concepts, peer group concepts, and parent-child concepts.

Selman (1980) presents an example of the interpersonal stages in the friendship concept domain. Children's ideas about friendship pass through Stage 0, momentary playmate, and Stage 1, one-way assistance, in which friendships are significant but understood simply, linearly, and egocentrically. Friends are more important to adolescents. Friends are important throughout the rest of life as well, but they are especially important to adolescents, and these social cognitive stages may give us an indication of one reason why.

By adolescence many youngsters would be in Stage 2, fair-weather cooperation, when they reach puberty, although some would be experimenting in Stage 3, intimate and mutually shared relationships. They are moving from a sense of friendship based on flexible reciprocity to a sense of friendship based on a conception of friendship as mutual, continuing, central, and important. This notion of friendship is tremendously supportive. It goes beyond the obvious concrete reward idea of friendship in Stage 1, but does not leave behind an element of concreteness. Friends are there, through thick and thin, and that is one reason for having a friend.

Adolescence, as will be said repeatedly through this book, is a time of immense change, with many unknowns within and outside the individual. There is probably no time of life in which friends are seen to be more important and there is probably no time of life when they are truly more important. And this is precisely because moving into and through first job, new high school, first period, first ejaculation, first boyfriend or girlfriend, first lover, first time away from home — first, first, first, second, second, only — can be lonely and scary, particularly alone, without a friend.

Adolescents no longer feel "right" turning to their parents over conflicts with friends. The development to Stage 3 seems almost a necessity. Stage 3 in the friendship domain almost smacks of adolescent idealism, but idealism may be concrete as well as abstract. In this stage adolescents recognize that individuals differ from one another and seem to expect and appreciate that friends therefore will not always get on perfectly. They can continue friendships through conflict and learn genuine, mutual understanding (Youniss, 1980). However, the importance attached to friendships and the magnitude of involvement with persons one sees as different, unique, and worthy, possibly for the first time, oftimes results in possessiveness and overinvolvement.

Stage 4, autonomous interdependent friendships, the in-depth and societal perspective-taking stage, implicates fuller formal operations as the sense of friendship becomes one of possibilities, possibilities for each friend and for the friendship. Circumstance, as one moves into later adolescence, may force a form of autonomous interdependent functioning in friendships, but circumstance need not force a change in the conception of the friendships. That is to say, you and your friend graduate from high school and go different ways, enter different schools and/or jobs, marry or not, and so on. You go on to live your independent life, your autonomous life, and can still in some manner maintain your friendship. But the friendship may continue to be understood by both parties or either party at Stage 3. If understood at the Stage 4 level, the friendship has a different quality as it has different meanings.

A still-to-be-answered question surrounds the precise relationship between intelligence — both quantitative-verbal and qualitative — and social intelligence, that which allows development of the ordered stages of social cognition. Marlowe's (1986) work is a good example of the growing body of knowledge in this area. He posits both that social intelligence is independent of verbal and abstract intelligence and that social intelligence is multidimensional, composed of five factors—prosocial attitude, social skills, empathy skills, emotionality, and social anxiety. Although these findings need replication before we can put much faith in them, they do indicate the complexity of people's ways of knowing about interpersonal issues. Just as general or academic intelligence is affected by emotions and attitudes, social intelligence must be affected as much or more by these factors.

One acts in the world as one understands the world. This applies in circumstances where the central issue is morality, as it does in dealings with others—friends, family, authority figures, and strangers. This chapter has described how changes in understanding one's world in the areas of moral judgments and social relations related to changes in thinking—cognitive development—affect people during adolescence.

CHAPTER 5
Sex-Role Development

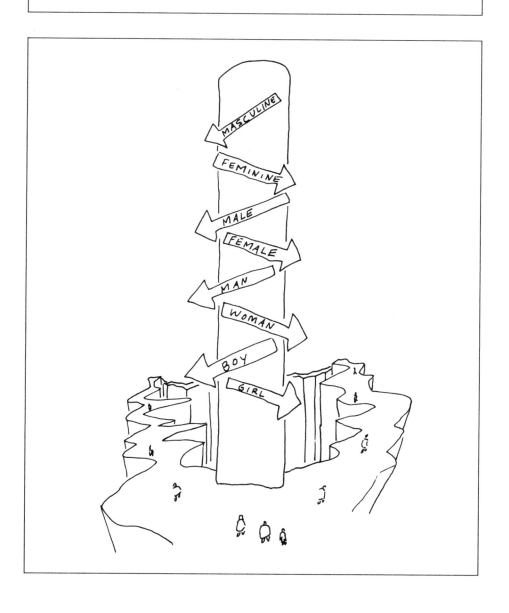

When a child is born, the parents immediately ask two questions: "Is it healthy?" and "What is it?" (except for the occasional overexcited and confused new parent such as myself who asked the nurse immediately upon the birth of our first child, "How old is it?"). The answer to the question "What is it?" is either "A girl" or "A boy." After determining the physical condition of the baby, the single most important question parents ask about their new child is its sex. With the information that "we have a daughter" or "we have a son," the new parents may begin to muse about and conjure up differentiated images of what life in the ensuing years will be like as they raise a boy or a girl. It is not unusual for the new father to begin the next day painting the baby's room pink, if he has a new daughter, or blue, if he has a new son. And the baby, on coming home a few days later, would not be able to discriminate or understand why there is a walking-talking doll in her pink room or a large professional football on the shelf in his blue room, the gift from grandma or grandpa. But these gifts are the beginning inputs in the child's socialization into an appropriate sex role and indicate the continuing sex-role expectations.

PSYCHOLOGICAL SEX DIFFERENTIATION

Much of the current controversy over the role of women in our society, and internationally, hinges on the issue of whether and how males and females differ in the broadest psychological connotations. Toward an understanding of this issue, here we will explain, discuss, and interpret four points: (1) how the differences in the psychological nature of man and woman develop, if indeed they exist — the development of psychological sex differentiation; (2) what these differences are; (3) where our society is in relation to such theories and facts, i.e., the maintenance of traditional sex-role stereotypes; and (4) how the developing adolescent deals with his or her sex-role identity in our changing times.

Three major psychological theories have been advanced to explain the process of psychological sex differentiation — that is, the developmental process whereby male children grow to act, feel, and think like older boys and adult men in the society, and female children grow to act, feel, and think like older girls and adult women in the society.

The first of the theories grew out of the Freudian and psychoanalytic theoretical traditions and emphasizes that sex differentiation occurs through a process of imitation. The idea is that children, most probably unknowingly, choose a same-sex model. The children try to emulate, to imitate, this person's behavior. This person acts as the model for the child's behavior, and the child attempts to model his own behavior according to his perception of the behavior of his same-sex model. Within this theory, most likely the child will choose his or her parent as the model.

Social-learning theory, with its emphasis on the occurrence and effectiveness of positive and negative reinforcement in influencing psychological sex differentiation, is the second major theory. In essence, this theory presumes that parents, other family members, and others in the society positively reinforce (boys by rewarding and praising them for behaving as they think boys should or negatively reinforce them by discouraging them from behaving in feminine or unmanly ways). In like manner, the social-learning theory would see girls receiving positive reinforcement for behaving in ways that the reinforcers, parents and others, see as feminine and receiving negative reinforcement for behaving in ways that are seen as masculine. Boys or girls, whether they understand what is happening or not, would then behave in the sex-appropriate manner in order to receive the reinforcement.

The third theory of psychological sex differentiation relies on a cognitive-developmental interpretation. In this theory the child comes to recognize himself or herself as a boy or girl, sex types himself or herself, and develops a conception of, and begins to categorize, behaviors and activities as appropriate to one sex or the other. So by age 4 or 5, the boy knows he is a boy and wants to do "boy things" and the girl knows she is a girl and, in keeping with her gender identity, wants to do "girl things." (Once at dinner our children, when quite young, had a choice of chocolate or strawberry ice cream for dessert and all chose both. But apologetically, our then 5-year-old daughter turned to her 6-year-old brother and said, "You know, chocolate is a boy's color and pink is a girl's color." Scornfully, he looked at her and retorted,

"Everyone knows that," and they changed their requests to "gender-appropriate" ice creams.)

The believers in each of these theories have maintained that their own theory is sufficient to explain the process of psychological sex differentiation. However, it is becoming clearer that there is considerable overlap among the theories. As an example, the controversy between the social-learning and the cognitive-development advocates continues unabated, yet a prime proponent of the social-learning view, Mischel, can point to the areas of overlap and the possibilities from drawing the viewpoints together. In effect, he says that the social-learning view can accommodate cognitive development formulations about the role of cognitions and self-concepts of sex-role identity as influences on personality. However, he feels that the cognitive development view places too much emphasis on these positions to the exclusion of the valuable aspects of the other position. He says, "The question is not the existence of such cognitions and self-concepts, but rather how adequately they in themselves account for complex sex-typing and socialization phenomena" (1970, p. 59).

In the opinion of this author, the value of the cognitive development theory does not lie solely in how adequately cognitions and self-concepts "in themselves account for complex sex-typing and socialization phenomena." Rather, the adequacy and value of the cognitive development theory lies in its explanatory power while subsuming the notions of the other two theories. "A child's conception of what is appropriate behavior for a male or female will depend both upon what he sees males and females doing and upon the approval or disapproval that these actions elicit differentially from others" (Maccoby and Jacklin, 1974, p. 2).

Both because the cognitive development view can accommodate the other two theories to a considerable degree, and because it is useful in explaining and understanding developmental change, as in adolescence, we agree most closely with it and the following conclusions of Maccoby and Jacklin:

> We believe that the processes of direct reinforcement and simple imitation are clearly involved in the acquisition of sex-typed behavior, but that they are not sufficient to account for the developmental changes that occur in sex-typing. The third kind of psychological process—the one stressed by cognitive-developmental theorists such as Kohlberg—must also be involved. This third process is not easy to define, but in its simplest terms it means that a child gradually develops concepts of "masculinity" and "femininity," and when he has understood what his own sex is, he attempts to match his behavior to his conception. His ideas may be drawn only very minimally from observing his own parents. The generalizations he con-

structs do not represent acts of imitation, but are organizations of information distilled from a wide variety of sources. A child's sex-role concepts are limited in the same way the rest of his concepts are, by the level of cognitive skills he has developed. Therefore the child undergoes reasonably orderly age-related changes in the subtlety of his thought about sex-typing, just as he does with respect to other topics. Consequently, his actions in adopting sex-typed behavior, and in treating others according to sex-role stereotypes, also change in ways that parallel his conceptual growth. (1974, pp. 365–66)

The sex-role development discussed to this point has all occurred in childhood. The child comes to adolescence with a "sex-role identity" that "usually refers to an awareness and acceptance of one's biological gender and an awareness that there are culturally defined attitudes and behaviors which are associated with gender" (Dreyer, 1975, p. 207).

Although there are a variety of sex-role identity types, which will be discussed later in this chapter, it has been considered that, in almost all individuals by the time of adolescence, sex-role identity is so firmly embedded as to be practically immutable. Even in extreme cases such as gynecomastia (breast growth in the male) and hirsutism (abnormal body-hair growth in girls), gender identity does not come into question. The adolescent so afflicted wants medical treatment to return his or her body to normal, to the body characteristics associated with the sex with which he or she identifies. Money and Clopper (1974) point out that incongruous pubertal development, the extreme cases, do not correlate with bisexuality or homosexuality. Dating and romantic involvements follow the earlier gender-identity differentiation.

Since sex-role identity is essentially fixed prior to adolescence, the problem for adolescents is one of sex-role preference. Sex-role preference refers to the choice an individual makes to adopt a particular set, or constellation, of attitudes and behavior that are sex-typed. At a time when roles in society (economic, familial, and social) were clearly defined as appropriate to one sex or the other — sex-typed — the adolescent's problem was minimal, i.e., a male, with male sex-role identity, chose male sex-typed attitudes and behavior. Today that choice is not as clear and, seemingly, will be even less clear in the future.

This implies that today's adolescents cannot rely for establishing their sex-role identity and sex-role preferences on a well-defined set of culturally defined attitudes and behaviors which are associated with gender. Block has introduced a definition of sex-role identity that allows the individual to make sex-role preference determinations, be a mentally healthy person, and be adaptable to traditional, present, and future conceptions of sex role. Block says, "Sexual identity means, or will mean, the earning of a sense of self in which there is a recognition of gender secure enough to permit the individual to manifest human qualities our society, until now, has labeled as unmanly or unwomanly" (1973, p. 512).

Throughout this text specialized psychological terms are used as they are in the literature, with an attempt to clarify points at which the terms themselves are hazy or contradictory. One set of terms that will be clarified in later chapters are those having to do with the "self-regarding attitudes," particularly terms including the words *self* and *identity*. As you will then see, *sexual identity* and *sex-role identity* may not refer to an identity but to an aspect of self such that the terms might communicate more accurately if they were *sex self-concept* and *sex-role self-concept*.

Equally confusing are the terms *sex* and *gender*. Unger defines these terms in a way that would be very useful if they were utilized. She suggests that we use the term *sex* when we are discussing biological properties. Differences "existing within other persons with whom the individual interacts," what she calls "stimulus sex difference," have to do with social labels between the two groups, males and females. Here she suggests using the term "gender . . . to describe those nonphysiological components of sex that are culturally regarded as appropriate to males or to females. Gender may be used for those traits for which sex acts as a stimulus variable, independently of whether those traits have their origin within the subject or not" (1979, p. 1086). Almost all of the differences discussed in the following sections would be gender differences. Because the bulk of the research literature has called them sex differences we will have to use that term most of the time, but the reader is cautioned that the differences most often are gender differences and that sometime in the future the terminology may change to represent the nonphysiological nature, the social nature, of these differences.

In the next section of this chapter we will summarize the scientific justification for the sex differences that our society has labeled as unmanly or unwomanly, before returning in the ensuing section to whether society still considers these differences valid.

SEX DIFFERENCES—MYTHS AND REALITY

The title to this section promises more than the text can deliver. The most complete review and analysis on this topic is Maccoby and Jacklin's book, *The Psychology of Sex Differences*. After an exhaustive review, in which they attempt to account for the biological, psychological, and social factors that might produce sex differences, they summarize their findings. However, they clearly admit the tenuous nature of their findings, a natural result of comparing so many studies varying greatly in samples, data-collection strategies, and theoretical assumptions. Even though the "realities" of sex differences presented by Maccoby and Jacklin may not be the final answer, their conclusions do represent the most advanced state of the art on these issues.

Maccoby and Jacklin looked at the beliefs, and possibly myths, about sex differences and categorized their findings in three ways: (1) those beliefs about sex differences that were unfounded, (2) those that they felt were fairly well established in the scientific literature, and (3) those that remain open questions, either because the research literature is insufficient or because the findings themselves are ambiguous. Included in the category of unfounded beliefs are "that girls are more 'social' than boys, . . . that girls are more 'suggestable' than boys, . . . that girls have lower self-esteem, . . . that girls are better at rote learning and simple repetitive tasks, boys at tasks that require higher-level cognitive processing and the inhibition of previously learned responses, . . . that boys are more 'analytic,' . . . that girls are more affected by heredity, boys by environment, . . . that girls lack achievement motivation, . . . that girls are auditory, boys visual" (1974, pp. 349–51).

The beliefs that girls have greater verbal ability than boys, that boys have greater visual-spatial ability, and that boys have greater mathematical ability are considered to be well founded. A fourth belief that Maccoby and Jacklin considered to be fairly well established in the social science literature is that males are more aggressive than females. This finding is important in its own right but is particularly noteworthy in that it is the only social personality characteristic or trait on which sufficient evidence exists to conclude that males and females differ.

For the beliefs that girls are more fearful, timid, and anxious, that boys have a higher activity level, that males are more competitive, that males are more dominant, that females are more compliant, and that girls show more nurturance and maternal behavior, the evidence is either too scanty or too contradictory to justify conclusions pro or con.

You may ask yourselves, as Maccoby and Jacklin asked themselves, how these beliefs, how these stereotypes about sex differences, continue to be perpetuated when the facts do not substantiate them. It appears that here, as in so many areas of our lives, we look for the confirmation of our beliefs and trust only the evidence that supports them. The beliefs and stereotypes presented in this section, whether corroborated or not, along with other similar stereotypes have, in general, long been accepted. They have influenced behaviors and decisions and the course of people's lives. There is much talk of changing sex roles and "exploding the myths." How rapidly are sex roles really changing, and how is this affecting adolescents?

SEX-ROLE STEREOTYPES—PERSISTENCE, CHANGE

The persistence of sex-role stereotypes and the lower status of women in society seem well illustrated by Aristotle, who said that "woman may be said to be an inferior man" and by the continuation of this theme through the late nineteenth century, as in Tennyson's comment that "God made the woman for the man, and for the good and increase of the world." It is only since the onset of the Industrial Revolution that in the Western World questions have been openly and actively raised about whether "the woman's place is in the home" and male dominance related to strength.

Many years ago Adler also concerned himself with the role that the sexes occupy in our society and lamented the inequality and resulting feeling of inferiority of many women and men who felt that they were not masculine enough. In 1910 he wrote:

> The search for the sexual role usually begins in the fourth year of life and increases the child's curiosity. . . . Not knowing the significance of his sexual tools, the child seeks the difference between the sexes in dress, hair, bodily and mental traits, and in doing so, often makes mistakes. . . .
>
> To this is added the arch evil of our culture, the excessive pre-eminence of manliness. All children who have been in doubt as to their sexual role exaggerate the traits which they consider masculine. (Ansbacher and Ansbacher, 1956, pp. 54–55)

Even in 1927 Adler wrote, "The advantages of being a man are, under such conditions [as exist in our society], very alluring. We must not be astonished, therefore, when we see many girls who maintain a masculine ideal either as an unfillable desire, or as a standard for judgment of their behavior; this ideal may evince itself as a pattern for action and appearance. It would seem that in our culture every woman wanted to be a man" (Ansbacher and Ansbacher, 1956, p. 108).

The mythical sex differences appear to be still with us, but are changing, as the following examples will show.

Williams, Bennett, and Best studied the awareness and the expression of sex stereotypes in young children and found that over 60 percent of the kindergarten and second-grade children examined held the belief that males are more aggressive, strong, adventurous, coarse, independent, loud, dominant, and ambitious, and females are more appreciative, emotional, sophisticated, and softhearted. They summarized their findings as follows: "(a) knowledge of sex stereotypes appeared to develop in a similar manner among both boys and girls, (b) kindergarten children show an appreciable degree of knowledge of adult sex stereotypes, (c) this knowledge increases to the second-grade level but shows no further increase during the next two years" (1975, p. 640). This finding speaks both to the validity of the cognitive-developmental theory of sex-role differentiation and to the persistence of sex-role stereotypes. Clearly these children have differentiated beliefs of how males and females behave to incorporate into their gender identity and for use in sex typing. Moreover, these young children believe these stereotypes today. As they develop, is there any reason for their stereotypic beliefs to alter if the greater society, their parents, their teachers, and the media do not show these beliefs to be incorrect?

Ponzo and Strowig (1973), in a study of sex-role identity of high school students, used an adjective checklist to ascertain the norms for behavior descriptive of, and appropriate for, teenage boys or girls. They found 65 adjectives for males and 59 for females that discriminated significantly between the sexes and that were along traditional sex-role stereotype lines.

Bieliauskas (1974) reported three studies of high school and college students carried out in the 1970s which did not show that the male "above" and female "below" valuation of the sexes had changed. He concluded that as long as the masculine superiority idea was maintained, the masculine protest would remain.

A hopeful note in this regard was struck by Ponzo and Strowig, who found what they termed "an emergent trend" in the sex-role identity of their high school subjects. These subjects showed sex-role identities that blended the behaviors traditionally held to be either male or female. Although hopeful, Ponzo and Strowig concluded:

> In the present decade and in the decades to come it seems likely that for personal optimal development a person will require a sex-role identity that is a blending of attributes to be appropriate for only one or the other sex. Subjects' responses indicated that their sex-role identities were more in the emergent direction than the traditional, but that they viewed appropriate male and female behavior along traditional lines. These lingering traditional stereotypes may cause conflicts among teenagers over appropriate ways to behave, and may restrict them from freely adopting emergent sex-roles that appear to be more conducive to academic success. (1973, p. 141)

Curry and Hock studied sex-role ideals in early adolescence and found that boys posited more differences than girls: "For the male ideal, girls stressed emotional expressiveness and altruistic empathy significantly more than boys. For the ideal female, girls stressed these same two dimensions more than boys, but also stressed task-oriented competence more than boys" (1981, p. 779). They suggested that changing cultural roles of women had begun to affect the sex-role ideals of early adolescent girls.

It is probably worth pointing out here that change in the roles of women has clearly occurred and continues but the exact nature of the sex-role change is as yet undetermined. Thornton and Freedman (1980) note that all groups of women have been affected and that more women than ever are in favor of equal roles for women. In a study comparing over 5,000 graduating high school seniors in 1964 and 1975 Lueptow showed "considerable social change in the liberalization of orientations of both sexes consistent with general value changes in the broader society over this period." However, he found

> no evidence of sex-role change toward masculinization of female roles. What change there is suggests a different dimension of change: liberation and intensification of feminine patterns consistent with the changes in the broader society, but not consistent with current conceptions of changing sex roles that are formulated in terms of masculinizing female roles. Finally, higher levels of achievement value orientations in the female students in both cohorts point toward a redefinition of sex-role content regarding achievement. (1980, p. 48)

What Lueptow seems to be suggesting is the possibility that women may fill different roles and positions than in the past and may share and divide tasks in different ways but may continue to do so in ways that cohere with their own sense of gender, or gender identity. Or it may be that changes which have occurred in adult sex roles have not filtered down to the adolescents studied.

In terms of adolescent development a number of issues are raised:

1. Cannot the content of the same areas, especially socially based areas, be different between the sexes?
2. Might not changes in thinking about and understanding of sex roles follow some developmental order, as we have seen in cognitions in other areas?
3. Does it not make sense that children and adolescents, as well as adults, show more variation, within and between age and sex groups, in their thinking about topics in which there are no clear, absolute answers, as in morality, and about topics where the practices of society are in flux, as in sex-appropriate behavior, than about topics such as math or physics, which are usually used in determining basic cognitive levels?

Remembering the discussion about Gilligan's view of gender differences in moral judgments, we might make the insignificant jump to conclude that girls and women may see themselves in, and think about, social roles differently than do boys and men. In speaking about achievement values, Lueptow notes that we may not have paid attention to the "differences between excellence and accomplishment on the one hand and winning out in assertive, aggressive competition on the other. Females may be high achievers and weak competitors" (1980, p. 57). It may be a strength of women that they are not as assertive and aggressive as competitors and thus their fulfilling of social roles that call for achievement may be quite different from men's manner of fulfilling the same roles. In this way there might continue to be sex-role differences in social roles, even when the social roles per se do not demand the differences.

One of the ways in which we may look at and understand society and social living is in terms of social conventions, e.g., mores, customs, stereotypes and etiquette. Turiel (1975, 1978a, 1978b) found that children and adolescents develop through a sequence of affirmations and negations of social conventions, wherein through seven levels they alternately accept and reject the validity of conventions. He suggested that sex-role stereotypes are one form of social convention. Turiel posited a theory of partial conceptual structures such that thinking about one aspect of a conceptual domain should be related to thinking about other aspects of that domain but not other domains. Carter and Patterson tested these notions with children through grade 8 and found that "changes in children's conceptions of sex role flexibility occurred concurrently with changes in social-conventional flexibility but were unrelated to changes in children's conceptions of the natural law," which suggests "that sex stereotypes and social conventions are not two separate areas of social cognition but are different aspects of the single conceptual domain of social convention" (1982, p. 812).

Turiel's ideas and Carter and Patterson's findings speak to two issues raised earlier. Sex roles, as understood by children and adolescents, follow a developmental sequence like that for social convention in a broad domain of social cognition. This type of thinking, this conceptual domain, is related to but different from that of the domain of natural law on which much of the cognitive-developmental testing is based.

EFFECTS AND PROBLEMS

In childhood, the individual by and large has come to a conclusion about his or her own identity by sex and its coherence with the stereotypes, as he or she understands them and their acceptance by the society for his or her sex and the opposite sex. We have seen that children hold views of male and female sex roles and stereotypes that are similar to, but not identical with, those held by many adolescents and adults.

However, to conclude that there is no sex-role development in adolescence, nor any reason for this development to occur, would be wrong. Most adolescents hold a firm and relatively unchanging sex-role identity.

If the sex roles, the sex-determined role standards, operative in the society were in agreement with the sex-role identity of the individual, there would be no reason for change. If the sex roles in the society were functional for the society and its members, there would be no reason for the adolescent to change or alter his or her sex-role identity. If the sex roles in the society were static, and thus the same for the individual in adolescence as when he learned and adopted them in childhood, there would be no reason for change. If the sex-role standards and stereotypes for children themselves were the same as the sex-role standards and stereotypes for adolescents and then for adults of different ages, there would be no reason for change. If the individual did not develop new abilities and perspectives, as in cognitive development in adolescence and, more pertinent, as in social conventional development, there would be no reason to question and change.

However, none of these *ifs* are true for most or all adolescents. The traditional sex-determined role standards are not desirable for several reasons, which Ellis and Bentler (1973) point out. First, in keeping with Adler's position, differential esteem is accorded male roles and female roles, and the female roles are inferior. As much evidence attests, both for the group and the individual, the attribution of inferior qualities and ascription to inferior roles produce negative social and emotional outcomes. Secondly, people are not satisfied with the traditional sex-role standards. When asked what kind of person they would like to be like males and females both reply that their "ideal person" is not the same as the sex-stereotypic traditional person. That is, they would prefer to be an amalgam of male-valued and female-valued traits rather than solely described by the traits valued for their own sex.

> Finally, a significant amount of literature suggests that traditional sex-determined role standards are not only nonfunctional but perhaps dysfunctional. For example, traditional sex-determined role standards appeared to have negative consequences for personality development, marital harmony, originality in females, and in males, level of achievement motivation, and problem-solving performance. In general, writers have suggested that traditional sex-role standards produce unnecessary internal conflicts and are incompatible with both individual and societal interests. (Ellis and Bentler, 1973, p. 28)

Overall, the traditional sex-role standards are undesirable because they are demeaning and restrictive. They restrict or negate the potential to develop a sex-role identity according to Block's definition. As long as individuals are concerned with whether their behavior, image, and identity are unmanly or unwomanly, they expend energy on those concerns and limit their potential to develop and manifest purely human qualities.

So most adolescents today come into this period with a conception of themselves as budding men and women. From Adler's time to the present, there has been support for the position that masculinity means not being feminine and femininity means not being masculine. The height of being a he-man means being "all man," not feminine at all. The height of femininity implies being truly "the little woman," helpless — "Frailty, thy name is Woman." The John Waynes, Clint Eastwoods, and Hugh Hefners "walking tall" through our high school corridors avoid at all costs, and there are many, showing any feminine characteristics. The Shirley Temple, Phyllis Schlafly, Scarlett O'Hara southern belles who walk next to them would never let on that they are capable or knowledgeable — "Why I could never do that, you're so big and strong."

These extremes of sex-role stereotypes continue, and adolescents who adhere to an extreme ideal, or have adopted a stereotypic traditional sex-role identity, feel diminished in relation to this extreme. Moreover, the females may feel doubly put down by not being even the extreme female, who is not herself as good as the extreme male.

Persons adhering to these extreme masculine or feminine sex identities or aspiring to this level of sex typing, as well as those relatively few persons who maintain a sex-reversed identity (the masculine female and the feminine male) are all restricted and limited by the boundaries of masculine or feminine behavior they feel appropriate to them. The type of sex-role identity described as an "emerging trend" by Ponzo and Strowig was considered to be a hopeful sign in that individuals of this type could express themselves behaviorally and emotionally from a fuller scope of potential behavior, masculine and feminine.

The emergent-trend type appears to be similar to what Bem termed the "psychologically androgynous" individual. She develops the thesis that "because his or her self-definition excludes neither masculinity nor femininity the androgynous individual should be able to remain sensitive to the changing constraints of the situation and engage in whatever behavior seems most effective at the moment, regardless of its stereotype as appropriate for one sex or the other" (1975, pp. 634–35). In support of this thesis, she cites studies that have shown consistently that high-femininity females exhibit high anxiety, low self-esteem, and low social acceptance and that although high masculinity during adolescence for males relates to better psychological adjustment, in adulthood high masculinity correlates with high anxiety, high neuroticism, and low self-esteem. Moreover, children and adolescents of both sexes who are more highly sex-typed are found to be lower overall in intelligence, spatial ability, and creativity.

Bem ran two studies, one of which was designed to elicit stereotypically masculine behavior—independence in a conformity-demanding situation —and the second of which was designed to elicit stereotypically feminine behavior—playing with a kitten when given the opportunity. The idea was simply that androgynous persons of both sexes could excel, could display the masculine independence or feminine playfulness, whereas nonandrogynous persons, highly sex-typed persons, could only excel in or display sex-appropriate behavior. Overall, her thesis was supported by the results of the study, although the feminine females could not be said to have exhibited either the masculine independence or the feminine playfulness, from which we can again infer that the feminine-female role and type is more seriously debilitating. Bem concludes that "the current set of studies . . . provides the first empirical demonstration that there exists a distinct class of people who can appropriately be termed androgynous, whose sex-role adaptability enables them to engage in situationally effective behavior without regard for its stereotype as masculine or feminine. Accordingly, it may well be . . . that the androgynous individual will someday come to define a new and more human standard of psychological health" (1975, p. 643).

We are able to talk about masculinity and femininity and even androgyny, some combination of the two, with relative ease and some good degree of common understanding. However, we should realize that these terms reflect large constellations of behaviors, attitudes, and feelings that do not go together as one, they are not an unbreakable block. Bem (1974) sees masculinity and femininity as independent dimensions and the androgynous as people higher in both. Spence and Helmreich (1978; Spence, 1982) have investigated clusters of qualities that have been posited as central to male-female differences and the continuance of traditional sex roles, the instrumental and expressive characteristics. Their findings are similar to Bem's in that the high instrumentals are mainly men, the high expressives are mainly women, and a third group, high in both, are seen as androgynous. *Instrumental* refers to relations with, adapting to, and seeking and reaching *external* goals, goals outside the self, while *expressive* concerns *internal* affairs with others, integrative relations, and regulation of patterns of behavior and tension levels (Parsons and Bales, 1955).

Instrumental and expressive characteristics relate to male-female differences as discussed by Gilligan in the previous chapter. They are core characteristics associated with the traditional roles held by men and women and functional to the maintenance of these roles. Using the instrumental-expressive concepts, we may have a clearer idea of a central element of masculinity and femininity, but they are not isomorphic. Instrumental and expressive characteristics may be seen as modes of being that may relate to gender identity for some, or many, people but need not. An individual may see him- or herself as of one gender and, by virtue of other needs and senses of self, elect to be more or less instrumental, expressive, or both. As society and social roles differentiate between the sexes and demand, in a sense, that instrumentality, expressivity, and other characteristics that have been known as masculine or feminine are appropriate mainly or only to one sex or the other, it seems more likely that boys and girls will pick this up and be more as they "should." As society does not make these demands and the signs and symbols to children of both sexes are less clear, the children may put together their own constellations of characteristics that do not diverge substantially from their own sense of themselves as male or female.

There are, then, persons, described as androgynous or of the emergent trend, for whom the traditional sex-role standards are not as limiting because they can choose to behave as they wish regardless of the sex-role demands. These persons, it would seem, should be prepared readily to accept changes in sex-role standards within the society toward a more egalitarian system. That is to say, as the restrictions on males performing "feminine" behaviors and vice versa are lessened, these persons almost automatically fit in. But what of the individuals who have accepted and adopted the traditional sex-role standards?

Resistance to changing sex roles can be expected, and does exist, particularly from persons who have maintained and adopted the traditional sex roles for themselves. It is easy to see how threatening it might be for a male of the John Wayne type who finds respect for his total masculinity diminishing and women encroaching on his territory. When we consider the antagonism that has long been felt and shown toward persons with sex-reversed identities, it is possible to generalize this antagonism to greater numbers of people who show what has been considered sex-inappropriate behavior and characteristics during a time of changing sex roles. Changing sex roles in the society may provoke problems, if not change, for the adolescent who has entered this period with the traditionally appropriate sex-role identity.

The three considerations raised thus far in this chapter regarding the necessity for change in sex-role identity or new developments in sex-role identity are (1) the restrictive and limiting nature of traditional sex roles, (2) the varying adaptability of existing sex-role types — masculine, feminine, and androgynous, and (3) the demands made, particularly on people with traditional sex-role identities or sex typing, in a society with changing sex roles, which may refer to problems and issues of adult development as well as adolescent development. Yet these issues may be more pressing, more immediate and critical, for adolescents because they are meeting them at a stage where they are expected to deal with them for the first time.

In the life-task chapters that follow, sex differences will be noted and discussed. However, sex differences will not be emphasized. Taking a somewhat futuristic view, and assuming that the readers of this book will be concerned with adolescents in some capacity in the future, gross traditional sex-difference stereotypes may be considered a cultural artifact, a historical anomaly, still with us to some degree but in the process of change. Many adolescent boys will be concerned that they are not as manly as they "should" be. Many adolescent girls will choose occupations because they are "feminine" occupations. Many adolescents will find the sex typing of behaviors and life-styles an issue in their decisions. But if this chapter has done nothing more, it has tried to show that, although the stereotypes still exist, they are changing; that, although many children and adolescents still identify themselves by sex in the traditional ways, there are significant numbers who do not; and, lastly, that there is almost no valid psychological or scientific justification for the belief in the stereotypes.

Personality Development

This chapter is about personality. The next is about self and the one after is mainly about identity. *Personality* is the more inclusive term and concept. However, each of these concepts has a distinctive place in our understanding of adolescents. It is intended that cumulatively these three chapters will impress the reader with the stability of adolescents' personality, the change and development of their senses of and evaluations of their "self," and the developments that may lead to a sense of identity and the difficulties, crises, of this development.

Adolescence is characterized as a period of change. So far we have discussed developmental change in physiology, cognition, and conceptions of morality and social living. From many perspectives, certainly that of many parents, it would appear that there is considerable personality change during adolescence. The position will be taken in this chapter, supported by both theoretical and research literature, that little or no personality change occurs in adolescence. The phenomena that look like personality change in adolescence and the type of research that has given credence to the personality change thesis will be examined.

DEFINITIONS OF PERSONALITY

It is probably impossible, and certainly not worthwhile, to discuss personality without defining it. "Personality" as used by psychologists does not mean degree of personableness or likability or congeniality, which is how it is more frequently used by "normals" (nonpsychologists). Within the psychological literature there are many definitions of the term that seem to depend on the theory under study. "Personality consists concretely of a set of values or descriptive terms which are used to describe the individual being studied according to the variable or dimensions which occupy a central position within the particular theory utilized" (Hall and Lindzey, 1957, p. 9).

After examining almost 50 definitions of personality, Allport defined it as "the dynamic organization within the individual of those psychophysical systems that determine his unique adjustment to his environment" (1937, p. 48). Allport later summarized a discussion of the structure of personality, saying:

> The most comprehensive units in personality are broad intentional disposi-
> tions, future-pointed. These characteristics are unique for each person, and
> tend to attract, guide, inhibit the more elementary units to accord with the
> major intentions themselves. This proposition is valid in spite of the large
> amount of unordered, impulsive, and conflictful behavior in every life. Fi-
> nally, these cardinal characteristics are not infinite in number but for any
> given life in adult years are relatively few and ascertainable. (1955, p. 92)

Maddi, an important contemporary personologist, that is, a student and specialist in personality theory and research, defines personality as

> a stable set of characteristics and tendencies that determine those common-
> alities and differences in the psychological behavior (thoughts, feelings, ac-
> tions) of people that have continuity in time and that may or may not be
> easily understood in terms of the social and biological pressures of the im-
> mediate situation. (1980, p. 10)

Personality definitions emphasize a set, or the organization, of an individual's ways that make him appear distinctly and consistently different from others and distinctly and consistently like himself. The essence of an individual's set of characteristics or tendencies resides in the simplicity of its organization and its "continuity in time."

In a way, you recognize this when you meet someone again after a long period of time and think, "Same old Joe." You may be reacting to his superficial mannerisms, which are more peripheral to personality, but you may also be reacting to his modus operandi, the way he copes, which you remember, or to the feeling you get from him, which you also remember. That is, this long-lost friend will have a pattern to his behavior and will have a goal or goals in relating to which you react. Although he will have changed in many ways, some of the attitudes he expresses or certain of his behaviors are peculiarly him and bring back that "old feeling."

Adler's (1929) conception of life-style, which at times he equated with self, man's own personality, and the unity of the personality, bears a lovely resemblance to the juxtaposition of individual uniqueness and social-biological pressures in Maddi's definition:

If we look at a pine tree growing in a valley we will notice that it grows differently from one on top of a mountain. It is the same kind of a tree, a pine, but there are two distinct styles of life. Its style on top of the mountain is different from its style when growing in the valley. The style of life of a tree is the individuality of a tree expressing itself and molding itself in an environment. We recognize a style when we see it against a background different from what we expect, for then we realize that every tree has a life pattern and is not merely a mechanical reaction to the environment.

It is much the same way with human beings. (Ansbacher and Ansbacher, 1956, p. 173)

PERSONALITY CONSISTENCY

It is within the stability, organization, and consistency of a person's thoughts, feelings, and actions as part of his culture and as uniquely himself that the meaning of personality lies. It is important to note that consistency is an element in the definition of personality. In some manner the distinctive characteristics that differentiate one individual from others in the psychological and behavioral realms must be consistent over time so that the individual can psychologically and behaviorally be "himself" to himself and others. A number of theorists have discussed this.

Very simply, in the Adlerian perspective, the individual comes to his own view of himself and his world and determines where he must be to be OK — getting there is his goal. This goal, called at times "fictional final goal" or "guiding self-ideal," is developed early and held with only slight alteration through life. "The goal of the mental life of man becomes its governing principle, its causa finalis. Here we have the root of the unity of the personality, the individuality" (Adler, 1923, in Ansbacher and Ansbacher, 1956, p. 94). The goal is a personal creation and is therefore unique for each person, depending as it does on the "meaning he gives to life." An individual's life-style is not clearly evident to himself or others. It is expressed vaguely in all the ways he strives for his goal. The individual cannot articulate his goal but strives for it in any way that he can, whether it appears consistent or inconsistent. "When a person appears to be inconsistent, the very inconsistency may be consistent" (Manaster and Corsini, 1982, p. 32).

There are some crucial points in these positions from Adler. The individual has his own conception of his goal, which he consistently strives to reach, but in the process of striving, he develops his own strategies to reach his goal. That is, his behavior is aimed toward his goal, but the observer may not recognize the consistency because he may not recognize the goal.

By the time a child is five years old his attitude to his environment is usually so fixed and mechanized that it proceeds in more or less the same direction for the rest of his life. His apperception of the external world remains the same. The child is caught in the trap of his perspectives and repeats increasingly his original mental mechanisms and the resulting actions. (Adler, 1930, in Ansbacher and Ansbacher, 1956, p. 189)

Allport discussed personality unity both as striving and in relation to the self-image. Referring to the unity-through-striving doctrine, Allport cites the position that "what integrates our energies is the pursuit of some goal" (1961, p. 380). He also refers to Lecky's work, one of the long-standing references on self-consistency. Lecky defined personality "as an organization of values which are felt to be consistent with one another" (1951, p. 152). "Behavior expresses the effort to maintain integrity and unity of the organization. . . . In order to be immediately assimilated, the idea formed as the result of a new experience must be felt to be consistent with the ideas already present in the system. On the other hand, ideas whose inconsistency is recognized as the personality develops must be expelled from the system" (1945, p. 135). Lecky's theory, stressing maintenance of the unity of the system, also seems to present a form of equilibrium and a process of assimilation and accommodation to new experience imposing on the existing personality schema.

In adolescence, with all of the changes that occur, emotional crises, instability, and reorganization appear. During this period, when the adolescent may be adapting and revising his values and outlook, Lecky points out that "the need for unity is most acute" (1951, p. 159).

David Glass, in a very complete review of theory and research in consistency and personality, shows the continuing viability of the concept as well as growing sophistication in its use. He says:

> One of the older doctrines in psychology holds that man cannot tolerate inconsistency among his cognitions and that he continually strives to eliminate it. The existence of inconsistency makes him uncomfortable, makes him feel something is wrong. . . . Two elements are inconsistent if, for any reason, they do not fit together. Cultural values, personal standards, or past experience may dictate that the two do not fit. (1968, pp. 788–89)

The psychology of Alfred Adler is often called *individual psychology* because it is based on the doctrine of the unity of the personality. "This name, which is so often misunderstood, is derived from the Latin word 'individium,' which literally means 'indivisible' " (Dreikurs, 1953, p. 56). This discussion has illustrated by definition and theory the indivisibility, the unity, the consistency of the individual, of personality.

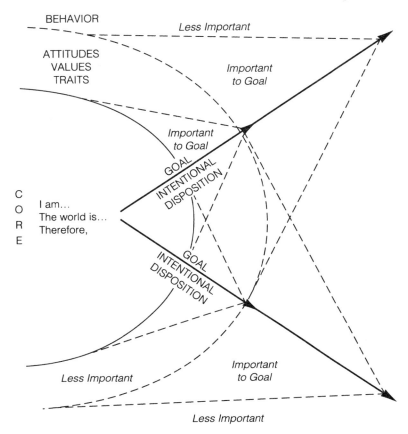

Figure 6.1. Personality consistency described as the core notions and goals. Attitudes, values, traits, and then behavior are more important to the personality, and more consistent, as they are more closely related to the individual's goals as felt by the individual in each role, situation, and age.

As this discussion has proceeded, I hope you have come to a conclusion and a confusion. The conclusion I hope you came to is that the individual's personality must be a consistent whole as he sees himself. This is illustrated in Figure 6.1. If he sees or feels inconsistent internally or about his behavior, if his thoughts or behavior are to him not like him, he will feel uncomfortable. To alleviate this discomfort he will act, mentally or behaviorally, to bring himself back into a self-perceived state of consistency.

Let us construct an example, using a key dissonance-reducing phrase, a phrase of a type often used by adolescents to make what they *want* to do consistent with what they think they *ought* to do. In counseling sessions, young men often say, in essence, "She's really a great girl. I like her. I'd like to make it with her. But I don't know whether she is that kind of girl. If she is, I'll try. If she isn't that kind of girl, or if I can't tell, I guess I shouldn't do anything. But I really like her. *I could even* love her." As the monologue continues, the young man can build his interest, dedication, and passion for the girl to the point where all his actions are justified in the name of love. Certainly, he understands, the most noble and pure of youth in the heat of the moment, with love in his heart, cannot be held accountable if he oversteps some bounds. And the bounds of proper behavior for the youth may not be thought, by him, applicable if he is in love—reason enough to be in love for an honorable young man who needs to be consistent in word and deed. "I could even love her" (if necessary).

There must be an infinite number of ways in which the objectively inconsistent and illogical can be construed by an individual as consistent and logical within his personality system. In like manner, what appears on the surface as logical and consistent may be inconsistent in the context of a person's goal. In many instances an adolescent will reject or avoid an opportunity for what would appear to be substantial personal social recognition. His act makes no sense to someone who understands the societal reward system. But it is entirely consistent and makes good sense to the adolescent whose personal goal is, for instance, safety—not standing out, not being noticed, not receiving special recognition—comfortable, inconspicuous safety. As disjointed, irrelevant, and incomprehensible an individual's behavior, attitudes, and feelings may seem, we can only conclude that they are consistent within the unity of his personality.

Having expanded on the conclusion, the confusion persists. Consistency has been used in two ways: personality consistency as it exists within the individual at any one time and consistency of the personality over time. It is more usual to refer to these two types of personality consistency as "personality consistency" and "personality stability," respectively. In order to emphasize the position being taken here, that the same dynamic which influences consistency at one time also influences consistency (stability) over time, reference will continue to be made to "two types of personality consistency." As shown in Figure 6.2, the need for unity and consistency at any one time precludes great and continuous change over time, because changes over time demand inconsistencies and disunities at many places along the time span. Once an individual develops the schema of his self-image, world image, and personal goal (his life-style or personality), he will maintain it intact over time. Personality, or "life style enables us to organize ourselves, to evaluate

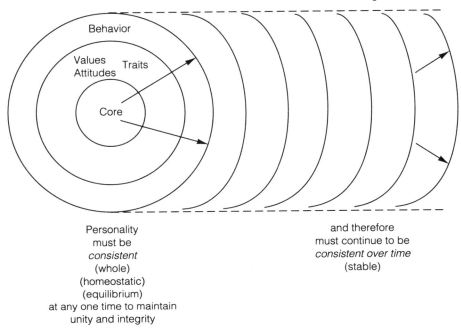

Figure 6.2. Personality consistency at any one time and over time. Major personality change would demand inconsistency (disunity, loss of personal integrity) at any one time, and, therefore, over time would cause personal, emotional, and behavioral instability.

new situations, to simplify life, to make predictions and in general to cope with life" (Manaster and Corsini, 1982, p. 98).

As in almost all issues in psychology there is dispute over these conclusions. Ample theory has been cited to show both the existence and the need for personality consistency at any one time and over time. Research does not exist to prove the complete unity of the personality at any one time—it would have to investigate the whole personality and the personality as all of its parts. But there is research on aspects of personality consistency over time, and this is cited in the next section.

RESEARCH ON PERSONALITY CONSISTENCY

The magnitude of difficulties in conducting and interpreting research on personality consistency over time—personality stability—is immense. There are two traditional approaches to doing this kind of research in which the question is the similarity or difference between ages on one or more personality variables. They are cross-sectional and longitudinal research.

In cross-sectional research, subject samples from more than one age or stage group are compared on the personality variable under investigation. If the age samples are comparable on other variables, such as sex, socioeconomic status, ethnicity, etc., the differences and direction of differences found between the age groups will be presumed to have a developmental function. That is, in interpreting the data, the investigator assumes that in specific basic aspects when the subjects in his sample were or will be the ages tested, they will be the same or very similar on these aspects. For example, if you were testing 15- and 20-year-olds using a cross-sectional design, to conclude that the differences or similarities found between the age groups showed consistency or inconsistency of a developmental nature, you would have to assume that the 20-year-olds were like the 15-year-olds when they were themselves 15 and that the 15-year-olds will be like the 20-year-olds when they become 20. There are many variables (child rearing, economic situations, or world events) that might intervene to make this assumption false.

The other research strategy for looking at developmental change or continuity is the longitudinal design, in which the same people are retested at two or more ages. In this type of research it is possible to study the developmental interrelationships within the same individuals over time. Longitudinal studies are limited because they (1) are quite expensive to run, (2) obviously take a long time to conduct, (3) lose subjects from beginning to end, which interferes with the assumption of random sampling, (4) are affected by the national and world events peculiar to the time of the study, and (5) either have to give the same tests over and over or have to give different tests for age-appropriate reasons at different ages, wherein test comparability is questionable (Kuhlen, 1952). Even with all the limitations, "where one is concerned with developmental processes through time, repeated testing in a longitudinal design is essential" (Holtzman et al., 1968, p. 132). Therefore this section will concentrate on longitudinal studies to explore the question of personality consistency into and from adolescence.

We will look first at some longitudinal studies in which the subjects were first tested or interviewed in childhood, or even infancy, and later reexamined in adolescence. Anderson (1960) concluded, from five- to seven-year follow-up testing of all subjects who had been 4th to 12th graders in a Minnesota county, that intelligence measures were more important predictors of later adjustment than were personality measures, which had little predictive validity. MacFarlane, Allen, and Honzik (1954) correlated behavior problems, such as sleep restlessness and food finickiness, with personality characteristics, such as shyness, dependency, and irritability, measured at various times between 21 months and 14 years. They found that the size of the correlations (the degree of relationship) varied greatly across ages, even between the close ages tested.

Neilson (1948) asked judges to match personality sketches of 15 children, based on Shirley's famous observations of children until they were two years old, with independently developed sketches prepared from test and interview data taken when they were adolescents. The judges were able to match the early childhood and adolescent sketches at better-than-chance rate.

A number of studies hypothesized and found relationships between personality deviations or behavior problems in childhood and similar disturbances in adulthood (Bender, 1953; Eisenberg, 1956; Morris, 1956), despite therapeutic interventions in some instances. As in these clinical studies, which show the persistence of disturbed personality and behavior, Bandura and Walters (1963) show the persistence of antisocial childhood behavior into adolescent delinquent behavior, citing Glueck and Glueck (1950) and McCord, McCord, and Zola (1959).

Several studies indicate significant consistency between personality variables or patterns from early adolescence through to late adolescence or adulthood. Schoeppe and Havighurst (1952) reported that the degree of achievement on a number of the developmental tasks investigated were essentially determined by 13 years of age. Gardner and Moriarity (1968) pointed out that the patterning of psychological defenses at preadolescence were more fully developed than had been thought before and were similar to the patterning in a group of adults. Tuddenham (1959) was justifiably impressed with the stabilities of personality ratings he found in a 19-year follow-up study of subjects, who were then approximately 33 years old, from the adolescent growth study of the University of California's Institute of Human Development. Peck and Havighurst (1960) in the "Prairie City" study found high correlations between conscience development and emotional independence at ages 10 and 16. Offer and Offer (1970) in a 7-year follow-up study of adolescent boys with average self-images found consistency in coping styles, problem areas, and responses to the problems, and adherence to parental value systems.

Kagan and Moss, authors of one of the most important and influential studies of this type, carried out on subjects from the Fels Research Institute's longitudinal population, came to the following conclusions, one of which was dramatic in its appearance in so many instances. A few behaviors exhibited during the ages 3 to 6 period, and many of the behaviors exhibited by children from 6 to 10, predicted fairly well adult behaviors that theoretically would be related. Among the adult behaviors that were related to reasonably similar, or analogous, behaviors or behavioral tendencies in child-hood were "passive withdrawal from stressful situations, dependency on fam-ily, ease-of-anger arousal, involvement in intellectual mastery, social interac-tion anxiety, sex-role identification, and pattern of sexual behavior" (1962, p. 266).

The strongest influence on consistency, Kagan and Moss found, was the appropriateness of an individual's behavior for his or her sex as defined by the culture. "The individual's desire to mold his overt behavior in concor-dance with the culture's definition of sex-appropriate responses is a major de-terminant of the patterns of continuity and discontinuity in his develop-ment" (1962, p. 269). They go on to say that everyone has an idea of "the person he would like to be and the goal states he would like to command" (p. 271). The question of development of an "ideal self" is considered in the next section, whereas the personal goal has been discussed with reference to Adler earlier in this section. "It would appear that the desire to be an 'ideal male' or 'ideal female,' as defined by the individual, comprises an essential component of everyman's model" (p. 271) and carries considerable weight in maintaining personality in a consistent pattern as the individual pursues his ideal self and personal goal.

In concluding this section, the difficulty remains in confirming the de-gree of personality continuity that the theorists affirm and that these studies indicate. Individuals may change their behaviors, attitudes, and values in many areas that are not central to their personality or life-style. If these be-haviors, attitudes, and values are studied to test their consistency over time, because the investigator believes them central or basic, low but significant correlations may be disappointing.

It seems, with the enormous room for error in measurement and method, and the unique personality patterns and constellations under study, that sig-nificant relationships in group data clearly indicate the presence of extremely strong threads of personality consistency over time. Overall, the research with global personality characteristics shows a moderately high degree of con-sistency over time, whereas research focused on more specific traits shows lit-tle consistency. Almost by our definition of personality, these should be the findings if personality is consistent at any one time and also continuous over time. We must agree with the conception of dynamic consistency as defined by Yarrow and Yarrow (1964), in which they point out that one would not expect a person to exhibit exactly the same overt behavior and personality characteristics at two different ages. Although this would produce high-level consistency data, it does not account for developmental transformations in which the new behaviors are dynamically related to earlier behavior patterns and functions. It is at this level of analysis that consistency is high.

WHY ADOLESCENT PERSONALITY APPEARS INCONSISTENT

DEVELOPMENTAL AND SOCIAL REASONS

The onset and growth in formal operations for many adolescents opens new vistas for thought and behavior. Almost as a form of reality testing, adolescents try out their new thoughts and behaviors with friends, parents, and others to assess their reactions, as well as the adolescents' own reactions. In addition to this reality-testing function, trying out new hypotheses and potentials in thought and action can be very stimulating and just plain fun. In toto, as reality testing and as an enjoyable facet of being an adolescent, this process has been referred to earlier as an experimenting effect of the development of formal operations in adolescence.

You can ask yourself whether you felt a thrill, an excitement, when you "overdid" a behavior or emotion when you were an adolescent. Having been crossed, or at least contradicted, by your parents, you got angry. As you stamped out of the room, during a momentary pause, you looked for some way of really showing your anger. Although it "wasn't like you," you slammed a door, kicked a wall, or threw a pillow. Or the first time you "lost in love" — which may have been when your favorite pop star married — you lay across your bed, sobbing and sobbing and enjoying the tears. Maybe you remember fiercely stating and debating a point or cause that you believed in at the time, but knew you wouldn't believe in forever. It might have been when you told your doctor father that you had decided to make pots, or your potter father that you wanted to be a doctor. It might have been when you sat by the pool and expounded on the socialist state, or when you explained the justice and rationale of the domino theory to your antiwar friends. You may remember sitting up half the night with your best friend, detailing your hopes and fears and very firmly saying what kind of person you were — it felt great to be able to lay this out clearly and definitely, but you doubted much of what you were saying. Even if it wasn't like you, you knew you could try it — whatever it was. So you tried on a style, or position, or behavior, and even if it didn't quite fit, you enjoyed the act and the fact that you could do it.

Much of the perceived inconsistency in adolescent behavior reflects the individual adolescent's experimenting with the new potentialities of formal operational development. However, as has been shown, not all adolescents develop formal operations.

There is a second major factor in the apparent inconsistency and lack of continuity in the personality of the adolescent. The adolescent starts to move from a limited area (home, immediate neighborhood, old friends) that he understands into the greater community which presents many tasks, roles, and situations that he does not understand. As the adolescent approaches new arenas — new schools, work experiences, new friends, dating, clubs, and organizations at school, church, in the community, and so on — he may not know how to behave. He may be unsure of what is expected of him and of how adequately he is able to perform in each of these arenas and specific situations.

As well-adjusted, competent, self-assured adults, we probably approach a new situation with some caution, attempting to gather relevant information so we know as much as possible of what to expect. Regardless of our understanding of, and expectation for, the new situation, we enter it with some degree of confidence that we can adequately handle it. To put it another way, our behavior in all situations, whether new to us or not, has to be acceptable because we have come to understand and accept, individually, that we can do what we can do, that we are what we are. With the sense of competence and self-assurance of normal, adjusted adults, we take the position in all our undertakings that we are OK.

An adolescent embarking on and passing through the new situations and tasks that are presented to him does not know whether he is OK. He does not know whether the style he has used before will satisfy in these new situations. He does not have the breadth of experience to feel confident that he can generalize style and understanding to the new tasks. Rather, he tries to find the appropriate style from modeling competent others he knows or has seen, even in movies or on television, anticipating what he has seen them do or acting as he thinks they would in the same situation. In a concrete way, he tries on the behavior he senses as appropriate or most effective for the roles in which he finds himself.

To some extent, when you observe a boy on his first date, you see him open the door as his older brother would, walk with the slouch or swagger of his entertainment or sports idol, criticize the movie with the verve of the "Today Show" 's movie critic, and treat the waiter as his father does. His date may exude the purity of Rebecca of Sunnybrook Farm, carry herself like her favorite actress, and act as reticent and unsure as she feels or as assertive as Bella Abzug. She may at times be like her mother, sister, friend, or idol. It is not that either of these adolescents loses himself or herself in the process. It is only that they do not know yet how they should, can, and will behave in these particular new situations. In the process of fitting themselves into new roles, they attempt to use available and preferred models as guides until they can behave naturally and comfortably as themselves. And parents, teachers, and friends see them as inconsistent during the times they are experimenting.

It is important to remember that the choice of models and styles of coping the adolescent uses, even if transitory and unusual for him, will be in keeping with his personal goals and his personality. But it may be very difficult to determine this while observing bits of behavior rather than patterns of behavior.

The point here then is that adolescent behavior and personality appear inconsistent when the adolescent is "experimenting" with new cognitions and/or learning about new situations in order to find his attitudinal and behavioral style, i.e., that style which best fits his personality and moves him toward his personal goals.

RESEARCH-METHOD REASONS

In the section on research in personality consistency and continuity, we have seen that longitudinal research investigating general, or broad, personality variables and patterns finds considerable continuity from childhood through adolescence into adulthood. We have also seen that there have been, for good reason, few complete and competent studies of this nature. Therefore most of the studies of consistency or change over time in adolescence have been cross-sectional. The results of these studies have reinforced the view of inconsistency and discontinuity—apparently unjustifiably so.

One research strategy speaks to this issue and attempts to control the factors that put the findings of longitudinal and cross-sectional research at such variance. Before discussing this strategy, and in order to understand it, a few words about the meaning of "generation" are needed. In chapter 2, reference was made to parent and child generations. Approximately a 25-year age difference was posited between the parent and the child generations. The ages of the members of the parent generation could cover a broad range, as could the ages of the members of the child generation, but the differences between their ages would remain constant. In this context, a generation includes a broad age range of persons with a common attribute, i.e., parent or child, and, for that matter, obviously, an individual may be a member of both generations.

Generation may also refer to groups with more general or presumed common attributes or attitudes that relate to their common age, whatever the range, and the commonalities in social history they hold by virtue of living at the same ages at the same times. There have been many recent uses of the term in this way — the prewar generation, the postwar generation, the Sputnik generation, the now generation, and even the Pepsi generation.

What is the range of age that constitutes a generation? Put another way, in research on personality and attitudes, when a difference between two age groups is found, does it relate to differences in common social history (generational differences) or to differences resulting from maturation and additional experience (developmental differences)? What is the smallest age increment that produces differences?

We would all expect, and indeed research has found, differences in many cognitive, behavioral, and attitudinal variables between 20-year-olds and 60-year-olds. Clearly, some of these differences are generational, unless you believe that the 20-year-olds will not differ from the 60-year-olds when they become 60. So, too, some of these differences are developmental, unless you believe that the 20-year-olds will be the same at 60 as they are at 20. This is clear and understandable when we speak of 20-year-olds and 60-year-olds. But do these same types of differences exist between, say, 12- and 14-year-olds or 15- and 18-year-olds, and, if so, to what degree? This question prompted the previous question: What is the range of age that constitutes a generation?

In the course the author teaches on adolescent development, on a number of occasions a student has made a point about today's adolescents through reference to a younger sibling. The point has always been that the younger sibling was different from the student, more extreme in some behavior or attitude when the student was the sibling's age or when the student was in my class. The differences between the students' ages and their siblings' ages were as little as two years and as much as eight years. This might indicate very informally that differences of the generational type exist between persons whose ages are even two years apart.

When referring to an age group, those persons born within a specified period of time, such as persons born in 1942 or persons born from 1955 to 1960, the term *cohort* is used. Cohort is a much more specific term than *generation* and can be operationally defined by year(s) of birth. The use of the term and concept *cohort* facilitates developmental research, including the generational factor.

This brings us back to the new model for research into these issues, which, though in a state of development, refinement, and controversy, holds much promise. The model, proposed by Schaie (1965), has as its goal to distinguish the contributions of cohort, chronological age, and time (year) of

Cohort	Time of Measurement						
(Year of Birth)	'72	'73	'74	'75	'76	'77	'78
1960			14				
1961			13	14			
1962	10	11	12	13	14		
1963		10	11	12	13	14	
1964			10	11	12	13	14
1965				10	11		
1966					10		

Figure 6.3. Schema for research design according to Schaie's trifactorial model (entries are ages) (From K. W. Schaie, "A general model for the study of development problems," *Psychological Bulletin* 64 [1965], 92–107. Copyright © 1965 by the American Psychological Association. Reprinted by permission.)

measurement in developmental research. The design is simply shown in Figure 6.3.

There are three types of design within this schema. They are known as (1) the cohort-sequential design, which is formed by the cells that make up the horizontal parallelogram, (2) the time-sequential design, which is formed by the cells that make up the vertical parallelogram, and (3) the cross-sequential design, which is formed by the cells within the square. The elaborate technical aspects of these designs and their analyses will not be dealt with here. From Figure 6.3, one sees that in this cohort-sequential design, one-year age cohorts are followed longitudinally and that by commencing testing with cohorts on successive years, time of measurement effects can be controlled. Similarly, there are advantages from each design over both simple cross-sectional and longitudinal designs.

Wohlwill differentiated "between age, time and cohort effects in the following terms: Cohort effects represent systematic alterations in the shape or course of the developmental function, while time effects represent temporary variations or aberrations superimposed on the developmental function. Age effects, finally, are those embodied in the generalized function as such, once cohort and/or time effects have been extracted" (1970, p. 173).

Baltes and Nesselroade (1972) utilized the rationale of Schaie's model in one-year longitudinal sequences with five cohorts of 1,249 adolescents, 12

1/2 to 16 1/2 years old, in a study of personality development. Using the High School Personality Questionnaire, composed of 14 personality trait factors, they found moderate stability overall, with some personality traits more stable than others, and a pattern in which subjects, with increasing age, exhibit slightly higher stability. The authors have interpreted stability in terms of "the stability of the environmental fields to which individuals are exposed during the time interval considered" (p. 254). Although there were many sex differences on traits, sex and cohort differences in trait stability were not pronounced. It can be concluded that, differentially, the personality traits tested show moderate stability across all cohorts. However, the differential stability of traits in cohorts, i.e., traits changing in different ways from one testing to the other in the various cohorts, imply that "the nature of adolescent trait change appears less dictated by age-related components than by the type of social change patterns which are setting the environmental milieu for adolescents of all ages over a given period of time" (p. 244).

Further, referring to social and anthropological interpretations of adolescence, "the authors feel that none of these theoretical propositions would have assumed that 1-year cohort differences would be of the magnitude reported" (p. 254). In fact, very few developmental researchers doing cross-sectional or longitudinal research would have assumed one-year cohort differences of this, if any, magnitude. If the data collected at either the first or second testing were analyzed separately as cross-sectional data, conclusions would have been drawn showing great change and "developmental" patterns. Although "future endeavors aimed at more fine-grained analyses of the mechanisms involved in the developmental linkage of ontogenetic and historical change components" (p. 255) are needed badly, this study illustrates how the new research strategy may get at personality consistency, and how traditional cross-sectional results have maximized the potential for making adolescent personality appear inconsistent.

In another study, Nesselroade and Baltes (1974) studied 1,849 students, ages 12 1/2 to 17 1/2, who were tested using three trait-theory-oriented batteries of ability and personality measures in 1970, 1971, and 1972. They summarized their findings:

> In the case of personality dimensions, time difference rather than cross-sectional (cohort) age differences dominated the picture. This finding delegates a lesser role to chronological age in the nature (direction, rate) of adolescent personality development than to the historical time period during which development occurs. . . . It was found, for instance, that all adolescents (largely independent of their age) showed a significant decrement in superego strength, social-emotional anxiety, and achievement from

1970 to either 1971 and/or 1972 and an increase in independence during that same time interval.

With regard to sex difference, male and female adolescents differed on most personality dimensions in the expected directions. However, it was surprising that only a few significant sex by cohort and/or time interactions were obtained, suggesting that most of the sex differences had emerged prior to age 12. There was tentative evidence to indicate that, if further sex-role development occurred from 1970 to 1972 in the 12–6 to 17–6 age range, it was in the direction of increased sex differences.

Examination of various . . . personality stability coefficients indicated that females show higher average stability than males; that there are wide differences among dimensions in the magnitude of associated stabilities with some dimensions exhibiting trait-like features; that stability, by and large, increased with cohort/age; and that the 1971–1972 time period produced higher 1-year stabilities than the 1970–1971 span. These developmental differences in stability, then, were also related to historical time as much as they were to chronological age. (pp. 69–70)

The most potent finding in this study, as described in the previous quotations, is that the major differences in personality were found, not between age groups and not between cohort groups, but between *time* of testing groups! Very clearly, something or things in the total environment at that time had the effect of influencing the nature of the pool of personality dimensions in this sample of adolescents. That is, across ages, there was a systematic change in certain personality dimensions from one year to the next, and one particular year, 1970–71, produced more change than the other.

This finding is important, not only for its methodological implications, but because it shows the sensitivity of even personality dimensions, which are like, but broader than, personality traits, to historical time period effects, to "the times."

(In this book, the organization and logic have implied previously that this finding was the case. That is, the first chapters of the book are an explication of the principles, theoretical laws, if you will, of adolescence, while the latter chapters on the life tasks and deviations attempt to show these principles in operation within particular time periods, within particular contexts, which are called the *situational element.*)

In addition to their important statements about historical time-period effects, Nesselroade and Baltes (1974) reinforced two other points made in this and the previous chapter. The first is that sex-role development as evidenced through consistent and explicable differences between the sexes "has emerged prior to age 12," and, if anything, becomes more marked during adolescence. The second is that even with the changes attributed to historical time effects, there is great and increasing stability in a number of personality dimensions during adolescence. Nesselroade and Baltes say, "the average magnitude (of stability coefficients, .57) is fairly high for personality dimensions. The general pattern is one of increasing stability with increasing age and decreasing stability as the time interval increases" (1974, p. 52).

These findings imply that as times change, differing pressures, preferences, freedoms, and restrictions exist and that personality dimensions are amenable to change under such conditions, but, by and large, persons will retain a similar ranking relative to other persons on important personality dimensions. That is to say, in a time of high anxiety, the adolescents who are highest on anxiety would also be highest on anxiety when the times were less anxious, when they and others would exhibit less anxiety. The adolescent who was a wild extrovert in the mid-1960s, when adolescents in general were more outgoing, would also have been more extroverted than others in the silent 1950s, when he would have been more unusual.

The findings of this study indicate that there are no substantial cohort effects, whereas there are many sex and time effects. This seems to mean, in our context, that the major determinations, adjustments, or assumptions of personality attributes have occurred prior to adolescence, with large sex differences. It further means that the time effects, the historical-environmental effects, have large, almost across-the-board, effects on personality variables. The implication is that personality consistency over time is not put into question further by these findings. Rather, consistency over time, stability, exists for individuals in relative ranking but the "quantity" or "amount" of a variable may alter as a result of time, as a result of "the times."

It must be repeated that considerable controversy surrounds this research strategy. Whether it is possible to statistically justify the conclusions made using it is questionable (Adam, 1978). Nonetheless, anyone who wants to understand adolescents must remember the factors this design stresses — time of testing and cohort, as well as age.

Adolescents seem, or have seemed, to change more than adults. We have said that there are physical and cognitive-developmental reasons for the changes and for the apparent changes as they are viewed. It may be that there is more consistency over time with age, over greater periods of time in adulthood than in adolescence. This may mean that adolescents, having not yet come to terms with the wider world, are more affected overall than adults.

CONSISTENCY: SITUATION VERSUS TRAIT

One aspect of the continuing controversy over the "consistency problem" has been viewed as the situational specificity versus the trait-determined influence on behavior. The questions are: "Are people consistent from one situation to another on a particular personality trait?" (which would support the trait approach if they were), or "Are people different from one situation to another because of the influence of specific situations on behavior?" Bem and Allen (1974) make the claim that individuals will only be consistent across situations on a particular trait if that trait is important to them (is an integral part of their personality). Therefore, Bem and Allen proposed research designs using an ideographic, rather than a nomothetic, approach.

To determine the importance and variability of traits among their subjects, they in effect asked: "In general, how friendly are you?" and "How much do you vary from one situation to another in how friendly you are?" They found that individuals who said that they did not vary to any great degree from one situation to another did, in fact, vary less across situations than did individuals who said they did vary. And, interestingly enough, variability across situations was not related to self-rated degree of friendliness.

Although Bem and Allen do not take the consistency position rather than the situational position, but "believe in both propositions," their strategy and findings seem to support the consistency argument. They say, "In short, if some of the people can be predicted some of the time from personality traits, then some of the people can be predicted some of the time from situational variables" (1974, p. 517). We might say that in situations where a trait that is central to an individual is not central to the situation, the influence of the situation would be greater than the influence of the trait. Conversely, when a trait that is central to an individual is important in a situation, the trait influence would be greater than the situational influence on the exhibiting of the trait.

As this type of research grows, it will be necessary to deal with the importance and meaning of situations to individuals in the same way that Bem and Allen have begun to deal with the importance and meaning of traits. Studies of consistency and stability of personality in adolescence will be initially, until research solutions are reached, confounded by the changing, developing meaning of situations for adolescents. We cannot expect that an adolescent in a new school will exhibit important traits to the same degree that he will when he gains a sense of his belongingness in that situation. A conscientious student may not reveal himself as generally conscientious until such time as he is given additional areas of personal responsibility. Do we expect people to be consistent in situations that are foreign to them, that they do not understand? They may have a consistent approach to unknown situations, but it need not be the same as their "normal" behavior. Adolescence, as the one stage past childhood where continuously new situations arise, must be studied with this in mind. An adolescent cannot be consistent in a situation that he does not understand—he cannot know how he could be consistent, be himself, in such a situation. Some good portion of adolescent anxiety and insecurity, as well as inconsistency, may arise when the adolescent does not know how to act—how he, himself, should act—in new and unfamiliar situations.

Before closing this chapter, an important definitional and cautionary note is necessary. At times, theorists, and probably all of us, insert the concept and the term *self* in place of *personality*. Personality, as we have seen, is the greater system, organization, set of characteristics—behavioral and attitudinal—that, in toto, is consistent at one time and over time and gives the individual his unique quality. Self is one aspect of personality. According to the Adlerian view we discussed, the life-style, or personality, is composed of at least the self-view, the world view, and personal goals. Self as a phenomenon is composed of many facets also.

Personality consistency and continuity have been strongly presented and supported in this chapter. Personality, life-style, does not change dramatically from childhood to adolescence to adulthood, without therapeutic help or traumatic impetus. The self, in its many facets, may change in many ways, and certainly in adolescence may waiver. Change in self, or sense of self, is an important issue in adolescence and will be discussed in the next chapter and the following one, which speaks to Erikson's notions of identity and the "identity crisis."

The Self

CHAPTER 7

Personality has been discussed as a global notion having to do with core characteristics, enduring basic attitudes about the self, the world, and the person's way of fitting into the world. The emphasis on core, basic, central aspects as the definition of personality led, logically and practically, to the conclusion that the basic characteristics of the individual's personality are stable, consistent, and, although adaptable, essentially unchanging through life. The self, in many of its definitions and aspects, need not be so stable, and the situation of adolescence may provoke a good bit of instability in the self-concepts of adolescents.

The term *self*, or *self* with a hyphen, *self-*, is so frequently used by everyone, including psychologists and educators, that it demands definition wherever it is used. This is because *self* has very different meanings to lay people and psychologists and philosophers of different schools.

Common sense and empirical observation tell us:

> The self . . . is not a mental construct, but a living organism, a person. When I say that I cut myself shaving this morning, I do not mean that I cut a mental construct. Likewise, if you hit ME, that "I" who got hit is not some "ego" of Freudian theory. We are talking here not about one's self-concept or self-image but about the existing reality. And this reality is the same referent when we say "I understand," or "I choose," or "I run." (Royce, 1973, p. 885)

Cooley's (1902) definition of *self* was "that which is designated in common speech by the pronouns of the first person singular, 'I,' 'me,' 'mine,' and 'myself' " (p. 136). We all use the first-person singular and have a sense of self—a sense of oneself as knower and as an object, as known (James, 1910). We may grant, then, that persons have a feeling or a sense of self and that

114

"the self is the person" (Royce, 1973, p. 886). If the self, then, is the person, and you will agree intuitively that you (the person) are yourself, and if personality is, as Maddi (1968) said, "a stable set of characteristics and tendencies that determine those commonalities and differences in the psychological behavior (thoughts, feelings, actions) of people that have continuity in time" (p. 10), then what of *self*—what aspect(s) of *self*—may be relevant in a discussion on development and dealt with as part of a separate life task?

The constructs made up of *self* with a hyphen—most importantly, *self-concept*—form the nucleus of the personality, according to Lecky (1945). The position taken here is that a holistic, phenomenologic view envisions the person and the self as the same, while, as stated in an earlier section, personality describes the set or organization of an individual's ways that make him uniquely himself and that are consistent, to a large degree, over time. The self-concept, which is a key element in the nature of one's personality, is a concept that implies active intellectual awareness and control. Therefore, the self-concept, and related self-constructs, may be seen as possessing possibilities for developmental change in conjunction with intellectual and environmental change and may be thought of as part of the life task self, over which one may assume active control, may have an effect.

Two definitions of self-concept should assist us in seeing the cognitively active nature of the construct. Rogers, who defined the self as "an organized, fluid, but consistent conceptual pattern of perceptions of characteristics and relationships of the 'I' or the 'me,' together with values attached to these concepts" (1951, p. 498), includes in the self-concept only those aspects of himself that the individual is aware of and feels some control over. In Snygg and Combs' definition of self-concept, "those parts of the phenomenal field which the individual has differentiated as definite and fairly stable characteristics of himself" (1949, p. 112), the operative word is "differentiated," illustrating cognitive activity.

McCandless (1970) conceives of self-concept, which is an extremely complex construct, as including three major components: structure, function, and quality. Within his conceptual framework, in the structure of the self-concept, such terms as *rigid* or *flexible, congruent, simple*, or *complex, broad* or *narrow* apply. In the function of the self-concept, such things are included as self-evaluation and prediction of success or failure, and in the quality of the self-concept, the primary components are high or low self-esteem and self-acceptance versus self-rejection.

Within this very useful framework, the function of the self-concept is a theoretical given. That is to say, theoretically, the self-concept operates in certain ways, functions in certain ways, regardless of the rigidity, congruence, complexity, or narrowness of the structure of an individual's self-concept, or the approving or disapproving, accepting or rejecting nature of the quality of an individual's self-concept. The self-concept functions as a standard for evaluating and predicting one's performance or potential performance socially (as others might see it), objectively (if there is an objective measure of the behavior), and personally (as it relates to the structure and quality of one's self-concept), and it functions to limit performance for the purpose of maintaining and enhancing itself—i.e., a person behaves as he thinks he can or should for the person he thinks he is.

Epstein (1973) sees the self-concept as a "theory that the individual has unwittingly constructed about himself as an experiencing, functioning individual" (p. 407). The functions of the self-concept or self-theory, as Epstein says, are "the maintenance of a favorable pleasure/pain balance, the assimilation of the data of experience, and the maintenance of self-esteem" (p. 411). The functions of the self-concept must be remembered as operating as the self-theory of individuals. For the youth who feels himself neglected, average performance in scholastic or sporting competition may best fit his self-theory and its functions. By receiving C grades or running in the pack in a long-distance run, he maintains a pleasure-pain balance that is favorable for him—he need not be picked out or picked on for running first or last. The C grade and running in the pack fit his expectations for himself and therefore are easily assimilated pieces of data and serve to maintain the level of self-esteem he has developed.

Epstein's (1973) developmental aspects of the self-theory begin first with the child's learning that he has a *body self* by virtue of simply recognizing that his body is one of many human bodies but is separate, distinct in certain ways, and his. The development of a body self requires only a low level of cognitive ability, whereas the next development, of an *inferred inner self*, requires a somewhat greater and abstract level of cognitive ability. Epstein shows that as one sees others who are behaviorally as well as physically identifiable, feels continuity in one's own experience, and feels emotions, needs, and defensiveness about aspects of one's own being, one concludes, or infers, an inner self of one's own. Lastly, in response to social demands, at a simpler, lower cognitive level when young and at a more abstract, higher cognitive level when older, one develops a *moral self.*

Self-concept develops with experience and new cognitive abilities. A general, overall self-concept is presumably quite stable and built on a multifaceted, hierarchically organized set of specific facets or categories about oneself (Marsh and Shavelson, 1985; Shavelson, Hubner, and Stanton, 1976), as seen in Figure 7.1. With age, more and more discrete and specific

GLOBAL SELF-CONCEPT = *COMPONENTS · *X* + OTHER COMPONENTS
WEIGHTED PLUS OR MINUS.

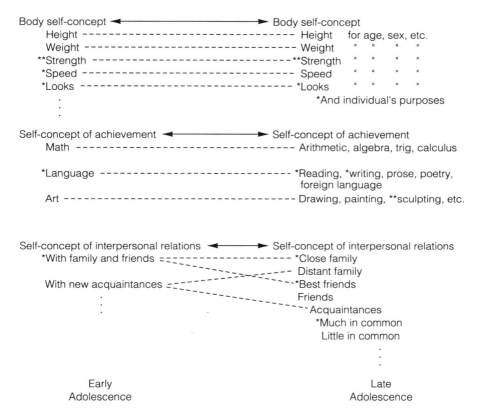

Figure 7.1. Scheme of global self-concept and examples of components and differentiations in adolescence. There are many possible components of self-concept. The examples in this figure are typical components of adolescence. The asterisked components and differentiations are hypothetical examples for one adolescent of those more important to the personality and personal goals, and would form a hierarchy as they are related to the goals.

facets of self-concept develop. Some of these may be important to the individual's sense of self and core characteristics, and others may not. Thus, some facets should relate strongly to global self-concept and others not, and some facets should be more strongly grounded in the personality than others—that is, they should mean more to the individual at a basic level and thus be less changeable than others.

From this discussion of the self and self-concept it may be seen that the biological changes at adolescence may potentially upset or alter the aspect of the self-concept called the body self and thereby make the self life task difficult. Cognitive, moral, sex-role development at adolescence may have effects on aspects of the self-concept. And, as has been shown in earlier chapters, as these developments differ among groups of adolescents, the teacher, parent, or psychologist may anticipate differing types of problems with self according to the group memberships of the individuals with whom they deal.

THE SITUATIONAL ELEMENT

It would appear that as developmental changes occur in a youth's body or thought, there is the potential for upset in his thoughts about himself, his self-concept. Tanner (1971) points to the effects of hormonal and other pubertal physiological developments on self-concept in early adolescence. Offer's (1969) study found both parents and adolescents agreeing that the adolescents experienced their greatest personal "turmoil" between the ages of 12 and 14. Moreover, events that occur with some frequency for large groups of adolescents, or all adolescents in a particular culture, may have the effect of creating upset, or "turmoil," in self-concept also, of fulfilling the potentiality. It is these events that are here being termed "the situational element."

A very good illustration of the situational element in the self life task is a study by Simmons, Rosenberg, and Rosenberg (1973), in which they first investigated whether there is self-image disturbance in adolescence; if there is, at what age, or ages it occurs; and, finally, what "triggers" the disturbance.

They studied a random sample of 2,265 pupils in grades 3 through 12 in Baltimore. The sample was 63 percent black and more heavily working class than the national average and reflected the population of Baltimore. They noted the fact, which from our discussion of group differences would have concerned us, that the study was cross-sectional and did not include dropouts as members of the older student population. They studied self-consciousness, stability of the self-image, global self-esteem (a general, overall feeling toward oneself), and specific self-esteem (an average of self-assessment on eight characteristics, such as smart, good-looking, helpful, honest, etc.).

Simmons, Rosenberg, and Rosenberg found a marked change for the worse on all measures between the 11- and 12-year-old groups. In general they found the 12-year-old group much lower than the younger groups on all self-image measures, with some further deterioration thereafter, leveling off around age 14 for self-consciousness and specific self-esteem and improving after age 14 on stability of self-image and global self-esteem. From these findings one might conclude that puberty is the chief determinant of self-image disturbance. However, Simmons, Rosenberg, and Rosenberg went on to analyze the effects of changing schools and moving into a junior or senior high school on children of the same age. Their conclusion points to the importance of a situational factor's influencing the rate or amount of upset youth feel toward themselves. They say:

> In sum the data indicate increased self-image disturbance associated with the transition from elementary to junior high school. The reason does not appear to be solely the age change (with its associated biological changes); for at ages roughly equivalent, the seventh graders still show greater disturbance. Nor does it simply appear to be the shock of transferring to a new school; furthermore, the transition from junior to senior high school shows no such effect. Perhaps puberty does not in itself disturb the self-image but heightens vulnerability to environmental circumstances which threaten the self-concept. (p. 564)

The situational element, going to junior high school from elementary school, may disturb the young adolescent's self-image. Simmons, Rosenberg, and Rosenberg do not find that moving on to senior high school is similarly disturbing. This would seem to point to the value of the junior high school in preparing its students, through organizational and social structures, for senior high school. However, it also points to the development of categories or facets of the self-concept that the adolescent did not previously have, such as a category of ability to move to a new school. Once they have established that they can change schools and cope, they should, logically, be less affected by future changes of school, which is what Simmons, Rosenberg, and Rosenberg show. Those who cope better with school, in part because of their abilities and higher IQ and in part because of their sense of self and sense of competence, will continue to cope better, which facilitates achievement (Manaster, 1972) and maintenance of their senses of self and competence.

What other "events" occur for most, or all, American youth? There are situational elements that affect self-concept in the life task areas of school, friends, and love. But in the continuity of self, there are no events that hold for all youth, except in interaction with other life task areas, because of differences in the paths that people take through life. Therefore this discussion will continue first by expanding on the cognitive-developmental effects on self-concept in adolescence and then by looking at sex, social class, and race differences in self-concept in adolescents.

"NORMAL" SELF-CONCEPT DEVELOPMENT

It must be repeated and remembered that probably the most frequent and continual description of adolescence is as a time of stress and upset. The classic psychoanalytic theory, as expressed again by Anna Freud (1969), predicts that disturbance in the ego-defense system, the maintenance and protection of self, will occur with the biological and sexual developments at adolescence. McCandless (1970), too, says that ideas about oneself, particularly heterosexually, change dramatically with adolescence. And both Erikson and Lewin stressed the same phenomenon of a normative crisis for adolescents. As this treatise is attempting to show, there are very usual, normal reasons for upset in adolescence, many of which are situationally fomented in interaction with developmental change.

But how does self, or self-concept, itself develop in adolescence? Monge (1973) studied the "connotative structure" of adolescent self-concept using seven-point semantic-differential scales to rate the concept "my characteristic self (yourself as you most often feel about yourself)" on 21 polar adjective pairs, such as smart-dumb, confident-unsure, relaxed-nervous, and rugged-delicate. Monge's idea of "connotative structure" includes comments that McCandless would refer to as structure and quality. It may therefore be thought of as the connotative structure, referring to the elements that make up the structure and quality components of the self-concept.

Looking at over 2,000 male and female public school students in grades 6 through 12 in central New York State, Monge was interested in the continuity or discontinuity of the structure of the self-concept over these years. Although he found differences in self, he found that "there was a very high degree of structural simplicity across grade and sex in the ratings of self-concept as shown by the emergence in all of the analyses of the same four factors" (p. 391). The four factors were named (I) Achievement/Leadership, (II) Congeniality/Sociability, (III) Adjustment, and (IV) Masculinity/Femininity. Granting the problems for inference caused by the cross-sectional design, dropouts from the older grades, and limited prepubescent data from girls because they mature earlier, Monge concluded that "the evidence for a restructuring of the self-concept around and after pubescence was very slight for boys and modest for girls" (p. 391). Monge, then, does not agree that major discontinuities in self-concept and psychological development occur around pubescence.

This finding is important but may be influenced by the method used. Factor analysis determines which variables, or items on a test instrument, go together. This "going together" is determined statistically, through the factor-analytic statistical technique, and the researcher decides that the factors produced statistically are conceptually meaningful. It is possible using factor analysis to determine, as in Monge's study, for a specified number of items making up a test, the most meaningful number and character of factors for subjects of various ages and grades for the whole sample and to determine the match between the factors for age and grade samples. This is what Monge did. He did not find striking differences across the subsamples; he was not really looking for them, but he did not find them.

Mullener and Laird (1971) were specifically looking for changes in the organization of self-evaluations — in a sense, changes in the structure of the quality component of self-concept — and chose a method that would help them find such changes if they existed. They hypothesized that "with age, individuals reveal an increasingly differentiated use of categories of personal characteristics when evaluating themselves" (p. 233). Their sample was composed of 24 students in a 7th-grade honors program, 24 college-prep high school seniors, and 24 evening college students. From a 40-item questionnaire in which the subjects evaluated themselves on a 6-point scale in each of 5 content areas, evaluation scores were determined, as was a variance score that was taken to measure differentiation in evaluation of self, i.e., more variance equals more differentiation. To test the intellectual level of the subjects, the Shipley Institute of Living Scale was given and showed mental ages of 16.7, 17.3, and 17.7 for the seventh-grade, twelfth-grade, and adult groups, respectively. The mental ages of the groups were then roughly equivalent, and the seventh-grade group was really (considering their age) brighter than the older group. So if intellectual level was the crucial variable in differentiation, no differences would have been found. However, these are not average groups, and the relationship that might be found between intelligence and differentiation using the full range of intellectual levels could not be illustrated with this study.

Mullener and Laird found that with age "there was a change from relatively global to relatively differentiated self-evaluations, changes that have been shown to characterize development of other cognitive products" (p. 235). They also found that subjects who did not differentiate as much, who had low variance scores, had higher evaluation scores than did those subjects who had high variance scores. So as well as finding greater differentiation at higher ages, greater differentiation was related to lower self-evaluation.

The differentiation of self-evaluation was measured by Mullener and Laird within five areas at all ages. These five areas were achievement traits, intellectual skills, interpersonal skills, physical skills, and social responsibility. In a general way, these areas resemble the factors of achievement, sociability, adjustment, and masculinity-femininity found across ages by Monge. It is as if Mullener and Laird assumed structural similarity of self-evaluations across ages and investigated differentiation within this structure.

Mullener and Laird referred to the general conception that greater cognitive differentiation occurs with higher levels of development, which is a conception based on the work of Piaget and Werner. Achenbach and Zigler (1963) studied the self-image disparity, the difference between the real self and the ideal self, using a developmental rationale. They predicted a positive relationship between self-image disparity and maturity level, assuming that (1) with greater maturity a person will make more demands on himself because he will see and feel more demands from society and will feel more guilt when he cannot fulfill those demands, and (2) with greater maturity a person will differentiate more within his real self-concept and thereby see more ways in which he does not measure up to his ideal self. They found the relationship they predicted with adults.

Katz and Zigler (1967) explored the same hypotheses in greater detail with children and their findings are more important to this discussion. Katz and Zigler's sample was made up of 120 fifth-, eighth-, and eleventh-grade students, half of whom, at each grade level, were low IQ (means 91, 93, and 94 for the three grades, in ascending order) and half of whom were high IQ (124, 127, and 125 for the three grades respectively). Looking at the disparity between real and ideal self they found that "real-self scores are more negative than ideal-self scores. The magnitude of this difference between real and ideal scores is influenced by both age and IQ" (p. 344). There were "greater differences between real and ideal scores at grades 11 and 8 than at grade 5. The high-IQ subjects exhibit a greater discrepancy between real and ideal scores than do low-IQ subjects" (p. 344). They then looked at the real-self scores separately. They found the real-self ratings more negative at grades 11 and 8 than at grade 5. For the real self, the high-IQ subjects had more positive feelings than the low-IQ subjects in fifth grade, the real-self ratings were similar in the eighth grade, and by eleventh grade the low-IQ subject ratings were less negative than for the high-IQ subjects. For the ideal self it was found that "the older or brighter the child, the more positive was his ideal-self" (p. 345).

Because a positive relationship was found between self-image disparity and chronological age and IQ, these findings support the hypothesis that there is an increase in self-image disparity with increasing maturity. By comparing and analyzing the scores on the various instruments used in the study, Katz and Zigler concluded that support was also found for the developmental rationale "that self-ideal disparity is a function of two underlying factors

Predictor	DF	R^2	R^2 Change	F-Ratio	Significance
		Entire Sample			
Cognitive Score	1; 221	.089	.089	21.56	$p < .0001$
Sex	2; 220	.112	.024	5.88	$p < .02$
SES	3; 219	.113	.001	$f < 1$	$p > .70$
		Younger Sample			
Cognitive Score	1; 132	.043	.043	5.93	$p < .02$
Sex	2; 131	.058	.015	2.03	$p > .10$
Age	3; 130	.067	.009	1.31	$p > .20$
SES	4; 129	.068	.001	$f < 1$	$p > .70$
		Older Sample			
Cognitive Score	1; 87	.14	.14	14.28	$p < .0001$
Sex	2; 86	.19	.05	5.29	$p < .03$
Age	3; 85	.21	.02	1.65	$p > .20$
SES	4; 84	.22	.01	$f < 1$	$p > .40$

Figure 7.2. Age, sex, SES, and mean cognitive development score as predictors of ideal-self score: stepwise multiple linear regression analyses (From Manaster, Saddler, and Wukasch, 1977.)

related to maturity level, namely, capacity for guilt and cognitive differentiation" (p. 350).

By asking adolescents to describe "The Person I Would Like to Be Like," researchers have found a sequence of categories that indicates the developmental maturity of the ideal self. Manaster, Saddler, and Wukasch (1977) hypothesized that development of the ideal self, and therefore presumably other developmental changes in the self in adolescence, are related to, are functions of, cognitive development. They analyzed written passages for cognitive-developmental level, from concrete to formal operations, and "The Person I Would Like to Be Like" for over 200 12- and 13-year-old (the younger sample) and 15- and 16-year-old (the older sample) working- and middle-class boys and girls in the north of England.

A regression analysis was run in which the variables of age, sex, SES, and cognitive-development score were used to predict ideal-self score. As shown in Figure 7.2, whether all subjects were combined in a single analysis or whether the younger and older samples were analyzed separately, the cognitive score was the most significant predictor of ideal self. In a general sense, adolescents who are still in the concrete operations stage are more apt to think of their ideal self in terms of their parents or heroes or other glamorous adults. But adolescents who have moved to formal operations may begin to think of who they might be in terms of combinations of imagined or real persons.

"Feelings about the self are relatively stable from moment to moment and from year to year," concluded Savin-Williams and Demo (1984, p. 1100), while their study "contribute(s) to the composite of recent longitudinal research indicating systematic increases in self-esteem throughout adolescence" (Wallace et al., 1984, p. 253). Chiam (1987) predicted this same increase in his Malaysian adolescent sample and found it for boys but less consistently so for girls, which reminds us of the situational factor in what might otherwise seem a developmental given. It may be that in areas of the world where women's traditional roles maintain, girls are less able to develop confidence in their self until they have established their traditional place in society.

Using these studies, what might we say in general about the development of the self-concept in adolescence? The basic structure of the self-concept remains pretty much the same throughout adolescence for individual adolescents. Those with higher IQ become able to differentiate more about the many facets of their selves and also become able to refine their ideal selves as they differentiate their perceived world, but in general all adolescents come increasingly to recognize their selves as adequate.

This may result in greater anxiety as the disparity between real and ideal self grows, and general concern as the adolescent perceives many smaller, differentiated areas in which he varies from the global way he has seen himself before. The anxiety need not be debilitating; it may be healthy. And whatever "crises" occur may be the same. Yet the potential for such a crisis is greater in the older and brighter adolescent. Such a crisis or set of concerns may never occur in the vast number of adolescents of average or below-average intelligence. In a longitudinal study of the self-concept of low-income youth, Barnes and Farrier found that their subjects' self-concepts changed minimally in the 10 years after fifth grade. They concluded that their data supported "Coleman's (1978) focal theory that youth face and deal with conflicts one at a time and, thus, do not undergo great changes during this period" (1985, p. 203). If one has fewer discriminated facets to one's self, it should be easier to deal with issues related to these in an orderly way than if one has discriminated one's self into a great number of facets.

People evaluate themselves globally and specifically for each facet of their self-concept producing self-esteem. We know that particular facets of themselves in relation to their personal goals will be more important than others and therefore they will weight some facets more than others in producing their global self-esteem. Some aspects of self, some abilities, are relatively easy to verify — i.e., running speed, spelling ability — whereas other aspects of self are not easy to verify — i.e., being a good person, being liked. Felson (1981) and Bohrnstedt and Felson (1983) found that adolescents' perceptions of easily verifiable abilities contribute to self-esteem, whereas with difficult to verify abilities the adolescents' self-esteem determines their perception of that ability. For example, Hoelter found that "evaluations of athlete, son/daughter and student have positive effects on self-esteem" while "effects of friend and club member evaluations on self-esteem are small and nonsignificant" (1986, p. 138). How important each role or ability is to the adolescent's sense of self, the discrimination ability the adolescent has in specifying aspects of abilities and self, and then the adolescent's performance on abilities that can be verified all feed into the adolescent's self-concept and self-esteem.

This section has alluded to the effects of intelligence, cognitive development, and age on development of the self-concept in adolescence. In a sense it has pointed to two extremes in the development of self-concept. At one extreme are adolescents who are younger, less bright, and less cognitively developed. They, at that time in their own development, do not seem to differentiate to any great degree in their thinking about themselves, have a relatively lower opinion of themselves, but also have a relatively lower opinion of the self they would like to be. As they grow older they may differentiate more, but still not to a great extent, and their self-concept relative to others is higher. The sense of who or how they would like to be does not rise appreciably, and therefore the real self–ideal self disparity does not grow. It may be that with cognitive development in adulthood, they become more like the other extreme group, but knowledge in the field on these issues is limited. It may be that little or no additional development occurs for these people in this area.

Is this first extreme group typified by the child who did not do very well in grammar school, and possibly in high school either (remember the relationships of both self-concept and intelligence with school achievement), but who later developed an area of competence that was satisfying? In grammar school, low achievement in the basic academic areas was part of an undifferentiated, or less differentiated, self-concept. As he or she ages (and finds competencies as a working person, in a craft, with secretarial or clerical skills, socially, and/or around the home), the global self-concept reflects this feeling of competency, of adequacy. And this less differentiated feeling of adequacy is not too distant from the conception he or she has of the person he or she would like to be.

Adolescents in the other extreme group are brighter and experience greater cognitive development as they age. When in grammar school, achieving at higher levels, they feel pretty good about themselves. In the same way as the first group, their self-concept at that age is not very differentiated and their achievement is reflected in their self-concept. However, as adolescents in this hypothesized group develop, they differentiate more aspects, or subsets, of self and more possibilities for how they could be. They see areas in which they are very distant from their heightened level of ideal self. These feelings may promote reformulations of many aspects of their selves and accompanying upsets may occur. As the persons in this group are more likely to attend college and thereby have a prolonged adolescence, a longer psychosocial moratorium, they may be the group that experiences crises of identity.

NORMAL PROBLEMS / NORMAL CRISES

Adolescents have problems. Some adolescents have crises. But let's face it: everyone has problems, and at one time or another everyone faces crises. Yet to many contemporary adolescents their "self" is a problem. Chabassol and Thomas (1969) compared studies of adolescents in the United States and Canada carried out in 1936, 1959, 1961, and 1968, in which subjects ranked 15 items as greater or lesser problems to them. A most interesting change from 1936 to 1968 for both males and females was found. In 1936 males ranked mental hygiene 13, and females ranked mental hygiene 9.5 of the 15 problems. In 1968 males ranked mental hygiene 3, and females ranked it 2. Clearly, mental hygiene (concerns with one's self and personal adjustment) is an increasingly important problem for college-age youth. The 5 most prominent problems for males in 1968 were, in order, money, study habits, mental hygiene, personal and moral qualities, and philosophy of life. The 5 most prominent problems for females were money, mental hygiene, personal attractiveness, study habits, and home and family relationships.

Allport (1964) discussed "crises in normal personality development" using his undergraduate class as subjects. His approach and conclusions seem relevant to high school–age youth also. He said a crisis "is a situation of emotional and mental stress requiring significant alterations of outlook within a short period of time" (p. 236). The changing role prescriptions that accompany the move from high school to college are more extreme than those that accompany the move to high school, but the crisis potential is similar. Allport notes that the freshman in college does not sense the feeling of crisis as much as in the sophomore year, because as a freshman the youth is trying to please the folks back home. But in the sophomore year "suddenly it becomes no longer tolerable to live one's life for the edification of the people back home" (p. 237). The youth feels at a crossroads between the past and the future and for many the choice is clear. So, too, high school teachers know the reticence of some early students to participate, and they find that when these students are truant they may be found "hanging around" their old junior high school or grammar school. The junior high school and grammar school teachers, initially quite happy to be visited by a former student, often find the student unhappy and tearful as he or she reminisces about the good old days, the sure, secure days of junior high or grammar school. The student may also be returning to where he is still a "big man."

Allport speaks of four areas of conflict, four crisis areas. The first is the intellectual crisis, which comes in high school for superior students who are bored and unchallenged, or who, in moving to a new school level, find suddenly that they are not able to maintain their superiority academically and are devastated by the competition. Next are the crises of "specific inferiorities" in which "besides the sense of intellectual inferiority . . . , we encounter deep disturbance due to physical handicaps or to plain physical appearance" (p. 238). The individual will have made adjustments and developed strategies for dealing with his real or felt inferiority or weakness in previous environments. Through adolescence new situations may arise in which he feels unable to cope because of his perceived inferiority and this may spark a crisis. Allport speaks, too, of crises due to religious and ideological conflicts, sexual conflicts, and family conflicts. These areas of conflict are analogous to the life task areas, and the "specific inferiority" area, the "inferiority complex" area, is analogous to the life task self.

Adolescents differentiate their "selves" into more discrete units, life-task-area, situation-specific units. Some will differentiate more than others. Presumably, cognitive-developmental differences will affect differentiation. That is, brighter and higher cognitive-level adolescents may construe their "selves" in a greater variety of ways than less able adolescents. Also adolescents with more life options, because of their own abilities or background, SES, which opens more options, may differentiate their "selves" to match and compare with the attributes they think important to these options.

To some extent on entering adolescence, self-concept and certain facets of the "self" appropriate to the life tasks exist along with global self-concept. Children have a body concept, a self-concept of their own body. However, the physical changes at puberty and after demand a reevaluation of body concept. "All the changes in the body, not only in sexual development and function but also in physical size and strength, necessitate modification of earlier established mental images of the body" (Committee on Adolescence, 1968, p. 74).

The modification for each adolescent would depend on the perception of change by the adolescent, which would relate to actual change and the importance of the body concept to the individual. But every adolescent's body changes and the potential for difficulty, or crisis, exist for every adolescent in dealing with his body concept. If the "normal problem" of body change and adaptation of body concept becomes a "normal crisis" for an adolescent, more change, or effect, on the global self-concept, or other aspects of self-concept, would be presumed. A social, popular child who is a late developer, or who feels changed to a relatively ugly adolescent from an attractive child or a relatively weak adolescent from a strong child, may no longer or temporarily feel socially or completely adequate and have a lower global self-concept.

As adults, most of us probably get up in the morning, wash up, throw on some clothes (which we hope go together and look all right), and proceed with our day. Maybe during the day, because it is convenient or even necessary, an adult might glance at himself or herself in a window or mirror and tidy up. What does a typical adolescent do? He or she probably spends considerable time early and throughout the day checking his or her carefully selected outfit, combing, recombing, and restyling his hair, and examining how he looks. Are there any new pimples, new hairs?

For adults, the question "How do I look today?" can generally be answered "Like I looked yesterday." For adolescents, it is a real question, which they answer by frequently inspecting and modifying the way they look, and incorporating this information into their changing body concept.

The self-concept and its differentiated parts may be affected by adolescent situations and affect feelings about self and performance in these situations. The new situations of love and sexual behavior, few and lesser known social situations in a wider community, a larger, more distant school with greater variety of course offerings and required skills, and demands of occupational and educational choice are all problems and potential crises for most adolescents. The adolescent's self-concept affects his coping with these problems, and the effectiveness of this coping, when the adolescent can verify its effectiveness, in turn affects his self-concept.

CONTEMPORARY "NORMAL PROBLEMS": ACTIVIST EXAMPLE

This section emphasizes the continuing normality of problems and crises in American adolescence. From the Chabassol and Thomas data, we might expect that problems and crises of the self are increasing, but Allport points to the continual presence of the usual human, life task conflicts. In the 1955 study "Youth's Outlook on the Future," Gillespie and Allport compared the attitudes of youth in a number of countries and concluded that American youth were more self-centered and more privatistic, i.e., less interested in, or evading issues of, wider ideological and international concern. In replicating portions of the Gillespie and Allport study some 20 years after the original data were collected, Kleiber and Manaster (1972) found considerable change over time and also greater differences within their sample.

Kleiber and Manaster divided their sample into activists and nonactivists on the basis of participation in demonstrations or confrontations and found that "while there was a general trend away from conservatism and traditional values in all our subjects, the activists reflected far greater changes" (p. 232). The activists were more involved with social problems than the nonactivists, who seemed to be content with primary involvement in their own personal lives and futures. The nonactivists were more similar to the 1950 sample, whereas the activist group seemed to be moving away from privatism. From this we might have concluded that the wider issues and therefore the life tasks other than self were taking on greater import for American youth, but we had to realize that this change was negligible in the majority of nonactivist traditional college and certainly high school youth.

Comparing a 1982 sample with these earlier samples, Manaster, Greer, and Kleiber (1985) found current activists "to be about as conservative as the nonactivists were a decade ago. In this regard, today's activists and nonactivists appear to be more similar to each other than they were in the 1971 sample." They conclude "The present findings, building on those before, begin to support Gillespie and Allport's 'safe' assumption that 'youth's attitudes, values, and philosophies of life reveal the impact of both national culture and of the current situation. . . . ' The data seem to indicate that American students' interest in ambition for a 'rich, full life' continues unbridled, and may even smack of privatism now as political and social conditions are relatively stable. But, as our 1972 study revealed, these interests and ambitions can become more subdued when social conditions become more threatening" (p. 110–11).

Although the majority of youth in the 1960s and certainly in the early

1980s were not practicing activists, the activist's role is open to today's youth. This same situation pertains to other life-styles also.

> We live in an age of extraordinary culture contact and conflict. The electronic revolution, coupled with the revolution in transportation, enables us to confront alien values within our living room or to immerse ourselves physically in alien cultures after a flight of a few hours. The days when one could live in parochial isolation, surrounded only by conventional morality, are fast disappearing. Conflict of ideologies, of world views, of value systems, of philosophical beliefs, of aesthetic orientations, and of political styles confront every thoughtful man and woman, wherever he lives. If such confrontations stimulate moral development, then we live in an era in which technology and world history themselves provide new facilitation for moral growth. We are all today a little like Redfield's peasants who move to the city, living in a world where conflicting cultures and moral viewpoints rub against us at every turn. (Keniston, 1970, pp. 588–89)

Whether the technologies of today along with the abrasions of culture contact and conflict are positive in the sense of developing higher level morality in larger numbers of young people is a moot question. There is no question but that Keniston is correct in pointing out that parochial isolation is dead. We are all, and all youth are, made continually aware of the vast spectrum of political and social ideologies, mechanisms, and strategies, i.e., activists' outlets and options, available in pursuit and support of such ideologies.

Block, Haan, and Smith (1973) discuss adolescent political-social behavior in terms of two dimensions: the "degree of involvement" of a youth with political and social issues, ranging from the uninvolved, apathetic youth to the involved, active youth, and acceptance or rejection of the traditional values and the authority of society's institutions, ranging from the adolescent who is accepting and conforms to society's values and institutions to the adolescent who outwardly rejects society's authority. There has long been in this country the option for adolescents and adults to be distant from the political process and political issues. They may have been apathetic or they may have been mildly interested; however, their involvement was minimal. The option of being more involved was, of course, always open. Although the option of rejecting the society's values and institutions was open, it was seldom taken, and when it was, it was seldom publicized, except in the instance of behaviors that were thought to be traitorous. For whatever reasons, and Keniston's are as compelling as any, the rejection of society's values, institutions, and life-styles occurs among far more young people today than in the past, and we all, including young people, know it.

Block, Haan, and Smith review the literature on activism and apathy in contemporary adolescence. They pose a number of types of youth who vary on the dimensions: degree of involvement, acceptance or rejection. In very simplified form it appears that there are youths who are active and rejecting in keeping with the values of their parents or supported by the values of their parents, just as there are youths who are active in rejecting society as well as actively rejecting their parents. There are youths who are uninvolved and accepting, the politically apathetic individuals who make up the majority of contemporary youth, and youths who are uninvolved and rejecting, the alienated youth. Interestingly, Kerpelman (1970) noted a similarity between activists on the right—active and accepting—and activists on the left—active and rejecting—in that both were high on "autonomy." "All activists—left, middle, and right—were found to need less support and nurturance, to value leadership more, to be more socially ascendant and assertive, and to be more sociable than their ideological counterparts who are not politically active" (Block, Haan, and Smith, 1973, p. 325). This picture of the activist, regardless of political persuasion, is one of a self-confident, high-self-concept person. There is, of course, the question of support from family and peers in choosing a political and social position at the extremes of involvement and rejection or acceptance. But it can be seen that in many individual cases, the autonomous, self-confident adolescent is willing to take the extreme position with minimal, but some, support.

We should also remember that in any group movement there are followers as well as leaders. The excitement, the notoriety, and the sense of community in mutual commitment provide ample support for the less self-confident, lower-self-concept, youth in activist roles.

> Why strip naked and bellow words of four letters in public?
> Poor young things, can it be none of you have any friends?
> (Auden, 1972, p. 50)

These findings and thoughts about activism have pertained primarily to college-age youth. Although it is clear that activism and protest increased in the high schools through the 1960s and is still with us to some extent today, there have been virtually no research studies on activist adolescents below the college level. My first experience of the filtering down of activism and protest to the high school and junior high school levels occurred a few years ago. A strongly worded, but I think humorously intended, petition was circulated by University of Chicago Laboratory School students to the administration and around campus. The petition stated that "little people have rights, too" and demanded that all doorknobs and urinals in the school be lowered.

Almost the only study of high school student involvement in social-political activism is by Leming (1974). The activist sample consisted of students taking an elective course in community involvement and a second group known as the "Memorial 100," a group of 100 students who had been suspended by the administration of the high school in Madison, Wisconsin, where this study was undertaken, when they demonstrated inside the school against the war in Vietnam. Leming looked at moral reasoning in relation to activism because some studies have indicated high moral-judgment levels among left-oriented activists and because activists generally protest most loudly their own morality. Comparing the activist group with nonactivist adolescents in the same high school, Leming found little difference in their moral reasoning. Most of the students were at Level II, Kohlberg's conventional level of moral reaoning; but more activists were at Stage 3, the good boy/nice girl orientation; and more nonactivists were at Stage 4, the law and order orientation.

The activist group was composed of two differing types of activists — the community-involvement course group, who were not rule or law breakers, and the "Memorial 100" group, who had shown themselves to be rule and law breakers. Twenty-two percent of the community-involvement group and only 4 percent of the "Memorial 100" group were at Stage 4, the law and order orientation. Twenty percent of the "Memorial 100" group could not be scored on the moral-reasoning global score. That is, no predominant level or stage of moral reasoning was found in these students' responses to the Kohlberg moral judgment stories. Leming considered that this indicated that these students were in a transitional period and were uncertain about their moral views.

In the "Memorial 100" sample, 65 percent were at the Stage 3 level of moral reasoning. As "a particular mode of reasoning determines how we perceive or interpret the world around us, clearly this 65 percent see right and wrong actions predominantly in terms of peer-group or good-boy orientations" (p. 524). Within the operation of this orientation, acting as a good boy should mean to these adolescents adhering to the norms of their peer group, and most therefore include an activism component. Leming's data clearly indicate that, among some adolescent groups at least, and presumably among many, there is a norm for activism. This norm operates as an option among the value and behavior potentials for high school youth. Of the activist group in Leming's study who protested beyond the bounds of law, fully 85 percent either judged the morality of actions on the basis of good-boy orientation or without a clear orientation. Yet there were twice as many principled reasoners — Level III activists — as there were nonactivists. One wonders, but feels intuitively that he knows, who the leaders were in the activist group.

Merelman notes, from his study of political activists and nonactivists, "that the egalitarian and conflictual aspects of political involvement appeal to some young people as a means of immersing themselves in a uniquely worthwhile activity. . . . Politics helps fill their lives with meaningful work over which they can exercise control" (1985, pp. 64–65).

A discussion of activism as it relates to adolescence through high school is necessarily short because so much is not known and so little is known. The purpose of this exposition was to illustrate how adolescents differentially involve themselves in phenomena and behaviors that are not inherent in the life tasks, but may be a part of the life task having to do with friends and community and need to be considered and accepted or rejected by all youth in contemporary culture. The data do not clearly and directly indicate the relationship between self-concept and activism. But they do indicate that, at least for moral development, those adolescents who feel that going along with the crowd, being a good guy, is right behavior and those adolescents who do not have a clear orientation, clear perspective, on right behavior are apt to behave as activists when the times seem to call for it. If going along to be a good guy or because you are not sure what else to do, from a moral-judgment viewpoint, relates to the same kind of thinking about self-concept, the appropriateness of this discussion would be assured.

In a sense adolescents are called upon to make decisions of "degree of involvement" and "acceptance or rejection" in their behaviors in all of the life task areas. In love and sex, friends and community, school and work, we see that the sense of oneself affects degree of involvement and acceptance or rejection of the traditional and normative ways of behaving. In each of these life tasks, problems and crises may arise. But for the adolescent today, even in high school, questions regarding social-political activism, drugs, alcohol, life-style, etc., are all encountered and must be answered by and for the individual. The process of answering may relate quite significantly to self-concept considerations and may feel like a major problem or crisis to the adolescent. And the answer of the individual adolescent may, too, provoke a crisis.

SEX DIFFERENCES IN SELF-CONCEPT

Issues of the type just described are particularly noteworthy in examining self-concept as we consider personality in adolescence. These types of problems appear to ebb and flow. They become more or less popular among adolescents, and receive greater and lesser news and media coverage accordingly. Remembering the discussion of personality consistency and research strategies in developmental psychology, these problems would seem to affect more adolescents during periods when they are popular and newsworthy. During these times, and across time, these issues would show themselves in the time effect in cross-sequential developmental studies.

Some problems seem to be with adolescents continually. Fleege (1945) listed the major problems confronting the adolescent in the conclusion of his extensive study of adolescent boys. His list, starting with most frequent and intense, included sexual adjustment, vocational choice and decision, feelings of misunderstanding and lack of understanding from adults, few social opportunities, financial difficulties, and difficulties with school. Adams (1966) asked 4,000 boys and girls, ages 10 to 19, to identify their own personal problems and those of their peer groups. School, interpersonal relationships, family, and money were the most frequently reported problems. Boys more frequently mentioned school and financial problems; the girls more frequently mentioned interpersonal and family problems.

Morgan (1969) reviewed studies of junior high school and senior high school students with the Mooney problem checklist. At the junior high school level, school problems were most frequent and problems concerning money, work, and the future, self-centered concerns, and interpersonal relationships followed. At the senior high school level, adjustment to school and work was the most frequently mentioned problem, followed by personal-psychological relations and current and future financial, vocational, and educational problems. All these problems may be seen as fitting neatly into the life task areas.

Although there is overlap and interrelationship among the other four life task areas, the life task self affects, aids, or interferes with feelings about and success in the other four life tasks. Therefore, in the other four life task chapters, there are discussions of how the self, self-concept, interacts with them. Hurlock (1975) notes four conditions that influence the self-concept of the adolescent which are covered in the life task chapters and three conditions that influence the adolescent's self-concept which are not covered. She notes that sex-appropriate appearance, interest, and behavior help in achieving favorable self-concept, that a close relationship with the same-sex family member facilitates sex-appropriate self-concept, that peers influence self-concept, and that the adolescent's level of aspiration also does. Names and nicknames, given to the adolescent either by family members or peers, may be a source of embarrassment, and the adolescent may feel ostracized and ridiculed when the name or nickname is used. Age of maturation may have a positive effect on self-concept when those maturing early are treated more like adults, but it may have a negative effect on self-concept when late maturers are treated like children. Appearance is particularly important to adolescents, and being or feeling that he is different in appearance may influence the level of an adolescent's self-concept. "Being different in appearance makes the adolescent feel inferior, even if the difference adds to his physical attractiveness. Any physical defect is a source of embarrassment which leads to feeling of inferiority" (Hurlock, 1975, p. 197). Of the many changes that become issues or problems for adolescents, whether affecting or affected by the self-concept, all are social and/or cognitive, with the exception of the concern with appearance that is a function of physiological change.

We usually think that while adolescents are all more concerned with appearance and attractiveness than adults are, adolescent girls are even more concerned than boys. Both the Douvan and Adelson (1966) and the Coleman (1961) studies support this notion. However, Maccoby and Jacklin, in their study of the psychology of sex differences, "encountered very little additional evidence for or against this view, except for the isolated facts that girls and women are somewhat more likely to want orthodontic treatment" (1974, p. 160). They point out that the traditional stereotype of girls in front of mirrors, thinking about clothes and the way they look for hours at a time, if it were ever valid, is now probably changing very rapidly. Although they cite some evidence that girls may be more interested in physical attractiveness than boys, they point to the unisex movement, men's hair stylists, curlers, and dryers, and the colorful, varied, and showy clothes that men and adolescent boys now wear.

In fact, in their study of sex differences, Maccoby and Jacklin find remarkably little difference in self-esteem between the sexes across all age levels through adolescence. In our discussion of self-concept earlier, we observed its relationship to sense of competence in much the same way that U'Ren does—"A sense of competence, a sense of doing or achieving something that is valued, is crucial for the development and maintenance of self-esteem" (1971, p. 470). From this position we would hypothesize that both males and females, having, as we have seen, essentially equal self-concepts, would show equal degrees of self-confidence and senses of competence in approaching task situations that are *equally valued*. However, Maccoby and Jacklin present 15 studies in which confidence in task performance was measured. There was no difference between the sexes in 4 of the studies, whereas men and boys had more confidence in their task performance in the other 11. It appears that through high school, boys and girls do not differ consistently on locus of control, but in college, girls tend to become more external. Looking beyond the locus-of-control variable as early as the grade school years, males exhibit a greater sense of personal strength and potency.

By the college years, Maccoby and Jacklin see a "male cluster" in which there is greater self-confidence in task performance, higher sense of potency, and a greater personal sense of internal control. The "female cluster" is "amorphous" but describes women as more competent socially, more attractive, acceptable to others, and less shy. It is as if men and women, boys and girls, have carved out for themselves the traditional sex roles and stereotypes, which do give satisfaction, self-esteem, and sense of competence, at least to the degree that they have accepted the traditional roles and stereotypes. Within the areas that are more important to them, the male and female clusters, each sex may have a higher feeling of self-worth but in toto there would be no difference, *if* they value their sex-appropriate clusters equally.

However, in recent years, as the societal perception of the value of the traditional female role has decreased and the perception of a valued women's role has become less clear, the general self-esteem of girls has been found to be lower than that of boys during preadolescence and early adolescence (Hare, 1980; Simmons et al., 1978; Simmons and Rosenberg, 1975) and later adolescence (Conger, Peng, and Dunteman, 1977; O'Malley and Bachman, 1979). Both girls' and boys' high self-esteem has been shown to be related to masculinity (Lamke, 1982). In this regard, the consistency of the personality traits that are associated with sex, instrumental and expressive traits, is of interest. Phye and Sola (1984) sampled females from their sophomore through senior years in high school and found these traits to be very stable. While the traits may remain stable, with little or no change in adolescence, the evaluation of the traits can change with time and at times. Thus, in effect, self-esteem may change when self-concept, and personality, do not.

RACE AND CLASS DIFFERENCES IN SELF-CONCEPT

It had long been considered, and a review of the literature to the early and mid-sixties concurs, that in studies comparing the self-concept of blacks and whites, blacks had lower scores. More recently, there is a growing body of literature that not only denies the earlier studies, but even shows positive and high self-concept scores for those black, Mexican-American, and Puerto Rican children and adolescents who are disadvantaged (Carter, 1968; Havighurst and Dreyer, 1971; Simmons, 1978; Simmons et al., 1978; Soares and Soares, 1969, 1970/1971, 1971; Trowbridge, 1970a, 1970b). Trowbridge (1970a) found that regardless of whether schools were more or less equally integrated or predominantly black or predominantly white, and regardless of SES or neighborhood, disadvantaged boys and girls had consistently higher self-concepts than advantaged children. Powell and Fuller (1970) tested 617 students and found higher self-concept scores for black students in all black, or predominantly black, schools. Black boys had higher self-concept scores than white boys regardless of the racial composition of the school. Soares and Soares (1971) found that

> (a) disadvantaged children view themselves and think that (i.e., their classmates, teachers, and parents) look at them more positively than do advantaged children; (b) elementary school children have higher self-images than secondary school students. Therefore, in comparison to elementary school children, both disadvantaged and advantaged high school students showed a diminishing self-image. (p. 428)

As we have noted numerous times, personality characteristics and self-concept are founded on a child's perceptions and conclusions. The child comes to the initial conclusions about himself, his initial self-view and self-concept within his home, immediate neighborhood, and early school. The people, the children, around the child are most likely to be similar to him in SES and race for a variety of social, historical, and economic reasons. His early perceptions, his models, his significant others have probably not reflected prejudices against him as being different or inferior because of class or caste membership. Rather, he most probably has been among equals, and the self-concept he develops is reinforced by those with whom he is closest and has most in common. "At first the child sees only that part of life and of the human community which is bounded by his environmnet, the family in which he is living. To him this environment means 'life' and the members of the family seem to be 'society' and he attempts to adapt himself to them" (Dreikurs, 1953, p. 43). The family is the first and most important set of significant others. Carter (1968) felt that Mexican-Americans did not have lower self-concepts than Anglos because they had their own peer group and ethnic group against which to evaluate themselves and develop their self-concept.

Within any group (sex, race, or ethnic) there is no reason for development of low self-concept relative to another group. However, as groups define themselves and are socially defined, they may differ in areas of strength and weakness, areas of high and low self-concept. We have just seen this between the sexes in the clusters of attributes that are most important to each. Even between socioeconomic classes, the important, relevant issues for status within that class and self-esteem of its members are available to all — individual differences in the creation of self-concept account for the differences. "There is no indication that the distribution of self-acceptance in a group is related to the social prestige of that group in American society" (Rosenberg, 1965, p. 56). However, as has been illustrated numerous times, there are differences in aspects of self-concept and these aspects of self-concept in relation to attitudes and behaviors in the life tasks. The point here is that the importance and relevance of an aspect of an individual's self-concept to some degree reflects the importance and relevance it has for the individual's group and that the related behaviors have for the group.

A study of race, gender, and SES effects on self-esteem in late adolescents by Richman, Clark, and Brown (1985) may serve to illustrate the particularity of these issues—i.e., that in fact, no one is of a socioeconomic status and not also of a gender and of a race, and thus each person represents their individual interaction of the three variables. "Concern with one status group can lead to neglect of people's multiple group memberships that may relate to an issue" (Grant and Sleeter, 1986, p. 207). They found that with the exception of school self-esteem, "black students were significantly higher than white students on all general and area-specific self-esteem measures" (p. 561). They found numerous interactions among race, gender, and SES and found "in general, high SES females were lower on several measures of area-specific self-esteem than other gender by SES groups. Furthermore, white females were lower in general self-esteem than were black students and white males" (p. 563). They speculated considerably about these findings. It seems safe to consolidate their speculations about the low self-esteem of high SES white females by saying that at this time in history these girls are unsure of what they should be and seem to be trying to be all things to all people. Therefore whenever and wherever they find themselves deficient or failing has an influence on their sense of self, because their sense of self is less clearly societally defined. "Carver and Ganellen (1983) found that young women overgeneralize a specific failure and express their perceived inadequacies in self-punitive behaviors" (Richman et al., 1985, p. 563).

How can this chapter be concluded? Some adolescents, more intellectually able, develop views of their selves in more abstract, wider frameworks. Most adolescents further differentiate facets of their selves as they are forced into a wider world where they must "measure up" in new ways. Each new situation and new option may provoke a "crisis" of "Am I up to it?". "It," the situation or area of ability, may be more or less relevant to the individual and his or her sex/class/race designation and may more or less affect, or be affected by the individual's behavior, self-concept, and self-esteem. And for many adolescents, their self fits their world and their future so that crises are few.

From within any group, and for any person, high self-esteem, self-confidence, is possible. The low-self-concept person will try to avoid areas of failure but agonize when he cannot avoid such situations. The high-self-concept person need not avoid tough situations and may provoke them to prove, or prove again, his own worth to himself.

Self-concept pervades all life tasks. Adolescence is the time to test it. Many adolescents do. Francoise Mallet-Joris illustrates this beautifully in "the saga of Daniel," her son:

> At fifteen there was a rock-'n'-roll phase. . . . At sixteen he began to display a lively interest in the opposite sex. Young ladies whose Christian names I didn't even know were always disappearing into his room, . . . like ladies in B-feature movies.
>
> He began playing the clarinet. And drinking a little.
>
> At seventeen he became a Buddhist.
>
> He began playing the tuba. His hair got longer.
>
> At eighteen he passed his baccalaureate. Shortly before that, there was a period when he was always covered in jewels, like a Hindu prince or a movie extra. . . .
>
> The jewels disappeared. He began playing the saxophone and the guitar. He hitchhiked 2,500 miles. . . .
>
> He returned home more or less without shoes. . . . He cut off his hair and began studying for a degree in economics. That is the saga of Daniel.
>
> Where is the upbringing in all that? If Daniel, who will be twenty-one this year, is a good son, a good-looking boy, serious yet with a sense of humor, endowed with both imagination and common sense, did I have anything to do with making him so? No, nothing, nothing. And yet yes, something, one tiny little thing, the only thing perhaps that I have given him, yet the only thing too, I sometimes tell myself with pride, that it was important to give him: confidence. (1971, pp. 81–82)

Identity and Theories of Adolescent Development

CHAPTER 8

Developmental and psychological theorists may refer to adolescence as it fits their theories or as it presents exceptions to their theories; others have developed theories about adolescence itself. From one context or another, theories and thoughts about adolescence have existed from the early Greeks to the present. By today the list of theories of adolescence is immense. In this chapter three theories are chosen for presentation because of their historical and current importance: personality theory à la Freud, Lewin's social-psychological theory, and, most widely used today, the neoanalytic theory of Erikson. Although other and additional theorists might have been covered, an understanding of these three, in my opinion, subsumes the major trends in contemporary thinking about adolescence.

FREUD'S THEORY

Sigmund Freud (1933, 1953) concluded his hypothesized series of stages, in which the child passes through the "oral," "anal," "phallic," and "latency" stages, with the "genital" stage, which commences with the onset of adolescence. In this stage, because of pubertal physiological changes, the instinctual balance presumed to prevail during the latency period is upset as the sexual impulses exert themselves, resulting in the "subordination of all sexual component instincts under the primacy of the genital zone" (S. Freud, 1953, p. 337).

The primary tasks of adolescence, according to Freud and in Freudian language, include the subordination of pregenital part drives (the incomplete, immature childhood drive) to genital primacy and the resolution of any oedipal conflicts revived at this stage. The latter demands object loss (detachment from parents and their internal representations) and object

142

finding (establishment of mature heterosexual object relations). The primary tasks for the ego in adolescence are modification of the superego, establishment of an ego ideal and more ordered character structure, establishment of sexual identity, and identity formation. Basically, these tasks are necessitated, within the Freudian theory, by the physiological changes at adolescence that unleash the genital sexual instincts that need to be restrained by the person, both to hold himself or herself together and to remain acceptable to society.

Lidz, in describing the psychoanalytic view of adolescence, said, "It has been customary to examine the youth's oedipal transition and to seek to understand his adolescent problems largely as recrudescences of the oedipal difficulties. . . . The intense sexual drives of adolescents tend to follow earlier attachments in seeking outlets, and the oedipal configurations must be reworked and once again resolved" (1969, pp. 105–6). Of course this statement continues the emphasis on sex and the relationships between the sexes that is so central to Freudian theory. It also implies consistency of personality and coping styles from childhood to adolescence. The crux of the task is to "rework" relationships and to try again previously used methods for finding fulfillment as a result of and accounting for the new, revitalized sexuality.

The latency period, the years just prior to puberty and the genital stage, is a period of quietude in the sexual area, according to Freud. It is the time when, in the juvenile and preadolescent eras, according to Sullivan, the child becomes social and an orientation toward living is established, norms of behavior in many settings and situations are internalized, and appropriate role behaviors are learned. It is the time for the development of what Sullivan calls a "chum" relationship.

From our discussions of cognitive, moral, and sex-role development we can see the latency period as a time of consolidation. It is the time during which the child "puts it together" concretely. He has the rudimentary capacities for understanding and functioning in his society. This period allows him to build on these capacities, these basic concrete perceptions, and to test them within his somewhat limited world. It is a period of intense but definite, because of the concrete operational cognition, socialization. The child can fairly clearly determine what is expected of him, in his various roles, in order to become a part of society. In this period he, again concretely, figures out how he personally is going to meet these expectations — how he is going to fit in.

The latency period is, then, a time during which little physical or cognitive change, as well as little situational or social change, occur for the child.

During this period, the child develops his basic stance and style, his understanding and manner of relating. With the onset of puberty he has to retest his stance and style with his new "powers" and in new settings and social situations. Within the Freudian framework this need not be that upsetting—indeed, if the previously used techniques work well, it should not be.

However, what of the difficulty inherent in reworking the oedipal conflicts? Chronologically the last time the oedipal issue came up was about the time the child started school, i.e., moving out from home into a broader social sphere. It is an issue of power and attachment. The attachment theme is dominant. The child asks, "Who gets? Do I get?" the source of warmth, nurturance, love? In the genital stage, at adolescence, the child again moves into a broader social arena. And again he must ask himself whether he is going to get the qualities of warmth and security he desires and from whom.

At both times when the oedipal issue arises, the child has to look out for himself, his objects of love, and/or his sources of love, when change appears to jeopardize the strength of his attachments to the objects. He is called on to maintain such a source and, because of either limited knowledge or limited confidence, he tries to hold on to what he has with the ferocity of a person clinging to the side of a cliff. As the adolescent desires love and support and sex, he or she is very apt to think of mother and/or father as the most likely sources. They have given it before, albeit in ways not wholly consistent with the adolescent's fantasies. But they have probably been the comforters, with hugs and kisses, and encouragers ("we love you, you can do it"), and sex symbols of sorts—the parent of the opposite sex being the only adult of the opposite sex the adolescent has ever seen live, in person, in the nude.

The process of detaching oneself from parents (in the sense that identifications are loosened and one sees oneself for the first time as an independent self rather than as a filial appendage) is referred to in Freudian jargon as "object loss." Similarly, acquiring new tender love attachments is "object finding." This may be harsh language, but the tension implicit in the "loss" of security and love from home and the need to "find" same as an independent person is clearly conveyed. This Freudian language and these concepts should not be taken literally, but they are helpful as descriptors of an adolescent's movement to independence and mature sexuality with the accompanying potential for distress and confusion.

Included in the primary tasks of adolescence according to Freud were those having to do with ego development. Referring to these tasks in the order they were presented earlier, many behaviors that are strictly forbidden in childhood are open, to some degree, to adolescents. It is incumbent on the adolescent, particularly in the sexual area, to modify the superego, to lessen the severity of the strictures he holds. As he develops a sense of who he would like to be, that is, as he establishes an ego ideal, he is able to modify his superego because he has a high standard set for himself which allows new thoughts and behaviors that he previously did not allow himself.

The ego must incorporate the altered limits and new abilities into a unity that is consistent. This unity must cover the areas of morality and character, sense of sexual identity, and a total holistic formation of personal identity. The biological changes of the genital stage require redeveloping stability and order in character and identity.

Freud's importance in psychology and the psychology of adolescence cannot be underrated, even at a time when his followers and revisers, and other contemporary theorists, seem to hold sway. Freudian language, and particularly the Freudian emphasis on the sex drive, do not help the theory's acceptability today. However, the underlying notions in the material just presented continue to be important in understanding adolescents. If we expand motivation, as the neo-Freudians have, to include the full thrust of meanings that moving from childhood implies (physiological—strength, size, looks, and sex—and social—all of the new situations), we see the adolescent asserting himself in many ways that are not necessarily sexual in nature.

Freud speaks then, if we accept this elaborated notion of motivation, of accepting one's new sexuality while becoming an increasingly independent individual who must develop an identity, make new attachments, understand how societal rules apply at this new age level, and resolve the problem of wanting to remain close to one's family of origin while becoming personally more independent. In defining the developmental tasks, Havighurst acknowledged that Freud's insights were integrated into the tasks. Freud's descriptions of the dynamics of the individual adolescent's struggle with these changes remains valuable. That Freud's notions can continue to be modified to contemporary adolescence also speaks to their value.

LEWIN'S THEORY

In the future history of our psychological era there are two names which, I believe, will stand out above all others: those of Freud and of Lewin. Freud will be revered for his first unravelling of the complexities of the individual history, and Lewin for his first envisioning of the dynamic laws according to which individuals behave as they do to their contemporaneous environments. Freud, the clinician, and Lewin, the experimentalist, these are the two men who will always be remembered because of the fact that their contrasting but complementary insights first made of psychology a science which was applicable both to real individuals and to real society. (Tolman, 1948, p. 4)

Kurt Lewin was not a psychologist or theorist who concentrated on adolescence. In order to demonstrate his basic theoretical construct, he included adolescence in his discussion. "The field-theoretical approach is intended to be a practical vehicle of research. As is true with any tool, its characteristics can be understood fully only by the use of it in actual research. Therefore, instead of stating general methodological principles in abstractum, I prefer to discuss the problem of adolescence and the definition of a social group as an illustration" (Lewin, 1939, p. 872). Lewin's illustration of his theory through adolescence provides a number of important insights. In order to understand the adolescence illustration, the theory in brief will be presented first.

Lewin called his theory "field theory," stating that "field theory is probably best characterized as a method: namely a method of analyzing causal relations and of building scientific constructs" (1951, p. 45). Lewin's field theory is very technical, with scientific-mathematical terms involving topology theory and vectors. Topology, a branch of geometry, deals with spatial properties and logical derivations thereof without requiring assumptions of quantitative relationships (Cartwright, 1959, p. 59). Lewin (1936) felt that through the topological approach one could determine which events in a given life space are possible and which are not, and with the vector concept, which events are more and which are less probable.

Field theory emphasizes a holistic, macro approach. Lewin saw behavior as a dynamic whole, not only the sum of its parts but different from the sum of its parts. Lewin felt that although both the whole and the parts are equally real, the whole has definite properties of its own. He concentrated his efforts on the dynamics of the whole and the interdependence of the parts.

A last general property of field theory is its emphasis on contemporaneity. Although Lewin did not neglect the importance of personal history, where relevant, his primary interest was in the interdependence of forces of the present situation, in the dynamics of "contemporaneous properties."

The key to Lewin's theory is the concept of the life space, the psychological field in which behavior occurs. The life space represents "the person and his environment . . . as one constellation of the interdependent factors" (1951, p. 240). The constellation that is the life space can be represented by a formula in which B (behavior) is an F (function) of the P (person) and his E (environment). P and E are interdependent variables, and E refers not to the physical environment but to the total psychological, internal and external, environment. Inasmuch as *P* and *E* together make up the *LSp* (life space), the formula is

$$B = F(p,E) = F(LSp)$$

Lewin graphically demonstrated the dynamics of the life space in two ways. He mapped the life space showing goals, barriers, and the like, i.e., topological representation. He also attempted to show forces acting on a person to cause movement toward or away from a goal.

Four directing principles of field-theory analysis have been summarized by Cartwright (1959): (1) only what is concrete can have effects, (2) every concrete aspect of a situation must be included (3) in any given field, events are interdependent, and (4) only what is present in a situation can influence its outcome (contemporaneity).

One may become confused by Lewin's stress on contemporaneity when we have placed so much emphasis on consistency. The notions are not incompatible. In fact, Lewin's position reinforces the consistency argument. He is saying, in effect, that past events do not cause behaviors in the present situation. However, what the individual remembers from the past, the conclusions the individual drew from the past, and the beliefs the individual therefore carries into a situation are concrete aspects of that situation and may thereby affect that situation. An individual's personality, a stable set of characteristics and tendencies, is present in all situations for that person — it is the person's framework for determining life space, for determining what *P* and *E* are so that *B* occurs.

TRANSITION TO UNKNOWNS

Lewin calls the period of adolescence a "period of transition," pointing to several ways of characterizing the nature of the transition. Figure 8.1 shows the clarity of the space of free movement for the child and for the adult as well as the difference in the number of activity regions available to each. The child has far fewer regions accessible to him than does the adult. Lewin (1939) says:

> The actual activity regions are represented. The accessible regions are blank; the inaccessible shaded. (a) the space of free movement of the *child* includes the regions 1–6 representing activities such as getting into the movies at children's rates, belonging to a boy's club, etc. The regions 7–35 are not accessible, representing activities such as driving a car, writing checks for purchases, political activities, performance of adults' occupations, etc. (b) the *adult* space of free movement is considerably wider, although it too is bounded by regions of activities inaccessible to the adult, such as shooting

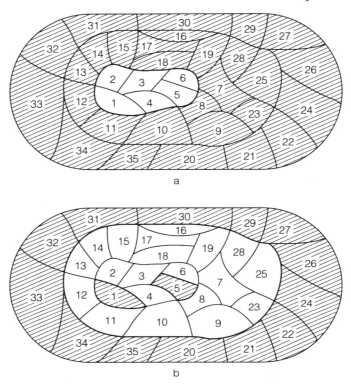

a

b

Figure 8.1. Comparison of the space of free movement of child and adult (Reprinted by permission from K. Lewin, "Field theory and experiment in social psychology: Concepts and methods," *American Journal of Sociology* 44 [1939], 868–97. Copyright © 1939. Published July, September, November, 1938; January, March, May, 1939. Composed and printed by the University of Chicago Press, Chicago, Illinois, U.S.A.)

his enemy or entering activities beyond his social or intellectual capacity (represented by regions including 29–35). Some of the regions accessible to the child are not accessible to the adult, for instance, getting into the movies at children's rates, or doing things socially taboo for an adult which are permitted to the child (represented by regions 1 and 5). (p. 875)

Figure 8.2 represents the space of free movement of the adolescent. This figure, or topological map, indicates the growth in the number of activity regions with adolescence and the closing of some regions that had been accessible to the child. The figure also shows the "unknown" quality of the life space of the adolescent. According to Lewin (1939):

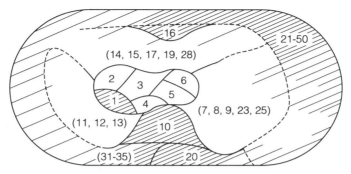

Figure 8.2. The space of free movement of the adolescent as it appears to him (Reprinted by permission from K. Lewin, "Field theory and experiment in social psychology: Concepts and methods," *American Journal of Sociology* 44 [1939], 868–97. Copyright © 1939. Published July, September, November, 1938; January, March, May, 1939. Composed and printed by the University of Chicago Press, Chicago, Illinois, U.S.A.)

The space of free movement is greatly increased, including many regions which previously have not been accessible to the child, for instance, freedom to smoke, returning home late, driving a car (regions 7–9, 11–13, . . .). Certain regions accessible to the adult are clearly not accessible to the adolescent, such as voting (represented by regions 10 and 16). Certain regions accessible to the child have already become inaccessible, such as getting into the movies at children's rates, or behaving on too childish a level (region 1). The boundaries of these newly acquired portions of the space of free movement are only vaguely determined and in themselves generally less clearly and sharply differentiated than for an adult. In such cases the life-space of the adolescent seems to be full of possibilities and at the same time of uncertainties. (p. 876)

As a child, one knows what one is allowed and able to do and what is prohibited by society or personal ability. An adult, too, understands with considerable definition where he is free and able and where not. The adolescent, moving from the limited activity regions of childhood, finds himself with great "unknowns."

A child belongs to a specific group, child, and probably a small neighborhood school or block group of friends. With adolescence he undergoes "a change in group belongingness." He is no longer, and does not want to be, considered a child, and he physically moves into new schools and neighborhoods, coming in contact with, and becoming a part of, new groups. Change in group belonging is always important, to adults as well as adolescents.

When, as with many or most adolescents, the change in group belongingness is major and has not been experienced before, it is extremely important.

Referring to Figure 8.2, Lewin states, "The uncertain character of the adolescent's behavior and his conflicts can partly be explained by the lack of cognitive clarity concerning the adult's world which he is going to enter" (1939, p. 876). The early adolescent may not know what the adolescent world holds as he enters it, much less the adult world.

Lewin points to another area that has been "known" with surety until adolescence brings change — one's own body. "More or less strange and new body experiences arise and make this part of the life space which is so close and vital to the individual strange and unknown" (1939, p. 876).

The time dimension of the life space also becomes an unknown region in adolescence. Until adolescence the child has not had to deal with time to any great degree. His day and his immediate future were set out for him, and the distant future was not even an issue for him. With adolescence, plans for one's activities and life become one's own responsibility. These plans must involve the present, immediate, and distant future in ways that satisfy one's own values and goals while still being realistic.

In this regard I will never forget my first day in high school when a staff person asked me to fill out a card showing the courses I wanted to take in my first two semesters. I had no idea what to do and did not particularly care. All I was concerned about was the location of my locker and who I would sit with at lunch. The spring term seemed so far off — as if no action now could affect what happened then.

This last anecdote in the context of Lewin's theory and topological maps leads to mention of a newer view of how adolescents resolve their confused situation with so much unknown all around them. Coleman (1974, 1978), in his "focal theory," asks, "If adolescents have to adjust to so much potentially stressful change, and at the same time pass through this stage of their life with relative stability, . . . how do they do it? The answer suggested by the focal theory is that they cope by dealing with one issue at a time. They spread the process of adaptation over a span of years, attempting to resolve first one issue and then the next" (1979, p. 9).

We must consider the focal theory as we try to partial out the specific problems adolescents face in particular situations and while we attempt to understand and place the "search for identity" and the "identity crisis" in the context of the adolescent's everyday life.

MARGINAL MAN

Lewin restates his opinion that the child group and the adult group are clearly defined, in contrast to the adolescent group, which is ill defined. The adolescent or youth culture may be seen as a functional attempt to give definition to this group. The issue of whether an adolescent subculture exists will be discussed later, and only slightly reduces the weight of Lewin's argument that "the adolescent does not wish to belong any longer to the children's group and, at the same time, knows that he is not readily accepted in the adult group. In this case he has a position similar to what is called in sociology the 'marginal man' " (1939, p. 881).

The marginal-man position of the adolescent is graphically illustrated in Figure 8.3. The marginal man is characterized as a person standing on the boundary between two groups, not belonging to either and uncertain about his belongingness. A person in this position, belonging partially to two groups but not fully to either, may exhibit symptoms of emotional instability and sensitivity. He may "tend to unbalanced behavior, either to boisterousness or shyness, exhibiting too much tension, and a frequent shift between extremes of contradictory behavior" (Lewin, 1939, p. 882). Descriptions about adolescents of this type are frequent, but seldom are they within a conceptual framework which explains the forces that cause them. Lewin's description of the marginal man is like the description of a frustrated man on an island in the middle of a lake trying to get the attention of someone on shore to prove he is worthy of being brought in.

Lewin likens the adolescent as a marginal man to the same marginal status of some "members of an underprivileged minority group," thereby preconceiving the "student as nigger" concept by almost 30 years.

Lewin's treatment of adolescent marginality was tested by Bamber with a sample of over 400 14- and 15-year-olds. His adolescent subjects seemed to see three developmental worlds, or circles, in which the overlap is slight between childhood and adolescence and considerable between adolescence and adulthood. Adult subjects, conversely, distinguished greater overlap between childhood and adolescence than between adolescence and adulthood. Adolescents saw their own age period and also adulthood as attractive, while adults did not find adolescence an attractive period. Although Lewin's approach was supported by this work, Bamber "concluded that Lewin's theory of the adolescent marginal man is an oversimplification" (1973, p. 5).

The theory may be too simple to catch the subtleties of the scope of positions adolescents may see and feel themselves occupying in the many situations they confront. However, the theory and conception of the marginal

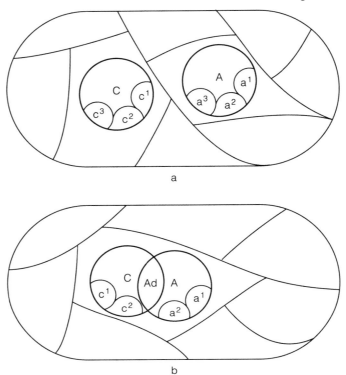

Figure 8.3. The adolescent as marginal man (Reprinted by permission from K. Lewin, "Field theory and experiment in social psychology: Concepts and methods," *American Journal of Sociology* 44 [1939], 868-97. Copyright © 1939. Published July, September, November, 1938; January, March, May, 1939. Composed and printed by the University of Chicago Press, Chicago, Illinois, U.S.A.)

man describes very well the amorphous world of adolescents as so many feel it. The self-description of this 15-year-old girl illustrates her feelings of marginality, in-betweenness:

> I'm a very impressionable romanticist, and an individualistic realist besides. I'm a mature young woman, and I'm still a little girl. I want so much, yet I quit too soon. I have so many dreams, but I forget to chase them. I'm afraid of people and even more afraid of myself. I love people, and sometimes I kinda like me. (Bravler and Jacobs, 1974, p. 204)

ADOLESCENT EXTREMISM: SITUATIONAL AND COGNITIVE COMPONENTS

The adolescent stands on the brink of first the adolescent world and then the adult world surrounded by question marks, unknowns, and feeling like a marginal man—a true member of no respectable group. Some symptomatic behavior has been alluded to. But how does a young person in this position feel and act? From Lewin's theory there is a logic and lawfulness to the adolescent's reactions to the overall situation of being an adolescent.

The adolescent is moving from one region to another. The very fact of movement and change, particularly the dramatic change at adolescence, makes him more flexible. Lewin says, "A period of radical change is naturally a period of greater plasticity" (1939, p. 878).

The adolescent's movement is to more or less cognitively unstructured regions or situations where he has marginal status and an in-between-groups position, with baffling changes in his own body and needs. This position is untenable unless the adolescent actively copes with himself and his environment. He is unsure and confused. Of necessity he is open to new ideas and behaviors because he brings a limited, if already patterned, repertoire of coping mechanisms with him into adolescence.

If he sees his life space as described here, he will show "shyness, sensitivity, and aggressiveness, owing to unclearness and instability of ground," be in "more or less permanent conflict between the various attitudes, values, ideologies, and styles of living," and have "emotional tension resulting from these conflicts" (Lewin, 1939, p. 883). He will be ready to take extreme positions and behave outlandishly—this is one way of giving structure and definiteness to his hazy world and partially formed ideas. Extreme attitudes and actions are most likely to bring responses from others. The responses may not be positive but may help in convincing the adolescent of his existence, if not his value, and in clarifying the limits that are imposed that give structure to his field.

The adolescent will also be ready to shift his position radically. Trying to find his place in this unclear field, the adolescent may take an extreme position. Although holding this position may have value, as just shown, the adolescent prefers, as does anyone, to have social support for the position he holds. It may be that one strong friend is sufficient to support his maintaining a radical attitude for a long while. It may also be that he finds that he loses friends, or respect from important others, because of this attitude. It is then quite easy for him to change his position completely to regain lost support—to see if he feels greater belonging when holding this new position.

Great emphasis is placed by adolescents, and by most American adults, on belonging to groups, specific groups. To the extent that a group, its leadership or leader, has specific ideals, values, and goals, whether they are overt or simply understood, it holds great promise for fulfilling the adolescent's needs for structure and belonging. These seem to be "the reasons behind the readiness of the adolescent to follow anyone who offers a definite pattern of values" (Lewin, 1939, p. 881).

The insights conveyed by Lewin's theory to the understanding of the adolescent's tendency to take extreme positions, follow extremist leaders, and make radical shifts in attitude and behavior are immensely important. To recognize the generality of Lewin's theory, consider the persons who assassinated or attempted to assassinate John Kennedy, Robert Kennedy, Martin Luther King, and George Wallace. Although much can be said about each assassin personally, without doubt they were each marginal men, and each one showed extreme behavior and affiliations before attempting the most extreme act of all. Obviously this is not to imply that marginality demands extremism. Rather, marginality makes extremism seem a viable personal option for some persons, their only way of seeking recognition, belonging, and structure in their lives. At times it must seem this way for some adolescents.

It is worth considering the similarity between the behaviors Lewin attributes to the marginal adolescent and the behaviors attributed to the adolescent searching for an identity.

ERIKSON'S THEORY

Erik H. Erikson, as a psychoanalyst and cultural anthropologist, amplified Freud's stage theory, attributing the crisis at each stage to the demands of society. Theoretically, Erikson's stages meet the criteria for stage theories in that one must successfully cope with the crisis at one stage in order to be successful at the succeeding stages. However, one can pass through the stages on the negative side. "Resolution of each crisis in ensuing life-stages adds a new quality to the ego — either a positive or a negative dimension" (Stendler, 1964, p. 242).

The stages and areas of development that Erikson (1959) discusses in his most important monograph on the adolescent stage are presented in his worksheet, Figure 8.4. The crucial stage for adolescents according to Erikson is V, Identity vs. Identity [or Role] Diffusion. In this section, the meaning of ego identity and the ego-identity stage as it relates to formal operations will be examined, as will Erikson's concept of the adolescent period as a psychosocial moratorium. Lastly, Erikson's stages will be considered in light of social-class differences.

	A Psychosocial Crises	B Radius of Significant Relations	C Related Elements of Social Order	D Psychosocial Modalities	E Psychosexual Stages
I	Trust vs. Mistrust	Maternal Person	Cosmic Order	To Get To Give in Return	Oral- Respiratory, Sensory- Kinesthetic (Incorporative Modes)
II	Autonomy vs. Shame, Doubt	Parental Persons	"Law and Order"	To Hold (On) To Let (Go)	Anal-Urethral, Muscular (Retentive- Eliminative)
III	Initiative vs. Guilt	Basic Family	Ideal Prototypes	To Make (= Going After) To "Make Like" (= playing)	Infantile- Genital, Locomotor (Intrusive, Inclusive)
IV	Industry vs. Inferiority	"Neighbor- hood," School	Technological Elements	To Make Things (= Completing) To Make Things Together	"Latency"
V	Identity and Repudiation vs. Identify Diffusion	Peer Groups and Out-Groups; Models of Leadership	Ideological Perspectives	To Be Oneself (or Not to Be) To Share Being One-self	Puberty
VI	Intimacy and Solidarity vs. Isolation	Partners in Friendship, Sex, Competition, Cooperation	Patterns of Cooperation and Competition	To Lose and Find Oneself in Another	Genitality
VII	Generativity vs. Self- Absorption	Divided Labor and Shared Household	Currents of Education and Tradition	To Make Be To Take Care of	
VIII	Integrity vs. Despair	"Mankind" "My Kind"	Wisdom	To Be, through Having Been To Face Not Being	

Figure 8.4. Erikson's worksheet (Reprinted by permission from E. Erikson, "Identity and the life cycle," *Psychological Issues* 1 [1959], 166.)

EGO IDENTITY AND FORMAL OPERATIONS

In order to understand Erikson on adolescence, it is important to have a feel for "identity," or "ego identity," and "identity formation," as well as how "ego identity" relates to self. I say "have a feel for" because the differences between these terms, as well as the definitions of the terms themselves, are fraught with subtle distinctions that demand an in-depth understanding of psychoanalytic theory and personology. This feel for the terms Erikson uses should be sufficient for our purposes.

Erikson (1959) says that "identity" relates both to an individual's *unique* development and his link with the *unique* values of the people he sees as *his* people. It is important, then, to an understanding of identity to show concern for an individual's personal uniqueness, emanating from his own personal history as he has perceived and constructed it and his identification with a group to which he feels he belongs. Erikson's own words for defining identity and his uses of it might best illustrate the multiplicity of views and approaches to the term:

> It is this identity of something in the individual's care with an essential aspect of a group's inner coherence which is under consideration here: for the young individual must learn to be most himself where he means most to others—those others, to be sure, who have come to mean most to him. . . . At one time, then, it (identity) will appear to refer to a conscious *sense of individual identity;* at another to an unconscious striving for a *continuity of personal character;* at a third, as a criterion for the silent doings of *ego synthesis;* and finally, as a maintenance of an inner *solidarity* with a group's ideals and identity. (1959, p. 102)

The simplest definition of identity I know is from Diane Said Arbus, the late brilliant photographer: "We've all got an identity. You can't avoid it. It's what's left when you take everything else away" (1972, p. 10).

If one looks at ego as the subject and at self as the object, one sees the ego organizing the developing self or selves, and to some extent, ego identity subsumes self and ideal self. "Identity formation thus can be said to have a self-aspect, and an ego aspect" (Erikson, 1959, p. 149). Certainly self and ego, either as felt or as conscious facets of the person, exist in some way from early childhood. Their development is lifelong, and thus identity formation should be considered lifelong. Whether we consider a teenager trying to incorporate new social experiences in high school into his sense of individual identity or a retiree wrestling with what remains as uniquely *him* after years of feeling solidarity with his work group, the continuous process of identity formation and reformation or refining is evident. As one develops, "it is the ego's function to integrate the psychosexual and psychosocial aspects on a given level of development, and, at the same time, to integrate the relation of newly added identity elements with those already in existence" (1959, p. 115).

Identity, then, incorporates elements that are conscious and unconscious, consistent and changing, general-social and personal-constitutional, and that result from personal internal constructions of reality (effective defenses) as well as social fulfillment through effective coping (successful sublimations). Depending on the manner in which one is studying human behavior, one or more of the elements of identity are considered.

Erikson uses "the term *ego identity* to denote certain comprehensive gains which the individual, at the end of adolescence, must have derived from all of his preadult experience in order to be ready for the tasks of adulthood" (1959, p. 101). At times the adolescent's sense of identity, as internal and external pressures are exerted, becomes conscious, almost to the extreme. Working with himself, to accommodate his felt needs and the demands he perceives (and which may exist) from society, the adolescent may be forced face-to-face with himself. Very consciously, he attempts to piece it together to make some sense, that is consistent and integrated, of who he is. This total sense of integrated, consistent self and/or ego identity is what must be gained by the end of adolescence.

However, most of the time one's sense of identity is not conscious. Rather it is a felt sense of adequacy and continuity. "An increasing sense of identity . . . is experienced preconsciously as a sense of psychosocial well-being" (1959, p. 118). This sense of identity, particularly as a feeling of greater or lesser well-being, is common to everyone at one time or another and is frequent in adolescents. It is hard to describe. Different people feel it in different ways. Many adolescents experience a somatic reaction of real intensity to their sense of well-being in particular situations or in expectation of experiences. Why the somatic reactions appear where they do is difficult to determine. In discussing this point I always tell my classes how, as an adolescent, I felt my qualms of confidence in the pit of my stomach. Although they have suggested some compelling, if not very complimentary, reasons why this prominent portion of my physique should carry such psychological importance, they can also remark on the diverse ways in which they physically felt their growing sense of identity in relation to specific situations.

The adolescent may feel intensely all the setbacks and gains in the process of identity formation. Erikson states, "The end of adolescence thus is the stage of an overt identity crisis" (1959, p. 113). As he explains the tasks of adolescence, he enumerates, in different language than mine, the life tasks that will be expanded on in the latter portions of this book. In the following quote one can see the emphasis on integrating and successfully coping with the life tasks of love and sex, work, friends and community, and the cosmos in successfully dealing with one's self: "The integration now taking place in the form of ego identity is . . . more than the sum of childhood identifications with the vicissitudes of the libido, with the aptitudes developed out of endowment, and with the opportunities offered in social roles. The sense of ego identity, then, is the accrued confidence that the inner sameness and continuity prepared in the past are matched by the sameness and continuity of one's meaning for others" (1959, p. 50).

Is Identity Crisis a Normative Crisis?

Erikson's emphasis on identity crisis and identity formation in adolescence has been extremely influential. The question posed in this section is whether an identity crisis per se is a normative crisis for all adolescents, for some adolescents, or not at all. The question will be attacked from two points of view: (1) in terms of Erikson's data and its generalizability, and (2) by differentiating the social or life tasks separately.

Erikson makes use primarily of three kinds of data in building and supporting his theory—biographic, pathographic, and theoretical. Although he has been associated with empirical study of "ordinary" individuals, much of his clinical experience has been with "mildly disturbed young people" who were Harvard students. He has been keenly interested in famous and unusual people. He says, "The autobiographies of extraordinary (and extraordinarily self-perceptive) individuals are a suggestive source of insight into the development of identity" (1959, p. 110). He himself is an extraordinarily self-perceptive person who worked through, with considerable time and psychic energy, his own identity crisis.

From my own experience, which is not to be compared with Erikson's in depth or time, but may be comparable in breadth and diversity of types of individuals, the identity crisis—in fact, the issue of identity itself—appears minor to many adolescents. This is not to say that the internal dynamic of integrating new abilities and experiences at adolescence does not occur. But rather that this integration is not so difficult as to be disturbing—it falls within the realm of normal day-to-day coping with life's problems. Moreover, the struggle that is the essence of the identity crisis as described by Erikson is cognitive. After all, one's self is cognitive; it is one's own mental construct.

It appears that the identity crisis of adolescence, as described by Erikson, is to a substantial degree a function of the development of formal operations at its higher levels. The identity crisis may thus be a reintegration of the social and physiological development of adolescence. The basic personal constructs about self and the world previously formulated in concrete terms are reinterpreted, that is, restated to oneself in the broader and more abstract schema of formal operational thought. With this view of the identity crisis, it may be that only those persons who reach formal operations to a high degree would find it possible, and maybe necessary, to undergo the reintegration that might cause distress of a crisis nature.

The study by Arlin (1975) cited in the chapter on cognitive development, which posits two parts to the formal operations stage — problem solving and problem finding — may bear on this question. Could it be that the identity crisis in Erikson's sense is a function of problem finding, the second part of formal operations or the stage after formal operations? If that were the case, then only a small, advanced, and older number of adolescents would have identity crises. Does this in turn sound like the differentiation made by Keniston between adolescents and youth dealing with their own identity question? "The adolescent is struggling to define who he is; the youth begins to sense who he is and thus to recognize the possibility of conflict and disparity between his emerging selfhood and his social order" (Keniston, 1975, p. 9). In this sense, adolescents through high school may have a problem-solving struggle with their selves, whereas those who later pass through the period called "youth" find problems with their identities that may cause a crisis.

An identity crisis may be "normative" at Harvard, and among persons such as George Bernard Shaw, Martin Luther, and Saint Augustine, whom Erikson wrote about. But it is not so with the "common" man — with those persons who are not cognitively equipped and/or socially encouraged (note the next section on the psychosocial moratorium) to examine themselves in depth in situations of great personal choice, with great potential for personal flexibility of action.

If this position is defensible, it becomes incumbent on educators, psychologists, and counselors to reexamine their use of the identity-crisis concept. It may be that many adolescents are being pushed into introspection when the nature of their problem or crisis is not as deep or extensive as the theory being applied by the educator or "helping" professional would imply.

This brings us to the second attempt to answer the question about the extensity of the identity crisis. Obviously, adolescents have problems. But many of the problems adolescents face are simply the result of ignorance in coping with their selves in relation to one or more life tasks. With experience, and counseling — more probably from peers and parents than from professionals — they can overcome the problem.

Some adolescents have problems that are neurotic in nature — the way of acting or thinking that they have employed as children is not amenable to functioning as an adolescent and then as an adult. Either they feel very discomforted by the discrepancy between their view of themselves and the world and see the discomfort as the problem, or else they act as they feel they should and find no approval or acceptance from peers, parents, or adults, which bothers them. In either case, the personality, the pattern of behavior and thought, developed to find a place as a child is not suitable for an adolescent or adult. Distress ensues, and professional remediation is called for. This description of neurotic disturbance at adolescence with reference to the life tasks relates well to Erikson's description of the unsuccessful or negative side of the identity stage, identity diffusion. He says, "A state of acute identity diffusion usually becomes manifest at a time when the young individual finds himself exposed to a combination of experiences which demands his simultaneous commitment to *physical intimacy* (not by any means always overtly sexual), to decisive *occupational choice,* to energetic *competition,* and to *psychosocial self-definition*" (1959, p. 123).

Lastly there are those adolescents whose problems grow from, or are magnified by, the confusion they are having with who they are and what to be. Proportionally, the fewest number of adolescents have problems that are strictly neurotic-personal, a greater number have identity problems sometime in adolescence (and which may be when they are in their twenties), and the greatest number of adolescents have difficulties and problems that are the result of limited knowledge and experience as they confront new situations. In this last group, unless they are psychologically unprepared, their personality is in conflict with the demands of the new situations, and they learn to cope and grow as a result. It is these problems that are normative. Most adolescents do not get to an identity crisis.

In the introduction to a section of their book of first-person accounts of aspects of their adolescence by college students, primarily from Harvard, Goethals and Klos presented their view of the prevalence of the identity crisis:

> It is our opinion that college students typically do not have a firm sense of identity and typically have not undergone an identity crisis. College students seem to be in the process of identity-seeking and seem to experience identity crisis toward the end of senior year or during their early postcollege experience. A male or female's disillusionment with first-job experience or

graduate study, or a female's disappointment with being at home with small children is often the jolt that makes them ask what their education was for and why they are not as delighted with their lives as they had been led to believe they would be by parents and friends. . . .

What students often interpret as an identity crisis in college may be more of a crisis of "instrumental competence" or a crisis of "interpersonal competence." A person who is unable to choose his course and then work or who is unable to get along with significant peers may be experiencing a problem of autonomy or of intimacy, in its adolescent sense. (1970, p. 129)

In the sense of this discussion of identity and the identity crisis, Goethals and Klos' comments reinforce the notion of the importance of the life tasks. The crisis comes, or is felt to be a crisis, in college within the context of dealing with the life tasks in a transitory situation. Noncollege youth encounter the tasks earlier and directly from high school, without an extended period removed from home and work. Theodor Reik concluded, "Work and love — these are the basics. Without them there is neurosis." The "identity seeking" in college appears to be a searching for a footing that cannot easily come in a situation where work and love take on the unreal aura they do in American universities.

MARCIA'S MEASUREMENT OF IDENTITY STATUS

Marcia (1966) developed the Identity Status Interview to determine subjects' crises and commitments to an occupational goal and to attitudes and beliefs in the ideological areas of religion and politics. Crises have to do with examination of alternatives with the goal of establishing a firm commitment, while commitment refers to a stable investment in one's beliefs with supporting activity. Marcia's method is limited because it focuses only on occupation and ideology, although it is being extended to other areas, such as dating, friendship, and sex roles (Grotevant, Thorbecke, and Meyer, 1982). Also a global identity status designation may not be appropriate because adolescents are more apt to be at different levels in different areas. Moreover, Marcia developed the interview with college students, and it appears that high school students' responses reflect less considered, more superficial choices and thus may be coded at achievement status when they are actually foreclosing (Raphael and Xerlowski, 1980). Nonetheless, Marcia's technique and notions are thought-provoking and have stimulated a good bit of research.

The identity statuses typically begin with *identity diffusion*, in which the adolescent is not questioning alternatives or trying to make a commitment. In the *identity foreclosure* status the adolescent has not explored alternatives to any degree but has made a commitment, usually at the suggestion or under the influence of others he or she values. Adolescents in the *moratorium status* are questioning and searching for and among alternatives without coming to commitment and usually with a sense of their own uncertainty, which may feel of crisis proportions. Having come through these statuses in some fashion, possibly with fits and starts and reversals, an adolescent who comes to choose his or her alternatives and a stable commitment is said to be in the *identity achievement* status. These statuses may also be seen to relate to concrete decision making and confusions of nonformally operational youth (Figure 8.5).

Young people in the identity achievement status tend to show more formal operational performance and receive better grades in college (Ginsburg and Orlofsky, 1981; Leadbetter and Dione, 1981; Marcia, 1980). Although it cannot be said definitely that formal operations are necessary for identity achievement, the indications that this is so are quite strong and underlie much of this discussion. Remembering that some, especially young, people may be labeled as achievers who are actually foreclosures, the percentages of boys in the moratorium and achievers statuses found by Meilman (1979) are indicative of the age trend that supports the need for formal operations notions. Among 12-year-olds, Meilman found no boys in moratorium or achievement status. No boys were found in moratorium at age 15, though 4 percent were said to be achievers. At age 18, 4 percent were in moratorium and 20 percent achievers, while at 21 and 24 these percentages had risen to 12 percent for moratorium and 40 percent and then 56 percent for achievement. There appear to be lower age boundaries for identity achievement (Archer, 1982), and with age, increasing concern for and ability to develop one's self in ways that are sufficiently global to encompass the breadth of adult roles and beliefs.

PSYCHOSOCIAL MORATORIUM

Erikson postulates adolescence as a second latency period, which he views as a "psychosocial moratorium." The adolescent period has been described in many ways, but "psychosocial moratorium" is particularly descriptive. Rather than seeing adolescence merely as a period between childhood and adulthood, Erikson's term describes society in both a functional and an active manner. Adolescence is a period in which society takes a relatively hands-off posture, allowing the adolescent to experiment behaviorally and attempt to find himself and his place. The hands-off posture refers to the laxness of society in enforcing rules on adolescents that apply to adults, as well as a general

	Identity Status (Formally Operational)	Concrete Decision Making
Foreclosure	Commitment without exploration, usually by suggestion, ascribed status	Same. Possible statements: "Dad said there's money in computers." "We're all Democrats."
Diffusion	No commitments No questioning	Same. Possible statements: "I'll decide when . . . . . . I need a job." . . . I can vote."
Moratorium	Questioning, searching— alternatives, possibilities, various hypotheses	Questioning, searching— known and new options
Achievement	Formation of stable commitments in line with broad sense of identity	Decisions and commitments made in line with sense of self

Figure 8.5. Identity statuses and related confusions and decisions. Adolescents, probably formally operational, may move through certain periods of decision and indecision on the way to achieving identity. Marcia (1966) delineated these identity statuses. Nonformally operational adolescents also need to make decisions and commitments about ideology, occupation, interpersonal relations, etc., and their behavior and decision making could appear similar to that of their peers who are formally developing identity. The decisions of the nonformally operational adolescents would be concretely related to their self-concepts.

attitude that diminishes responsibility of adolescents relative to adults. The functional reason society takes this stance is to give adolescents time to mature and experience so that when it is time for them to enter the adult world, especially the occupational world, they will be ready, emotionally and educationally.

Erikson's multicultural viewpoint is seen in this quote: "Societies offer, as individuals require, more or less sanctioned intermediary periods between childhood and adulthood, institutionalized psychosocial moratoria, during which a lasting pattern of 'inner identity' is scheduled for relative completion" (1959, p. 111). Differences exist between societies and between groups and individuals within societies in the length of the sanctioned intermediary periods, the psychosocial moratorium.

In our society, it is presumed that when a person stops going to school, he or she will take on a full-time career, in or out of the home. There are a great number of points at which individuals stop going to school. Some may stop at some point before finishing high school (which includes persons even today in the United States who never begin high school), and others finish high school, have some college, graduate from college, do some post-graduate study, or complete postgraduate study. The age range of these points is great—from eleven or twelve to the late twenties, at least. Individual differences in ability, interest, and personal circumstance influence how much school a person will complete. However, social-class and ethnic-group memberships carry differences in opportunity for and probability of extent of schooling. As an example, statistics show that less than half of the Mexican-Americans in the Southwest complete high school, whereas over half of the middle- and upper-middle-class Anglos go on to at least some college. The probabilities then show that, on the average, as leaving school indicates the end of the moratorium, one group will have at least three to four more years than the other to come to "relative completion" in development of "a lasting pattern of 'inner identity.' "

IDENTITY AND OTHER CRISES IN ADOLESCENCE

Not everyone has an identity crisis during adolescence, or even during young adulthood. We can only hypothesize about why this is the case. It may be, as has been mentioned, that attainment of formal operations is related to the identity crisis. The identity crisis in this case would be, in a manner of speaking, a crisis of formal operations as applied to oneself.

It may be that dwelling on issues of personal identity is a luxury that comes with an extended psychosocial moratorium. Adolescents who are not pressed into the adult social and occupational world, most probably because they are pursuing courses of higher education, are granted the time, and to some extent are expected, to look closely at themselves and their future.

However, not every adolescent is granted this time or possesses these capabilities. The majority of adolescents come to the end of their schooling with, at most, a high school diploma, and maybe even some college or an additional technical training course of some sort squeezed in after high school. They are pressed into the adult world. They need to find a job. They want to get married and move out of their parents' home. The questions for psychologists, teachers, and counselors are whether these adolescents experience an identity crisis, and whether there is any need for them to do so.

It appears that the identity crisis relates to cognitive development, the psychosocial moratorium, and related personal and social variables (such as IQ, SES, etc.) and does not occur for many adolescents, and need not.

In this chapter, the works of Freud and of Lewin have indicated a number of personal and social difficulties that all adolescents encounter. Overcoming these obstacles and meeting these life tasks are sufficiently difficult that adolescents at all social, intellectual, and maturational levels may feel the crisis of achieving them.

Adolescents may also successfully pass through adolescence, with all of the difficulties mentioned, without crisis. Could it be that many adolescents do cope well with this stage? Could it be that more could? This certainly seems possible.

Might there be an element of delaying the inevitable in this position? That is also possible. Crises in the life tasks may occur throughout life. Does an early crisis preclude a later crisis? Is there an advantage to the early crisis? The theorists presented in this chapter have raised many questions while giving us their perspectives. Some of these questions, as they pertain to the adolescent stage, will be looked at further in the following chapters.

From Adolescence
to Adolescents

CHAPTER 9

BELONGING AND DEVELOPMENT

Adler said:

> For almost every child, adolescence means one thing above all else: he must prove he is no longer a child. . . . Very many of the expressions of adolescence are the outcome of the desire to show independence, equality with adults, and manhood or womanhood. The direction of these expressions will depend on the meaning which the child has attributed to being "grown-up." (Ansbacher and Ansbacher, 1956, p. 439)

When Adler spoke of the "will to power," inferiority and superiority, and social interest, he was speaking, very simply, of the theme that unifies all human life—belonging—to belong, to fit in, to be one with one's fellow humans. The notion of compensation refers to the degree to which the individual feels he has to be better than others to make up for the degree to which he feels he is not up to the level of others, i.e., "Someone with my faults and weaknesses must be stronger or nicer or smarter, etc., than the others in order to belong."

The Adlerian position may be seen as similar in some ways to that of Erikson or Lewin or certainly Rogers, Maslow, and White. The point in all of these is one of fit and belonging. Fitting for yourself to be yourself, and fitting in with others, belonging with others.

If we take this conception of belonging, of knowing one's place and acting therefrom, as the central theme in life, we should start with the conceptions children have as they move from being children to adolescents and then adults. When Adler speaks of the major task of adolescence, the major meaning of adolescence for the individual child, he says that the child must prove that he is no longer a child. Adler is speaking to the problem of learning how to belong to new and larger groups, fitting into new situations, and fitting into new roles.

The conclusion reached earlier about personality consistency and personality development led us to believe that a child as a unique individual comes into adolescence with certain conceptions of himself and the world and of how he must act in that world. He has had a notion of his body, but changes occur in this body as he goes through adolescence. These physical changes he has to cope with. For many children moving into adolescence, the ways in which they think about the world change. They move from concrete to formal operations. The child's ideas about what constitutes right and wrong and the inputs into decisions about what is right and wrong also change in line with the moral development stages of Kohlberg, as do the child's thoughts on being a friend and a member of social groups.

Basically it is these changes that take place within the developing adolescent. These changes are not purely physical and internal, however. As the child grows into adolescence, as she changes and begins to look like an adolescent and more like an adult, more is expected of her, new ways of behaving and new situations are open to her, and she is expected to act at least like an adolescent and maybe like an adult.

We are brought, then, to the problem of the new adolescent's attempting to maintain herself as a unique individual (that is, to hang on to the personality that she has developed as a child—and thereby to know herself) in situations where it is not altogether appropriate still to be a child. At one and the same time we are expecting her still to be herself, to be the Sally or Judy or Meg that she has always been, and we are expecting her to be this old self while trying to fit in, to belong, in these new groups with her new body and her new thoughts.

The general thrust of Erikson's position, which has been so heavily accepted by people who think about and work with adolescents, is that the overriding emphasis in adolescence is on finding oneself, establishing an identity. The thrust of Lewin's position is one of fitting into groups and, in a sense, seeing oneself and believing oneself to be a part of groups— eventually moving from the adolescent marginal-man position to being a full-fledged adult. A combination of personally, individually feeling that one belongs and accurate perceptions that one does in fact belong is a major thrust of adolescent development. And it would be remiss not to add that this is the thrust of development throughout the remainder of the life cycle.

ADOLESCENCE — SOCIETAL MICRO PERSPECTIVE

With this somewhat strange conception of a changing yet consistent person seeking belonging in new age-graded groups, the next issue has to do with influences on the adolescent in the new situations and roles of adolescence. Lyle Larson, speaking about the variety of influences on the adolescent, and particularly the influence of family, has developed a hierarchical structure of social influence, which is shown in Figure 9.1. He says:

> The basic assumptions of this approach to the structure and process of social influences are summarized below.
> 1. Role-learning is a lifelong process occurring throughout the positional career of the individual.
> 2. A hierarchical pattern of influence characterizes all levels of the influence posture (between and within).
> 3. The influence hierarchy is not static but dynamic and position-situation specific.
> 4. The influence hierarchy at any given point and time involves the articulation and theoretical integration of the variant structures, processes, and linkages within the influence posture. (1974, p. 319)

These assumptions and the hierarchical structure in Figure 9.1 are presented to show the complexity of influences on the individual adolescent. Larson refers to the hierarchical levels as filters. Filters 1 to 4 are characterized as the secondary system, while filters 5 to 7 are seen as of primary salience to the individual.

Filters 4 to 7, as more primary before late adolescence, are the influences about which the child had some awareness and which influenced him for better or worse through childhood. His family, neighborhood friendship clique, and teachers (his reference sets, defined as the base of significant others whom the individual takes into account when he acts [Goodman, 1965]) relate to each other. The child fits in and relates to them. They influence the child and present to him, filter to him, the norms, values, and ideologies of his culture, subculture, and time in history.

In order to understand the full scope of influences on the adolescent as he comes to assume new roles, meet new situations and the life tasks in adolescence, this hierarchical structure is useful. At the base of the structure, "Attributes of individual as final filter (age and personality)" is the individual with his own personality — his own approach to belonging. Influencing each individual are the primary groups with their many ways of relating and interrelating. At the secondary normative and behavioral system levels are the influences of social class, race, and education as they filter the dominant culture

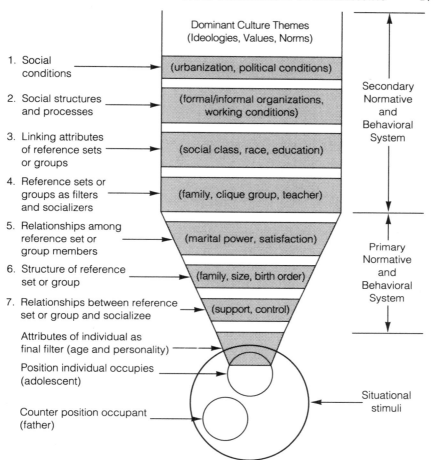

Figure 9.1. The hierarchical structure of social influence (Reprinted by permission from L. E. Larson, "An examination of the salience hierarchy during adolescence: The influence of the family," *Adolescence* 9 [1974], 317–32.)

themes at any and each historical time. There are an incredible number of influences filtered differently at different times by different groups, communities, institutions, families, and *each* individual.

Within this framework, which shows the "big picture," it seems amazing that we know as much about human behavior as we do, still recognizing that we know as little as we do. Clearly, to predict an individual adolescent's successes and failures in the life tasks, his situations and roles, we must know the individual. To predict, discuss, and understand the problems of adolescents, we must deal in probabilities and generalities resulting from empirical research, much of which has classified people according to groupings at the secondary levels.

Therefore, in the remainder of the text we will discuss adolescents, individuals, who are changing in specific ways in line with the developmental criteria, within certain influence groupings at the primary and secondary levels.

ADOLESCENCE—CULTURAL MACRO PERSPECTIVE

Figure 9.2 sets forth a number of proposed relationships implying probabilities for cognitive development, and associated development and difficulty in adolescence, for persons growing up in differing societal and subcultural settings.

Most of the hypothesized relationships that follow have been suggested in previous chapters. The data cited in these chapters have led to these hypotheses. In time, as they are tested, their validity will be proven or disproven. However, at this point in time, in this author's opinion, there is justification for presenting the hypotheses because they can assist in understanding adolescents in general and individually. Nonetheless, as a cautionary note, the following "tentative conclusions" by Neimark are presented:

1. There is a stage of thinking beyond and different from concrete operations.
2. That stage is not universally attained by all individuals and may not be stable within an individual over time.
3. Differences among cultures in proportion of the society's members attaining the level of formal operations undoubtedly exist. . . .
4. Within-culture differences undoubtedly exist, also. . . .
5. Among individual-difference variables, general level of intelligence appears to be an important factor. It is probable that a minimal level of intelligence, in terms of mental age, is a prerequisite for the attainment of formal operational thought. (1975, pp. 585–86)

Before explaining the meaning of the relationships implied in Figure 9.2, an important caution must be restated. All the relationships hypothesized from this figure, as well as most relationships and research findings presented in this book, are based on probabilities determined from group data. Probabilities are a means for understanding group phenomena, for understanding the differences between, and the similarities within, age, class, and national groups. But the reader must be cautioned, and we all must continuously remind ourselves, that in human psychology there are no perfect

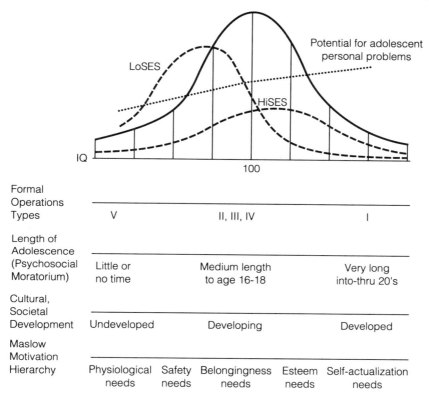

Formal Operations Types	V	II, III, IV			I

Length of Adolescence (Psychosocial Moratorium)	Little or no time	Medium length to age 16-18		Very long into-thru 20's

Cultural, Societal Development	Undeveloped	Developing	Developed

Maslow Motivation Hierarchy	Physiological needs	Safety needs	Belongingness needs	Esteem needs	Self-actualization needs

Figure 9.2. Relationships in a macroscopic perspective

correlations, no 100 percent probabilities. The exceptions to the high proba-bilities, the generally low levels of probabilities and correlations in most studies, should remind us that one never knows an individual from the prob-abilities revealed in group data. If you find an adolescent to be as — or to put it in the vernacular, where — the theory predicts, you may presume that some of the probabilities have applied. But the probabilities, the predictor varia-bles, did not cause the person to be as he is. The predictor variables tell us about types of persons. No matter how many predictor variables we may ap-ply, no matter now high the probabilities, we may only know and under-stand an individual in all of his or her uniqueness from knowing him or her.

Now back to Figure 9.2. Measured intelligence by definition constitutes a normal curve in the population from which it was derived. The lower- and upper-SES groups together form the total population, but the lower-SES groups predominate at the middle to lower portions of the normal curve of

IQ while the upper-SES groups predominate from the middle to upper portions of this curve. The five cognitive developmental types in adolescence (see chapter 3) relate to measured intelligence, although at this time the exact nature of the relationship is unknown. Suffice it to say that, in general, the higher an individual's IQ, eventually the more developed will be his formal operations, and thus presumably formal operations will be used in more aspects of the individual's thought and life. Conversely, low-IQ persons will not develop formal operations to any extent. The line labeled "Potential for adolescent personal problems" refers to the confusions, the affect, and the behaviors associated with the development of formal operations adolescents who will find their new potentialities upsetting in many facets of their lives. This means also that the upsets related to development of formal operations, such as an identity crisis, should be more prevalent among high-SES adolescents than low-SES adolescents.

The duration of adolescence, although so often assumed to be very long in this country, varies greatly among individuals. We can equate, simply, the end of schooling and the undertaking of job and family responsibilities with the end of adolescence, the end of the psychosocial moratorium. A shorter adolescence is anticipated for persons of low IQ, low SES, and little formal operations. They will be less likely to experience the personal upsets related to attaining formal operations, but they will be more likely to have social difficulties resulting from lower ability and poorer coping skills. They may be school dropouts, be un- or underemployed, have delinquency problems, and thus have a shorter moratorium period.

At the other end of the length of the adolescence scale are most probably persons of high intelligence, and more probably of higher social status, who have had the indulgence of the society through a long psychosocial moratorium. They have been given the time and access to the educational and cultural facilities of the society in order to develop themselves in many ways. They have had the time, the inputs from their surroundings, and the cognitive ability to see and meet the personal-emotional challenges of prolonged adolescence. In a sense, the long adolescence, the long period of time of the psychosocial moratorium, allows persons at this end of the scale to meet, anguish over, and then presumably conquer these challenges. Put another way, the long psychosocial moratorium serves to facilitate meeting these personal challenges whether the person wants to or not.

A central thesis throughout this discussion has been that there exists great variety in the significance of, and necessity for, personal upset in adolescence. It is proposed here that theorists and researchers considering adolescence, and educators and counselors dealing with adolescents, respect these variations and not demand of all adolescents the upsets, thoughts, and feelings associated with high IQ, developed formal operations, and a long psychosocial moratorium. It is as if the unity of the theory about adolescents has the effect of many adolescents' being forced through counseling, institutional structure, curriculum geared to presumed problems and an identity crisis, and the attitudes and understandings parents and teachers carry into a mold or set that is not appropriate for them.

The scales labeled "Cultural, Societal Development" and "Maslow Motivation Hierarchy" are included to place these relationships in a broader perspective and thereby to shed more light on these relationships within the American culture. The scale of cultural development ranges from the least developed nations and "primitive" cultures to the most developed, modern nations. The Maslow Hierarchy scale runs parallel to the societal-development scale.

Primitive cultures and very underdeveloped countries are primarily involved in satisfying the basic deficiency needs, the society providing sustenance and safety for its members and citizens, and individuals doing so for themselves. As countries develop, more persons within the country are satisfied in their basic deficiency needs and are able to confront the issues of belonging and love, and then move to the growth needs. In the most developed countries, the great majority of normal, adjusted adolescents and adults are thought to be satisfied in their deficiency needs and to be dealing with their growth needs. The emphasis on esteem needs and, particularly, self-actualization needs is feasible to more persons in developed than in succeedingly less developed cultures. As Nehru said, "Poetry and culture have little place in a poor man's hut; they are not meant for empty stomachs. It is an insult to talk of culture to people who have nothing to eat." The differences in the level of the hierarchy at which the majority of persons, of large groups of persons, are involved in the various societies relate also to the development of a middle and upper-middle class in the society—the more developed the society, the greater the middle class.

It is important to note that even in the most developed countries, such as the United States, there is great variability in the need levels among the populations. "In our society [physiological] needs are seldom dominant, at least in the greatest segment of the population. That is to say, they are chronically gratified; few people fear starvation" (Cofer and Appley, 1964, p. 676). But many people are concerned about where their next meal is coming from and fear for their personal safety. These persons, most at the lowest socioeconomic levels of our society, are surely far less involved in personal issues of esteem and self-actualization.

Persons at the lowest socioeconomic levels of our society, in some ways like persons in underdeveloped societies, are shown to have probable deficits in three of the four influences on cognitive development: maturation of the nervous system, active experience, and environmental effects. The fourth influence, equilibration, is a dynamic that functions in all persons, though on different contents and cognitive structures.

The maturation of the nervous system and, as we have seen, related physiological maturation influence and correlate with cognitive development. There is strong, but hotly debated, evidence that genetic influences account for much of the difference in intelligence scores between social classes. In addition, however, there are presumably nutritional and other bases, which may be subsumed under the physiological and safety needs, that influence cognitive development. Persons at the lowest socioeconomic levels of developed, as well as less developed, countries are more likely to have deficiencies in the physiological and safety needs and therefore are more likely to be deficient or slow in the maturation of the nervous system.

Active experience with a variety of stimuli is the second influence on cognitive development. One of the primary reasons for the Head Start Program has been the wealth of material showing that low-SES children do not get this active involvement, particularly with some structure. This was evident in the many children who entered inner-city schools who were not able to count or discriminate among colors. Children in the lowest strata of undeveloped countries have active experience within a very limited range, with limited structure, and are also therefore deficient in experience by comparison.

Lastly, the lower strata in countries at any stage of development have more limited contact with the cultural and educational opportunities of the country, the variety of environments, and the breadth of language styles and nuances.

The three influences on cognitive development are less satisfied or available to persons at the lower socioeconomic levels of undeveloped and developed countries. This position, in general, is accepted as it applies to children. This discussion implies that the influences continue through adolescence and have a proportionally greater effect as they limit both potential for future activities and opportunity in wider environmental spheres.

Let us construct a hypothetical, but typical, lower-SES youth with measured intelligence in the normal range but below average. In early adolescence, say at age 15, he has attained at best, little if any, formal operations, in limited areas of his experience. His high school achievement is barely adequate and he is encountering greater academic difficulty as his courses introduce more abstract concepts, which seem vague and irrelevant to him. Some kids he knows are leaving school, some are trying to finish high school, a few are hoping to attend college. He would like to have more money to take out his girlfriend and would love to have a car. His father has had a variety of laboring and semiskilled jobs, and the son aspires to some kind of skilled job.

He has limited ability and has, fairly realistically but without much informational base, limited his occupational aspirations. He may have other cultural or artistic interests; he may have other dreams. But probably not. He has not been exposed to these areas; the concrete possibility has not presented itself. And he does not have the cognitive ability to explore possibilities for himself that do not have tangible referents in his reality.

The genetic-maturational, experiential, and environmental influences served to limit his cognitive development. His cognitive-developmental level and his intelligence limit both his potential and his aspirations. As he fulfills his potential and aspirations, his experiences and environment will probably not expand to any great degree beyond what he has known. Therefore there will not be experiences or environmental influences to foment further cognitive development, there will be little "external disturbance" to upset his cognitive equilibrium.

This hypothetical case may look like the proverbial dead end for persons without ability and status. In some sense it is true, and change agents are being sought, although the person described does not necessarily feel unhappy with his life and situation. However, this section attempts to place these relationships in a macroscopic perspective.

There is an adaptive value to differential cognitive development across social classes and, similarly, across countries varying in development. No society, to this time, has been able to develop or accommodate all its members at the highest cognitive-developmental level. Quite simply, the cognitive abilities of formal operations are necessary for certain levels of occupations, such as those in higher management and government, academia, and the professions. Formal operations are not required to any degree for the majority of workers at lower bureaucratic jobs and semiskilled and laboring jobs.

As societies develop, as the need for a middle and upper-middle class grows, the society needs more persons at higher cognitive levels. As the society develops, nutrition and education improve and facilitate cognitive development among at least certain portions of the populace.

On the individual level, there is a question of whether persons with higher cognitive abilities and more education are satisfied with occupations and life-styles that do not involve these abilities. That is to say, within a population, those persons who are "overeducated" for the job they hold, with growth needs probably unfulfilled, would presumably be dissatisfied with their life situation. It is therefore more functional, both for the personal satisfaction of individuals and the satisfaction of the ability needs of the society, that the cognitive ability "pool" within a society relates in size directly to the needs of the society at its stage of development.

Thus, taking a macroscopic view, the adaptive value of differential cognitive abilities within a society is understandable. However, this is in no way presented to deprecate the possibility of a society of the future in which deficiency needs are met and a happy and satisfied populace functions at its highest potential.

DURING ADOLESCENCE BEING ADOLESCENT

In 1872, Herbert Spencer wrote in his *Principles of Biology*, "Life is the continuous adjustment of internal relations to external relations." Cognitive development, moral development, sex-role development, personality development, and physical development are all internal changes. If the adolescent lived in a world that was otherwise unchanging, these internal, personal changes would demand adjustments. If the adolescent's view of himself, the world, his body, and right and wrong changed and nothing else around him changed — he went to the same school, played the same games with the same friends, was expected to function interpersonally and heterosexually as he had as a child, etc. — he would have difficulty adjusting to the internal changes. If the adolescent's internal relations did not change — there was no developmental change with adolescence — but he was asked to change schools and friends, to begin to decide on a vocation, to develop heterosexual attachments, to think of the meaning of life, and to begin a transition to adulthood, he would have difficulty adjusting to the external changes.

There is a logic to much of the external change in adolescence to conform with the internal change. Dating and expectations of more intimate heterosexual relations accompany physical changes and heterosexual interests. Adult-like strength and abilities occur as they are needed for work. Many laws allowing assumption of civic responsibility are timed to coincide with assumption of other responsibilities. Recognizing that society, too, is changing, it just may be doing so to become compatible with generalized changes among adolescents. At any one time, aspects of external demands may be out of step with internal changes occurring in large numbers of adolescents. But in the main it may be assumed that the changes society expects from adolescents during their adolescence are functional, assist them on the road to adulthood, and smooth the path.

This kind of analysis may satisfy the academician, but it does not make adolescence satisfying for the individual adolescent. He must cope with both internal and external changes and still be himself, cope as he knows how for him. The remainder of this book explains how adolescents in general adjust their new internal relations to their new external situations. Generalization follows generalization. That is the best we can do, both because that is as far as the science has moved and because *each* adolescent does it his own way. "No two human beings have made, or ever will make, exactly the same journey in life" (Sir Arthur Keith).

CHAPTER 10
Love and Sex

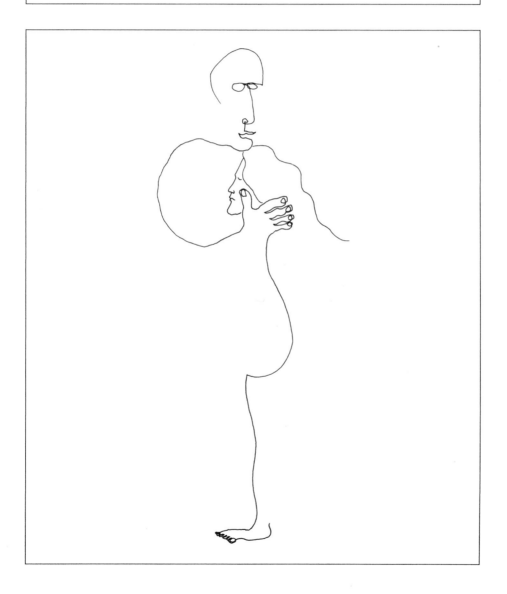

CHAPTER 10

Beyond its biological function, sex *can* be a pleasure. Beyond biology and pleasure are psychological meanings and goals. Sex may serve many different personal psychological functions. Culturally and socially, sex may serve various functions and is limited and sanctioned in many ways. If a person is confident, content, and knowledgeable about himself, and has made an informed peace with the expectations and demands of his society, sex is easy, natural, and a pleasure. Unfortunately, many adolescents have serious doubts about themselves and are ignorant of the physical and social facts and attitudes about sex. For them, the whole question of sex is anything but easy, natural, or pleasurable.

Love is a word that describes a crucial and necessary quality of relationship. Love may be natural and pleasurable, although maintaining a love relationship is seldom easy. Love, like sex, may have a variety of meanings and functions psychologically and socially.

Sex and love have a place in the lives of children, which is quite separate and, in a sense, removed from the child's control. The child is severely, and probably properly, limited in her contacts with others to first her family and neighbors. Should love and warmth not be forthcoming from her parents and family, she does without and holds dearly to whatever little passes for love and interest in her. Sex in childhood is merely the noting of physical differences, the learning of some physical sensitivities, and beginning explorations that raise issues and questions of morals and standards.

With adolescence, the young boy or girl is faced with new demands, new situations, in which the task of love and sex must be faced. A few points need to be made. First, life for anyone is fuller, brighter, and means more when one has a "loved" one or ones. The capacity or ability to love serves also to fill and broaden the potential for enjoying one's life. A person who is unable to love — for whatever psychological or social reason — is deficient, and is missing out. In the parlance of youth, love most commonly refers to romantic love. In its fullest meanings, love refers to the selfless and complete relating of one person to another and must therefore include love of parent for child, and vice versa, love between friends, and may include love of God and country. However, as we are speaking of youth and the life task love and sex, heterosexual love and sex will be our primary topic. The development of the capacity to love and to enjoy sex is the global task.

The old song said, "Love and marriage go together like a horse and carriage." In this day of the horseless carriage, love and marriage may constitute the romantic ideal but are not by any means the universal situation. Love and sex may go together, too, but not necessarily. It is said that this life task in adolescence involves the development of the ability to integrate love and sex. Ideally and traditionally, this may be true. However, it would appear, as we examine the evolving attitudes and behaviors in this task, that three related capacities may be developed: the capacity to love, the capacity to function and enjoy oneself sexually, and the integrating aspect, the capacity to love someone with whom one enjoys sex. It seems that this separation allows for both the traditional and the new forms of love and sex relationships accepted by adolescents of differing social-class levels, subcultures, and sexes.

The developmental tasks associated with each life task overlap and interrelate, as do the life tasks themselves. Many of the developmental tasks may be associated with the life task love and sex, particularly because an adolescent's sense of self, ethics, friends, and community all impinge on his ability, knowledge, and freedom in love and sex. However, the three primary developmental tasks relating to love and sex are achieving newer and more mature relations with age-mates of both sexes, preparing for marriage and family life, and achieving emotional independence of parents and other adults.

It may be, if the reader is disenchanted with the institution of marriage and is doubtful about its future, that preparation for marriage and family life appears to be a false goal, or an unnecessary task. As Havighurst says, "Marriage is not becoming less important. . . . It is being readjusted, as an institution, to the changing economic and social and religious characteristics of the society" (1972, pp. 60–61). It is hard to imagine that the institution will change to the degree that maintenance of a long-term and secure heterosexual relationship and at least some responsibility for rearing children will not be a basic part of marriage.

It may also seem curious that achieving emotional independence of parents and other adults is presented as being essential in the love and sex task.

Certainly it is important in the establishment and maintenance of friendships also. Without emotional independence, an adolescent or an adult cannot establish an active love relationship or a sexual relationship, or both, that is his or her own. When an adolescent who is emotionally dependent on one or both parents attempts to form a love relationship, he feels severe limitations because his source of support and fulfillment is not his partner but his parent. He may view his partner through his parent's eyes and evaluate his payoff from the relationship as much or more in terms of his perception of his parent's reaction, positive or negative, as in terms of what he feels and experiences in the relationship. His behavior is reactive—a reaction to real or expected behavior from his parents—and the love relationship cannot be what it could be.

On the other hand, the adolescent who develops a sense of emotional independence from parents and other adults but who does not develop a close heterosexual relationship with an age-mate feels very much that he has missed out and is at loose ends. Emotional independence from parents fosters the need for the interdependence of a love relationship.

This, then, is the task. What is the situation?

THE SITUATION

Sex, like all human sexual behavior, becomes patterned. Individuals as members of groups of various sizes need to know what is expected of them culturally, how others will act, and how they should act. The expectations in an area of behavior, such as love and sex, are determined by many factors, historical and cultural, immediate and social, personal, psychological, and biological. These factors interact with and influence each other.

The pattern of approved, usual, or normal sexual behavior in adolescence in America at this time, or at any time, will be static or changing in conjunction with changes in the influencing factors. At this time the ages of biological development at adolescence have been changing, as we have seen. This is surely not the sole cause of the current changes in behavior in this area, but may well have been influential. So, too, the great social changes, the loosening of tradition, may be influencing changing attitudes and behaviors in the love and sex area. With these great changes, the adolescent finds himself in immediate social situations that would not have occurred before, or at so young an age. His adaption to these new situations as part of his total life situation, in view of all the pressures he feels, becomes the current norm.

Much of what is called here "the situation" is substantially obvious to anyone who has lived through it himself. As this part of the book is written primarily about adolescents in the United States, the overall situation should be familiar to most American readers. The situation should also be highly similar to that in many developed Western nations, and to that among the middle and upper classes of many developing nations (albeit with specific cultural differences, such as, say, chaperoning in Latin cultures).

As a child comes through puberty and shows development in secondary sexual characteristics, and as this occurs among the child's peers, the child is expected to show heterosexual interest. These expectations may be more or less obvious to the child as they are conveyed by his peers, older siblings, and parents, as well as by the institutions in which he participates. As examples, the child who has been used to choosing one or two activities from a list made up for children of his age by his local YMCA, church, or park district will find that included in the "age 12 list" may be social dancing, boy-girl parties, or even a sex-education class. Birthday parties he attends may be boy-girl parties, and the party games may be, for him, shockingly heterosexual. Parents may suggest that an age-mate of the opposite sex be invited to accompany the family on an outing. From a much earlier age the child may have been teased about "loving" or being "loved" by an opposite-sex age-mate. But now it has more meaning and may be less a tease than a compliment or threat.

The child does not just succumb to social pressure and express heterosexual interest. The individual child's rate of physical development relates slightly to his interest in sex and sexual feelings. However, social pressure from age-mates and opportunities for expression of heterosexual interest socially seen as typical for an age are more important facilitators of dating and other heterosexual activities (Dornbusch et al., 1981).

There are probably as many variations and themes in sexual patterns of behavior around the world as there are cultures and subcultures. What is considered natural in one culture for people of a certain age is considered unnatural in another.

The one essential, incontrovertible fact is that in one way or another, at one age or another, sex, meaning sexual intercourse, regardless of what comes before or after, is practiced in all viable societies! We may want to go a step further and state that with the onset of puberty, it is acknowledged in all cultures, maybe through encouragement or maybe through discouragement, that the ability to have sexual intercourse and interest in relationships with the opposite sex develop and exist at this time. This book is intended to pertain primarily to American adolescents. Therefore, the behavior patterns relating to sex and love that exist in the various subcultures and regions of this country (and to some degree in other developed nations) will be explored herein.

THE DATING SYSTEM

For one adolescent, love, sex, and the social structure, the system called dating, which allegedly supports these behaviors, may fit together comfortably and efficiently. For another adolescent, these behaviors may not mix well at all, to the extreme situation in which they may be almost mutually exclusive. That is, in the extreme case, an adolescent may be dating for purely social, fun reasons; have sex in an illicit and separate portion of his life; and love, if he loves at all, an unattainable person at a distance. Certainly this extreme is not a comfortable, or ideal, way of dealing with the life task. In the main, however, there is a merging of love and sex within a loosely established system. Due to the obvious overlap, it is difficult to speak of the areas of love, sex, and the system for facilitating heterosexual interaction, the dating system, exclusively. It is more difficult to speak of them at the same time, which is why the remainder of this chapter will be broken down into separate sections on dating, sex, and love. But we cannot forget that the adolescent is living these all at the same time. He must, says Offer, "plow his own way through the maze of adult double standards" (1966/67, p. 311) and wrestle with the direct and indirect influences from friends and family. As he balances these influences with his feelings, his experiences provide the testing ground for matching feelings and fantasies with the external world.

Dating is a system whereby adolescents may enjoy themselves in heterosexual relationships while learning about their strengths, weaknesses, and coping strategies in social situations and their preferences for qualities in a mate. By saying that dating is a system, we do not assume that this means only the formal aspects of the system. Dating is an evolution from previous courtship practices that were very formal, with clearly proscribed manners. The formal element in current dating practice still includes the boy's calling the girl and asking her if she will accompany him, at a specific time, to a designated event, movie, party, meal, what have you. The girl accepts or rejects the offer and, if she accepts, a date has been made and they go on said date. But this is only the formal portion of the whole arena that allows boys and girls to be together, and the directionality is more fluid than in even the near past, i.e., girls are more likely to be the initiators, to phone the boys, than would have been the case as recently as 20 years ago.

This capsule statement of the dating system seems simple and sweet, with obvious differences in the sex roles within the system. There probably are places in the United States where this simple-sweet system operates in the idealistic, encapsulated form just presented. But by and large this system is much more complex, not as sweet, and predicated on assumptions of sex differences and sex-role differences that may be seen either as changing or as having changed, all in the context of the adolescent's peer group norms and expectations.

The female adolescent, it would appear, is more likely to be socialized into a flexible role with a clearly identifiable model and a clearer set of standards for her behavior that is approved by her peers. The male role, on the other hand, although highly rewarded, is fairly specific and includes a greater number of potential models and more leeway for deviation from parental standards. Thus, for the male, although the potential for conflict with parents exists through deviation from their standards, and the potential for conflict exists with peers through deviation from peer standards, there also exists great potential for conflict with and punishment from the culture as a whole for deviation from the specific male role. For these reasons, one would assume, as has repeatedly been found, that males experience a great deal of anxiety in the area of sexual behavior.

In our culture today, with the continued assumption of changing sex roles propounded throughout the media, adolescent boys and girls must have a less precise view of how to proceed as males and females than did their adolescent predecessors. This is not to say that it will be more difficult to proceed through adolescence and life, but merely that less clearly defined sex-role standards are of less assistance to the adolescent. Moreover, the dating system cannot function as clearly, formally, simply, or sweetly as in the past.

According to Staton, there are developmental stages of heterosexual maturation into which the dating system fits. These are: "(1) sexually undifferentiated behavior, (2) sexual segregation, (3) heterosexual group activities and associations, (4) tentative pairings-off within the group, (5) double dating, (6) dating numerous people for various types of activities, (7) going steady and becoming engaged, and (8) marriage" (1963, p. 397).

Hurlock (1967) presents a kind of stage theory to explain the transition from sex aversion in childhood to a merging of sex and love, as in marriage. The first stage in this progression, according to Hurlock, is the crush—a strong emotional attachment usually directed toward an older individual of the same or opposite sex. The crush is the beginning of the movement of affection outside the home and thus the beginning of independence. Crushes also function as a step in the development of a permanent identity through the process of choosing a person one would like, a person one would like to be like. Girls tend to form crushes earlier, in keeping with their earlier maturation and earlier development of heterosexual interests, and to maintain them until boys of their own age group are ready for heterosexual relationships or until they develop relationships with older boys who are already interested.

According to Hurlock, the first heterosexual relationships with age-mates are of the type often referred to as puppy love. These awkward, playful, sexually tinged, aggressive, short, but intense affairs provide the adolescent with the opportunity to appraise members of the opposite sex, to begin to learn self-confidence in heterosexual relations, and to discern the patterns of heterosexual behavior that are positively sanctioned in her peer group.

The next stage is dating. This evolves through the stages mentioned by Staton, from heterosexual group activities through pairing off in a sort of informal dating structure, then double dating and dating numbers of people, and then the more intense relationship of going steady, which is Hurlock's following stage. Hurlock lists twelve functions that dating serves. These can be summarized by saying that dating allows the adolescent to learn about himself in relation to a member of the opposite sex, to clarify sex roles, to experience different situations, to experiment socially and sexually, to unromanticize some of his ideas about sex and love, and to have a good time socially.

An elaborated framework for analyzing dating was delineated by Skipper and Nass (1966). In their analytic framework, they saw four functions of dating placed on a continuum from most instrumental to most expressive: (1) a form of recreation, (2) a form of socialization, (3) a means of establishing status and achievement, and (4) a form of courtship. They saw the functions of dating on this continuum as expressive of the primary motivation of the individual involved in the process of dating.

Moreover, Skipper and Nass developed the notion that there is a relationship between the place on a continuum from instrumental to expressive in the primary motivation for dating and the degree of involvement in dating and relationships themselves. This notion relates well to the conception of sex-role differences that has been developed. Males would be seen as more likely functioning in dating situations at the more instrumental side of the continuum, recreation and socialization, whereas females would be seen as functioning at the other, more expressive extreme, seeing dating as a form of courtship. Also, then, males would be less likely to be emotionally involved in the dating system, whereas females would be more involved.

By placing dating into a more global category of "the premarital dyad," which includes dating, courtship, and mate selection, the importance and overall function of dating is more readily understandable. In sum:

(1) The dating period covers approximately 6 to 8 years and generally begins between ages 14–16 for both sexes; (2) transition from single-sex associations to the courtship continuum has probably become less abrupt and traumatic as heterosexual relationships have begun developing earlier in life; (3) though the transitions may be easier, anxiety is still prevalent for many youths and is not limited to initial dating experiences; (4) conflict between adults and youth concerning dating and courtship probably peak somewhere along the continuum and then decline as adult norms seem to be more influential at the beginning and ending of the experience; (5) age appears to be the most influential factor in dating frequency, but the consequences of variation in age at initial dating and going steady seem unclear; (6) it appears that there are at least two kinds of going steady experiences (steady and steady dating) with differing antecedents and consequences . . . ; (7) the effects of varied dating patterns are unclear and await the evidence from more comprehensive and longitudinal studies. Though some support for the educational value of dating appeared, so did evidence associating early age of dating and accelerated heterosexual activity with early age of marriage and possibly greater marital stability. (Moss, Apolonio, and Jensen, 1971, p. 1)

This listing, interestingly enough, includes some reference to conflict and anxiety as well as a framework for forecasting some lessening of conflict and anxiety. "Having a steady" and "going steady" imply an intensity to the relationship and a commitment to continue for some period of time in the "steady" situation, while implying also a greater future orientation in the going-steady situation. A growing acceptance of the steady relationship as well as the earlier commencement of heterosexual relationships and activities would seem to point to a greater acceptance of a natural meaning to the dating system. The conflicts and anxieties that dating arouses in the adolescent can easily be seen from the perspective of (1) the individual's fighting for greater independence from his parental home, yet concurrently being concerned with giving up some of that independence in a relationship, and (2) the adolescent's approaching the whole area of sexual relations, which, despite the frequent and constant demand for and offering of more and more sex education, seems to perpetuate itself as an area that holds the aura of the unknown, no matter how much is known.

Husbands suggests that the American dating system is dysfunctional. The frequent turnover of partners and the superficial nature of the relationships result in always trying to make good impressions, lessen the ability to learn about personalities, increase the tendency to be dissatisfied with partners, and reduce "opportunity to experience the open expression of sexual antagonisms" (1970, p. 460).

If Husbands is referring to the dating system or the "dating" stage separately from the later stages of going steady and engagement, or without regard to the dating system as part of a total premarital dyad that includes courtship and mate selection, he is probably fairly correct. It would appear that in dating, prior to the commitment implicit in going steady or engagement, a greater degree of dallying, fun for its own sake, and education in the broadest social skills is occurring. More frequent dating, more experience in dating, leads to more confidence and satisfaction in dating and with dates (Herold, 1973, 1979). Much of early going steady includes a tendency to break off the relationship if things are not going just the way one wants them to and before one openly expresses oneself. However, it may be, as we look at the section on sexual relationships, that more future-oriented, more open and intense relationships are developing among adolescents today and that these orientations are active within dating.

SEX

Any young adult or adult in this country who can look back 10, 20, or 30 years can see the tremendous increase in the visibility of explicit sex as a topic for discussion and as entertainment in all the media and probably in day-to-day life as well. In this section, we will look at the changes in attitudes of adolescents toward sex, assuming that all will agree that the changes in attitudes are dramatic. However, prominent researchers in the field of sexual behavior, such as Packard (1970) and Simon and Gagnon (1970), seriously question whether there has been change in actual behavior in the sexual area in recent decades. A noted authority, Reiss, stated: "There is a widespread belief that much has changed in terms of premarital sex behavior in the last twenty to twenty-five years. However, the evidence from all the available major studies is in strong agreement that although attitudes have changed considerably during this period, that many areas of sexual behavior, such as premarital coital rates, have not" (1966, pp. 125–26).

There is then some difference of opinion about whether behavior change in premarital sex has occurred in the same way as attitude change. Some observers maintain that the openness and freer attitudinal and verbal expression by today's teenagers is not matched in their sexual behavior — which is essentially the same as that of their parents at the same age. Others feel that significant changes have occurred in sexual behavior as well as attitudes.

In 1964 Ehrmann, reviewing marital and nonmarital sexual-behavior research from the beginning of this century, took the position that a sexual revolution had occurred over these years in which both men and women, and particularly women, were participating much more in premarital coitus. Much of the dramatic change in frequency of premarital coitus seems to have occurred between the generations that would be today's adolescents' parents and grandparents or between the generations of today's adolescents' grandparents and great-grandparents. However, to determine the current situation regarding sexual behavior of adolescents, and the degree to which the change is felt as change, research over the last 20 years is probably most pertinent.

Research into premarital and adolescent sexual attitudes and behaviors since World War II includes a few studies at the high school level and many more at the college level. Many difficulties arise in attempting to gain permission from schools and parents to quiz high school–age people about their sexual behavior. For our purposes here, to understand the love and sex life task for adolescents through high school, the paucity of research in this life task area on this age group demands that we infer to some degree from studies of older adolescents both in college and not in college. In order to make these initial inferences, an analysis of the breakdown of high school–age youth into subgroups may be of assistance.

Thornburg (1974) divides adolescents into three distinct peer groups: high school youth, noncollege youth, and college youth. In fact, in order to understand adolescents through high school, it is more accurate and more valuable to think of this age group in terms of three subgroups: (1) those who are not in school—a dropout group (with whom we are not dealing specifically here), (2) those who are in high school but will not go on to college, and (3) those who are in high school and who will go on to college. Nationwide, approximately 50 percent of high school graduates go on to college. Therefore, data representing college youth and noncollege youth, at post–high school age, should represent the attitudes and behaviors of these two groups at the earlier developmental stage. In inferring back to high school–age youth overall, therefore, where socioeconomic differences or educational-plan differences are not noted, we would expect the attitudes and behaviors for high school–age youth to fall somewhere between those attitudes and behaviors noted for the college and noncollege youth. This conclusion must be tempered by the obvious fact that the attitudes and behaviors of younger adolescents as a group appear to be more conservative and less permissive than those of older adolescents as a group.

In comparing college and noncollege youth, Thornburg summarized the findings of a 1969 CBS News survey titled "Generations Apart":

> It could be said, as compared to college youth, that noncollege youths are (1) more conservative, (2) more prone to traditional values, (3) more religious, (4) more respectful, (5) more work-oriented, (6) more money-

oriented, (7) more patriotic, (8) more concerned about moral living, (9) more conforming, (10) more accepting of the draft and war, (11) less activism-oriented, (12) less sympathetic with activists, (13) less drug-prone, and (14) less sexually permissive. (1974, p. 336)

Although Thornburg concludes that noncollege youth are less sexually permissive than college youth, Kinsey's 1948 data showed that lower-class males, who were far more likely to be noncollege, had a much higher incidence of premarital intercourse than did college males. Of the dropout group—males not going beyond grade school—50 percent had experienced intercourse by age 15 and three-quarters had experienced intercourse during adolescence, whereas only 10 percent of college-educated youth had experienced intercourse by age 15 and not even half had experienced intercourse throughout their adolescent years.

However, Reiss (1967) feels that a sampling bias in Kinsey's data might have accounted for much of the difference between socioeconomic and education-level groups, in that many of the lower-class interviews in Kinsey's sample were with prisoners, and Kinsey's upper-class sample was predominantly conservative. Reiss found no relationship between sexual permissiveness and socioeconomic status. Conger (1973) concludes that, although, historically, working-class youth had the highest incidence of premarital intercourse at any given age, over the two previous decades tremendous increases in intercourse among college-educated youth, and most particularly among the college-educated girls at the liberal elite coastal colleges, had lessened if not erased the social-class differences. The difference between male and female incidence rates is smallest at these "prestige" institutions, but there, as everywhere, the male incidence rate is still higher than the female rate. However, the male-female difference was lessening dramatically.

The following is important for inferring from college-age studies to high school students' attitudes and behaviors: "The higher incidence of premarital intercourse among today's youth, in comparison to those of their parents' generation, is accounted for largely by the age at which it occurs (as well as by its greater openness). After all, the incidence among college girls currently is no higher than it eventually was for their mothers, but among the latter it began at a later age, and usually only with their future spouses (estimate of the mean age of first coitus among contemporary American college students range from 19–22 for females, and 18–20 for males." (Conger, 1973, pp. 262–63).

Cannon and Long, reviewing a greater number of studies of premarital sexual behavior in the 1960s, concluded that "apparently there is not a single major study that has been made in the late 60's that has found premarital coital rates that were the level of those found in the late 50's and early 60's" (1971, p. 40). Using comparable samples of college females for the years 1958 and 1968, Bell and Chaskes (1970) reported that, in a dating relationship, 10 percent of the girls in 1958 and 23 percent of the girls in 1968 had premarital coitus. The proportion of girls having premarital coitus while going steady moved from 15 percent in 1958 to 23 percent in 1968, and, while engaged, from 31 percent in 1958 to 39 percent in 1968. Bell and Chaskes also reported significant reductions at each dating level in guilt connected with coitus.

Christensen and Gregg (1970) studied changing sex norms in the United States and Scandinavia using comparable samples from universities in 1958 and 1968. Looking only at the data for the United States sample, which is referred to as the intermountain sample (a Mormon sample) and the midwestern sample, we note a sizable increase in coitus rates from the 1958 sample to the 1968 sample. In analyzing the comparisons of 1968 with 1958, Christensen and Gregg produced additional generalizations that pertained to the American sample and to the Scandinavian (Danish) sample. In the United States the rate for males was about the same, whereas the rate among females increased dramatically. This suggests a convergence between the sexes in behavior as well as attitudes. A sharp rise in premarital coitus for both sexes, slightly higher for females, in Denmark brought the rate of incidence to 95 percent, with 100 percent of both sexes approving such behavior.

Analyzing their data in light of Reiss' (1969) conclusion that America is moving toward the traditional Scandinavian pattern of "permissiveness with affection," or permissiveness with commitment, Christensen and Gregg conclude that "while the emerging American pattern seems to be toward the traditional Danish norm of premarital sex justified by commitment, the emerging Danish pattern may be away from both commitment and restriction, toward free and promiscuous sex" (1970, p. 625). From this cross-cultural data one is inclined to conclude that as far as regional, religious, socioeconomic, etc., differences are concerned, Conger's statement about adolescent sexual attitudes and values pertains to behaviors also — "the differences between some subgroups of youth appear wider than those between youth in general and adults in general" (1973, p. 254).

To continue to bring the attitude and behavior question forward, Chilman (1983) notes a sharp increase in nonmarital intercourse, especially among white females, since the late 1960s, with nonmarital intercourse occurring at younger ages and more frequently among adolescents who consider themselves committed. Yet there are important differences between groups of adolescents in attitudes and behavior so that, for instance, "whites who attend church tend to have more conservative sexual attitudes than whites who do not attend church" (this does not hold for blacks); "men have more permissive attitudes than women and blacks have more permissive attitudes than whites; however, . . . white men in New York were more permissive than black men in Virginia" (Dreyer, 1982, p. 567). All of this leads to the conclusion that increased sexual activity and permissiveness are a general trend in this country since early in the century (Miller and Simon, 1980).

INFLUENCES ON SEXUAL BEHAVIOR

The influence of friends, parents, significant others, and reference groups on adolescent sexual behavior may be a key to particularizing that behavior, thus promoting greater subgroup differences. Mirande (1968), testing among college students the hypothesis that "the sexual behavior of an individual will tend to be a function of the reputation of his peer reference group, irrespective of the direction of influence" (p. 573), found a close relationship between a student's sexual behavior and that of his or her two best friends, his or her reference-group standard. This relationship is even more significant for females than for males, for upperclassmen than for lowerclassmen, and for fraternity- and sorority-affiliated students than for nonaffiliated students, leading the author to suggest that "they tend to seek out groups which reinforce their psychological predisposition" (p. 577).

Kaats and Davis' (1970) data illustrate both the influence of significant others and reference groups or selective perception on the part of the adolescent. They found significant differences in the amount of disapproval the adolescents felt from close friends, fathers, brothers, and clergymen according to whether the adolescents were virgins or nonvirgins.

Reiss developed the proposition that "there is a general tendency for the individual to perceive of his parents' permissiveness as a low point of the permissive continuum and his peers' permissiveness as a high point, and to place himself somewhat closer to his peers, particularly to those he regards as his close friends" (1967, p. 139). In Reiss' study, 66 percent of the students perceived their sexual standards to be similar to their parents' standards, 77 percent perceived their sexual standards to be similar to their peers', and 89 percent saw their standards as similar to those of their very close friends. Davis' (1970) study shows the interrelationship of personal attitudes and reference-group influence. He found that girls who believed sexual intercourse to be acceptable when in love, who were very much involved in a dating relationship, and who considered that several of their girlfriends had had sexual intercourse were much more likely to have had sexual intercourse themselves (only 21 percent had not); whereas of those girls who did not believe that premarital sexual intercourse was acceptable even when a person is in love, were not involved in a dating relationship, and did not think that several of their girlfriends had had sexual intercourse, all were still virgins. Billy and Udry found among junior high school students that "white females are influenced by the sexual behavior of both their best female friend and best male friend" (1985, p. 21).

Reiss (1967) shows a clear relationship between the stage of a dating relationship, the degree of affection or commitment, and the level of intimacy that is acceptable to students. Approval of petting when there is not affection in the relationship is 34 percent for males and 18 percent for females, whereas when the couple is in love and possibly engaged, the approval of petting is 83 percent for males and approximately 78 percent for females. When there is no affection in the relationship, 21 percent of the males and 11 percent of the females approved full sexual relations, whereas when the couple was in love and possibly engaged, almost 50 percent of the males approved of full sexual relations and approximately 41 percent of the females approved.

Roche's findings are similar, indicating "that men are more permissive than women, but only in the early stages of dating" and "coincide with Schulz et al.'s (1977) conclusion that 'men and women in strong effective relationships were about equally likely to engage in premarital sexual intercourse' (p. 162)" (1986, p. 119).

If emotional involvement and affection are primary reasons for participating in premarital intercourse, it would seem logically to follow that an absence of affection would be the primary reason for not participating in more intimate heterosexual behavior. Ehrman (1962) rank ordered reasons for not going further in all heterosexual behavior with acquaintances, friends, and lovers for both male and female adolescents. The main reasons for control, for not going further in heterosexual behavior, among the females in their relationships with acquaintances and friends was that they were just not interested in and had no desire for sexual behavior with these categories of persons. On the other hand, moral restraint was the most important reason for control with lovers. The second most important reason for females' not going further with lovers was fear, whereas the second most important reason for not going further with acquaintances and friends was morals. In contrast, the two most important reasons given by males for not going further in all heterosexual behavior were "date would not" and "respect for date."

A number of the issues that have been discussed so far were investigated in a recent U.S. national probability sample survey of 15- to 19-year-old females by Kantner and Zelnik (1972), which revealed that premarital intercourse is beginning at an earlier age and is becoming more widespread. Ninety-two percent of the total sample, which included approximately 2,800 white and 1,400 black girls, had not been married. The likelihood that a never-married woman has experienced coitus rises from 14 percent at age 15 to 46 percent at age 19, and about twice as many never-married blacks have had intercourse as whites. The differences between blacks and whites were not striking with regard to frequency of intercourse and number of sexual partners. The permissiveness-with-affection concept seemed borne out in that sexual relationships were restricted in over half the cases to the man they intended to marry. Furthermore, they experienced coitus with relatively moderate frequency, two times or less in the month prior to the interview. Poverty status seemed to have an effect on black females under 19, who were more likely to have had premarital sexual experience than were those who were less poor. This effect did not pertain to whites. Reiss (1968) also found that his data indicated that white youths are more restricted sexually than black youths, though Dreyer (1975) points out that the differences in sexual behavior are lessening between the races as well as between the sexes and classes.

Broderick studied 10- to 17-year-old black and white adolescents living in the same urban industrial community on an index of social heterosexuality that permitted interracial comparisons by sex and by age. For 10- to 13-year-olds, he concluded that

> the white children showed the traditional pattern, with girls far more romantically oriented than boys, although at about the same level in terms of actual heterosexual interaction. Negro boys, however, showed none of the heterosexual reserve of the white boys. They did not trail the Negro girls on any item except attitude toward marriage, and in, fact, showed a higher level of heterosexual interaction at 12–13 than the girls did. This high level of preadolescent heterosexual interest and involvement among Negro boys, together with an apparent progressive disenchantment with marriage, suggest that the pattern of socio-sexual development in the Negro subculture may differ markedly from that of the dominant culture. (1965, p. 203)

To further confuse this pattern, a study by Harrison, Bennett, and Globe (1969) comparing premarital permissiveness among Mississippi and Virginia adolescents indicated that both white and black adolescents in Mississippi tended to display more permissive attitudes, especially regarding the acceptability of premarital intercourse. These were rural groups, who are usually considered to be more conservative in the area of premarital sex. They found the permissiveness-by-affection rule to hold in that affection was seen as a prime factor in determining acceptability of advanced sexual activity and neither racial group appeared to be particularly promiscuous. Although blacks were considered to be somewhat more permissive by the authors, this difference fit the condition of permissiveness in engagement or love. Sex differences by race showed white females to be less permissive than white males, with no sex differences among blacks.

A variety of polls and surveys attest to the continued high rate of adolescent sexual activity. A study carried out in Culver City, California, a city that advertises itself as "the heart of screenland," showed 29 percent of middle school and 54 percent of high school students to be sexually active (*Parade Magazine*, February 1, 1987, p. 11). A poll run by *People* (April 13, 1987), which mentioned how difficult it was to get school administrators to cooperate with the study, also found that 57 percent of high school students were not virgins.

We have seen in this section that sexual attitudes, and particularly sexual behaviors, are related to age, sex, religiosity, political and social attitudes, parental, peer, and best-friend attitudes and perceptions, societal mores and norms and their change, personality, and geographic differences. In fact, sexual attitudes and behaviors in adolescence are related to inputs and influences at all levels of the culture and the society. This makes for enormous individual variation within communities and between communities and geographic areas, and yet we see national trends in change to a more permissive standard.

Sexual Behavior and Cognitive and Moral Development

From a developmental point of view, it appears natural that with greater age adolescents would exhibit more sexual behavior, both for social reasons as they become more independent and for biological reasons. There has also been a certain natural logic to the double standard in the pre-pill days, as well as to social-class differences in sexual behavior. Younger marriages among lower socioeconomic groups — persons who would be classified as noncollege youth or dropout youth — might be construed as justifying or allowing more premarital sexual activity. Allen and Martin (1971) report that 30 percent of the brides from families earning less than $3,000 per year go to the altar pregnant. The poor cannot afford birth-control devices or abortion, and free services are not being adequately delivered. The greater availability of birth-control devices, abortion, and sex education to the middle-American adolescent could in itself almost portend the diminution of the double standard among older middle-American adolescents, as we have seen in the Vener and Stewart study (1974). A study of the effects of moral development on the selection of premarital sexual standards carried out at eight coeducational colleges in the northeastern region of the United States adds a significant dimension to our understanding of adolescent sexual attitudes and behavior.

Jurich and Jurich (1974) related Kohlberg's moral-developmental levels, tested with two of Kohlberg's moral dilemma stories and two additional stories dealing with premarital and marital sexual problems, to five classifications of premarital sexual standards, four of which had been developed by Reiss (1960) and a fifth which they found empirically in piloting their study. Reiss' four standards are (1) the traditional standard (supported by law and church, dictating total sexual abstinence before marriage), (2) the double standard (allowing males sex before marriage but demanding total sexual abstinence for females), (3) the sexual-permissiveness-with-affection standard (linking the morality of premarital sex to the existence of love between the partners), and (4) the permissiveness-without-affection standard (a hedonistic standard dictating that sex is legitimate with anyone at any time under any circumstance). The fifth is the standard developed by Jurich and Jurich, labeled nonexploitive permissiveness without affection (which allows premarital sex, including intercourse, for both sexes without love, but includes the proviso that any sexual exploitation by either partner is immoral).

Jurich and Jurich found that subjects who held the nonexploitive-permissiveness-without-affection standard were at the highest level of moral maturity among subjects in their sample. The subjects who held to the permissiveness-with-affection standard had moral maturity scores significantly lower than those with the nonexploitive-permissiveness-without-affection standard, but their moral maturity scores were significantly higher than those of the subjects who held the other three standards. Those subjects who advocated the double standard, the traditional morality standard, and the permissiveness-without-affection standard did not significantly differ on moral maturity among themselves.

Jurich and Jurich interpret their findings in terms of the level of intellectual sophistication necessary to function at any of the sexual standards. The permissiveness-without-affection standard can be applied to all people in all situations and requires no sense of reciprocity, no sense of a moral order. The traditional morality standard demands only a desire to maintain the social order but may otherwise be applied to everyone in all situations, and therefore may be seen as a slight progression in the level of moral and intellectual sophistication necessary. The double standard demands an evaluation of whether one's partner fits the moral order, is good or bad, and therefore whether the standard applies in the particular situation. If the female partner is deemed "bad," the relationship with her will take on the aura of the permissiveness-without-affection standard because this evaluation and decision must be made in each new relationship and situation. The double standard also requires a slightly more sophisticated moral and intellectual approach.

A major step in level of cognitive moral sophistication is needed to adhere to a permissiveness-with-affection standard. In this standard, the individual must evaluate for himself and his partner whether there is a mutuality of feelings that can be considered in both cases to be love. These determinations are very difficult and subtle, and require an empathy and honesty that are not always within the capability of even more intellectually sophisticated adolescents.

Allen and Martin (1971) show how the pursuit of this standard is often erroneously construed by adolescents in the quest for sexual gain and the confusion of love and sex. Allen and Martin say that love is taught to adolescents to be a marvelous thing that "happens." When it occurs, it brings unqualified happiness and changes sex, which until then was considered bad and forbidden, to a "good" and "right" thing. A developing adolescent begins to experience sexual desires and wants to express his sexuality. However, he has learned, and it is well known to him, that sexuality without love is bad. Therefore, the adolescent decides that his feeling of desire is naturally love and proceeds as if he were functioning on the permissiveness-with-affection standard. These evaluations are extremely difficult.

The adolescent has grave difficulties distinguishing between the state of being "in love" and the interpersonal feeling of "loving" another person. Adler pointed out that the healing power of love is severely limited if it exists at all. Were the healing process not much more difficult, "it would be enough to surround every problem child, the neurotic, the alcoholic, the sexual pervert, with love in order to cure him" (Ansbacher and Ansbacher, 1964, p. 306). Adolescents often look to "love" to heal their wounds, to cure their hurts. So little in the scientific literature investigates love in adolescence, yet so much of the literature of adolescence is about love. The popular music of adolescents is a training program in winning and losing in love. And the panacea for the problems of adolescents, to many is to be "in love." To be "in love" means all is right with the world, the sky is blue and the clouds are pink, there is Muzak in the park, and nothing else matters. To "love" someone means an enduring and deep emotional regard for someone. It may rain, there may be troubles, life goes on, but through it all, the regard, the "love," prevails. Adolescent experimentation in the full bloom of being "in love" leads to the realistic ability to "love," to mature love. Trying to determine whether applying the permissiveness-with-affection standard is built on "love" for the other person or on being "in love" is a sincere problem for the adolescent. And it is sometimes useful for immediate purposes not to make that distinction.

The highest level of sophistication is needed to pursue the nonexploitive permissiveness-without-affection standard. To function at this level, the person has to determine before engaging in premarital intercourse for each person in each situation whether there is any way in which participation is exploitive of the partner and thereby invalidates or makes the sexual act immoral. In terms of intellectual sophistication, this standard requires the highest level and the most effort, although this does not speak to level of morality itself. One always has to ask the question why, both for oneself and for one's partner, and cannot rely on consensual love.

> Phyllis was sixteen, and I was a freshman at college. Sexually she was much older than I. She was no virgin. She didn't do it for anybody as the rumor stated, but she had "been around." She just did it for love. It took her two dates to love me. (Goldburgh, 1965, p. 26)

As a conclusion and a caution, Jurich and Jurich state:

> The present study has given evidence to support the description of the logical prerequisites required for the formulation of each sexual standard. This is not to say that one standard is more moral than another but that certain standards require a greater level of cognitive moral development. Although they are different in a systematic way, that does not imply that a sexual standard requiring a high level of cognitive moral development is better or more functional than a standard requiring a low level of moral maturity. In fact, a low level of moral development may be highly functional in a specific environment. Therefore, no value judgment shall be placed upon this ordering of premarital sexual standards. (1974, p. 740)

The influences that have been seen to bear on sexual behavior in adolescence all filter through that final influence, the individual. In a longitudinal study of high school students, Jessor and Jessor (1975) looked at personality variables and views of the environment (sense of control and beliefs related to the environment). They hypothesized that there would be differences between virgins and nonvirgins on these variables and that the differences toward the nonvirgin position would be evidenced by virgins in the testing before they became nonvirgins. In fact, they did find a pattern of differences among the virgin and nonvirgin groups and the pattern was found "to obtain prior to the initiation of sexual intercourse experience and to constitute therefore a transition-proneness that significantly predicts becoming a nonvirgin during the subsequent year" (p. 480).

The nonvirgins and those high school students who were more probable to become nonvirgins in the coming year showed less conventional values and outlooks in their immediate environment, parents, and peers, which supports and facilitates the changing status. Moreover, "the nonvirgins — and those virgins who are going to have sexual experience in the subsequent year — consider independence important, have loosened their ties to the family in favor of greater reliance upon friends, and have also engaged more in other nonconventional or transitional behavior" (pp. 480–81). This study strongly supports the notion that the various influences on sexual behavior obtain through the attitudes and decisions of the individual adolescent. Moreover, the individual adolescent makes these decisions in the context of a relationship, and thus the moral judgments of both partners and their judgments about their relationship are involved in their eventual sexual behavior (D'Augelli and D'Augelli, 1977).

CONTRACEPTION AND PREGNANCY

There has been, then, some speculation about the relationship between cognitive development and sex behavior. Pestrak and Martin (1985) looked at whether adolescents, particularly young adolescents, may not have "reached the level of cognitive development to be able to develop genuine intimacy, understand the complex, interpersonal aspects of a mature sexual relationship, and properly practice birth control" (p. 981). They conclude that level of cognitive development may well affect intimacy and the nature of sexual relationships while pointing out that "there is no guarantee that after a more sophisticated cognitive level is reached, a healthy and satisfactory sexual relationship will be achieved" (p. 985).

The speculation that adolescents may not have reached a level of cognitive development sufficient to practice birth control properly, presumably early formal operations at least, does not appear valid. Pestrak and Martin suggest that the use of the IUD would be the most effective birth control method for teenagers because they do not have to make so many attributions and decisions on a day-to-day basis. That is probably true. However, the attributions that teenagers have to make to use birth control — acceptance and acknowledgment of their sexuality and their sexual activity and realistic expectations about future sexual experiences — would seem to be easily made, concrete judgments. The decision to be ready, "anticipation in the present" (p. 986), seems to be the problem and, at a superficial level, no more difficult than remembering to bring a swimsuit if you are going somewhere there is a pool. The issue regarding use of birth-control devices does not seem to relate to cognitive development.

"Knowledge, as measured by sex education courses and self-reported birth control knowledge, has no effect on the chances that a black or white female will experience an out-of-wedlock birth as a teenager. However, when adolescents and their parents hold values that stress responsibility, the adolescents' chances of experiencing an out-of-wedlock childbirth are significantly reduced" (Hanson, Myers, and Ginsburg, 1987, p. 241). Values more than knowledge affect chances for illegitimate births. Adolescent pregnancy also seems to depend more on values and attitudes than on knowledge, although this is not to say that without knowledge behaviors would not be different. That is, sex education, though not as good or as prevalent as it might be in the schools, is still plentiful and available, and most pregnancies, and the misuse or lack of use of birth control, are not due to lack of knowledge. "Many teenagers have sex, often reject birth control, get pregnant, and have children — not because of ignorance, but because they see those actions as ways to keep a relationship alive, or escape their own families, or achieve something in a life filled with failure, violence, uncertainty" (Leon Dash in *Carnegie Quarterly* 31 [1986] p. 3).

A study of teenage pregnancy in 37 industrialized countries by the Alan Guttmacher Institute found that "in every country, when respondents were pressed to describe the kind of young woman who would be most likely to bear a child, the answer was the same: economically and emotionally deprived adolescents who unrealistically seek gratification and fulfillment in a child of their own" (*Carnegie Quarterly*, 1986, p. 3).

The Guttmacher Institute study also found that the teenage pregnancy rate in the United States is the highest in the developed world. "In 1984, an estimated 1,004,859 girls under age 20 became pregnant — about 11 percent of the female adolescent population; 47 percent of this number gave birth, while 40 percent had induced abortions, and the remainder miscarried" (p. 2). They estimated that 40 percent of American teenage women become pregnant and that increasing numbers of those who give birth are unmarried.

Over half of births to teenagers occur outside marriage, and blacks are much more apt to have children outside of marriage. However, much of the rise in births to unmarried teenagers can be attributed to the fast rise in births to unwed white teenagers. Yamaguchi and Kandel used a risk factor modeling approach to predict premarital pregnancy and its outcomes—abortion, premarital birth, or postmarital birth—and found that "such variables as cohabitation, being black, having had poor grades and high peer activity in high school, use of illicit drugs other than marijuana, and having dropped out of high school are associated with a two- to threefold increase in the risk of a premarital pregnancy. Premarital births are overrepresented among blacks, as are abortions among users of illicit drugs other than marijuana" (1987, p. 257).

Very few adolescents are unaware of the possibility of birth control and few are unaware of some actual devices. Thus, not using birth control is just as much a decision as using birth control, and some adolescents need to make a subsequent decision about whether to have a child or not. Clearly some of the decisions not to use birth control are related to the decision to have a child, possibly for the reasons given by Dash. And for some, the decisions are separate, because they never believed that their decision not to use birth-control measures would lead to pregnancy for them.

The data show that unwed teenage mothers are more likely to be poor, are less likely to finish high school, and are more likely to then have low-status jobs and low income. Family-planning programs appear to have an effect on birthrates but not on pregnancy rates (Weed and Olsen, 1986). Knowledge, values, and attitudes may together be of greater import when girls are pregnant than they are before pregnancy. Even the knowledge of the effects of having a child seems insufficient in itself. However, my younger daughter once suggested to me that the information's lack of effectiveness may have something to do with its nature. She, at age 16, said that information about future income and employability doesn't make much sense to girls who are pregnant or thinking of getting pregnant. Either they don't care or they don't think that it applies to them. She said that if they could be brought to realize that they were going to be full-time baby-sitters, even if for their own children, and thus stuck at home, they might rethink their opinions.

This section has pointed out many associations between behaviors in the love and sex life task and developments, both cognitive and moral. To a large degree we have seen that progressions in these behaviors are more associated with these developments among the more mature or advanced adolescents. On the other hand, we have seen that sexual behavior is related to the attitudes and values of the times, with variation between subgroups, and to other deviant and nondeviant behaviors.

HOMOSEXUAL EXPERIENCES AND HOMOSEXUALITY

The gay community and the mental health community feel that it is harmful to call homosexuality "abnormal" and to apply that label to "normal" people. Such a label is not used by professionals, and the attitudes associated with that notion seem to be slowly changing in our society. Still, homosexuality is neither practiced nor accepted to the extent that it is usual, normative behavior. Approximately 4 percent of adult men and 2 percent of adult women say that their sexual orientation is exclusively toward members of their own sex (Chilman, 1983; Francoeur, 1982).

Homosexual experiences in adolescence are not infrequent. About 6 percent of female adolescents (Sorenson, 1973) and about 15 percent of male adolescents (Simon and Gagnon, 1967) have at least one homosexual experience. Yet these experiences are not the norm and these experiences are not "abnormal." They may provoke crises in cases where adolescents worry that they will become homosexuals, but for the vast majority of adolescents, the crisis as well as the homosexual behavior passes.

As Kiell (1964) noted, in general, homosexual activities in adolescence are normal with elements of experimentation and represent single or short-time occurrences with little or no long-term psychological effect. In fact, he says rather than forecasting homosexuality in later life, homosexual activities in adolescence are usually not present in the life histories of adult homosexuals.

A vast array of psychological, social, and physical factors are hypothesized by different theorists to influence or cause homosexuality. Most of this theorizing weights childhood and early childhood heaviest in determining future homosexual tendencies. Although adolescence may be a particularly difficult period for the adolescent who does become a practicing homosexual in adulthood, homosexuality is not truly developed in adolescence.

Homosexual experiences in adolescence are within the domain of this book. To understand their occurrence, two factors seem crucial: (1) the intensity of, and need for, the same-sex friendship group as a support and base from which to move into the greater adolescent, heterosexual social world, and (2) the influence of cognitive development to formal operations, with its extensions of possibilities for thinking about oneself, i.e., "maybe I am homosexual," "this is a way to act that can also be considered."

Even from Otto Fenichel's (1945) psychoanalytic perspective, the strong social component in these behaviors is apparent. He says that homosexual gatherings are preferred by many as a social outlet to avoid the excitement and temptation of the other sex. However, the sexual component asserts itself within these groups, too.

In arguing against a hereditary explanation of homosexuality, Adler points out the frequency and normality of homosexual experiences that are almost forced in some settings: "An argument against the hereditary view of homosexuality is the frequent occurrence of noncompulsive homosexuality, that is, casual homosexual experiences, in childhood, in boarding schools, on long journeys as in the case of sailors, or in the life of soldiers and of prisoners" (Ansbacher and Ansbacher, 1956, p. 425).

In setting that the adolescent devises and in others over which he has little control, i.e., same-sex settings of longer duration, homosexual experiences may occur. For the teacher, parent, or even the adolescent, without denying the self-questioning that may occur at the time (although the experience may be the result of the questioning rather than the opposite), we may tell the adolescent, "This is nothing to worry about." And the worry, if it occurs for the homosexual, should not be about the label "abnormal" itself, but about the long-range effects of behaving in a way that is negatively sanctioned by our society (no matter how unjustly), as well as the effects of limiting one's potential for heterosexual life and having a family with children.

An example of the view that homosexuality in adult males emanates from childhood perceptions, experiences, and conclusions is seen in the following early recollections of adult male homosexuals. Although these recollections were gathered in my psychotherapy practice and may not be representative of the life views of "well-adjusted" adult homosexuals, they also show that early on these patients found, or gave themselves, reasons for avoiding the opposite sex. One young man said his earliest recollection, at age 5 or 6, was:

> I was lying on the floor and made a caustic remark, and she [mother] kicked me in the crotch. It hurt—but she apologized. It was an enraged kick—but she immediately became soft.

Another young man said that at age 4:

> Mother was cleaning the house. I picked a thing off the floor. I went to blow into it. I thought it was a balloon. She was furious and hollered. It seemed like a long time, on and on. I couldn't understand how, over a balloon, but I knew there was more to it. Now I know it was a prophylactic. Whenever they are mentioned I think of this. (Manaster and King, 1973, p. 29)

Homosexuality does present problems, such as avoidance, as these recollections imply, but it appears to be under individual influence. The basic ideas about one's relationships and preferences originate in childhood, although, obviously, the decisions about preferences and acting on preferences are evidenced later. Homosexual activities in adolescence are not of this nature.

The pervasiveness of the notion of the normality of homosexuality in adolescence is illustrated in the following quote from the autobiography of Kenneth Clark, the guide and author of the television series "Civilization":

> And here I must make a confession that psychologists and advanced educationalists will regard as shameful. I have never felt the faintest inclination to homosexuality. I realize that it is natural for young people to form emotional and sometimes physical attachments to members of their own sex, partly out of fear of the unknown, partly from the structure of our educational system. For some reason I never did so. I was not one of those plump and pretty boys who attract the attention of their elders, and I never fell in love with my contemporaries. I do not think this can be explained by emotional poverty or lack of vitality, but by the fact that my premature devotion to the girls was so strong as to fill my fantasy-world and leave no room for homosexual attachments. (1974, p. 73)

Possibly the adolescent who feels no homosexual interest should also be cautioned "not to worry."

CONCLUSIONS AND AIDS

The life task love and sex brings together the full scope of influences on the individual in an area that is extremely personal. We have seen that the pressures to conform to expectations of parents and peers interact in this area, yet the adolescent chooses carefully the information he wishes to utilize. The adolescent chooses to follow the lead of those he or she feels have the most to offer on the question at issue. In particular, we have seen that as the adolescent's attitudes change, and as the influences felt are not as dependent on less mature emotional attachment to parents, the likelihood of more intimate sexual behavior follows.

The high school adolescents of today hold more sexually liberal attitudes and are more sexually active at a younger age than their parents were. In part this relates to the more open attitude toward sex that is prevalent throughout the society. But this also relates to new moralities available to the adolescent as a result of cognitive and moral development.

Sex differences (notably absent in the most recent high school data of Jessor and Jessor [1975]), race differences, and socioeconomic-status differences also appear to be decreasing. All in all, the responsibility for sexual behavior and attitudes seem to be on the individual adolescent, which is where it should be, if the adolescent has the facts and maturity to handle it.

In view of the existence and threat of AIDS, much of this chapter may be more of historical interest than indicative of current adolescent behavior and attitudes. And yet, some of what we have learned about adolescent love and sex behavior may be useful for predicting and understanding the effect of AIDS and AIDS education on these behaviors.

The problem was well put in an article titled "Kids and Contraceptives" (*Newsweek*, February 16, 1987): "The alarmingly high rate of teenage pregnancy and the fear of AIDS and other sexually transmitted diseases have opened up the debate over what to do about the precocious sexual activity of young people; what was once a matter of morality has become a matter of public health" (p. 54).

At this writing, in the summer of 1987, it appears that the magnitude of the threat of AIDS is enormous and that the questions about the reality of that threat for heterosexuals in general and for groups so far identified as at high risk are myriad. It is, at this time, too early to tell whether there are genetic components in susceptibility to the disease, whether other health and physical and emotional fitness factors play a part in who contracts the disease, how easily the virus is transmitted heterosexually, and on and on. The behaviors are known that make homosexuals and intravenous drug users high-risk groups. The safest approach for public health officials to advocate is that all individuals should use a "safe sex" option, i.e., abstinence or limited sexual contacts using precautions, such as condoms.

Whether AIDS will become a major epidemic and disaster is not now known. The potential for an epidemic exists, on the basis of current knowledge, and therefore the precautions suggested make sense. It appears that the threat of other sexually transmitted diseases has not been taken too seriously by adolescents. They believe that the diseases are treatable and thus their worries about contracting them have been mostly social — they are concerned about embarrassment and parental disapproval. That is not the case with AIDS, and publicity and educational efforts should reach a point where everyone knows that AIDS kills.

This threat presumably will reduce adolescent sexual behavior, perhaps very drastically. It may be, however, that changes in sexual behavior will be related to the factors described in this chapter as affecting current sexual practices. One would imagine that homosexual experimentation among male adolescents will be greatly reduced. One would imagine that the more cognitively developed adolescents subscribing to the nonexploitive-sex doctrine will at least be more cautious, if they do not limit their activity. But will adolescents who have not believed that pregnancy can happen to them believe that AIDS can? It is too early to tell. However we can strongly expect that the presence of AIDS in our society will affect the sexual behavior of our adolescents.

CHAPTER 11
School

Miss Van Buren's
7th Grade Class
C. A. Riley Jr. H.S.

CHAPTER 11

This chapter on school and the next chapter on work together deal with the life task that emphasizes contributing to the welfare of others through one's efforts. School, it is hoped, prepares one to make one's contribution. The full scope of learning that should occur in school, from the formal basics through the learning of social behaviors and social-institutional living, add to the individual's ability to make it, for self and for others.

Time spent working constitutes the major single portion of time in an adult's life. That is to say, if an adult works a 40-hour week, with the exception of sleeping, there is no other single activity that takes as much time. Although schooling often in and of itself does not take 40 hours a week, schooling and related extracurricular activities take up the largest portion of time in an adolescent's life. School is not only the major time consumer in the adolescent's day, but it is also the societal mechanism for assisting the adolescent to become a productive, contributing adult member of the society. Although there are exceptions — such as the dropout or the immigrant with little or no formal education who is very successful in business — there is a strong, long, and consistent relationship between success in school, number of years of schooling, and economic success. For the many who graduate and go directly to work, high school appears to be education for a job, while for the college bound, high school is preparation for additional education that may then lead to a job, to a broader and fuller life, or to both.

School is not now, if it ever was, solely for the purpose of education for a job. Regardless of the stated intent of various institutions, school and its surrounding formal and informal activities is a major socialization agent. Whether intended by the school authorities or not, it is where adolescents learn a great deal about the other life tasks also, sometimes through curriculum, but greatly through interpersonal associations formed in organized and

210

unorganized activities in and around the school. The developmental tasks of achieving assurance of economic independence and selecting and preparing for an occupation are still at the base of American schooling. The tasks relating to civic competence and socially responsible behavior are recognized and taught and equally a part of one's school life, i.e., one spends many full days in a large group, an organization, an institution.

The task of becoming a socially responsible individual contributing to others as both a citizen and an independent worker is the forerunner of becoming such a person as an adult. Therefore, for adolescents, because of the length of the moratorium, the time given to learn and develop the ways in which they can succeed in these life tasks, school is their form of work. It is from this perspective — school as the adolescent's work — that this chapter will proceed. We will look at school achievement in relation to personal, peer, family, and social influence.

THE SITUATION — THE SCHOOLS

In the United States schooling is mandatory for all children up to at least age 15 or 16, and most finish high school at about 18 or 19. With rare exceptions, children go to at least two schools — elementary and high school — or three schools — elementary, junior high or middle, and high school. There was a time, 25 years ago and more, when schools across the United States were much more uniform in organizational structure and curriculum than they are now. What has become known as the "traditional" school was then the standard. Moreover, the neighborhood grammar school and the local high school that combined students from a number of neighborhood grammar schools was also normative. This structure produced de facto racial segregation in great portions of the country, whereas de jure segregation was practiced in other regions. The attempt to eliminate racial segregation, which continues today, as well as the institution of a multitude of educational structures, teaching approaches, and curricula have produced a situation where generalizations may be made but exceptions proliferate. Evaluations and conclusions are more prevalent of the exceptional programs, making generalizations to the greater high school scene tenuous.

Schools have traditionally differed in "quality," some considered better and others worse for reasons such as monies expended per student, quality of facilities, innovativeness of programs, and success of graduates. Many of these differences in "quality" have related directly to the social class and ethnicity of the student body. Moreover, schools have differed in their curriculum orientation — that is, vocational or college bound or, unfortunately, custodial—with related prestige attached to the various curricula. Schools also vary in size and location and thus in community impact or involvement.

Teachers vary every bit as much as schools. In elementary schools, pupils traditionally spent the day with a single teacher and evaluated school each year on their feelings about that teacher. More grammar schools are now moving to team-teaching, open approaches, so pupils have the chance to interact daily with more teachers. In junior high schools, middle schools, and high schools, a student generally has a different teacher for each subject. Attitudes toward school are related on a day-to-day basis to attitudes toward certain subjects and teachers, but the qualities of a "good" teacher can be, and are, disputed. The teacher I think is good, that I like, may not be the teacher you think is good, that you like. And probably we are each right for ourselves.

All these factors, listed as contributing to the quality of a school or teacher, may be thought of as the school-related influences on the student's attitude and success in school.

The schools are under constant criticism and have been for many years. At a recent school board meeting in the author's city, the schools were criticized for being too conservative and for being too liberal, for being too narrow and academic and for being too social, and proposals were brought before the board to reinstitute "traditional" grammar and high schools, as well as to make the schools more open, flexible, and progressive.

It was easier to note the strengths and faults in the educational system when it was more uniform nationwide. Today, when myriad attempts are being made to improve the education of our young people, recognizing that many of these attempts will fail, prove fruitless, or be downright silly, there is little reason to believe that education for young people is any worse than it ever was. It may, in fact, be better and fuller. It is comparable to when having two rooms in our home newly painted makes the rest of the house look drab. In some ways, it was more comfortable to have the whole house with drab walls, but now that some improvement has been made, we feel called upon to complete the refurbishing. The gigantic American system of schools is in what must be a never-ending process of refurbishing. How successful are we to this point?

An indicator of the continuation of the general progress being made in education is that the 1970 census findings can be restated for today:

- A greater proportion of Americans than ever before is going to school.
- We are starting school at an earlier age and staying in school longer.
- For the first time, the average American adult has completed high school.

- People who live in urban areas have a higher level of education than those in rural areas.
- Although a higher percentage of whites finish high school than blacks or those of Spanish ancestry, these minorities are closing the gap.
- There is a definite relationship between level of education and the kinds of jobs people hold, and how much they get paid. (*We the Americans: Our Education*, U.S. Bureau of the Census, 1973)

Silberman pointed out that "three students out of four now finish high school; in 1929, three out of four did not go beyond the eighth grade" (1970, p. 17). According to the 1980 census, in 1900 11 percent of 14- to 17-year-olds were in high school, whereas in 1980 94 percent were enrolled. Slightly more than 73 percent of the 17-year-old population have graduated from high school in recent years, down from the 75 percent level in the late 1960s and early 1970s. The dropout rate among 18- to 19-year-olds in 1981 was 16 percent for whites, 19 percent for blacks, and 26 percent for students of Spanish origin (U.S. Bureau of the Census, February 1983).

In answer to the question, "How functionally competent are U.S. adults?" the authors of a national survey conclude, "not as competent as we thought. Overall, approximately one-fifth of U.S. adults are functioning with difficulty" (Adult Functional Competency, 1975, p. 6). Knowledge and skill competencies in areas such as consumer economics, government and law, community resources, reading, and problem solving were ascertained. Even remembering that many older adults were in school a long time ago, and that many are immigrants who received little education in their country of origin and none here, the results caution us in our optimism about advancements and improvements in education.

Students who should be doing well, as opposed to those who are not even functionally literate, are those who intend to attend college and who therefore take the Scholastic Aptitude Test (SAT). From the mid-1960s, scores on the SAT declined steadily, the verbal score more than the math, until the early 1980s, when they seemed to bottom out and begin a slight upturn. Many reasons for the decline have been given, from nuclear fallout to too much television viewing (Sternglass and Bell, 1983). The greater number of minority students attempting the SAT and going through high school is certainly part of the reason for the decline. However, possibly, in concert with all the other reasons, the major reason is too broad to be included as a researchable variable — the nature and mood of the times. A much more diverse high school student population, affected by the Vietnam War, Watergate, the progress of the Civil Rights Movement and the Women's Movement, seeing themselves entering a postindustrial, service economy in a less strong and stable America that is having trouble competing in the world economy and determining its political and moral place in the world, may well have lowered motivation for school achievement. The schools received a great deal of the blame for the decline in SAT scores. Did not the confusion in the schools—the lack of core curriculum, the grade inflation, the constant change in standards and in boundaries for desegregation—reflect the lack of direction in the society? Might not the decline in SAT scores have been, in the students, a reflection of the same lack of direction?

Havighurst (1966), acknowledging the truism that "everybody has un-realized potential," points to three specific groups who are not being served by the schools as well as they might: the socially disadvantaged and educationally maladjusted adolescent, the underdeveloped and underachieving adolescent, and the potentially superior but uncommitted adolescent. The editor's introduction to a recent issue of *Education and Urban Society* stresses the degree to which these groups are not being served in America's cities. It points to the fact that "school systems in most major cities fail to graduate anywhere from 25% to 60% of the students they enroll is both an ill kept dirty secret and a major indictment of American education" (1987, pp. 227–31).

The task of the schools, to educate everybody, under the general direction of federal and state laws, rules, mandates, and bureaucracies and the specific instructions of local boards and administrations is so difficult that no one in education is ever satisfied. The numerous reports in recent years with contradictory suggestions for improving education are indicative of the magnitude of the problem.

Yet wherever we are in the evolution and adequacy of the schools, each adolescent, as he or she proceeds through junior high school and high school, is exposed to some combination of all the factors mentioned here, and these, in interaction with the student's personal attributes and the other social and personal influences on him or her, culminate in the student's attitudes and success in school, and, to some degree, in occupational life.

ADJUSTMENT WHEN CHANGING SCHOOLS

Belonging, fitting in, knowing where you stand in relation to others—these are, as has been said, crucial feelings for the individual. Our system of schools disrupts the actuality of belonging and fitting in as students are made to change schools, from elementary school to middle or junior high school to high school, and for a good number of students, there are arbitrary changes from year to year for purposes of desegregation. This is not all bad, as it prepares youngsters for future changes of locale and job and status. However, it is not necessarily easy. For some students the change from one school to another is a gentle readjustment, while for others it is difficult and for a few it is traumatic. Although efforts are oftimes made to soften the effects of these transitions through orientation meetings and social functions, a number of influences may affect the quality of this transition.

Family and socioeconomic influences may include transition from a school in which one is primarily similar to the other children in socioeconomic status or race to a school where one is less similar to the majority. The new school may be located some distance from the child's home and bring him into an area that is more foreign to him than was the location of his old school. The transition may be more difficult because zoning regulations or busing procedures for integration disrupt existing peer relationships and bring a student to a new school without a core friendship network. The new school may be organized differently, be much larger, be more demanding. Yet through it all, the student brings one constant with him: his own conception of himself and his abilities and strategies for coping with new situations. Nottelmann's "results indicate that entry into secondary school represents significant change from elementary school, but that most children negotiate the transition without undue difficulty" (1987, p. 441).

Recently I saw a college freshman who utilized none of these strategies for adapting to the greater college scene, including orientation week, fraternity rush, and organized campus activities, and consequently he had a very difficult and lonely first semester. He slowly developed his own group of acquaintances and friends, and with their mutual support, moved into some of the more formal campus activities. He reported that prior to attending both junior high school and high school, he was very anxious and cried at night, not knowing why, for two weeks before the start of each. His personal strategy for becoming a part of a new institutional organization was to be extremely selective in choosing friends and associations. This was a difficult and discomforting strategy that put him through a period of unhappiness but eventually led to a good adjustment.

The study by Simmons, Rosenberg, and Rosenberg of disturbance in the self-image at adolescence suggested that environmental variables may have a stronger effect than age in producing greater instability of the self-image and somewhat lower self-esteem in early adolescence: "Children who had entered junior high school appeared more disturbed along these lines than their age-peers still in elementary school" (1973, p. 553).

The difficulty in adjustment, in adapting, to any situation is in the final analysis most directly a function of the individual's coping strategies and coping style. According to Murphy (1962): "coping strategies are the child's individual patternings and timings of his resources for dealing with specific problems or needs or challenges" (p. 274), and "a given child may develop a large range of coping devices and strategies or he may limit himself to very few. The total range determines his coping style" (p. 321).

Coelho, Silber, and Hamburg (1961) define coping behavior from a personality-social viewpoint as having two broad components. The first component of coping behavior has to do with the effectiveness of the behavior in accomplishing specific tasks. The second component has to do with the "cost to the individual" in dealing successfully with these tasks. If a behavior accomplishes, or increases the likelihood of accomplishing, a task within limits that are tolerable to the individual and tolerable, in the sense of successful, to the group in which he lives, then it may be said to "serve coping functions," i.e., to be successful coping.

The coping strategies, the coping style, developed through childhood have been aimed at dealing primarily with family first, and then peer and grammar school associations. The first encounter of these strategies with a broader and possibly very different situation is in the movement to new schools. The schools may or may not be terribly different, the peer and family influences may be supportive, and a child with poorly developed coping strategies may still make a smooth transition to middle school or high school. Conversely, all the factors influencing this transition may be negative and may make the transition potentially more difficult, and yet a child with a large range of coping devices and strategies may make this transition smoothly. And lastly, as in the case of the college student cited earlier, the transition may not be smooth because of the nature of the individual's coping strategy, may therefore be very costly to the individual, but may in the long run be very effective.

For the most part, adolescents like school. Bachman et al. (1981) found that 45 percent of high school students said they liked school very much or quite a lot and 40 percent said they liked school some. Even if we recognize that students who had dropped out were not included in this sample of seniors, only 10 percent said they did not like school very much and 4 percent did not like school at all. Interestingly, Gesell (1956) showed that liking for school drops most sharply at ages 12 and 15, approximately the ages at which school transition occurs.

In general, adolescent girls (as well as boys) have a very positive attitude toward school (Konopka, 1975). If they have been treated badly because of racial discrimination or labeling as a delinquent, their attitudes are more negative. But many girls enjoy school. When asked "what they expect of school, they spoke of friendship and understanding, but also of learning. Often the subjects they preferred were those we consider difficult" (Konopka, 1975, p. 4).

With all of the criticism, all of the problems, all of the trauma and potential for trauma and personal difficulty in school, with unrealized potential great in some groups but existing in all, by and large children go through school liking it, adjusting to each school in turn, wanting more, and benefiting from their achievements therein. This 14-year-old-boy's statement seems typical:

> When it comes to school, I can honestly say I don't like it a whole lot, but I don't hate it. I like coming back and seeing people I haven't seen all summer, and I like getting into a class that is really interesting and there's a good teacher. He or she will help you and kid with you, and you look forward to that class and really get something out of it. I try harder in a class that's interesting. (Bravler and Jacobs, 1974, p. 137)

"All accounts of adolescence stress both the sense of questioning and the parallel discovery or search for a new self of the adolescent." One "problem of meaning . . . is the problem of whether the high school has meaning to the adolescent." High school has had "a double meaning to the adolescent. . . . First, it was the locus of the peer culture in which he found his immediate identity. . . . Second, on the academic side, it was a point of connection to a place in the adult world" (Kohlberg and Gilligan, 1971, p. 1055).

SCHOOL ACHIEVEMENT

School achievement has been used as a criterion variable in innumerable researches. Lavin (1965), in his book *Prediction of Academic Achievement*, lists 29 types of variables used as predictors of school achievement. Although there is a group of school critics who contend that schools overemphasize achievement, the reasons for this great interest in school achievement and in predicting school achievement seem to be threefold. First, school achievement, in the form of grades and standardized achievement test scores, is a standard, however reliable, that is accessible for all children in our country. Second, it is also, for the vast majority of children, a stressed and understood goal. It may be said that with very few exceptions, parents would like their children to do well in school. They may not equally convey their desire to their children or actively support and affirm their wishes, but school achievement is generally a desired goal of all parents for their children. Third, in the face of the myriad, ever-growing, and conflicting demands on schools to educate, train, and socialize beyond the basic academic curriculum, achievement in the basic academics is the basis for schools. School achievement is therefore the one quantitative indication we have of results of behavior that are sought after, or the ideal, for all children.

THE PERSONAL, SELF-INFLUENCE

> The self-concept construct has been utilized by several psychologists in research related to academic underachievement and overachievement in education. Though their studies are based on different assumptions and hypotheses, it is not difficult to find some logical truth in the belief that certain types of self-regarding attitudes may affect academic performance. For example, if the child perceives himself to be able, confident, adequate and a person of worth, worthy of respect rather than condemnation, he has more energy available to spend on academic achievement. On the other hand, if he perceives himself as worthless, incapable to cope with life's problems, he may fail in spite of being intellectually capable of achieving more. (Bhatnagar, 1966, p. 178)

One aspect of the self that necessarily has a strong personal influence on achievement is intelligence. Regardless of whether or not you believe that intelligence is primarily a function of heredity or environment, by the time an individual reaches puberty and adolescence, his measured intelligence is very stable and will change by little more than the amount expected from measurement error over the course of the remainder of his adolescent and adult years. One would expect that adolescents of very high or low measured ability would have correspondingly high or low achievement levels in high school in the great majority of cases. "Studies suggest that for the high school level, ability and grades are correlated at about .60" (Lavin, 1965, p. 56). Curry (1962) showed that deprived home conditions have a more serious effect on school achievement as intellectual ability decreases. That is, when the child or adolescent has above-average intelligence, he can more probably overcome a deprived environment. Lavin's and Curry's conclusions lead one to believe that the ability-achievement relationship would hold true to extremes of intellectual ability regardless of social class.

Manaster (1969), using a sample of 10- and 14-year-olds of average intelligence, removed the effects of intelligence in predicting achievement and found a significant relationship between sense of competence and achievement. Sense of competence as a construct may be seen as falling within the global self-concept, or self-regarding, attitudes. Sense of competence, as developed by White (1964), is considered to be the individual's subjective perception of his ability to solve problems in general or to solve specific types of problems—his perceived ability to overcome the obstacles encountered in life. Although self-concept and the self-regarding attitudes are more global conceptions, whereas sense of competence is a more discrete, particularized concept, there is considerable overlap. Shibutani's use of self-esteem is much closer to the way in which Manaster used sense of competence. Shibutani says, "Much of what a person does or refuses to do depends upon his level of self-esteem" (1961, p. 433).

Purkey arrived at a definition of self that stresses its organized and dynamic aspects, in which self is "a complex and dynamic system of beliefs which an individual holds true about himself" (1970, p. 7). The organizational aspect of the definition of the self allows one to conceptualize and study the most global, all-inclusive self-concept, a concept such as sense of competence, which is more particular but still global, or any of the specific beliefs that an individual has about a certain aspect of himself. All of the specific beliefs about particular aspects of the self add to, weighted for their own importance to the individual, the total self-concept and constitute the organizational element of the definition.

One such specific belief, or aspect of the total self-concept, is "self-concept of ability," which we will define and examine to understand the "dynamic" quality of an aspect of self-concept. Brookover, Erikson, and Joiner saw self-concept of academic ability as "behavior in which one indicates to himself (publicly or privately) his ability to achieve in academic tasks as compared with others engaged in the same tasks" (1967, p. 8). This definition indicates the organized aspect of self-concept while implying that other concepts of self refer to other areas of behavior.

Marsh and Shavelson, who, you will remember, investigated the multifaceted, hierarchical structure of self-concept, found that achievement scores for math and English "were substantially correlated with the academic self-concepts, but not with the nonacademic scales" (1985, p. 117). Likewise, Zarb (1981), looking at separate aspects of self-concept, family, peer, and academic self-concepts in relation to achievement, found that "academic self-concept was the best single predictor of Grade Point Average for both the male and female samples" (p. 897).

In Zarb's investigation, "the Study Habits measure was the other significant predictor of Grade Point Average in both the male and female samples" (p. 898). "Miller et al. (1985) . . . showed that educational self-direction increases students' intellectual flexibility and that intellectual flexibility, in turn, leads to their exercising greater self-direction in schoolwork" (Miller et al., 1986, p. 374). They then found "that educational self-direction affects non-cognitive aspects of personality as well. . . . Greater self-direction in schoolwork . . . increases the self-directedness of the student's orientation. Greater self-direction in schoolwork also decreases the student's sense of distress" (p. 388).

Burke et al. point out that "the literature is replete with research on self-concept, academic achievement, and the relationship between these two educationally relevant variables" (1985, p. 260), but that a good number of academic self-concept measures are not equivalent and that this causes difficulties in interpreting studies. Still, studies continue to show in this country and elsewhere, for instance in Korea (Song and Hattie, 1984), the influence of home environment and social status on self-concept and achievement and the effect of academic self-concept on achievement.

These studies illustrate our growing understanding of the role of, and specificity of, self-concept in relation to school achievement. They also show the line from academic self-concept to academic coping behaviors, such as study habits and self-direction, and back to academic self-concept. That is, these studies begin to indicate more clearly that it is the particular sense of ability to do particular academic work that leads to doing that work well, they show that being able to do this work well is dependent, at least in part, on having relevant study skills and independent work habits and strategies, and they demonstrate that having these skills and habits and doing well affects one's sense of ability. This growing body of knowledge holds the promise of development of interventions at each of the different levels — self-concept skills, and performance — that, if effective, will be seen to influence all levels.

Brookover, Erikson, and Johnson (1967) found that students with low self-concept seldom achieved at above-average levels, but a good number of students with high self-concepts of ability did not perform at high or above-average levels as would be expected. This means that students who do not believe that they can do well will not, but that students who do believe that they are able to do well will still not necessarily do well. Brookover put this in the form of a "necessary but not sufficient" hypothesis, in that high self-concept of ability is a necessary but not sufficient influence in determining academic achievement. The potential effectiveness of feedback from self-directed education may prove to be the "sufficient."

SELF, SUBGROUP, AND ACHIEVEMENT

Patterson (1965) explained the self-concept of academic ability dynamic with particular emphasis on its meaning for black adolescents:

Once a child is convinced he cannot learn in school, the task of educators becomes almost impossible. He may well make trouble for his classmates, his teachers, and himself. A negative self-concept is just as crippling and just as hard to overcome as any physical handicap. In fact, a negative self-image may be even more crippling, because it is often hidden from the view of the naive or untrained observer. Most children who hate themselves act out this self-hatred by kicking the world around them. They are abusive, aggressive, hard to control, and full of anger and hostility at a world which has told them that they are not valued, are not good, and are not going to be given a chance. Such attitudes often continue to cripple an adult life. (pp. 4–5)

This description of the dynamic effect of low self-concept on achievement and school behavior is extreme for most cases but is illustrative of the extent to which some psychologists and social scientists view the influence of self-concept. When Patterson states, "The child with the negative view of self is a child who will not be able to profit adequately from school" (p. 4), he is in essential agreement with Brookover.

Although the dynamics of self-concept influencing academic achievement are apparently generally understood and accepted, conflicting views remain of the specific effects of this relationship when analyzed separately by sex and race. Whereas the assumption of the Conference on Negro Self-Concept introduced by Patterson was that black self-concept would necessarily be lower because of the press of the American color-caste system and therefore would result in "defeated behavior" in academic spheres, Coleman et al. (1966) indicated high self-concept and achievement motivation for both black and white students. Zirkel and Moses (1971) reported that black students had even higher self-concepts than whites, although the difference was not significant. Soares and Soares (1969, 1970) also found that disadvantaged children had higher self-perception than did advantaged children and concluded that "despite their cultural handicap, disadvantaged children do not necessarily suffer lower self-esteem and a lower sense of personal worth" (1969, p. 43). Whether the changing picture of black self-concept has to do with changes and improvements in measurement and research design or whether black self-concept has improved over the years it has been studied, the current conclusion is that "there appears to be strong evidence that blacks on average do not suffer from poor self-images" (Lay and Wakstein, 1985, p. 46).

Wylie (1963), investigating self-concept of academic ability, found that black students modestly estimated their abilities for college as compared with white students, but more blacks expressed the desire to go to college than did whites. However, the black-white difference disappeared when socioeconomic status was controlled. Wylie suggested that the lower level of black students' estimates of ability might be a function of their relatively low socioeconomic status overall. Lay and Wakstein (1985) found that among college-bound students, blacks and whites used the same dimensions of ability to evaluate themselves and that at the same levels of academic achievement in high school, larger percentages of blacks show high self-esteem than whites.

It might be suggested that some of the conflict in these findings relates to the generality of self-concept being investigated. That is, an adequate to high global self-concept is a reflection of the individual's assessment through experience of his ability to get on in general and an assessment of how he compares overall with his peers. Among lower socioeconomic groups, regardless of race (although it must be remembered that black and Spanish heritage groups have greater proportions at the lower socioeconomic levels), where emphasis on educational achievement is less than in the higher status groups, global self-concept need not be greatly affected by one facet, self-concept of academic ability, which might be less important to the individual adolescent.

Kleinfeld (1972), recognizing that "academic self-concept has been found to be strongly related to school achievement for both white students and Negro students" (p. 211), investigated the relative importance of teachers and parents in the formation of black and white students' academic self-concept. Although Brookover, Erikson, and Johnson (1967) had found that white students' parents' perceived evaluations were more strongly related to the students' academic self-concept than were the perceived evaluations of their teachers, Kleinfeld considered that "since Negro parents are less likely than white parents to be highly educated and expert on academic matters, their views on their children's academic potential may have less credibility than the evaluation of the teacher" (p. 211). Her findings confirmed Brookover's for the white sample, and her notion that black students' academic self-concept would be more strongly related to the teachers' perceived evaluation than their parents' was also confirmed. "The difference in the strength of the relationship between parents' and teachers' perceived evaluation and students' academic self-concept reached significance for the Negro females but not the Negro males" (Kleinfeld, 1972, pp. 211–12). Here we see sex differences operating more strongly on influences related to girls' self-concept of ability for blacks than on boys' self-concept of ability.

Boys do appear to suffer with lower grades, even when IQs are comparable. Teachers seem to be more harsh with boys and to be less accurate in their estimates of boys' achievement (Arnold, 1968). It may also be that because boys exhibit greater independence and are more restless, less conforming, and more assertive, they do not fit the model of orderly, disciplined, quiet behavior emphasized in most schools, and teachers may therefore underestimate their efforts and interests (McCandless, 1970).

A great number of motivational, interest, work-habit, and personality characteristics combine in various ways to determine school achievement. Overachievers, students whose achievement exceeds that predicted on the basis of their IQ scores, were found, in comparison with normal achievers or underachievers, to have better work habits and more interest in school; to be more persistent, more grade conscious, more responsible, more conscientious, and better organized; and to have higher self-esteem, greater acceptance of authority, more positive interpersonal relationships, a more realistic goal orientation, and better control over anxiety. Underachievers, on the other hand, combine some of the following characteristics: inability to delay gratification, greater impulsivity, less inhibition, poorer interpersonal relationships with peers, lower self-concept, low academic orientation but high social, pleasure-seeking orientation, and either unrealistic long-term goals or none at all. As is unfortunately the case when dealing with personality traits, the traits appear as separate and discrete labels of specialized aspects of behavior and do not necessarily cohere, or form a dynamic whole, to allow explanation and understanding of real people in real situations. The above listings are descriptive, but only of general trends. Some overachieving students may be overcompensating for feelings of inadequacy and inferiority. Some underachieving students may be disinterested and may begin to achieve when school catches up to them.

"Success in school depends less on the school than it does on what the youngsters bring to school with them (intelligence, ability to attend, perhaps degree to which they have developed inner control systems)" (McCandless, 1970, p. 277), and, we should add, although this is obviously related to development of internal control, a conception of their ability to succeed academically and an adequate or positive sense of competence.

McCandless' conclusion, which stresses the personal or self-influences on school success, was reached after reviewing the various contributing factors in this area. Among these is a most interesting relationship or nonrelationship between attitudes toward school and achievement. Lahaderne found no relationship between measures of students' attitudes toward their schools, schoolwork, teachers, and their scores on standardized achievement tests. Lahaderne described the typical classroom of her study, concluding: "In short, pupils were coaxed and compelled to adhere to a code of conduct that supported the order of the classroom. Thus, regardless of how he felt about school, the disgruntled pupil had little chance to do anything about it in the classroom" (1968, p. 324). She seemed to conclude that no correlation was found between school attitudes and achievement because bright children would be bored in such a classroom and slower children would be "bewildered."

Jackson and Lahaderne (1967) found that teachers were not at all accurate in assessing whether or not their pupils had positive attitudes toward school, schoolwork, or themselves, the teachers. To paraphrase P. G. Wodehouse, the teachers couldn't tell whether the students were actually disgruntled, but knew they were far from being gruntled. The assumption and logic of the argument in these two studies is that pupils have to present themselves in a manner that coheres to the orderly norms and standards of the classroom, that teachers in this setting cannot identify their pupils' satisfaction or dissatisfaction with school, and that the press to achieve is cloaked by this orderly behavior pattern.

"An alternative explanation might be that the individual brings a set toward satisfaction or dissatisfaction to the institution—that it is a reflection of a more pervasive personal orientation and that success or failure experiences within the institution have a limited influence upon it" (Jackson and Getzels, 1959, p. 295). Jackson and Getzels tested this alternative explanation on a large group of adolescents (whereas the Jackson and Lahaderne studies used sixth graders) using an instrument called the Student Opinion Poll. They determined two experimental groups—(1) the dissatisfied, and (2) the satisfied—which were made up of students who were considerably above or below the mean scores for the entire sample of 531 on this Student Opinion Poll instrument. The experimental groups were compared on a number of intelligence, achievement, personality, and teacher rating instruments. They also found that attitude toward school in neither group related to either intellectual ability or scholastic achievement. However, they did find that on each of the instruments that assessed psychological health or adjustment, the "satisfied" group attained "better" scores, i.e., the score indicating a higher, more adequate level of psychological functioning. In addition, teachers rated the "satisfied" boys higher than they did the "dissatisfied" boys, although this did not appear to be true for girls. This perhaps supports the popular expectation that girls are less likely to express negative feelings publicly than are boys. Jackson and Getzels summarized by saying that in order to understand dissatisfaction with school, data on psychological health may be more relevant than data on scholastic achievement. In addition, the girls who feel dissatisfied with school may be more likely to be feeling personal inadequacy, whereas dissatisfied boys may be characterized as having feelings that are critical of school authorities.

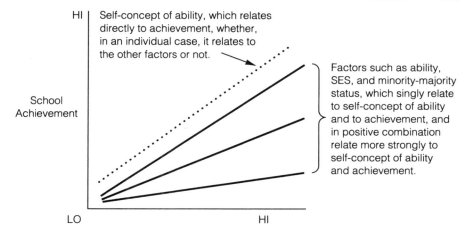

HI | Self-concept of ability, which relates directly to achievement, whether, in an individual case, it relates to the other factors or not.

School Achievement

Factors such as ability, SES, and minority-majority status, which singly relate to self-concept of ability and to achievement, and in positive combination relate more strongly to self-concept of ability and achievement.

LO   HI

Figure 11.1. Personal factors that relate to school achievement

Students with high academic self-concept have, according to Nelson (1984), families and classrooms that provide support and structure. Either helps, but both provide the most facilitative climates for development and maintenance of high scholastic self-concept.

This section, and Figure 11.1, have shown the continuing importance of self-concept and other variables pertaining to self and personality in relation to school achievement. However, it has also shown that as aspects of self and personality are related to variables such as sex, race, socioeconomic status, etc., the relationship of self-concept and achievement may be obscured. The interaction between the variables — that is, the ways in which the variables influence each other — in this instance, make less clear the major individual relationships with school achievement.

An adolescent who thinks well of himself and who has developed healthy and efficient coping strategies will probably be more successful in school than others. But influences on him not to succeed, such as low expectations of parents, peers, and teachers related to his race and/or class, can take their toll. However, the influence of the individual himself on the outcomes of his life, his achievement, are generally stronger than the other influences.

In the early 1960s I began teaching the fall semester in a school located in the center of a public-housing project on the west side of Chicago. The area was the most heavily patrolled in the city because it had the highest rate of violent crime. Almost all of the students qualified for free meals. We had a short written assignment the first day of class, and I was particularly taken with the paper by one young fellow. The theme was how he intended to make it to college and become an engineer. That first day, as he sat with a sparkle in his eye, dressed in a clean white shirt, I felt there was no stopping him, he would make it.

As the semester went on, the quality of his work never wavered. His attendance was perfect. Although he did not have the needed supplies, that was not unusual. All the teachers in the school bought supplies for the kids who could not afford them. Occasionally he dozed off in class. And his white shirt became progressively grayer. We spoke about life and his life, and eventually I had to request that outside agencies be brought in to help him. His mother worked the streets at night, slept during the day, and was seldom sober. He did not know who his father was, had no other relatives to turn to, and was locked out of the apartment most of the time. He had not slept in a bed for the first three weeks of school—he slept in hallways and stairwells. He was a poor, black, essentially parentless, urban ghetto kid. He had a sense of commitment, a desire, a feeling that he, himself, could make it. The year I knew him, he did.

This young fellow, on the basis of ethnicity and socioeconomic status, illustrates the following points, which cannot be overstressed:

> The socioeconomic status of students calculated on the basis of parent occupations and education almost invariably has a strong association with attainment of education and societal goals when the average attainment of large student aggregates is examined. On the other hand, using SES to predict an individual student's prospects for academic achievement, or future employment, is very liable to error.
>
> Students' ethnicity, especially their majority or minority ethnic status, relates strongly to the life prospects of aggregates of students, but again the prediction of individual achievement on this basis could easily be wrong. (Grannis, 1975, p. 1)

At the other extreme, while making the same point—and moving to the section on school influences—George Bernard Shaw said:

> "I was never in a school where the teachers cared enough about me, or about their ostensible profession, or had time enough to take any such troubles; so I learnt nothing at school, not even what I could and would have learned if any attempt had been made to interest me. I congratulate myself on this; for I am persuaded that every unnatural activity of the brain is as mischievous as any unnatural activity of the body, and that pressing people to learn things they do not want to know is as unwholesome and disastrous as feeding them on sawdust." He further asserted that even "experience fails to teach when there is no desire to learn." (Pearson, 1942, p. 14)

SCHOOL DIFFERENCES AND INFLUENCES

In the preceding section, we have seen the substantial degree to which individual differences in motivation, ability, sense of self-adequacy, and scholastic achievement are related. In this section, we will explore the influences of some particular facets of schools on achievement and pupil participation within those schools. This is a somewhat different perspective than is taken in most of this book. As adolescents develop, they are confronted with the life tasks, which present themselves differently and have potential for many successful outcomes for each adolescent. However, the life task as it applies to schools for adolescents is the one standard instance in which all adolescents confront the issues of their potential for contributing to their own lives and to mankind in a single, universally similar, institution outside the family.

In America, for all intents and purposes, every adolescent goes to school. There may be some differences between schools to accommodate particular handicaps, strengths, or interests of adolescents, but all adolescents go to school. Some adolescents, possibly because of other interests, but most usually with below-average ability and background factors that lessen or impede academic success, drop out of high school, but the great majority finish. These statements seem simplistic, but are stressing an important and oftimes overlooked fact. Compulsory education has been with us for many years. Of native-born school attenders, a high degree of literacy has been reached. Although critics galore will disagree, the paucity of findings showing impressive school effects on achievement may be the result of our having reached a plateau of good basic education for most of our adolescents. This is not to say, or even to imply, that higher levels cannot be reached through improvements, innovations, and changes in education. Rather, it is to say that maybe the inequities and differences among schools and school systems are not sufficiently great to allow empirical research findings that differentiate school effects.

What, then, are the findings on school effects? In a large-scale study of equality of educational opportunity carried out on behalf of the U.S. Office of Education, Coleman et al. concluded that: "Variations in school quality are not highly related to variations in achievement of pupils. . . . The school appears unable to exert independent influences to make achievement less dependent on the child's background" (1966, p. 297). Having reviewed studies at both the university and public school level, Nichols concludes:

> The largely negative results of studies of school effects suggest that in the United States, where some sort of education is available to everyone and the

mass media continually bombard us with seductive conceptual material (in other words, where very few suffer really drastic educational disadvantage), the family factor and the genetic factor are likely the major sources of individual differences in ability. (1973, pp. 138–39)

Johnston and Bachman say:

> There are differences between schools, to be sure, in terms of educational and occupational aspirations, test scores, values and attitudes, affective states, and so on. But when we ask what produces these differences, we find almost invariably that they can be attributed to individual differences in background and basic abilities. . . . In retrospect, the overall lack of differential school effects is not necessarily proof that schools are generally ineffective. It could just as well indicate that our schools, in conjunction with aspects of our culture, are succeeding in making equally rich educational opportunities available to nearly all who desired them. Perhaps a more realistic conclusion involves a balance between these two interpretations. (1973, pp. 236–37)

It may be that the key phrase in this quotation is "in conjunction with aspects of our culture." Differences between achievement levels of various minority groups have been attributed, at least in part, to differences in importance of education, attitude toward education, and view of what education may provide them, such as better jobs or a fuller life. These attitudes at specific levels pervade thinking within a subculture and affect the achievement levels reached by great numbers of pupils within the subculture. So too, the meaning and role of education as seen by vast numbers of the youth at any one time may be different from these views at another time.

When schooling is seen as a way of broadening oneself and an avenue for securing a better job and a better life by the majority of adolescents and adults, one would expect achievement levels nationally to be high or rising, with the most able, motivated, confident pupils still achieving above the average. However, during times when schools are under fire, either from critics or because the national economy is declining and myths of national glory are being shattered, one would expect achievement levels to be lowering — but the higher achievers will still be the individual students who are most motivated, with the most ability and the most self-esteem.

Hamilton summarizes the research on secondary schools, pointing out what the schools can do and the effect of other influences on their success:

> Secondary schools have the potential to foster adolescent development in four important ways that other environments either cannot do or cannot do as well: (a) they can teach adolescents knowledge and skills; (b) they can teach adolescents how to behave in a formal organization; (c) they can in-

troduce adolescents from diverse backgrounds to a common culture; and (d) they can engage adolescents in developmentally beneficial activities with their peers. The extent to which schools achieve this potential depends in large part on whether the other environments in which adolescents spend time reinforce or conflict with the schools' influence. In general, the environments of middle class white students reinforce the schools' beneficial influence, whereas those of lower class and minority students conflict in some serious ways with what the schools are supposed to do. (1984, p. 254)

There have been many innovations in public school education that have been largely geared to the three nonacademic areas and to the students whose environments are less supportive of educational achievement. Have these innovations or changes in educational practice negatively affected the achievement of students in reading and science nationally? Were these changes instituted consistently across the country in all school systems and are they so now? I think not in both cases. To some degree, there may be a lessening of academic emphasis in the public schools by teachers, administrators, and policy makers. However, the students who are being tested today and those who have been tested through the 1960s must all have been greatly affected by the events, changes, and atmosphere of the times, at least as much as by changes in educational practice. These "aspects of our culture," or influences of the times, may greatly influence national trends and changes in achievement levels. Would another sputnik affect achievement levels in science positively? Will a prolonged economic slump inspire students to perform at higher levels? The answers to these questions are certainly not clear. But the findings on school effects make illogical the conclusion that schools nationwide are suddenly less effective and are therefore producing lower achievement scores.

Efforts to determine the most effective organizational, structural, and personal attributes of school districts, schools, classrooms, and teachers have been extensive. The scarcity of findings relating these variables to student achievement is not for a want of looking. Some examples of studies and conclusions regarding school districts, schools, and teacher characteristics as they relate to student achievement follow and may assist in providing a better understanding of the immensity of the problem.

Bidwell and Kasarda (1975) used a "social-ecological" approach to ask whether, and how, various aspects of the organization of school districts in relation to environmental or demographic characteristics (what they called "environmental inputs") affect academic achievement level. This approach had not been well developed and previous research was uneven. Using data from 104 school districts in Colorado, Bidwell and Kasarda looked at the environmental conditions: school-district size, fiscal resources, percentage of disadvantaged students, educational level of adults, and percentage of population classified as nonwhite. These they related to organizational attributes (seen as the intervening variables): pupil-teacher ratio, administrative intensity—that is, the ratio of administrators to classroom teachers, professional support components, and the percentage of the total staff who held at least a master's degree. Both the environmental and the organizational variables were studied for their effect on reading and mathematics achievement. The researchers found that, as pupil-teacher ratios declined, as there were fewer pupils per teacher, achievement scores tended to rise. On the other hand, as administrative intensity rose, as there were more administrators in proportion to teachers, pupils' achievement scores went down. With better qualified teaching staffs, both math and reading achievement is higher. But administrative overhead seems to divert resources from teaching and instruction and has a negative effect on achievement.

In view of our previous conclusions regarding the paucity of findings about school effects on achievement, Bidwell and Kasarda's findings are especially striking. They clearly show that there are "certain ways in which the structure and staffing of school districts appear to transform inputs to school districts into outputs of student achievement" (p. 68). It appears from this study that by examining dependencies among the environmental and organizational aspects of school districts, particularly concerning qualifications of teachers, revenue, and size of district in conjunction with pupil-teacher ratio, effects of school on achievement may be seen.

The idea that "big is good" has long been a prevailing ethic in America (and an author writing in Texas must certainly be aware of that ethic). It has been incorporated into the thinking of educators because it has been assumed that larger school districts, and presumably larger schools, are better equipped to be effective and have more and more varied resources for instruction (Conant, 1967). Gump specifically asked the question of whether increasing school size produced a corresponding increase in variety of instruction. He very definitely confirmed this relationship, but he found it less than economical. It takes a 100 percent increase in size to realize a 17 percent increase in variety. "Since size increase, by itself, pays relatively poor dividends" (1966, p. 1), Gump suggests that educational planners look at strategies other than increased size.

From the perspective of behavior-setting theory (Barker, 1968), school activities may be seen as behavior settings—ecological-behavior units characterized by time and place, arrangement of people and objects, and patterns of behavior. Wicker (1968) summarizes work by Barker and his colleagues which indicates that the number of students in a high school relates to both the behaviors and the subjective experiences of the individual student in school-sponsored extracurricular activities. He concludes that students of small schools are more likely than students of large schools to become involved in a broader variety of activities, to attain more responsible positions in the activities they enter, to describe school activities in more varied ways, to achieve more satisfaction, involvement, challenge, and feelings for moral and cultural values, and to feel and report internal and external pressures — feel obligated — to attend, participate, and support activities.

Wicker conceives of the differences between large and small schools as relating, although not perfectly, to undermanning and overmanning of behavior settings. Undermanning was determined by calculating the number of students who attended an activity of that kind. The activities used for analysis were available at most high schools of any size — activities such as a varsity basketball game played at home, a class or club business meeting, a school play, an informal evening dance, a class or club money-raising project, and a school-sponsored or organized trip away from school. It seems clear that in a large school, unless it has an incredible number of activities, the number of students who are truly active in each setting would be a smaller percentage of the total group in attendance than would be the case in a small school, but more students would be available to participate in the large school. Wicker found "for five of the six kinds of behavior settings, undermanning is significantly greater in small than in large schools" (1968, p. 256). This conclusion means that in large schools, most activities are overmanned and some few are undermanned, whereas the opposite is true of small schools. In overmanned settings, fewer students who participate will be performers, whereas in undermanned settings, more students are likely to be performers. The average student, then, in a large school, would have fewer performances and experience in activities than would the average student in a small school. Through participation, the small-school student may feel greater confidence, more importance, more depended on, a stronger sense of obligation and responsibility for success, greater closeness with others, and a stronger feeling of accomplishment. Clearly, Wicker is supported in his feeling that school size, because of its effect on under- or overmanning and opportunity for individual performance, is an important influence on the experiences of students.

TEACHER CHARACTERISTICS AND INFLUENCES

Buxton (1973) studied four school systems in his analysis of adolescents in school. He refers to his conclusions as "sober" and "concerned," though some may consider them depressing: "What has determined the mismatch between adolescents and schools is to a large extent the unwillingness or incapability to adapt of the junior and senior high schools and the communities in which they serve. I have also come to feel that less than new 'programs' or facilities, a massive change in attitude of all persons concerned with the schools is necessary" (p. 123).

Although Buxton finds that, on the whole, students are not greatly enthusiastic about school, he also finds, in one of the few hopeful notes, that "it is typical for a student to believe that schooling can make a difference in his future" (p. 121). Another hopeful finding, which he found surprising, was that "on the whole, teachers are liked in every school, more by girls than by boys, and rather unclearly so by the more advanced students. . . . It nevertheless now suggests that teachers may be a positive resource for change" (p. 120). A most important aspect of studies of school effects or studies of teachers is teacher characteristics as they relate to student attitudes and achievement. It is to this feature of school effects that we now turn.

An extensive research literature into the relationship between teacher characteristics and student achievement exists, covering more than 50 years. By and large, significant relationships have not been demonstrated, but belief that a relationship exists continues. We all, from our personal educational experiences, can identify teachers we have had who are "better" and "worse," teachers from whom we have learned more, and teachers from whom we have learned less.

Heath and Nielson (1974) assessed a good number of reviews of the teacher-characteristics literature, citing Brim's (1958) conclusion and reiterating that reviews of the vast body of research on the subject do not show any consistent relationship between any teacher characteristic and teaching effectiveness. Mood, in the same vein, concluded that "we can only make the very useful observation that at the present moment we cannot make any sort of meaningful quantitative estimate of the effects of teachers on student achievement" (1970, p. 7). Heath and Nielson, citing background variables that we have not yet discussed, conclude that "given the well-documented, strong association between student achievement and variables such as socioeconomic status and ethnic status, the effect of techniques of teaching on achievement are likely to be inherently trivial" (1974, p. 481).

And yet the belief that a relationship exists between student achievement and the characteristics and behaviors of teachers has continued and begun to show some success. Rosenshine and Furst (1971), after reviewing some 50 studies in this area, propose 11 teacher-behavior variables they consider to be most promising. These are (1) clarity, (2) variability, (3) enthusiasm,

(4) task-oriented behaviors, (5) opportunity for students to learn material, (6) use of student ideas and general indirectness, (7) criticism, (8) use of structuring comments, (9) types of questions, (10) probing, and (11) level of difficulty of instruction.

Hamachek reviewed teacher variables related to motivation and learning and concluded that, in fact, there are characteristics that at least appear more consistently in teachers who are "high" or "low" in motivating students to learn. According to Hamachek, the characteristics that seem to be exhibited by teachers who are superior in "encouraging motivation and learning in students" are

> (1) willingness to be flexible, . . . ; (2) capacity to perceive the world from the student's point of view; (3) ability to "personalize" their teaching; (4) willingness to experiment, to try out new things; (5) skill in asking questions (as opposed to seeing self as a kind of answering service); (6) knowledge of subject matter and related areas; (7) skill in establishing definite examination procedures; (8) willingness to provide definite study helps; (9) capacity to reflect an appreciative attitude (evidenced by nods, comments, smiles, etc.); (10) conversational manner in teaching—informal, easy style. (1972, p. 237)

Excepting a few crucial cognitive and personality attributes that directly relate to the learning process, Ausubel is not at all enamored of the extensive research on personality characteristics because he sees a broad range of these characteristics as "compatible with effectiveness in teaching." He comes down hard on what he sees as an overemphasis on teacher characteristics presumed to relate to student mental health and personality development. It appears that for some teachers and teachers' educators today the sole standard and purpose of teaching are improved interpersonal relations and the development of positive self- and other attitudes. Teachers should not be selected for personality characteristics that theoretically relate to personality or mental health development. Their selection and evaluation should be according to "their ability to stimulate and competently direct pupil learning activity" (1968, p. 450). Ausubel goes so far as to cite evidence that pupils are primarily concerned with their teacher's ability to teach, and not merely concerned with having kindly, sympathetic, and cheerful teachers (Taylor, 1962). Recognizing the full scope of the teacher's role as socializer and "facilitator of personality development," Ausubel analyzes teacher characteristics as they relate to achievement within a perspective that sees it as "undeniable that the teacher's most important and distinctive role in the modern classroom is still that of director of learning activities" (1968, p. 450).

Teachers in this country, by virtue of their training and selection within the training institution, are generally above a certain minimal level of intelligence that is necessary to be an effective teacher, and therefore the relationship between teacher's effectiveness and teacher's intelligence is found to be low because of the limited and higher range of intelligence of teachers. Certain aspects of the teachers' academic preparation as well as their orderliness and systematic approach to running a classroom and teaching have been found to relate at fairly low levels to student achievement, although some presume that they have a somewhat larger effect.

Yet from all the teacher characteristic variables that have so far been investigated, and probably from the extensive number of variables that have not yet been investigated, the relationship with effective teaching produces at best low correlations. "The two principal exceptions to this generalization are warmth and understanding, on the one hand, and a tendency to be stimulating and imaginative, on the other" (Ausubel, 1968, pp. 453–54). These two exceptions fit well with Ausubel's statement that "perhaps the most important personality characteristic of teachers influencing their effectiveness is the extent of their personal commitment to the intellectual development of pupils" (p. 455). Teachers committed to student learning may not always appear warm and understanding to even a trained observer. But students in interaction with their teachers day after day come to know who is really interested and willing to make the effort and sacrifice to help them. This commitment, I believe, reaches the adolescent as warmth and understanding even if masked by a cold exterior. Commitment to the students' intellectual development, not commitment to a particular teaching style or commitment to maintaining one's personal status and protecting and defending one's self, demands being flexible. Commitment to the students' intellectual development demands that the teacher try everything within her ability and bag of tricks to stimulate and encourage the imagination and ability of her students. As Ausubel laments, however, commitment is a difficult factor to measure, and no objective evidence exists of its generally acknowledged value. Students who are bound and determined to learn will probably do so regardless of their teachers. But teachers bound and determined to teach may do so even with students less interested in learning.

A new approach, process-product, or process-outcome, research, which looks at the relationship between teacher behavior (rather than teacher characteristics) and student achievement, has proliferated and built a clear and useful base for better understanding student achievement and teaching. Brophy (1986) summarized this research and found that:

> At least two common themes cut across the findings. . . . One is that achievement is influenced by the amount of time that students spend en-

gaged in appropriate academic tasks. The second is that students learn more efficiently when their teachers first structure new information for them and help relate it to what they already know, and then monitor their performance and provide corrective feedback during recitation, drill, practice, and application activities. . . .

Those (teachers) who do these things successfully produce significantly more achievement than those who do not, but doing them successfully demands a blend of energy, motivation, subject matter knowledge, and pedagogical skills that many teachers, let alone ordinary adults, do not possess. (1986, p. 1076)

From all of the preceding discussion, our general conclusion must be that professional knowledge and skills as well as personal characteristics and motivation of teachers influence student achievement.

SOCIAL-CLASS INFLUENCES

The concept of social class is global. It cuts across other social groupings in our society, such as racial, ethnic, and religious groups. We may think of American society in toto as composing a single culture, the American culture — the attitudes, beliefs, and behaviors that are common to or most typical of Americans. But there is enormous variation within this culture. It is composed of subcultures that may be considered horizontal and vertical. By virtue of shared attitudes, beliefs, and behaviors, subgroups based on ethnicity, race, or geographic area may be seen as comprising the various subcultures that cut vertically across the American culture. We see these subcultures as vertically cutting across the horizontal layers, the ranked, structured, hierarchical levels of social classes. Ethnic, racial, and geographic subcultures cut across all levels of social classes. All groups — Catholics, Protestants, and Jews, Polish-Americans, Italian-Americans, Irish-Americans, whites, blacks, and Chicanos — may be found at all social-class levels from the lower to the upper. The relative distribution, or proportion, of each subcultural group in the various social classes may differ for historical and other reasons. Conversely, each social class — working, middle, and upper — cuts across the racial, ethnic, religious, and geographic subcultures.

> Social classes constitute subcultural groups. When people from the same social class meet and converse, they soon find they have much in common, even though they may come from different ethnic or religious backgrounds or from different sections of the country. They will find that they live in much the same kinds of neighborhoods, have similar eating habits, dress in pretty much the same ways, have rather similar tastes in furniture, litera-

ture, and recreation, and have about the same amount of education. (Havighurst and Neugarten, 1967, p. 9)

Try to visualize any axis at which a vertical subculture such as Italian-American meets the horizontal subculture of social class. There are ways in which the persons at that axis are similar in beliefs, attitudes, and behavior to all other Italian-Americans up and down the vertical ethnic subculture lines. So, too, these Italian-Americans are similar in beliefs, attitudes, and behaviors to most other persons falling along the horizontal social-class subcultural line. The combined wisdom of social-class studies in this country and across countries indicates that persons of the same social class, differing in ethnic, religious, etc., subcultures, will be more similar in their general way of life to the others of their same social class than they will be to members of their same ethnic, religious, or racial subcultures of other social classes.

Social stratification, the ranking of people hierarchically within a society according to their degree of economic and political power, and social prestige are recognized, if not readily accepted, by most people. They may with little difficulty, as Warner et al. (1960) illustrated, rank themselves and persons near them or of whom they are aware as being at the same level or higher or lower than they are in power and prestige on a social ladder, thus creating a social scale.

The major dimensions underlying the social-class structure in America have been defined by Kahl (1957). They are prestige (as shown in the amount of respect and deference a person receives), occupation (considered higher or lower on the basis of contribution to the welfare of others, particular or special abilities, and extent of reward), wealth (income or holdings), social interaction (whom one usually socializes with, one's own kind), class consciousness (seeing oneself or feeling oneself as working class or middle class, union/labor or management), shared value orientations, and the actual or perceived ability to control the actions or outcomes for other people (power or clout). In itself, occupation is probably the single best indicator of an individual's status. Occupation, like all of the dimensions, may be studied independently, but all are in general related. Persons high or low on any one dimension are likely to be similarly positioned on the others. This similarity across dimensions constitutes social class.

In respect to the dimensions of social class delineated by Kahl, children and adolescents cannot be said to possess most of the characteristics of the dimensions on their own behalf. They come, through the process of learning and socialization, to develop a class consciousness to some degree, value orientations, and social interactions with "their own kind." But in the main, children and adolescents derive their status and are members of a social class through their parents. The child and adolescent become a part of, learn to be a part of, the social class of their parents and experience their mobility or lack of social mobility. The child and adolescent may be said to have

> the experience of growing up in a certain social class. The existence of a so-cial structure based largely on occupational differentiation gives all people common perceptions of society and of the occupational and personal charac-teristics that determine status in that society. The membership of a person in a particular social class, then, gives him certain attitudes toward educa-tion, property, family relations, and certain occupational aspirations that he shares with people of similar social class in other societies. (Manaster and Havighurst, 1972, p. 4)

The adolescent in and from his family is part of a fairly clear social class. His associations and interactions with friends are more intimate, more com-fortable with "his own kind," with other adolescents of his same social class. The pervasive and multidimensional quality of social class makes it a difficult but important concept to use in explaining school achievement and family and peer influences on school achievement.

Swift (1967) has suggested that the use of the concept of social class is too crude to explain differences in home environment and differences in school achievement. However, research over the last 50 years has consistently emphasized that educational achievement of middle-class children is su-perior to that of working-class children, and correlations on the order of .30 to .35 between social class and academic achievement are customarily found. A study by Miller (1970) attempted to get at factors, clusters of variables, that would suggest explanations for social-class differences in achievement. More-over, Miller hypothesized that these factors, derived from variables thought to differentiate between social classes, would be more directly associated with academic achievement than would the global concept of social class. Almost 500 children from the top classes of 10 primary schools — 5 from middle-class and 5 from working-class districts — completed an inventory designed to elicit their own perceptions of their environment. Five of the 8 factors derived from the inventory responses may be considered to help "explain" social-class differences in educational development and achievement. The factors la-beled "desire for education," "intellectual enterprise," and "confidence and parental support" correlated positively with social class and with academic achievement, whereas the factors labeled "general deprivation" and "domi-nant parent-submissive child" were negatively correlated with achievement.

As shown in Figure 11.2, the variables generally found in the middle to upper social classes favor school achievement, whereas the variables found in the lower occupational levels are negatively correlated with achievement.

Generally Lower SES Students	Generally Middle and Higher SES Students
• Parents have less education • Less intellectual home environment • Parents stress behavior in school more than learning • Parents less involved in studies and school issues • Parents show less confidence and support • Lower educational and occupational aspirations • Peer group does not value education	• Parents have more education • More intellectual home environment • Parents stress importance of learning and education • Parents more involved in studies and school issues • Parents show more confidence and support • Higher educational and occupational aspirations • Peer group does value education

Figure 11.2. Some aspects of social class related to achievement

However, as Miller states, "this is only a weak tendency" (1970, p. 267). That means that a family of higher social class may have characteristics that have been found to relate negatively with school achievement. In like manner, a low socioeconomic family may exhibit those characteristics positively correlated with achievement.

This is an important point. In this study, as in so many others, social class is assumed to be different from the variables that make up social class. However, the differentiation is by no means perfect. As in any comparison between groups, particularly on global measures such as social class, we analyze degree of relationship or degree of difference. Almost always groups overlap, which in this instance is confirmed by Miller's statement that a family of high social class may have characteristics that are negatively associated with achievement, that more usually would be associated with families of lower social class, and vice versa. Miller concludes on the basis of his findings that there is a more direct association between the environmental factors and achievement than with social class, that the factors themselves have higher correlations with academic achievement than has social class, and that social class is of less importance in predicting or determining achievement—it is too vague a concept to be explanatory. Nonetheless, the notion of social class, with its easy access and general understanding by educators and to some degree the lay public, is valuable for predicting and understanding achievement. The more specific variables or factors would almost by definition be more clearly related to academic achievement, but would be much more difficult to determine in the individual case than would social class.

Although researchers' belief in the impact of socioeconomic status on achievement seems to ebb and flow over the decades, some effect is almost always acknowledged, and conclusions such as Stockard, Lang, and Wood's are most usual. Their results from a study of high school seniors who graduated from a predominantly white, western city, "suggest that the influence of social class is significant. . . . There was little indication that status variables were a less important influence on grades in the later years of school. . . . Social class and gender influenced students' grades. These influences consistently worked to the advantage of middle class females and to the disadvantage of working class males" (1985, pp. 17–18).

People working with adolescents, particularly teachers and others related to education, become very aware of differences in attitudes toward school, work habits, sense of competence or self-concept of academic ability, and educational and occupational aspirations as they differ by social class and relate to differences in academic achievement. These educators become equally well aware of exceptions to the "social class by academic achievement" relationship. It is thought by many that the expectations of teachers for students of differing social classes may influence the students' achievement. Conversely, however, the adolescents themselves are aware of and hold, with the variations within social classes of which we have spoken, expectations and aspirations for their own behavior and success that they think are appropriate to their own social class. Parents of middle- and upper-class children have traditionally been more interested in and more encouraging of their children's careers in school and afterwards than have parents of children in lower socioeconomic groups. Parents at the lowest level, the lower-lower social class, have been by far the least encouraging and expected the least of their children. School success has long-term implications for higher education, future occupation, future associations, and maintenance of social status or upward mobility. In addition to the direct influences on achievement resulting from class consciousness, varying satisfactions of basic needs (health care, home stability, etc.) related to social class may also influence achievement.

A study by Harrison investigates social class/home background, school success, and attitude of adolescents. This study assumed and found expected social-class differences while pursuing further the question of students whose performances are not as expected. Harrison started with the proposition that most students who succeed in school come from advantaged home backgrounds, whereas most students who do not succeed are from disadvantaged home backgrounds. But there are students who do not fit, who are inconsistent with, this proposition: advantaged students with expectations for school success who are not successful and disadvantaged students who are successful. "It was hypothesized that the attitudes of the inconsistent students would be incongruent with those of their associated majority group who, for the advantaged, non-successful students, were the advantaged, successful students, and, for the disadvantaged, successful students, were the disadvantaged, non-successful students" (1968, p. 334).

The hypothesis was confirmed. The attitudes of the inconsistent students were not congruent with those of their like majority groups, advantaged-successful, disadvantaged-nonsuccessful. With the exception of attitudes toward education, which did not distinguish between advantaged and disadvantaged or successful and nonsuccessful students, but was positive for all, the attitudes of the successful students were similar and the attitudes of the nonsuccessful students were similar regardless of advantaged or disadvantaged position. The successful students' views were more positive for the scales investigated, with the disadvantaged-successful students expressing the most optimistic view of the future of all groups.

On the scales investigated in this study, view of the environment (that man can/cannot gain control of his environment), attitude toward education (that it is of little value/of real value), attitude toward school groups (that association with school groups may be a waste of time/of real value), and peer-group attitude toward education (that the student's peer group did not/did value education), there are social-class, advantaged-disadvantaged, differences in attitudes and related differences in school success. Seemingly, a student with the preferred, positive attitude will be successful in school regardless of advantaged or disadvantaged status, whereas a student with negative attitudes will not be successful. But the fact remains that the attitudinal differences usually coincide with social-class differences and school success.

The conclusive and pervasive influence of social class on adolescents in school summarized by Charters still pertains:

> To categorize youth according to the social class position of their parents is to order them on the extent of their participation and degree of "success" in the American educational system. This has been so consistently confirmed by research that it now can be regarded as an empirical law. . . . It seems to hold in any educational institution, public or private, where there is some diversity in social class. . . . Social class position predicts grades, achievement and intelligence test scores, retentions at grade level, course failure, truancy, suspension from school, high school dropout, plans for college attendance, and total amount of formal schooling. It predicts academic honors and awards in the public school, elected school officers, extent of participation in extracurricular activities and in social affairs sponsored by the school, to say nothing of a variety of indicators of "success" in the formal structure of the student's society. (1963, p. 739)

THE DROPOUT PROBLEM

Briefly, following, is a framework for understanding the complexity of the dropout problem and a suggested approach for dealing with that problem that emphasizes within school methods. This section is an excerpt from a report I submitted to the Texas Legislature's Joint Special Interim Committee on High School Dropouts, in December 1987.

In brief, the framework outlined here states that dropping out is caused by one or both of two types of problems for the adolescent: (a) personal, family, economic, and social problems, and (b) school difficulties, academic or social. Usually if one type of problem becomes sufficiently serious, problems of the other type arise.

The greatest need for dealing with these problems is flexibility on the part of the school personnel so that they can (a) deal with other agencies to assist the child with personal, familial, economic, and social problems, and (b) appropriately use the vast array of potential options, from teaching methods to alternative school organization, to assist the child with school-related problems.

Who are the dropouts? One of the things I do at the University is teach, or educate or train school counselors. One Friday this semester I met a high school counselor at my house in the early evening for an individual session to go over cases she is seeing at her school. We can't get together during anything like normal hours, teachers and counselors don't have "normal" hours.

We talked about four kids she was counseling at school.

The first was a 15-year-old, ninth-grade, boy who sees the counselor regularly for support sessions, though the boy wouldn't call them that, he comes in "when he has to talk." He told the counselor about a dream he had been having that bothered him. It can be interpreted as a dream of defeat, of being held back and abused for wanting to run and fly and be more than he is. No one in the boy's family has ever graduated from high school and they don't want him to either. They want him to go to work.

The second kid was 16, living with her boyfriend, working 30 hours a week, attending school regularly and getting good grades, anxious, confused, and tired. She goes to the counselor for support and for guidance. Her parents had thrown her out because she missed curfew.

The 15-year-old boy who we then spoke about had been expelled from school for three days for coming to school drunk. His mother works two jobs to sustain herself and the four children. His father, when not in the State hospital, remains unemployed and depressed, generally in his room with the shades pulled. The boy was very angry about being expelled. He made Regionals in UIL math last year and is president of the computer club.

The last girl we discussed is 15 also. She has a friend who says he can get her a job with him at $8 an hour. The girl has five unexcused absences this semester. The rules are that she therefore cannot receive credit for her classes, which she is otherwise passing, so she told the counselor she thought she might as well drop out.

These cases are not unusual. We have held intensive seminars for school counselors at the University the past two summers. Following is a sampling of potential dropout cases the counselors discussed at the seminars. Cases where mothers encourage their teenage, and early teenage, daughters to have children because they had or it is not seen as a problem; cases where young girls have their fathers' children and their mothers agree to take care of the children; cases where family feuds encroach on the school day and boys and girls fight for their family's honor in halls and counselors' and principals' offices; cases where kids have to take care of their younger siblings on a routine basis and thus miss so much school they are held back again and again; cases where the kid can't go home because the mother brings men to the home at all times of the day and night; cases where adults in the home are going to abuse them if they come home; and cases from more affluent homes where the kid shuttles between parents in different cities at the parents' convenience and feels he doesn't belong anywhere, or where the kid hasn't seen a parent in weeks because the parents are at work or at meetings or even traveling, holidaying, in Europe; and cases where the kid is doing poorly in school because, he says, his folks only give him $20 for an A and $10 for passing while his friends get $50 for As, $40 for Bs and $25 for passing; and cases where the kid does poorly because there is no way he can achieve to the level his parents demand; and cases where the student can do all the work and pass tests with A grades but hates to go to class where he or she is invariably disinterested and often disruptive. And immigrant kids have additional types of problems. And kids with disabilities have additional types of problems. And foster kids have special problems. And kids who are gifted and talented have problems that some would think enviable, but problems nonetheless. . . . And that is a sample of the kinds of problems that kids in school have which influence dropping out.

The schools are repositories for all of society's ills and problems, and all of the ills and problems contribute to the dropout problem. Society has asked indirectly, even directly demanded in some instances, that the schools solve these problems. Unbelievably, to me, the schools try to do all of this. Our public schools, most of which are very similar, with only slight deviations one to another, try to accommodate all of the kids from all of the backgrounds with all of the personalities for all of the purposes.

Clearly the schools cannot, singlehandedly, solve all of our society's problems from racism to sexism to elitism, the balance of payments and the national debt. However, in the individual student's case the schools could, if given the flexibility and the resources, oftimes, alleviate the problem for the student and, overall, increase the numbers of students remaining in school to graduation.

CONCLUSIONS: NECESSARILY TENTATIVE

The concentration in this chapter about school and adolescence has been on academic achievement and success in school as defined by the schools and those who make these definitions for the schools. We have seen that there are enormous numbers of influences on the success of students, as individuals and as members of groups, that are relatively more and less important. And probably most important for the prospective teacher, the current teacher, the prospective parent, and the current parent is the enormous individual variation in ways of responding to all influences that have been mentioned.

It seems clear that adolescents from homes that foster educational achievement by virtue of parental interest and encouragement both personally and materially will more probably have higher aspirations and expectations, a more positive sense of their own abilities, a more positive self-concept, and more success in high school. That families from some socioeconomic statuses and ethnic groups rather than others are more apt to foster educational achievement is also evident.

The school an adolescent goes to, because of its own achievement ethic or one fostered by a high-achieving, higher social-status student body, may have a positive effect on academic achievement. The individual teacher, by virtue of education and skill, interest and commitment, may positively affect a great number of students, and still, many teachers may influence students for special, probably very human, reasons that we do not yet know.

Nonetheless, any one student, regardless of socioeconomic background, regardless of parental encouragement or the nature of his home life, regardless of biases and discriminations against him on the basis of sex, ethnicity, or race, may still regard himself as an adequate and able person and, if he has the ability as well as this conception of his ability, may well be successful.

Although this chapter has dwelled more an academic achievement, the schools that adolescents attend are also the settings for good portions of their activities in the other life tasks. In and around schools, friends are made and lost, organizations and extensions of activities into the community are joined and developed, stronger love attachments begin, exposure to persons of differing religious and philosophical orientations occur, and the individual — the self — reacts to and develops with all of these. Many of these issues are dealt with in their appropriate chapters, but many of the interactions spoken about in those chapters occur in and about schools. Moreover, the ability of adolescents to cope with the other tasks oftimes affects their academic and social success in school.

Work

The life task work "means contributing to the welfare of others" (Dreikurs, 1953, p. 4). The variety of ways in which one can work for the welfare of others is immense and probably endless. The connection between formal work, a job, and its contribution to the welfare of others may sometimes be indirect and obscure. As one produces, serves, as one's efforts culminate in the maintenance of life or improvement in the quality of life, one's work can be said to be contributing to the welfare of others. Concurrently, as a person benefits from her work, carries her own weight, she is not a burden on others and in most cases is contributing to the welfare of those close to her. Women who choose to be housewives contribute most directly to the welfare of others while maintaining a home and providing security, nurturance, and child rearing. The person who makes no efforts to maintain and advance lives of others in her immediate environment, in her family, or in her society in general cannot be said to work.

Mowsesian points out that since its inception the ethic in the United States is that work is a moral imperative, "a 'good,' signifying man's worth and dignity to self and society" (1986, p. 29). We come to define ourselves, and others come identify us, by our work. In some ways for all people, and in most important ways for some people, we are identified as our work and our success in our work.

WORKING HIGH SCHOOL STUDENTS

Our major interest in this text is adolescence through high school. Early adolescents are not likely to work for many reasons, not the least of which is state laws that prohibit adolescents below certain ages from working. The Department of Labor's Bureau of Labor Statistics generally considers 16 as the earliest age at which persons work, and its data, which begin with that age, show what has been a continuing trend, that somewhere in the area of 50 percent of high school seniors and a considerable proportion of high school juniors, both girls and boys, work for pay during the school year. Steinberg et al. (1982) estimate that by high school graduation 80 percent of all adolescents will have had some type of job.

Of those students who want to work, and who are therefore considered in the labor force, unemployment rates are "high relative to the rates for other segments of the population" (about 13 percent in 1979), but "the unemployment rates for youths in and out of school were about the same or slightly lower in October 1979 than in October 1970," with "the major exception . . . the situation among black youths: the unemployment rate of black students (34.2 percent in October 1979) had increased about 9 percentage points over the decade" (Bureau of Labor Statistics, *School and Work among Youth during the 1970s*, January 1981).

Some question the value of work for youth in school. Before looking at that question directly, it may be worth looking further at the effects of unemployment on youth, both as an indirect comment on the value of work and as an area of interest itself. "Studies on the psychological consequences of unemployment tend to point in the same direction—namely that unemployment causes stress, a lowering of self-esteem and a change in expectations. . . . If, for any reason, the young people are unable to find a job, they might lose self-esteem, become physically ill and might change their expectation of getting a job. Lowered job expectations will no doubt affect jobsearch strategies, which in turn lower the probability of getting a job, so confirming the belief" (Furnham, 1985, p. 121). The vicious circle of unemployment, which is found for youth as well as for adults, must, obviously, be more dramatic and devastating for youth whose personal views are reinforced by those around them, as is the case for ghetto black youth, among whom unemployment is highest. However, for the individual adolescent or the adolescent surrounded by others in the same boat, unemployment hurts in the present and may continue to hurt in the future.

If being unable to find work is harmful to a high school student, does it follow that working is helpful? The work high school students find is not usually directly related to the work they will do when they finish their education, either high school or college, or to their careers, the work that they will do for most of their lifetimes. Jobs for high school students are usually low-level service jobs, basic laboring jobs, floor sales jobs, and the like. In my area, kids put most of the groceries on the shelves, do most of the checking out, and carry the bags to the car. It is most usual to buy your fast food from a teenager at the counter, and the proverbial "soda jerk" is now a uniformed Baskin-Robbins or Swenson's employee, but still 16 years old.

Two curvilinear relationships found in the literature speak to the issues of who works and what they get out of it. Young (1979) and the National Center for Educational Statistics (1981) point to a curvilinear relationship between socioeconomic status and labor force participation: youth labor market participation increases from lower to middle income levels and then decreases at the upper-middle and upper income levels. Schill, McCartin, and Meyer surveyed over 4,500 Washington State high school students and found a curvilinear relationship between GPA and hours employed: "Students who work less than 20 hours have the highest average GPA, while those working more than 20 hours and those who are unemployed have lower GPAs" (1985, p. 160).

Juxtaposing these two findings leads to an interesting observation: those students who are least needy tend not to work, and those who are most needy tend not to work or not to be able to find employment; those who are unable to find work and those who do find work and work a lot, over 20 hours a week, do not do as well in school as those who do find work and work less. The middle-class students who hold reasonable part-time jobs do well in school. It seems as if those who work to make the most of the opportunity to work benefit most all around, whereas those who need to work the most and probably need to work hardest in school suffer in school for their extra outside work. In any event, "it appears that working in excess of 15 or 20 hours weekly during the school year is more than the average adolescent can handle without work taking its toll on health and on commitments to potentially important nonwork activities" (Steinberg et al., 1982, p. 394).

Work for pay for high school students may provide experience that allows and facilitates more sophisticated occupational decision making. But most high school students who work are doing so, it would appear, to promote values as found by Coleman (1961): high school boys highly value auto ownership and girls value physical beauty, social success, and nice clothes. Moreover, girls who work may be attempting to ensure economic security in order to marry early.

Rice gives seven reasons why the work experience in adolescence is helpful:

> By working the adolescent learns that work is an important and necessary part of life. . . . Working teaches the adolescent responsibility, cooperation, punctuality, and industry. . . . Working helps the adolescent learn social skills and how to get along with many different types of people in a variety of situations. . . . Through working, the adolescent develops au-

tonomy and independence. . . . Working helps the adolescent develop self-assurance, a feeling of self-worth, and to develop his own concept of self. . . . Work enables the adolescent to earn money for things he needs now and in the future. . . . Properly selected work can provide relevant training for the adolescent for a future career. (1975, pp. 400–401)

This list bears most strongly on the value of work in adolescence, summating in a young adult who is prepared to work and is knowledgeable about work. Job experience has been shown to relate to satisfactory vocational choice (Hurlock, 1975). These values of work also begin the process of developing vocational values that continually evolve throughout an individual's working years. By the time one is in the late twenties, primary vocational decisions have been made and stability of vocational choice increases thereafter. Sometimes people change jobs because their interests change, but by and large, job changes are within the same broad vocational categories. The adolescent who works seemingly has an advantage in having begun to appraise his occupational values and develop skills related to working.

The degree to which the reasons given by Rice for adolescents' work experience are helpful can be seen to overlap with, and ease the burden of, the following list of factors, which makes vocational choice difficult:

- The ever-increasing number of different kinds of work from which to choose
- Rapid changes in work skills due to increased use of automation
- Long and costly preparation, which makes job shifts impossible
- Unfavorable stereotypes of some occupations
- A desire for a job that will give an individual a sense of identity, rather than one that makes him feel like a cog in a large machine
- The individual's ignorance of his own capacities due to lack of job experience or vocational guidance
- Unrealistic vocational aims carried over from adolescence
- Unrealistic vocational values, especially concerning prestige and autonomy (Hurlock, 1975, p. 233)

Comparing these two lists, one can see that the adolescent who works and develops skills related to work, social skills, independence, self-assurance, and understanding of some occupations eliminates a number of the factors that make vocational choice difficult. This adolescent could then confront the difficulty factors that are inherent in the magnitude of occupational choices open to persons in a dynamic, developed, changing society.

VOCATIONAL CHOICE AND DEVELOPMENT THEORIES

It seems useful to introduce in this section some examples from the multitude of theories of vocational choice and development. There are theories of vocational choice grounded in the economic, cultural, sociological, and psychological disciplines as well as interdisciplinary theories.

A cultural and sociological theory of vocational choice described by Super and Bachrach (1957) includes a model in which the individual is seen at the center of a series of concentric circles that represent the social systems with which he interacts. These systems influence his occupational decisions and choices. Moving from the most distant social system to the social system closest to and most directly affecting the individual's decisions are the general cultural variables, such as Western, Eastern, or Eurasian; the subcultural forces, such as social class, geographic region, and racial background; community variables, such as ethnic group, peer group, and neighborhood; and finally, home, school, and church. At the center of the circle is the individual with his personality—seen in terms of traits or reality testings and subdecisions, perceiving the social systems of influences on him from his personal and biased apperception. And somewhere, probably clouding this entire picture, is serendipity.

Luck, fate, chance, and accident are the reasons given by most laymen for their vocational choices. This popular notion, called the accident theory of vocational choice, may be defined as follows: "Chance factors are the fortuitous, unplanned, unpredicted events which affect a person's vocational choice" (Crites, 1969, p. 80). Not only laymen subscribe to this theory—Miller and Form, occupational sociologists, studied the occupational background of a large sample of young people and concluded:

> One characteristic is outstanding in the experience of most of the case histories that have been cited. In their quest of a life work there has been a vast amount of floundering, and chance experiences appear to have affected choices more than anything else. It is the compounding of various experiences and influences which has finally crystallized into a wish for a certain occupation. Chance experiences undoubtedly explain the process by which most occupational choices are made. (1951, p. 660)

The social or behavioral scientist aspires to an understanding of any facet of human behavior within a framework, theoretical and then verifiable, of laws or rules that account for as much as possible of the variance and variability of the behavior in this area. A theory in the area of vocational choice based on accident or chance is alien to and discomforting for most behavioral scientists.

However, each of us, within our own experience, is aware of the operation of the accident theory, personally and among friends. You can think of people you have known in this situation and I will give you some examples of persons I have known. I know a highly successful businessman who left a university where he was a promising anthropology student, on the death of his father, because he had to support the family; a clergyman who, when "turned on by a campus minister," changed his major from pre-med; a bartender whose part-time bartending job became his career and who never returned for his second year in law school; a high school honor graduate who gave up a college scholarship and became an apprentice in a building trade when his father's bowling-team partner told him of an opening; a physician whose uncle said he would pay for her schooling if she would become an M.D., an option she had not previously considered; a talent agent whose connections and experience in this field began when she represented her first love, an entertainer, to the media, etc., etc. And I know a young fellow who had been offered a job as a truck driver who turned it down until the day he fell in love with a car in a used car lot. That day he dropped out of high school, took the driver's job, and put a down payment on the car, and he has been driving and out of school ever since.

"If I had known then what I know now" often prefaces the explanation or lament of a vocational decision that in retrospect an individual considers wrong for him. This may mean that as an adolescent this person did not understand the economic and status aspects of the job chosen, although in the main, adolescents seem to rank occupations about as accurately as adults do. Of course, there may be something peculiar to a particular job that made it a bad choice for the individual. The statement that began this paragraph reflects an individual's acknowledgment that the job chosen does not fit his personality or interests. That may be because he is more (or less) able — has a higher or lower sense of competence, self-concept — than he thought or felt when he chose the job. Or it may be because he has changed, developed, since that vocational choice. Psychological theories of vocational choice emphasize personality and personality traits, matching of interests and abilities with choice, self-concept commensurate with choice, and development of rationales and reality testing for making vocational decisions.

The idea behind all psychological theories is that the individual can systematically choose an occupation to enter, or at least that there is a substantial element of choice in the decision. Even in analyzing the previous examples of the accident theory of vocational choice, the psychological theories presume that a person would not make such a decision except as individual interests, values, sense of ability, and competence led him or her to do so.

The trait- and factor-matching theories of vocational choice, generally accepted in this country until the early 1950s, were first explicated by Parsons in a three-step process for choosing a vocation that a person was said to go through. With a clear understanding of himself and his aptitudes, abilities, strengths, and weaknesses, and knowledge of all aspects of various occupations, the individual was said to make his decision through the third step, "true reasoning on the relations of these two groups of facts" (1909, p. 5).

In a general way, the notion that by matching his abilities and dispositions with the demands of a particular occupation, an individual makes his occupational choice underlies the thinking of laymen and many counselors in explaining and understanding occupational choice. Unfortunately, the research relating occupations to the personalities of the members of those occupations has not supported this theory. Super and Crites observed that the assumed relationships between particular personality traits and choice and adjustment in certain occupations, as in "social dominance and selling, submissiveness and bookkeeping" (1962, p. 516), have rarely been found.

Borow (1973) points out that the trait-matching approach has proved static and does not account for the psychology of motivation and human development. The traits exhibited by a high school freshman that may be thought to relate to a particular vocational choice may not be the same traits exhibited by that student as a high school senior, and ambitions and aspirations may also change. One wonders whether the traits appropriate to the conductor of a major symphony orchestra are more easily specifiable than the traits appropriate for being in sales—whether selling door-to-door, representing a corporation, or being a sales engineer for an international conglomerate. Contemporary trait theory presumes that "the more generalized the activity, on a scale ranging from specific position, to job, to occupation, to occupational group, the larger is the number of (trait) patterns applicable to the activity" (Super and Bachrach, 1957, p. 102).

The psychodynamic and developmental theories of vocational choice elaborate on both the factors preceding choice and the changing factors or considerations in choice. The theories developed by Roe, Holland, Ginsberg, and Super are most prominent and illustrative of psychodynamic and developmental theories of vocational choice. Some short indication of the content of these most influential theories of vocational choice follows. The validity of the theories is not sufficiently established to allow one to conclude that there is *a* way of assisting adolescents in their career choice. However, counselors and parents are called on to give advice in this area. And teachers, explicitly and implicitly, offer advice in this area all the time. When a teacher turns a student on to a particular subject, a career option may be opening.

When a teacher encourages a student by rewarding a set of behaviors, the student may begin to work on the notion that this is something he can do well. And of course, when a teacher expresses a value judgment on the status or the sex-role appropriateness of a job, the teacher may be influencing the students' choices. Lastly, when students seek advice from teachers rather than presenting purely personal opinion, a sense of the field may be helpful to the teacher. For these reasons the following theories are presented.

ROE'S NEED THEORY

Roe's theory (Roe, 1956, 1957; Roe and Siegelman, 1964) is a need theory of vocational choice, one in which the desires and wants of the individual lead to preference for one occupation or another as the primary focus of the theory. Emanating from inherited tendencies interacting with childhood experiences and environment, a style or pattern develops for expending psychic energy and satisfying specific needs or levels of needs that the individual has developed. To some degree unconsciously, without conscious thought, the individual learns to satisfy the needs he feels, needs that have not been satisfied for him. In the process of satisfying his own needs, specific interests, attitudes, values, and abilities are developed and pursued.

Roe used Maslow's needs hierarchy to define levels of needs, from the lower-order needs (food, safety, love), which must be satisfied before the higher-order needs (understanding, beauty, self-actualization) may be pursued or become effective. Osipow presents three specific propositions from Roe's theory:

> (1) Needs that are routinely satisfied do not become unconscious motivators. (2) Higher-order needs, in the sense of Maslow's self-actualization need, will disappear entirely if they are only rarely satisfied; lower-order needs, in the Maslowian sense, will become dominant motivators if they are only rarely satisfied; in the event they become dominant motivators, they will block the appearance of higher-order needs. (3) Needs that are satisfied after unusual delay will become unconscious motivators under certain conditions. (1968, p. 18)

These propositions from Roe's theory seem to bear particularly on social-class differences in need satisfaction. Although Crites assumes that in modern society lower-order needs are usually satisfied "for most people most of the time" (1969, p. 97), it would appear that there are major differences between the lower, or lower-lower socioeconomic groups and the upper-middle and upper socioeconomic groups in satisfaction of the lower-order needs. In groups where there is economic insecurity, hostility, and violence in the environment and greater family instability, many children and adolescents will not feel that their lower-order needs are being satisfied, regardless of an objective determination that they are well off relative to their peers in Ethiopia. Roe concludes, and it must be remembered that her work began with studies of scientists and has continued primarily on professionals and university students, that the self-actualization need is paramount in the choice of a vocation, saying: "All that a man can be must be if he is to be happy" (1956, p. 29).

Although the research evidence does not strongly support Roe's theory as "an adequate representation of the crucial features of vocational development" (Osipow, 1968, p. 33), a generally unrecognized aspect of her theory is conceptually stimulating and possibly useful for counseling. The theory does not connect specific needs to specific occupations, but points out how any occupation may satisfy needs at some level. The theory "pertains to the relationship between levels of need and occupations, not kinds of needs and occupations" (Crites, 1969, p. 97).

This notion seems crucial. An adolescent may have, or see himself as having, a need to satisfy higher-order needs and do so as a craftsman, a farmer, or even on a production line. So, too, lower-order needs may be satisfied in occupations that presumably demand a human orientation and fulfill self-actualization needs but that also very highly satisfy the lower-order needs, as in such occupations as doctor, lawyer, and psychologist.

HOLLAND'S PERSONAL-ORIENTATION THEORY

Holland's theory (1958, 1964, 1966) is one in which a personal orientation, the style or pattern of dealing with the environment in preferred ways, should match the occupational environment (in a sense, a matching-occupation orientation) for appropriate occupational choice and adjustment. He proposes that to the degree that a person has a stable personal orientation, a well-integrated and consistent orientation, he will have clarity in vocational choice and stability in vocational behavior. The six orientations developed by Holland are realistic, intellectual, social, conventional, enterprising, and artistic. The literature contains some confirmatory evidence of Holland's theory. It is a more sophisticated version conceptually, but less precise in some ways, of the trait-matching theory. However, Holland does not speak to the issue of development of personal orientations and therefore adds little to developmental information.

GINZBERG'S DEVELOPMENTAL THEORY

Ginzberg's theory (Ginzberg, 1972; Ginzberg et al., 1951) is a developmental one that has evolved considerably to its most recent form. Ginzberg proposed movement through three primary psychological periods: a fantasy period, a tentative period, and a realistic period. The fantasy period covers childhood up to about age 11. Children by the age of 4 or 5 are able clearly to state vocational preferences, which reminds me of when my son at age 6 declared that he wanted to be a farmer, a drastic change from the astronaut he wanted to be the previous week. Through the fantasy period, because of insufficient information and a sense of inadequacy in their own childishness, children "play" at work and assume made-up work-role identities. In this play and in their acting out of occupational roles, children do not consider the various presses of occupations, such as abilities, training, economics and opportunities, potentials, and time perspectives.

The next period, the tentative period, is said to last from approximately age 11 to age 18 and is divided into three stages. The interest stage, ages 11 and 12, finds the child recognizing the need to consider and identify a career area and showing interest through identification of activities and areas that are liked or disliked, enjoyed or not enjoyed. In the capacity stage, ages 12 to 14, adolescents begin to put together the notion of ability, necessary and relevant aptitudes and education, with their areas of vocational interest. In the value stage, ages 15 and 16, issues of service to society, personal goals, and need satisfaction at all levels that the adolescent feels and is cognitively aware of come into play. At about age 18 or 19, the adolescent moves into the transition stage, during which the individual confronts the necessity of making concrete and realistic decisions about his vocational future that will have immediate and direct consequences for him.

The realistic stage begins at about age 18, and although Ginzberg earlier stated that it concluded as late as age 24, he concedes that realistic vocational choices and decision making may occur throughout one's lifetime. During the realistic stage, the adolescent is, in a sense, forced, either through termination of schooling or choice of continued schooling, to make efforts to resolve his questions of vocational choice. He attempts to coordinate the self-knowledge in the area of vocation that he has developed to this point with his knowledge of the openings and opportunities in the social and economic world. From his earlier interpretation, which viewed the adolescent as compromising with reality, Ginzberg came to see the adolescent as attempting to optimize personal satisfaction through career decision.

Although Ginzberg divides the realistic stage into further periods, these periods pertain to post–high school adolescence but do not differentiate between college students and nonstudent youths. Ginzberg's studies were mostly carried out on upper-income adolescents, primarily boys. He did investigate the applicability of this theory among underprivileged boys and using a female sample. He concluded that, in general, underprivileged, lower socioeconomic boys' and females' vocational development paralleled the development of the boys on whose data the original stages were built through the fantasy and tentative stages. At the realistic stage, however, there is divergence from his male, highly privileged sample. It appears that the variance in role and educational patterns that differentiates upper-middle from lower socioeconomic males and males from females upsets the progression of periods within the realistic stage. Moreover, the underprivileged boys' sample parallels the privileged boys' through the interest and capacity stages, but this parallel was obscure in the value stage of the tentative period and during the transition period. The value stage and transition stage would presumably be more difficult and more clearly defined for adolescents into, or well into, formal operations, and also more demanding of them in terms of their consideration of options and their greater potential occupational options. The particulars of Ginzberg's theory possibly overdefine the sequence and timing of the stages and thereby may limit its value. But the general theory is receiving some support in the research literature.

SUPER'S SELF-CONCEPT THEORY

Super's theory (Super, 1957, 1973; Super et al., 1957, 1963) is the most extensive of the psychological theories of vocational choice and development. Super's theory has provoked considerable research that has supported "the two fundamental aspects of his theory: that career choice is seen by the chooser as a way in which to implement his self-concept and that throughout life one is confronted with a series of career developmental tasks which specify the particular vocational decisions that must be made" (Osipow, 1983, p. 296).

In adolescence there develops a vocational self-concept that is part of the individual's global self-concept but is particular to, and developed in contrast and in evaluation with, others in the vocational world as perceived by the individual adolescent. The vocational self-concept is similar to the self-concept of academic ability discussed earlier. However, the self-concept of academic ability was developed through childhood as the child was participating in and able to measure himself in the academic arena. The vocational self-concept does not really spring to the fore until adolescence, when issues and press for a vocational decision begin. Super says that the adolescent has to "translate" his self-concept into occupational terms to develop the vocational self-concept.

Super has elaborated the concept of vocational maturity and defined it normatively as the correspondence between the vocational behavior exhibited by an individual and the vocational behavior expected for an individual at that age. Super specifies five vocational developmental tasks, which are crystallization of a vocational preference (14 to 18 years), specification of a vocational preference (18 to 21 years), implementation of a vocational preference (21 to 24 years), stabilization within a vocation (25 to 35 years), and consolidation of status and advancement (35 years plus). The ages given are typical of the age range at which these developmental tasks are reached and passed through, but they are not rigidly defined.

Implementation of vocational preference, which includes obtaining a first job in the preferred vocation, cannot without considerable wasted time occur for the high school graduate in the age range typically stated for it. The high school graduate who obtains a first job in the vocation preferred would probably do so at age 18 or 19. This age flexibility in the theory allows investigation of movement through the stages according to differing career-development patterns, a real advantage. Super (1973) has presented a problem-solving sequence, developed to foster understanding of computer-system use in vocational counseling. The general model of problem-solving steps to vocational choice that follows may be seen elongated or shortened according to the press for decision making on the adolescent. That is, the high school graduate who is not going on to college needs to reach the stage of implementation more quickly than does the college student. The sequence is

- Anticipation
- Awareness of the need to choose among alternatives
- Acceptance of responsibility for choice
- Awareness of factors to be considered
- Knowledge of sources and resources
- Crystallization
- Use of resources for exploration and information
- Clarification
- Awareness of the consequences of choice
- Specification
- Synthesis of information and the choice
- Implementation
- Action on the choice

Super feels that this sequence may be potentially useful in guidance and counseling. In fact, all of these theories have been useful in guidance as employed by trained counselors utilizing the measuring instruments developed for each. Super's sequence illustrates the steps the adolescent goes through, but is additionally helpful because it indicates for the teacher or adviser differing kinds of information the adolescent should be offered. It also appears that there is a parallel between the kinds of information and decisions an adolescent who is not going on to college makes in relation to a job and the kinds of information a college-bound adolescent makes use of in choosing a college. Super's sequence appears worthy of study for both of these purposes.

BLAU'S CONCEPTUAL FRAMEWORK

A conceptual framework integrating economics, psychology, and sociology, developed by Blau et al. (1956), places the vocational choice in a broader perspective, particularly as it reminds us that entry into an occupation is not solely determined by the preference of the individual, but is dependent too on the appropriateness of the individual for a job as determined by an employer and the availability of such jobs as determined by economic conditions. Occupational entry is seen as an interaction of vocational choice and occupational selection. "In choice, the individual compromises between preferred and expected occupations, whereas in selection the occupation compromises between ideal and available workers" (Crites, 1969, p. 110). Blau sees the determinants of occupational choice, selection, and entry divided between those factors that are influential prior to the time of entry into an occupation and those factors that are operative at the time of entry into an occupation. Blau therefore sees occupational choice as a long-term developmental process in which there are antecedent conditions for the individual (biological conditions, native endowment, socialization, and personality development), antecedent conditions for the occupation, and antecedent conditions for the selection agency (the physical-economic conditions and historical change), and both the individual and the agency antecedent conditions interact with the social structure.

The more immediate factors influencing the selection agency at the time of an individual's proposed entry into an occupation are the socioeconomic organization (division of labor, distribution and turnover, policies, stages of the business cycle) and the agency's demand, requirements, and rewards for a potential employee. The more immediate factors influencing the individual at this time include his sociopsychological attributes (knowledge, abilities, education, social position, aspirations, expectations, and motivations) and his immediate preparedness and appropriateness in terms of qualifications, characteristics, and values for that job. As conceptualized by Blau, it is within these nonstatic processes—vocational choice by the individual and occupational selection by the agency—in interaction at one point in time that occupational entry by an individual is determined.

ONE LIFE—ONE CAREER

Until recent times, most people who entered formal careers expected to remain in those careers throughout their lives, and, moreover, this singularity was seen as the ideal. Today, for many people, that is not the ideal, the expectation, or the reality. Occupations become obsolete and force change. People reach levels in occupations from which they see no challenge, excitement, or advancement, so they change occupations. People "burn out" in one occupation and seek another. People develop new interests, develop new values, realize themselves in ways that allow new priorities, and change occupations to further their personal development. The expectation for many, and increasingly more, it would seem, is that they will begin a career and, depending on their success and fulfillment, they will remain in it or not. The stigma of changing careers is minimal or nonexistent. In many cases, the moves are felt, and thought by others, to be positive. Much of the adult education movement is predicated on notions of life-long development and multiple careers.

Thus the usefulness of the career development theories (integrated in Figure 12.1), particularly in career counseling, is as aids in determining what a person might most benefit from doing first, or next. Not only is this view more realistic, but, because the adolescent can understand career choice in this light, making a decision feels less monumental and the process of decision making is consequently less anxiety provoking and potentially more reasonable.

CORRELATES OF VOCATIONAL ASPIRATIONS AND CHOICE

The story of how a little kid from anywhere grows up to be the holder of a particular occupational role is a fantastically complex one, as the theory section should have indicated. The full range of influences is operative on the child's and then the adolescent's aspirations, preferences, expectations, and choices. Depending on which measuring instruments are used, the sample, the geographical region, the specific hypotheses of the study, etc., the empir-

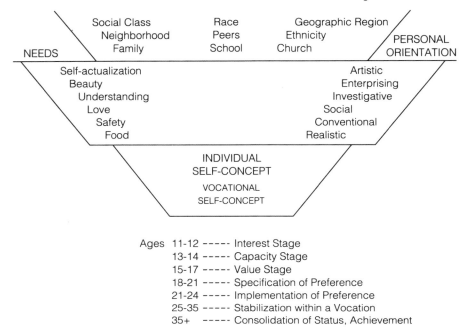

Figure 12.1. Social influences on personal needs and orientations that affect and interact with the individual's vocational concepts, preferences, and development: an integration of schemes by Super and Bachrach; Roe; Holland; and Ginzberg and Super.

ical findings are in agreement or in conflict. Research in this area in general has been going on throughout this century, and is, at this point, mammoth. In this section, conclusions that are generally agreed upon showing the influence, or relationship, between factors and their vocational aspects will be considered.

Intelligence has been shown to be related to vocational choice (Holden, 1961) and vocational preference (Porter, 1954). Perrone, using Roe's system for determining vocational preference, concluded that "the most significant finding of this study is that boys with similar scores on cognitive measures tend to indicate a preference for similar occupational groups" (1964, p. 978). Stubbins (1950), on a sample of over 200 male World War II veterans, obtained a correlation of .43 between intelligence and aspiration. Although for some reason he considered this a rather low correlation coefficient, it is rather high in comparison with most correlations in this field and provides ample indication of the relationship between aptitude and aspiration.

A number of aspects of personality (personality viewed from a number of positions) have been shown to be related to vocational choice. Super's hypothesis that "in choosing an occupation one is, in effect, choosing a means of implementing a self-concept" (1951, p. 92) has been tested and in general supported by a number of studies of education majors (Englander, 1960), nursing and education majors (Morrison, 1962), sixth graders (Holland, 1981), and twelfth graders (Blocher and Schutz, 1961). Oppenheimer tested Super's hypothesis using yet another measuring instrument and concluded that "people prefer occupations perceived as congruent with their self-concept" (1966, p. 194). Studies by Schutz and Blocher (1961) and Stockin (1964) lend support to the thesis in Holland's theory that a relationship exists between vocational choice and self-evaluation, which is defined broadly as including status needs, sense of competence and potential competence, and interpersonal evaluation of work. A study by Osipow, Ashby, and Wall (1966) among college students lends support to Holland's other major thesis that personality types relate to vocational choices.

Manaster and Perryman used their *Manifest Content Coding Manual* to analyze early recollections in order to differentiate between persons choosing different occupations—college majors in teaching, counseling, nursing, biological science, and accounting. The early recollection technique asks the subject to recall and relate the earliest scenes that can be clearly remembered. Differences found point to long-term, deeply embedded personality differences of a global nature between persons choosing different types of occupation. For example, the nursing and counseling majors were most similar in having a higher frequency of mentioning "mother" in their early recollections than did the biological science, teaching, and business groups. If a person has a life-style in which the "mother-helper-supporter" image is important, the fields of nursing and counseling seem natural occupational choices to manifest that life-style. The teaching, biological science, and accounting groups showed more neutral affects in their early recollections than did the nursing and counseling groups. There were indications that the counseling group showed more positive affect than the other groups and that the counseling and nursing subjects showed more negative affect than the other group. These findings "are consistent with the affective differences that might be expected to exist for people in these occupations. People choosing to be counselors and nurses live in a more 'emotional world,' i.e., more open to and active with emotion. On the other hand people choosing to be biological scientists, teachers and businessmen might be expected to see life in less emotional terms" (1974, p. 236).

Research on personality and vocational choice using the Manaster-Perryman technique continues and has come to show subtle differences in personality within major occupational categories. "Ostensibly there is little reason to suspect that engineering students of varying specialities should be different on . . . personality variables in any substantive way. . . . Notwithstanding this line of reasoning, it appears that the manifest content of ERs did distinguish between groups of students in chemical, electrical, and mechanical engineering" (Hafner, Fakouri, and Etzler, 1986, pp. 364–65).

Manaster, Friedman, and Larson (1976) analyzed questionnaire data collected from a large sample of high school graduates who had indicated that they would be premedical students when they enrolled in college. The data were collected in the summer before fall entrance to the university. Of this large pre-med group, 52 stated they wished to be surgeons, 29 expected to become pediatricians, 18 wanted to be psychiatrists, and 43 intended to specialize but had not yet decided on a field. Differences in self-assessment, future priorities, and recollections of early experiences were found among these future specialists — and it should be pointed out that at the very least, it would be seven years until they began their specialized training. The future psychiatrists were seen as reflective, confused, and less emotionally stable, with lower self-confidence than surgeons, who were seen as emotionally stable and saw themselves as well suited for their chosen specialization. The future pediatricians remembered their mothers as having stable dispositions and were the least complaining of any unsatisfactory family life. The psychiatrists, whose memories of their families were less favorable, were uninterested in family practice, whereas the pediatricians, whose memories were most favorable, obviously intended to go into family practice. Interestingly, and in keeping with earlier statements about needs and satisfaction available at different levels and different types of jobs, the group of future specialists who were undecided on a field appeared much more susceptible to external influences on their career and had the highest desire for status and monetary reward from their specializations.

Research on personality and vocational choice is fraught with contradictory findings and inconsistencies. Nonetheless, the field of research flourishes. It appears to be that with sensible and sensitive selection of personality variables and occupation and/or with broad, open instruments that allow subjects to show their personality characteristics, strengths, and predispositions (rather than solely the variables the researcher wants to look at), the personality-by-occupation relationship will be more strongly supported.

FAMILY INFLUENCES

The foregoing studies, particularly through analysis of early recollections, early family life, and personality, illustrate again what every student of psychology must by now know — the relationship between family (at least as perceived by the individual) and personality.

We keep coming back to the direct and subtle ways in which parents and family influence adolescents in all of the life tasks. In the choice of occupation, parents' direct influence, direct in the sense of open, overt, may have a decided effect on the adolescent. If at age 21 you can expect to be vice-president in charge of anything in your father's company, which will someday be your own, you may well have your vocational choice made for you. Traditionally, over 90 percent of farmers' sons choose to go into farming (Gottlieb and Ramsey, 1964). Parents in craft unions are often able to wangle apprenticeships for their children, and their children often take them.

Parents may steer, or try to steer, their child into a particular occupation by providing encouragement and training in the relevant area. They may go further. One thinks of extremes, such as Shirley Temple and Judy Garland, whose parents chose their occupations for them when they were children, with, as history shows, mixed outcomes. Or if you watched when the young Jimmy Connors played championship tennis on television, the camera would pan to his mother in the crowd, and the broadcaster mention, "She forced a tennis racket in his hand when he was four."

In terms of vocational interest and vocational choice, "identification with both parents influences the formation of vocational interest patterns, but identification with the father is more important than with the mother" (Crites, 1962, p. 269) for boys. The quality of the identification, in nature of attitudes toward parents, is seen in differences between occupational groups. Segal and Szabo (1964) found that accountants had more positive attitudes toward their parents and other people, and were more accepting of authority and rules, than were creative writers. Their interpretation was that the accountants' positive attitudes toward others were generalized from their attitudes toward their parents. Segal had earlier hypothesized a "seeking for the completion of multiple identification in creative writing students" (1961, p. 208), which may be a function of the more negative identification found for this group. Either positive or negative identification, either acceptance of the identification relationship or rejection of the role model, may equally influence career decisions and patterns: "Their importance may be more similar than it has been commonly realized. Each may serve as important occasions for self-definition" (Bell, 1969, p. 34). Permutations of "My son, the doctor" could include "My son, the doctor, is a bum" and "My son, the bum, is a doctor." Parents influence adolescents in the models they present for them, their wishes, hopes, and aspirations for them, and their motivational influence. Parents, particularly father for son, may be very concrete role models, as evidenced when the son follows in the father's footsteps. Although this occurs more frequently than would be the case if occupations were chosen randomly, the literature shows great variations in the extent of this practice. More importantly, adolescents tend to choose, enter, and remain in occupations at the same socioeconomic level as their fathers, or one level above. This may be more a function of family socioeconomic status, does not seem to account for family differences within socioeconomic levels, and will be mentioned again in the section on socioeconomic status influences.

Parental motivation — the support, encouragement, and ambitions that parents have for their children — influences the ambitions and aspirations of the adolescent regardless of his or her ability and social class (Douvan and Adelson, 1966; Simpson, 1962). Lunneborg (1982), in studying women graduate students in engineering, natural science, and architecture, found that both parents had supported the students' aspirations in nontraditional careers.

PEER, SCHOOL, AND SUBGROUP INFLUENCES

The influence of peers, teachers, and school on vocational interests and choices involve each other, as well as family and social class, to such an extent that a mixed, or composite, statement may be most informative. Armour, in his *A Diabolical Dictionary of Education*, observes that "in education, a peer group is a group of students of about the same age and ability who, also being about the same height, can peer at each other on equal footing. In this sense the 'peer' goes back to the Latin *par* meaning equal" (1969, p. 87). As is so often the case, there is a strong element of truth in humor. In this humorous definition there is the implication that peers, a group of friends and associates, stick together because they are on an equal footing, or stay on an equal footing in order to stick together.

The peer group, in toto, in a school, characterized by a similarity of socioeconomic status among the majority in that school, conveys the dominant values for that school and the total peer group. If the dominant values are upper-middle class, even the working-class adolescents in the school will be affected in choice of occupation by that dominant value climate. And this operates in reverse fashion if the dominant group is a working-class group. "The dominant climate of opinion within a school makes a significant impact upon students' occupational goals" (Wilson, 1959, p. 844). High school students who intend to go on to college are influenced in their vocational choice, in the form of college major, particularly, by favorite teachers or those few teachers whom they get to know well (Carlin, 1960; E. G. Johnson, 1967). Although peer influence is notable, parental influence is more important overall than peer influence (Simpson, 1962).

The composite situation appears to be that the adolescent will approach school and vocational choice in all probability with the expectations appropriate for, or held in common by, the majority of his socioeconomic status group. If his parents have been particularly encouraging and ambitious for him, or the opposite, his expectations and aspirations will be accordingly higher or lower than the norm for his own socioeconomic status group. If the majority group in his school is of the same socioeconomic status as his own, his tendency will be to adhere to the norms for expectations and aspirations of that dominant group. If the dominant group is different from his, there will be a tendency, particularly if supported by parental encouragement, for him to move toward the norms of the dominant group. In a mixed socioeconomic school there would appear to be more leeway, more potential for movement, in ambitions and choices according to the level of ambition promoted by the parents and assumed by the adolescent.

Studying academic achievement among working-class Mexican-Americans in junior high schools, Manaster and King (1972) predicted that the "clannishness," the sticking together, commonly attributed to Mexican-Americans would operate to a greater degree when the Mexican-American students were a minority in a school than when they were equal to or greater in number than the other students in the school. They found that there was a tendency for students, when a minority in a school, to show smaller variance on GPA. When the Mexican-American students were about equal in number to the others there was no difference, but when they were a majority their variance was greater. It appears that for this particular ethnic group, with the social characteristics attributed to it, minority status in a school has the effect of closing doors, closing opportunities, to students while accentuating peer influence, thus eliciting stricter adherence to group norms. Cherry found:

> Children from working class homes in schools with mainly working class pupils appear to have less interest in breaking with working class occupational traditions than do similar children mixing with pupils from more varied home backgrounds. Social class and the parent interest in education are shown to be of substantial importance in determining the ambition of children at non-selective schools. If the school is to counter the effect on job choice of poor family circumstances, the area from which it draws its pupils may be important in determining the acceptability of occupational information and guidance. (1974, p. 29)

If the schools, or the society, take the responsibility for instilling in children and adolescents the motivation to achieve vocationally at higher levels, then the effects and influence of socioeconomic status and sex on aspirations and expectations must be countered. Children and adolescents are socialized into the roles they occupy and the roles that surround them in the society. To a great degree, adolescents come to a common orientation of what is important. They accept the common values and common aspirations of their class. So, too, still today, the vast majority of boys and girls develop the values, aspirations, and expectations traditionally appropriate in the vocational arena for their own sex. Aspiration level has been shown to be related to family socioeconomic status and a variety of environmental correlates of family SES (Hollingshead, 1949; Thomas, 1956; Tseng, 1971; Youmans, 1956), as well as sex (Seward and Williamson, 1969), although the relationship between aspiration level and sex may be in the process of change (Seward and Williamson, 1970; Steinmann, 1963). Poole and Cooney found "that adolescents, regardless of gender, social class, or ethnic background, were aware of multiple occupational possibilities. Concerning self-preference, however, various social-environmental circumstances (gender and social class) militated against a consideration of multiple occupational possibilities for self" (1985, p. 251).

At a time in history when change appears so rapid and all-encompassing, many people, and especially many young people, tend to pay more attention to the changes than to the constants. For that reason, it seems worthwhile to emphasize a series of studies that indicate the continuing and pervasive influences of socioeconomic status and sex on occupational aspirations and expectations.

In investigating occupational aspirations and expectations, some form of measuring device must be used. There are many such devices available, which in essence ask the questions, "What job, kind of job, prestige level of job would you like to have?" and "What job, kind of job, prestige level of job do you expect to have?" The researcher must then, depending on the measuring instrument, calculate the occupational-prestige level of the answers for both the aspiration and the expectation questions. The concepts of level of aspiration as an idealistic goal and expectation as a realistic goal are well established in the literature (Haller and Miller, 1963; Stephenson, 1955). In order for the findings from investigations of occupational aspirations and expectations using these devices to be valid, to make any sense at all, the subjects taking the tests must understand the occupational-prestige hierarchy.

It appears that adolescents from the lower working class up are fully capable of understanding the occupational-prestige hierarchy and responding sensibly to questions of occupational aspiration and expectation. This does not apply to lower-lower class students, who are not as aware of the nature of occupational prestige (Tseng, 1971). In a major cross-national study (Peck et al., 1973) in which over 10,000 upper-middle-class and upper-lower, skilled working-class 10- and 14-year-olds were tested, generally accurate and adequate understanding of the relative positions of occupations on the occupational prestige hierarchy was found for children and adolescents in Brazil, England, Italy, Japan, Mexico, and the United States. The United States data, collected in the Chicago area and Central Texas, and made up of approximately 1,200 white 10- and 14-year-old male and female, upper-middle- and upper-lower-class students in each locale, found in both areas that males' aspirations and expectations were higher than females and that middle-class children's aspirations and expectations were higher than upper-lower-class children's. In studies of the same socioeconomic, sex, and age groups in Puerto Rico and Mexico (Manaster and Ahumada, 1970) and in India (Manaster, Ahuja, and Pannu, 1976), socioeconomic-status differences of the same direction and order were found for both occupational aspirations and expectations. Although due to a peculiarity in the Indian sample, the Indian females had higher occupational expectations than did the Indian males for the total sample, Puerto Rican and Mexican females' aspirations and expectations were lower than those of the males. In both studies the aspiration and expectation discrepancies between males and females were greater at age 14 than at age 10, leading to the conclusion in the Indian case that males who stay in school longer, the 14-year-olds in this sample, have higher aspirations and expectations than the younger males. Females who stay in school longer have lower aspirations and expectations than the younger females. The data, collected in 11 countries around the world, reinforce the notion of the enduring influences of socioeconomic status and sex on occupational aspirations and expectations, and presumably, therefore, occupational choice.

Work values, too, show the enduring influences of SES, sex, and subcultural group. Krau investigated these variables in a sample of ninth- and twelfth-grade Jewish, Arab, and Catholic students in Israel and found support for his hypothesis "that the source of work values is the subculture of the social group of affiliation, which has socioeconomic and cultural (national, religious) characteristics" (1987, p. 103).

VOCATIONAL CHOICE, SEX, ETHNICITY, AND THE FUTURE

It would be a joy to be able to say that the strictures, biases, and prejudices that have excluded females and minority-group members from particular occupations and occupational-prestige levels have vanished. It would be a joy to be able to say that "cultural pluralism" at its best is operative in America today. "At best, 'cultural pluralism' means that the separate groups coexist harmoniously, secure in their distinctive biological, religious, linguistic, or social customs and equal in their accessibility to natural resources, civil rights, and political power" (Havighurst and Dreyer, 1975, p. 269). Clearly we have not moved that far.

It would be equally erroneous to say that the barriers to equal occupational opportunities exist to the degree that they have in the past. "Cultural pluralism" at its worst is not operative. "At worst, 'cultural pluralism' means that the separate groups compete with each other for economic, social, and political power, regarding each other suspiciously as threats to their own survival and well-being" (Havighurst and Dreyer, 1975, p. 270).

Income and occupational status for minority-group members and females are still considerably lower than they are for majority-group males. But statistics abound to indicate that the situation is improving. That it has not improved enough to satisfy many and exhibit cultural pluralism at its best is obvious. Organized efforts of representative groups from these populations as well as the continuing efforts of governmental agencies hold promise of further improvement in time.

Yet the theme running through this book has been that in the final analysis, the individual, regardless of race, creed, ethnicity, or sex, has potential and responsibility for his or her choices, achievement, and way of life. The group figures, the probability statistics, are merely that. But they indicate the greater or lesser difficulty that might be expected by adolescents from particular backgrounds in meeting the life tasks, which ultimately are individual life challenges.

Women whose career choices are influenced by what they think men feel are appropriate women's jobs (Hawley, 1971), and/or who maintain preferences for typically feminine occupations even when this is contrary to their interests and potentials (Harmon, 1971), are clearly not meeting their individual potential. They are not taking full responsibility for their decisions and their future. The obstacles they see in the society are there. However, their efforts to remove these obstacles may take the form of choosing and striving for the occupation and way of life they desire, as well as working in the more organizational process mentioned above.

The efforts of readers of this book, future parents, teachers, counselors, and scholars, must be to support the individual children and adolescents with whom they work to realize (meaning both to understand and to fulfill) their potential. This means your efforts must be toward equality in the greater society *and* in your dealings with individuals, while also encouraging individual children and adolescents. Encouragement engenders the sense of competence youngsters need to make their own decisions. And encouragement suggests presenting them with the most enriching experiences, which will in turn allow them to choose occupations without regard to sex typing or the traditional domination of that occupation by a certain group (Almquist and Angrist, 1970). The future is bright to the extent that we make it so for ourselves and make it so that others may brighten their own futures.

CHAPTER 13
Family, Friends, and Community

CHAPTER 13

The life task of family, friends, and community is an evolving one. That is, when a child is preadolescent, his community and friends are severely limited, the family being the center of his life. In adolescence, the movement is essentially one from major emphasis and influences of family to greater influence and emphasis of friends and expansion into the greater community.

The developmental tasks that fit within the friends and community life task can be seen as evolving in this same order—family to friends to community (Havighurst, 1972). They are, first, "achieving emotional independence of parents and other adults (p. 55); second, "achieving new and more mature relations with agemates of both sexes" (p. 45); and third, "desiring and achieving socially responsible behavior" (p. 75).

The nature of the situation for this life task may therefore be broken down into these three major areas: the relationship and the relative influence of family; the relationship and the relative influence of peers as individuals and groups; and, lastly, the movement to, participation with, large groups, small groups, and intimate friends, i.e., being integrated as a member of the total community. Evolution and social change may be evident in these areas also.

THE FAMILY

The nature of the American family has, in the eyes of many social scientists and social philosophers, changed considerably in this century. Certainly we are a more urban people, and more dependent on each other, major institutions, and governmental agencies and institutions. There is no doubt that in many of our cities, and in many of our suburbs, there is a degree of personal isolation and therefore dependence on social institutions that is much different from the close-knit interdependent family that existed in the past. Nonetheless, the family in America today is still central in the lives of almost all children; it is still a crucial factor in emotional and social development. It cannot and should not be forgotten that the family is by no means lost in the modern technological society.

The family in America, by virtue of differences in socioeconomic status, ethnic and cultural background, rural, suburban, and urban setting, and geographic area, is extremely diverse. In this chapter we will attempt to look at the adolescent's movement from and problems within the family as she attempts to achieve independence, as evidenced in studies that investigate something of the dynamics of family and peers. A quote by Martineau indicates, I believe, how the influence hierarchy affects parents in responding to the dictates and contradictions of society and funnels the influences through to the child. Martineau says that "to one degree or another [the adolescent] absorbs the contradictory feelings that the parent has about his social status, his income, his jobs, his friends, and applies them to himself" (1966, p. 277).

Likewise, Lidz (1969) and Peters (1985) see the development of children into adolescents as an additional influence on parental behavior and interaction. The impact on the parents of the onset of adolescence in a son or daughter may be intensified due to the confrontation of the parents with the full spectrum of middle age. At this time, the parents attempt to come to terms with the limits of their own lives, their accomplishments, the frustrations they have encountered in meeting or not meeting their own ambitions and ideals. Their offspring at this same time confronts them with adolescent insecurities, rebelliousness, and resentments. From Lidz' point of view, the male adolescent seeks to assert himself and wants to be instrumental in the decision making of the family. If the parents are unable to surrender some of their prerogatives, the adolescent's drives are turned toward disruption of the family system. Females more likely seek to live out the expressive-affectional role in the family. Rebellion in this instance may take the form of open hostility or incitement of siblings to defiance.

Two studies by Cameron (1970a, 1970b) present evidence that youth envy adults their power and wealth, and the adults envy youth their sexual vitality and prowess. Conflict between generations on the basis of each's unfulfilled needs is evident here, as it is in Lidz' work.

Steinberg emphasizes a very basic point underlying contemporary adolescent-parent conflict. He notes that throughout history there have been accounts of dissension between parents and their adolescents. "But our predecessors enjoyed an important advantage over today's parents: Adolescents rarely lived at home much beyond puberty" (1987, p. 38).

ATTAINING AUTONOMY

We will look at the adolescent's movement toward independence within the framework of family or parental power and influence versus the adolescent's power and influence. The idea is that the more power asserted over an individual, the less his independence, and the adolescent's battle is therefore to move to an independent position from beneath others, parents', power. The adolescent wishes to develop a modicum of control over his own actions and, in the process of developing this control, to exercise some power of his own. At the same time he realizes, probably through his anxiety, that he is not intellectually, psychologically, or emotionally ready to deal with the world or to exercise power in a mature, adult-like manner. Lastly, his anxiety continues because he is fearful of too much separation from his parents. So the movement to independence is not like walking out of the house with head up, fully confident that "now as an adolescent I am a powerful, autonomous human being." Rather, a conflict exists within the adolescent between being fully autonomous and being able to rely on the protection of his parents. Thornburg says, "The ambivalent conflict is affected by the need to relinquish childhood ties on the one hand and to find sufficient independent behaviors that do not overpower the adolescent on the other" (1970, p. 474).

In one way the adolescent feels, maybe knows down deep, that he cannot handle, and does not want, too much independence and power, so he attempts to stay within the aegis of his parents; but at the same time he tries to demonstrate his independence and fights, or at least exerts himself, to wrest more independence from his parents. The parents then are put on the spot. How much independence to grant? The more independence, the more power over his own life, they grant to the adolescent, the more power they lose over him or her.

Salzman (1973) points to this problem from the perspective of parents who must be seen within the influence hierarchy as being influenced both from higher levels of the hierarchy and also from their children, their adolescents, at lower levels in the hierarchy. Salzman points to an implicit demand on the part of parents that youth conform to the standards set for them by their parents because the parents have raised them, are responsible for them and their further socialization and development. If the adolescent's standards differ excessively from the parents' standards, he will, from the parents' point of view, not be accepted by society. It is the responsibility of the parents, as the parents view it, to see that this does not happen. Moreover, the parents fear that if their child participates in behaviors that are not in keeping with the parental standards, and thereby deviant, it might have an adverse effect on the parents, emanating from the possibility of their being labeled as failures as parents. Salzman says, therefore, that parents are very hesitant to relinquish any of their power over their child and to grant their child independence, for if this independence is misused, it will reflect negatively on the parents. This is not something that parents readily admit, both because it reflects badly on their child and because they fundmentally wish to have their children grow to be independent, responsible adults.

There is then this two-way problem, or conflict, within both parents and their adolescent children. There is hesitancy on the part of the adolescent to accept too much independence and power over his own life, although he outwardly demands it. There is hesitancy on the part of the parents to give this power and independence, though the parent wants to give his child power and independence to enable him to grow and develop according to the best standards of the society as the parents perceive them.

Steinberg and Silverberg conducted research with adolescents to age 16 from a range of socioeconomic backgrounds on three aspects of autonomy. Rather than determine that autonomy is movement toward independence and away from parents, they found that "for most boys and girls, the transition from childhood into adolescence is marked more by a trading of dependency on parents for dependency on peers" (1986, p. 841). Thus the process of developing autonomy that we look at is not straightforward and unidimensional, but a wavering and borrowing, trading and covering so that one is not autonomous, not somehow independent and out there on one's own, before one is ready.

In a study of freshman college students and their parents, 184 nuclear families, Lerner and Knapp assessed the comparability of their attitudes toward contemporary societal issues. They found that, although parents and adolescents were fairly accurate in assessing each other's attitudes, there was a tendency for parents "to minimize discrepancies between themselves and their children, and a tendency for the adolescents as a group to magnify such discrepancies" (1975, p. 35). In terms of attitude consistency between parents and adolescents, the youth felt that the difference was greater than it was, whereas the parents felt the opposite. That may be a good guide for parents and teachers. As large as you feel the gap is, adolescents think it is larger.

Goodman (1969) spoke to the issue of this conflict when he developed three stages in the growth of autonomy: the "they-me" of infancy and childhood, wherein the child is subservient and dependent, powerless against "them"; the second stage, "I-me," occurring during adolescence, wherein the individual attempts to acquire power over his own self and his own behavior; and the third stage, the mature stage, called "I-them," wherein control over others has developed from control over oneself. Studying the adolescent in terms of parent, teacher, and friend reference groups, and home, family, school, and peer areas of behavior, Goodman hypothesized that in order to express a degree of autonomy and power the adolescent calls upon a different subgroup of his total reference group when interacting with each subgroup. The adolescents conformed more with parents in the peer role and more with their peers in their family role. In this way the adolescent was able to show his independence from parents by depending on and exclaiming norms of his peer group in the family-behavior area, while conversely calling on the norms of his parents when interacting with his peers. This very interesting juxtaposition of norm and behaviors is cunningly safe for the "marginal man" adolescent. Remembering Lewin's thesis that the adolescent is marginal in not being truly a part of either the child or the adult group, Goodman's study shows how the adolescent can keep his foot, so to speak, in both camps. The adolescent does so by being defiant of his parents when in their presence and under their direct control but still maintaining their protection by conforming to their expectations when he is out of their sight, out of their direct control.

When it is said that the influence of peers is greater in adolescence than in childhood, people often construe this to mean that the peer influence is so great as to exclude previous and current parent and family influence. The dynamics of the movement out of the total power scope of the family in adolescence certainly does not mean that the adolescent jumps completely into another realm of influence. Talk of the "generation gap" has implied that this kind of total jump has been made — that the adolescent's values, views, norms, attitudes, etc., are completely opposite from and opposed to those of their parents and all people over 30. A short review of evidence looking at differences in values and norms between parents and adolescents may give us some additional perspective on the nature of the generation gap, of the relative influence of parents and peers.

Solomon (1972) argues that a sense of family identity is a necessary aspect of a healthy adjustment to maturity. He says that autonomy is not reached until part of the parental image has been internalized. The values and norms held by the parents thus must in some way be internalized in order for maturity to be reached, and one would expect some congruence between parents and adolescents in terms of these norms and values. In Havighurst's description of the developmental task "achieving emotional independence of parents and other adults," he says the goal of the task is "to become free from childish dependence on parents; to develop affection for parents without dependence upon them; to develop respect for older adults without dependence upon them" (1972, p. 55). Solomon and Havighurst are in accord in seeing that, in the process of maturing, the adolescent takes the values and norms from his parents that enable him to function as an adolescent and will enable him to function better as an adult. The "childish" dependence on parents is what needs to be eliminated in the process of achieving emotional independence.

This developmental task, this process, is now being called individuation, a core proposition of which is "that central to all relationships, including marital, parent-child peer, and sibling relations, is the interplay of the two dimensions of individuality and connectedness" (Cooper and Ayers-Lopez, 1985, p. 15). Blos (1979) refers to adolescence as the "second individuation," pointing to the separation from parental influence as necessary for development of a mature sense of self. Cooper, Grotevant, and Condon (1983) see individuality in self-assertion and separateness and see connectedness in mutuality and permeability. The process of individuation implies a playing off, between and among parents and adolescent children, strivings for individuality through self-assertion and separateness against strivings for connectedness through mutuality, sensitivity to others' views, and permeability, a responsiveness to others' views. "From middle childhood through adolescence, parents and their children have the opportunity to use the increasing capacity of their developing children to make their contribution to individuation more mutual" (Cooper and Ayers-Lopez, 1985, p. 16). All of the perennial issues involved in this process, whether referred to as individuation or striving for autonomy, and related to conformity continue to have a place in assisting our attempt to understand adolescents. As the concept of and research on individuation illustrate, we can understand more about the purpose or function of adolescence as well as the process of being an adolescent.

A pertinent question at this point would seem to be, "Where do adolescents stand in relation to parents and peers on various values, norms, and attitudes?" Meisels and Canter (1971) asked adolescents to judge issues such as the Vietnam War, marijuana, modern art, etc., in terms of their own views, those of their friends, and those of their parents. The mean "self" scores placed the adolescents between their parents and their peers. They viewed themselves as somewhat more progressive than their parents but not as progressive as their peers. Munns (1972) compared male adolescent self scores and perceived scores for parents and peers on the Allport-Vernon-Lindzey study of values. The boys' self ratings and ratings for peers were quite similar for all value categories, while the ratings for fathers were similar on four of the six values. However, the mothers' values were seen as quite different. Although Munns does not make this point, on three of the six values, the male adolescents' mean scores were between those for parents and peers and, on two additional values, were between those for mother and peers. Both studies seem to indicate that adolescents see their values as falling between those of their parents and those of their peers. It is as if they want the best of both worlds, which certainly reflects on the power-independence conflict. Fasick posits, at least of the middle class, "that adolescents remain committed to the adult-related values of parents and maintain warm emotional ties with them. Close relationships with peers represent an extension of emotional bonds rather than transference" (1984, p. 143).

The three following studies indicate that parents' influence over their adolescents is dependent to some degree on the use of parent power. Permissiveness and parent tutoring in political areas were found to be important in transmitting a political role to adolescent children (Thomas, 1971), and control that is combined with affection was found to be influential in transmitting a "proper" societal role (Jessor and Jessor, 1974). Baruch (1972), studying the influence of the mother on attitudes toward women and work held by their adolescent daughters, found a tendency for daughters of nonworking mothers to devalue women's competence in competing with men. These studies point to the influence of parents on the values related to roles taken by adolescents, thereby integrating the previous studies, which looked at influences on values and influences on roles separately.

In a study by Gray and Gair (1974), adolescent girls rated themselves as they would like to be. This ideal self was then rated by their two best friends and their parents to find out how these two groups believed the subjects rated themselves. The parents and peers agreed with each other and with the adolescents' ideal self ratings, which would seem to indicate a good deal of understanding and empathy between the generations.

Nowicki and Segal (1974) showed that adolescent males and females perceived themselves as having approximately the same locus of control, the same sense of personal control over the outcomes of life situations, as their parents had. This seems to indicate the kind of influence that parental self-concept, or sense of self, has on the child's sense of self or self-concept.

A study by Brittain tested the hypothesis that adolescents would respond to parent pressures versus peer pressures, what Brittain called parent-peer cross-pressures, as a function of the content of the alternative presented by parents or peers and as a function of the specific situation in which the cross-pressures were presented. His ideas were supported, and Brittain offered some hypotheses to explain the pattern of responses produced in the study. The first hypothesis stated:

> The general social orientation of adolescents is of a dual character. Choices tend to derive meaning from either of two general reference groups, or both; the peer society in which many status and identity needs are gratified, and the larger society in which the status positions which one can aspire to as an adult are found. When choices pertain to the latter, parents are perceived as the more competent guides. . . . Adolescents, for example, perceiving themselves to be more like peers in regard to tastes in clothes and in regard to feelings about school, find peer-favored alternatives in these areas psychologically closer and more acceptable. But in other areas the greater perceived similarity is between self and parent. (1967, p. 389)

Brittain's study is particularly significant in the context of the previous articles, which show the continuous strong influence of parents on values, norms, and roles of adolescents. The findings of this study point clearly to the areas of values and behaviors where there are more probably disparities, and it seems that the perennial furor over hairstyles, dress, music, etc., points to this disparity. Parents, and maybe adults in general, seem to become more upset about hairstyles and clothes than about many other aspects of the adolescent's life. It would appear that this is because, using Brittain's rationale, these are areas where the adolescent's reference group is his peer group and he is more influenced and more conforming to the values and norms of his peer group. It is therefore an area in which parental power is minimized.

Munns (1971) queries the issue of the generation gap and takes the position that what is seen as a conflict between the generations is in actuality the result of the adolescent's making efforts to understand, explore, and define his own system of values. This, as we have seen, is the goal of Goodman's "I-me" stage. It would also seem to bear on Erikson's emphasis on the search for identity and the identity and role confusion in adolescence. From Munns' point of view, the adolescent is not much concerned with values and identity in the sense of "Who am I?" but is deeply concerned with the question of "Which way can I be?" According to Munns, the problem in the search for identity lies in the self, which demands in its fullest development the attainment of formal operational thought, something that, as we have seen, is not yet or may never be developed for many adolescents. This may therefore produce "muddled self-concepts." In view of the studies presented, it would appear that the great generation gap is really not very great at all. Moreover, it appears that because of social pressures, the "marginal" position, and the cognitive-developmental stage, or "between stage" of adolescence, the generation gap appears and feels to adults and adolescents alike to be greater than it is. And adolescents sometimes feel the need to show their peers where they stand—on the adolescents' side of the generation gap. "A . . . teenager found it pertinent to say to his parents: 'I hope you'll understand . . . some friends are coming over and I have to pretend I don't like you' " (*Individual Psychology News Letter*, 1973, p. 55).

The variety of child-rearing and parent-personality influences and variables that might influence an adolescent in his attitudes, values, behaviors, and norms is immense. In this chapter (and in this book) we are not getting into issues relating to specific personality types or specific child-rearing patterns and their relationship to specific adolescent behaviors. It is important, I think, at this point, to interject some negative findings as well as some more sociological variables into the issue of attitudes and values in general, and the issues of compliance or conformity to parents or peers.

Spencer, in a survey of attitudes and values of over 500 14- to 15-year-old boys in school in England, found no support for two hypotheses that appear generally supported in the literature elsewhere. First, he did not find that the social class of origin or the type of school attended provides criteria for determining the pattern of attitudes and values, what might be called "the subcultures," of these boys. Second, Spencer found no anticipatory socialization; that is, he did not find the adolescents adopting attitudes and values that are appropriate for the socioeconomic status that they expect to enter. In this book we attempt to look at influences that affect adolescents in general, but have numerous times referred to the importance of the individual. Spencer believes that his negative findings are in a sense accounted for by the importance of this individuality. Social surveys use broad variables, such as social class and type of school. As we have seen, this necessitates the omission of particular, individualistic aspects of these variables. This results, according to Spencer, in patterns of low correlations, such as he found, being "elevated into the position of being evidence of the role of family, or school, as a socializing agent" (1972, p. 10).

Yet it is through social surveys, and the kinds of generalizations and models they generate, that we are able to develop general pictures of what is distinctive in adolescence. We may then apply this knowledge and understanding in planning day-to-day activities with individual adolescents in which their specific personality and characteristics prevail.

A cross-national study by Thomas and Weigert (1971) investigated the hypothesis that conformity to significant others—i.e., best friend, mother, father, and priest—for middle-class Catholic male and female adolescents would increase as one moved across four selected samples from New York City; Saint Paul, Minnesota; San Juan, Puerto Rico; and Merida, Yucatan,

Mexico. Their data indicated "that it is primarily conformity to the expectations of authoritative others that is inversely related to the development of industrialization-urbanization" (p. 844). This type of conformity, conformity to authority, is differentiated from the other conformity, conformity to the expectations of best friend, that was also studied. "This type of conformity (category of best friends) is not consistently related to industrialization-urbanization" (p. 844). Thomas and Weigert seem to be showing a relationship between modernization and a decrease in conformity to authoritative others. This relationship may be predicated on the greater number and diversity of authoritative others who could exist in a more modern urban setting. However, they do not find that conformity to the category of best friends, peer compliance, is consistently related to the differences in modernization and urbanization of their four samples.

Brittain, comparing rural and urban adolescents with respect to peer versus parent compliance, analyzed items pertaining to dating, dress, glamour roles in the peer society, and informing, or communication with, agemates. Significant differences between the rural and urban adolescents were found: the urban group was more peer-compliant than was the rural group. In speculating about the interpretation of this difference, Brittain recalls the distinction Coleman "makes between the influence of peers as individuals and the influence of the peer society. It may be that there is a rural-urban difference with respect to the latter and that this difference may or may not be obscured, depending on how the data were analyzed" (1969, p. 66).

These last three studies have been interjected, in a sense, to confuse the issue. The hierarchy of influences is always operative. From Thomas and Weigert's study we can see the macroscopic cultural influences on conformity to, or compliance with, the expectations of parents and other significant figures in the adolescent's life. From Brittain's study we get an indication of the importance of geographic (which may be considered subcultural) influences on the adolescent's relationships vis-à-vis parent and peer. And although Brittain, citing Coleman, points to the influence of a peer society, Spencer does not see what are generally considered important influences— school and social class—as being sufficiently precise to help explain the development of adolescent subcultures. All of this is to say that this issue is anything but resolved.

If not resolved, however, the consistent finding of the relative importance of parents and peers by subject area, as in Wilks' research, wherein "parents were perceived as most important in certain 'future-oriented' areas, whereas for 'current' decisions, friends' opinions were more valued" (1986,

p. 323), is truly important for understanding adolescents' social dynamics. How these findings relate to developmental stages follows.

Saltzstein, Diamond, and Belenky (1972) investigated the relationship between Kohlberg's moral-developmental stages and conformity behavior, assuming that children would conform to individuals whom they viewed as having moral authority. In a group-pressure situation study to measure conformity in seventh graders, although Saltzstein et al. found little overall conformity, the Stage 3 moral-development, good-boy morality subjects conformed the most to their peers, as would be expected. The Stage 4 and Stage 5 subjects conformed the least, thereby demonstrating their own growing autonomy. This study seems to support the relationship between moral development and the kinds of power or parental influence that will be effective with the adolescent.

Weisbroth (1970) investigated the proposition that individuals with close parental identification would attain a higher level of moral judgment. She found that identification with parents was significantly related to a high level of moral judgment for males and that identification with the father was significantly related to a high level for females. Her position was that close parental identification contributes to personal and social adjustment, thereby giving adolescents the opportunity to develop positive self-evaluations and feelings of self-worth.

Remembering Munns' hypothesis that generational conflicts are related to a lengthening of time before adolescents reach Piaget's formal operations stage of cognitive development, recalling the relationship between Kohlberg's moral-developmental stages and Piaget's stages, and bearing in mind the relationships between development of and search for personal identity and intellectual or cognitive development, we are brought to the following attempt to summarize the material on parent versus peer relationships and compliance. Shainberg (1970) points out that identity formation often demands a fit between the real self and the ideal self because the individual is tied to a concrete operational thinking and therefore cannot free his ideal self as an abstract concept. The individual is therefore trapped in Goodman's "I-me" stage of autonomy formation with its emphasis on the concrete. To progress to the "I-them" stage requires the ability to abstract a "them" from the situation, over which the individual can then exercise some personal control. It would appear that before development of formal operational thinking, the adolescent is unable to abstract the standards of his various reference groups from given situations and make them a unified part of his moral principles. He is still tied to Kohlberg's third stage of maintaining good relations and is under the influence of referent power. The movement through the stages

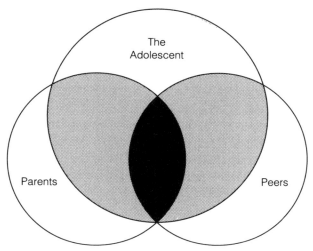

Figure 13.1. A view of the continuing influences of parents and peers as the adolescent individuates. The white areas signify the attitudes, values, and behaviors the adolescent sees in belonging solely to self, or parents, or peers. The gray areas signify areas of influence of parents or peers as the adolescent sees either parents or peers as more knowledgeable, expert, or current. The black area indicates attitudes, values, and behaviors the adolescent sees as congruent, in agreement, among self, parents, and peers.

of the growth of autonomy according to Goodman, going from dependence in the "they-me" stage, to conformity to reference group in the "I-me" stage, and finally to personal control in the "I-them" stage bears a close relationship to movement toward more autonomy and the highest level of moral development, the level of conscience, in Kohlberg's stages.

In summing up this section, and shown in Figure 13.1, we see a logic along certain lines. A conflict arises between parents and adolescents over the degree of autonomy the adolescent will be permitted to have. The adolescent will respond to his parents' use of authority on the basis of numerous influences, including the mode and manner of the exertion of that parental authority. The conflict will be more or less intense as the adolescent sees the area, or subject, of the conflict as more or less within the parents' area of expertise. The adolescent will balance his assertions against his parents with his support from his peers, and, to a degree, will reverse the balance with parental support against peers, depending on who has the expertise. He will also respond in relation to his stage of cognitive development, his stage of moral development, and his stage of autonomy development.

PEERS IN GROUPS AND AS FRIENDS

Peer groups and peers and friends provide the adolescent with the arena for much of the learning and developing that occur in all the life tasks. In general, friendships, the close friendships that an adolescent has, will be with some one or some few adolescents who are also members of his peer group. Differentiating between the functions of the peer group and of friendship presents a false dichotomy. This dichotomy must be viewed as two points on a social-interaction continuum, the adolescent learning and developing in two social areas, i.e., finding his place and interacting with a group of people, and learning how to interact more intimately with individual people. The remainder of this section will be broken down into functions of the peer group, structures of the peer group, and the functions and manners of friendship. The issue of conformity, to peers in groups and to peers as friends, will be discussed throughout.

Ausubel (1954) saw peer groups in adolescence as performing several functions. Probably the most important of these is to provide the adolescent with the chance to demonstrate his competence, which Ausubel calls "providing primary status." Primary status is considered such because it is the status that the individual adolescent learns through his own efforts, exerting his own abilities, and is different from the status he had as a child, which is termed "derived status," the status granted him by virtue of being his parents' child. Elkind (1969), in the Piagetian tradition, views adolescents as being in a stage of egocentrism in which they are so preoccupied with self-definition and self-interest that all friendships and social interactions are based on these egocentric needs and perceptions. So, too, Erikson's (1968) continued view of the identity crisis shows the importance of the many aspects of identity formation, including the nature of relationships. This is put succinctly by Oshman and Manosevitz:

> During the identity crisis the emerging adult is confronted with the task of reformulating all that he has been into all that he wishes to be. This reformulation demands a relinquishment of infantile sources of gratification, a transmutation of notions of youthful omnipotence, a selective assimilation of meaningful occupational and ideological alternatives, and a synthesis of childhood identifications. In this way, an individual can develop a sense of ego identity which will permit him to establish a symbiotic relationship with the society and preserve a sense of continuity for himself. (1974, pp. 207–8)

These views related well to the need for status, for gaining primary status, as a type of self-definition during adolescence and the assumption that the identity, or self-definition, is garnered through interaction with external sources.

In addition to the first function of the peer group, providing a source for developing primary status, Ausubel offers several other functions of the peer group. These additional functions are interrelated and lead to the development of the first function, primary status. Ausubel says that peer groups facilitate emancipation from home and parental influence and furthermore give focus to the adolescent's resistance to adult standards and authority. A study by Phelps and Horrocks adds weight to the notion of this function. Using a questionnaire about group membership, attitudes, feelings toward the group, activities with the group, and satisfaction with the group to study 200 adolescent boys and girls, they found that "the degree of emancipation from adult control appears to be a most important influence in the formation of patterns of informal group activities and attitudes" (1958, p. 86).

The other side of emancipation from parental influence is the focalization of resistance against adult standards and authority. Sherif and Sherif (1964) concluded, on the basis of numerous observations of adolescent groups, that group members often engaged in behavior that was not only socially unacceptable but was in fact in violation of the law. These behaviors included drinking of alcohol, traffic violations, destruction of public property, carrying illegal weapons, and buying and smoking cigarettes, which was illegal for minors in most communities. Douvan and Adelson (1966) found that even though adolescents stated that the reason for membership in many peer groups might be emancipation and resistance, they did not greatly change their emotional attachment and dependence on adult standards. The question of degree of resistance and emancipation from parental standards and authority has been referred to in the previous section. The Phelps and Horrocks and Sherif and Sherif studies show that the adolescent peer group supports this function and facilitates the movement to greater autonomy.

Relating to this support, the next function of the peer group that Ausubel discussed is that of providing certain norms for governing behavior. As the study by Dunphy (1963) presented later will show, the norms are intended and function to provide guidelines for learning different types of behaviors, values, etc., as the nature of the peer groups and the nature of the adolescents' interests change through the adolescent years. Sherif and Sherif show that peer-group members develop common practices, common evaluations, and shared tastes that become standards by which the adolescents appraise their own and their peers' behavior.

It seems crucial to consider the norms of the peer group as providing the adolescent with alternatives to the parental norms. We should try to view the adolescent as moving from a limited world of family and small community into a world with much more varied behavioral and attitudinal options. The adolescent takes giant steps as he moves away from the normative standards of his family. Accompanying these steps, logically, is considerable anxiety. By moving into and forming peer groups that set their own standards, the adolescent is able to deviate from parental standards and norms while still having support from other persons. It is hard to stress enough this difficulty for the adolescent.

If we try to think of the mass and maze of possible behaviors, attitudes, and values the adolescent sees around him personally, in his greater community, in school, and in the media, and if we try to see through his eyes the extreme difficulty of choosing values, attitudes, and behaviors that might feel consistent and coherent for him, we begin to grasp the nature of the adolescent's dilemma. If next we try to envision the adolescent constructing a coherent and consistent set of attitudes, values, and behaviors on his own and then acting out this pattern on his own, we may be able to conjure up the frightening, even awe-inspiring, range of social and personal difficulties that might be encountered. If one has to choose his own way of thinking and his own way of behaving—and it would seem that one does have to—how much easier and how much safer this is as part of a group that has norms or values and behaviors for people like oneself.

The last function of the peer group presented by Ausubel that will be discussed here is to serve as an arena that allows latitude for the adolescent to test himself in a variety of roles, to test the range of his abilities and emotions, and to test these within a group that conceptually, at least, will be more open and empathetic to the problems, the extremes, and the anxieties of adolescence.

In sum, the peer group supplies the adolescent with an arena that is sufficiently supportive, rigid in the sense of providing alternative norms from those of his parents, but flexible in providing opportunities for trying out new roles, skills, attitudes, and values, so that the adolescent may begin to answer the question, "Which ways can I be?" and can begin to derive his own "primary status."

PEER-GROUP STRUCTURE

Turning now to the issue of the structures of peer groups, we see that they have been variously described, starting with the "subculture" conceptualization that received impetus from the work of Coleman (1961), observations of age-mate reference groups (Sherif and Sherif, 1964, 1965), and analysis of the social structure of peer group developmentally by age (Dunphy, 1963).

Is there a youth culture? Are there youth subcultures? There is no universally accepted answer to either of these questions. Elkin and Westley (1955) believed that they had destroyed the myth of the adolescent subculture through their survey study which showed that an adolescent middle-class sample complied with the norms of their parents and held no hostile or resentful feelings against their parents. Berger (1963) concluded that what Elkin and Westley had "actually done is present evidence that certain adolescents do not share the norms of youth culture" (p. 319). Berger suggests that the characteristics associated with youth culture refer to a system that is normative for youthful persons. There may be young persons who do not adhere to the system and older persons who do. "Whatever it is that is normatively distinctive about youth cultures is probably not characteristic of all or even most adolescents" (p. 319), but the term and the idea have value.

Elkin and Westley's explosion of the myth of the adolescent culture relates directly to the previous section, which showed adolescents seeing themselves as somewhere between their parents and their peers on many issues, closer to their parents on important issues and closer to their peers on issues that fell within a "youth culture" purview. Berger's position is that most adolescents spend little if any time or energy involved with facets of behavior that might be considered part of the "youth culture." But he does say that the youth culture is attended to by certain youthful people and that there is no age bar to participation in youth culture. Funnily enough and very funny indeed, on one episode of the television show "The Odd Couple," Felix felt he was old, over the hill, so he and Oscar went to a purely "youth culture" discotheque. In support of Berger, not only did they lack the appropriate clothes and the appropriate language, but they lacked the essential ingredient of youthfulness. The audience enjoyed their time at the discotheque, but Felix and Oscar did not.

James Coleman's (1961) widely acclaimed and widely criticized study helps put the issue of subcultures into the framework of the influence hierarchy. Coleman's position, in generalized form, was that our society, changing rapidly, highly rationalized, can and does no longer rely on the family in the "natural processes" of education. These processes are now the business of formalized institutions, the schools, which are set apart from the rest of the society and which take longer to educate the child and adolescent in the fullness of contemporary education than the family did in the narrower life of the past. As a result of this institutionalization of education, society is no longer confronted with individuals to be trained or socialized into adulthood, but is rather confronted with "distinct social systems" in which adolescents to be trained offer a united front to the efforts toward their education made by the adult society. In the adolescents' decision making, he said that their peers are as important as, or more important than, their parents. Although the adolescent subculture bears a strong resemblance in its major characteristics to the adult society, there are nonetheless superimposed on this subculture variations in its character that are due to factors that differ from school to school and from community to community. Sampling from the 10 high schools, nominational procedure was used for identifying the "leading crowd" and the persons most outstanding in athletics, popularity, and activities in each school. The leading crowds in the various schools were similarly composed, with emphasis on the athletic boy and the popular girl and with far less emphasis on the brilliant student. More differences were found for girls, in that girls who were activity leaders from higher socioeconomic schools and girls who were popular in lower socioeconomic schools were more likely to be in the leading crowd.

Being an athlete and being in the leading crowd are of great importance in making a boy popular. In general, the boys in Coleman's study felt that school-related activities other than athletics were of considerably less importance in being popular with girls than they were in being popular with other boys. Just as athletics for boys shows a high relation with actual popularity, so do activities for girls, particularly in higher socioeconomic schools. The role of girls as objects of attention for boys was seen as very important by the adolescents, as exhibited in their values.

We must remember that Coleman's study dates from 1961 and that attitudes may have changed. However, a replication of Coleman's study by Eitzen (1975) indicates that athletics are still of primary importance to adolescents and their status within their high schools. He did find that differences exist between schools, which might suggest that in the future athletics will be of less importance in more urban, higher-SES schools. But in the years since Coleman's study, with the influence of his findings on education, athletics have not diminished appreciably as the major source of status within our high schools.

To the question "What does it take to be important?" the answer "good grades, honor roll" was ranked fourth out of the six items used for boys and fifth out of the six for girls for all schools. Regardless of this overall low standing, its position differs considerably in the various schools. Coleman continually illustrates differences among the schools based on school size, SES, urban, suburban, country setting, etc. But his point is that the "value climate" of the school is more than all of these.

The general picture derived from Coleman's work is one in which boys do not try for academic success as they might because it cannot get them status by itself. Girls try to do well enough to please their parents but not so well that their social status is jeopardized. And the leading crowd of a school, as the norm setter for that school, adds to more than the sum or consensus of the values of the student body with an extra middle-class weighting. The leading crowd appears to support the important background characteristics representative of the school and to accentuate them, whether they be lower or upper socioeconomic characteristics.

Acknowledging the influence of the school and school differences, and acknowledging the differences in value climates among schools, one must still remember the extent of diversity in personality and group types within schools. Reister and Zucker (1968) analyzed the informal structure of a high school and found a number of more or less distinct groupings. One clearly defined group, the "collegiates," appeared active, social, establishment-oriented, what might be seen as classic all-American high school students. Equally extant and equally a tradition in American high schools was the group called "the leathers." These are kids who act rougher and tougher than the others and who might at one time or another have been thought of as hoods. Another group, which was small at the time of this study, was called "true individuals." They would be primarily identified by their clothes and hair and over the last 20 years have been variously called "beatniks," "hippies," or "freaks." Reister and Zucker noted three other less distinct but still identifiable groups of young high school people with the following patterns of behavior:

1. "Quiet kids," who seem more independent, go their own way, and may in fact belong to an identifiable grouping but outside the school
2. "Intellectuals," students who were serious about their studies and interested in many or deeply interested in at least one topic or area of study
3. "Kids going steady," who spent a great deal of time with each other and maybe with other couples similarly involved with each other

The geographic and urban-rural effects on the values and social groupings in schools are evident to anyone who has traveled and, particularly, taught in various regions of the country. As I write this in Austin, Texas, I am aware that the high school students in the city could do a ranking of high schools on the basis of how numerous and how valued the "kickers" group is in each school. Kickers are either future cowboys or highly westernized, ranch- and rodeo-oriented people. What they "kick" is implicit in the nature of their preferred environment.

Although these studies begin to indicate the ways in which schools and adolescent peer groups are structured, they leave no doubt that the influences leading to differences in the structure of the groups in different areas do not overwhelm individual differences. As an example confirming this, Roff and Sells (1965) studied the relation between intelligence and socioeconomic status in groups differing in sex and socioeconomic background. They concluded that above-average intelligence in a peer group is an asset to the adolescent in a wide variety of social groups.

Peck and Galliani, studying intelligence, ethnicity, and social roles in adolescents, found for both Anglo-American and Latin-American adolescents in three Texas communities that intelligence was related positively to peer nomination as "brain," "wheel," "big imagination," and "average one," and related negatively to nomination as "daydreamer." Intelligence was not related to being labeled "quiet," "left out," or "wild one." "The intellectually above average individual tends, generally, to be more visible among his age mates than his intellectually less able fellow" (1962, p. 70).

Once one recognizes (1) that there are a variety of types of adolescent age-mate or reference groupings, (2) that these groupings are influenced in norms and behaviors by family and background variables as well as by value variables inherent in particular communities and schools, and (3) that the choice, either by individual adolescents or by peers, of inclusion in a particular group is related to personal interest and ability, i.e., personal characteristics of the adolescent and characteristics of the peer group, the peer group itself becomes of interest.

After many studies of adolescents, and especially an intensive study of 24 groups of boys in several cities, Sherif (1966) concluded that adolescent goals and attitudes are strongly affected by the status structure and norms of their group as well as by the interaction process within the group. While functioning as a group member, or acting with the internalized norms and goals of the group, the adolescent is still bombarded with influences, competitions, and conflicts within the context of other social ties and from other peer groups and adult authorities.

Clearly Sherif and Sherif (1965) are impressed with the complexity and multiplicity of influences and interactions in the functioning of age-mate groups and the development of adolescent attitudes, goals, and behaviors. Equally important is their conclusion on the generality of groups:

> We were impressed once again with the generality of group formations in all walks of life in this age period. . . . All have differentiated patterns

regulating their interpersonal relations. All have rules, customs, fads — in short, norms — regulating behavior in their activity. These are the minimum essentials of a group. . . .

These groups of adolescents were formed, or joined, on the members' own initiative. . . .

The individual had a hand in creating the properties of the group, or had selected it. . . .

Psychologically, therefore, the basis of group solidarity, of conformity to group norms without threat of sanctions, of the binding nature of group rules even when they conflict with those of parents and officials, lies in the personal involvement of members. (p. 286)

The functions of the peer group as explained by Ausubel are clearly seen in the generality of group formations found by Sherif and Sherif.

In addition to the striking similarity in peer-group makeup among these different groups, Sherif and Sherif found a considerable amount of similarity in attitudes and behavior across groups from different socioeconomic classes. They all held highly an image of individual success in adults as symbolized through the media, they were all strongly oriented toward age-mates as their reference sets, and they all held an intense interest in the opposite sex. Moreover, all of these groups were able to distinguish very clearly what adult authority considered to be right or wrong, while "the finding most common to all was the boys' insistent desire to do things on 'our own,' without adult programming or supervision" (p. 316). In analyzing the differences among the groups, the direction of differences in achievement, ambition, and adherence to middle-class values were as expected between the upper-middle-, lower-middle-, and lower-class adolescents. However, the conclusion was not that the upper-middle-class youth were more ambitious or achievement-oriented, but rather that the lower-class youth were as ambitious "relative to their own ideas of achievement, and even more ambitious relative to their own parents' achievement" (p. 318).

A most interesting and important aspect of the Sherifs' findings relates to the issue of conformity in adolescence. In analyzing their data, the Sherifs were surprised to find that in the schools serving high socioeconomic areas there was the least diversity of individual values and goals. Much greater heterogeneity was found in the values and goals of the student bodies of schools in the middle and lower socioeconomic areas. Only on questions that were strictly financial, such as income, spending money, and the like, was homogeneity, or like-mindedness, found in the schools serving lower socioeconomic groups to the degree that such like-mindedness was found in the high socioeconomic schools. Sherif and Sherif say, "These findings have led us to suspect that some theorists on lower class life may have overlooked the actual diversity within lower class settings, perhaps because of their preoccupation with specific social problems" (p. 321).

The greater homogeneity in upper-middle-class schools and upper-middle-class reference groups may be attributable to greater similarity of personal aims and goals, i.e., these people are more likely to go to college, more likely to have upper-middle-class jobs, and more likely to live in particular places. The middle and lower socioeconomic groups will be made up of adolescents for whom upward mobility is differentially important, and the tracks or ways of attaining desired mobility will be more varied. Also for those who feel unable to move upward in the social system, the variety of ways to entertain themselves, enjoy themselves, and hold the status quo must be greater than for the people who are trying to move up.

DUNPHY'S SOCIAL STRUCTURE OF PEER GROUPS

Dunphy (1963) studied the social structure of urban adolescent peer groups. His findings provided a framework for considering why there may be greater diversity within adolescent subcultures or large adolescent groups than might previously have been thought and supplied a picture of the general trend of changes in the social structure of the peer group developmentally, through the adolescent period. According to Dunphy, the social structure of adolescent peer groups is composed of two basic types of groups—crowds and cliques. The crowd is larger and is essentially an association of cliques, ranging in size from 15 to 30 members, or up to 4 cliques of 3 to 9 members each. He found no cliques with more than 9 members, which points strongly to the intimacy involved in a small group. Although they were the basic units of crowds, not all cliques were associated with crowds. One could be a member of a clique without being a member of a crowd, but clique membership appeared to be a prerequisite of crowd membership.

This is very interesting for observers and functional for adolescents. The adolescent becomes a member of a small group, which Dunphy is calling a clique, composed of three or more individuals, up to nine, with similar interests. They may be close friends from childhood days or newly found friends, but they have a strong feeling of "we," with strong emotional involvement individually among members and strong individual attachment to the clique. The aim of the individual adolescent, both as an adolescent and in terms of socialization into adulthood, is to be able to function comfortably and successfully with people in groups ranging from small to large. Therefore, a possible aim for most adolescents is to become part of a crowd. A crowd is larger, less closely knit, and more impersonal than the clique, although the crowd is made up of people who are more similar in terms of backgrounds, interests, likes, and dislikes. The crowd is most likely to function through particular kinds of activities, which may be of an athletic or social nature and provide the opportunity for interaction between the sexes. If we try to envision an adolescent moving into a new community or moving into a new school or merely progressing in the usual way from junior high school or middle school into high school, we see him encountering by himself many people he does not know. In other words, we start, I think, with a fairly lonely character. Not only would such an average adolescent be too anxious and unsure of his social competencies to attempt to plunge directly into membership or association with crowds, but this movement does not, I believe, fit the logic of movement into crowds at any age level above adolescence. Clique membership comes first.

The clique, the making of two, three, four, or five friends, gives the adolescent the chance to establish some degree of companionship, security, and acceptance, offers a place of belonging where he need not be as anxious, before he attempts any kind of movement into a larger social scene. Moreover, the clique allows him to try out social skills, evaluate his own behavior, and have others evaluate his behavior, and gives him some standards for behaving which, because of the relationship between the clique and the crowd, allow him to gauge his potential for success and acceptance in the crowd. Because he can rely on the closeness of the clique, the adolescent can blow off steam and act differently than he might otherwise while simultaneously developing skills and retaining support for movement into the wider arena of the crowd.

There are potential disadvantages, or what some considered to be disadvantages, in both the clique and the crowd. Primarily, these center around issues of exclusiveness. The clique or crowd may become snobbish and not accept certain other cliques or individuals as members, which may be difficult for the excluded. The clique or crowd may become of such importance to the adolescent that it causes tension with his family and a tendency to neglect other responsibilities. These problems are probably more crucial in the upper-middle-class areas, where there is less diversity and the standard of clique and crowd behavior is more commonly accepted. In such a setting, adolescents who are, or who feel, excluded would conceivably have few options for other directions of behavior and other types of cliques and crowds to join. However, group membership and the variety of groups that exist in a community and in a school relate to a broad range of individual differences and individual choices. We can consider that the clique/crowd manner is facilitative and satisfying for many.

The differing functions of the clique and crowd also lead to a tendency for their settings and activities to be distributed differently throughout the week. Most of the crowd settings occur on weekends, while most of the cliques meet on weekdays. The crowd settings — social activities, parties, and dances — are by nature more organized and therefore have to fall into "free time." The predominant activity of cliques is talking. Analysis of the incredible amount of conversation that occurs within a clique shows that it has an instrumental function in organizing and publicizing crowd activities and in evaluating them when they are over.

A superordinate grouping occurs in some high schools, where certain crowds or combinations of crowds are distinguished according to a particular status within the youth hierarchy. These larger groupings are called "sets." Sets are usually based on their members' social background, ethnic background, personality type, or some combination of these. For example, churchgoers may form one set, college-bound youth another, and playboys and playgirls — a highly social group — may form another. Sets rarely overlap, and even if an individual qualifies for two or more sets, he is generally assigned by his peers to the set for which they think he is most suitable (Stone and Church, 1968).

Another form of peer group that should be mentioned is the gang. Gangs may be differentiated from cliques and crowds in that they seem to have regular leaders, well-defined membership, and a clear-cut organization. Whereas clique members have greater mutual affection and spend more time interacting with each other as individuals, gang members seem to focus more on the activities of the group and the goals of the group. The gang member is more likely than the clique member to play a well-defined role and to adhere more closely to the more structured, intense rules of the gang, which tend to be rigidly enforced. Although gangs vary greatly among themselves and generalizations are difficult to make (Rogers, 1972b), research suggests that organized gang behavior is traditionally more a part of particular subcultures and is found only in specified slum areas in larger cities (Thrasher, 1936). Gangs are viewed by many as being abnormal to the American adolescent experience, although successive migrant groups and minority groups in urban centers have formed and still are forming and participating in gangs. Gangs seem to function in approximately the same way as other peer groups, with clique-type subgroups either forming the gang or together making up the gang. However, gangs are typified as being antisocial, and many gang members have antisocial attitudes and behavior and are often poorly adjusted in school. The brighter, better adjusted individuals in these same communities are not usually attracted to gangs (Crane, 1958). Gangs are more likely to be same-sex, male groups, with the opposite-sex, female groups participating as tangential cliques, or auxiliary units, to the gang.

Dunphy shows the structural changes in the typical makeup of adolescent peer groups through adolescence, as illustrated in Figure 13.2. Particularly noteworthy is the development from unisexual peer groupings and relationships to heterosexual peer groupings and relationships, as well as movement from smaller to larger groups, which in combination allow the adolescent in late adolescence to function with members of both sexes in large and small groups. Following is Dunphy's explanation of these structural changes:

> The initial stage of adolescent group development appears to be that of the isolated unisexual clique: i.e., isolated in terms of any relationship with corresponding groups of the opposite sex. This primary stage represents the persistence of the preadolescent "gang" into the adolescent. Stage 2 introduces the first movement towards heterosexuality in group structure. Unisexual cliques previously unrelated to cliques of the opposite sex now participate in heterosexual interaction. At this stage, however, interaction is considered daring and is only undertaken in the security of group settings where the individual is supported by the presence of his own sex associates. Interaction at this stage is often superficially antagonistic. Stage 3 sees the formation of the heterosexual clique for the first time. Upper status members of unisexual cliques initiate individual-to-individual heterosexual interaction and the first dating occurs. Those adolescents who belong to these emergent heterosexual groups still maintain a membership role in their unisexual clique, so that they possess dual membership in two intersecting cliques. This initiates an extensive transformation of group structure by which there takes place a reorganization of unisexual cliques and the reformation of their membership into heterosexual cliques (stage 4). While the cliques persist as small intimate groups, their membership now comprises both sexes. Stage 5 sees the slow disintegration of the crowd and the formation of cliques consisting of couples who are going steady or engaged. Thus there is a progressive development of group structure from predominantly unisexual to heterosexual groups. In this transition the crowd — an extended heterosexual peer group — occupies a strategic position. Membership in the crowd offers opportunities for establishing a heterosexual role. The crowd is therefore the most significant group for the individual, but crowd membership is dependent on prior membership in the clique. In fact, the crowd is basically an interrelationship of cliques, and appears to consolidate the heterosexual learning appropriate to each stage of development. The majority of clique members, therefore, possess a determinant position in an extended hierarchical arrangement of cliques and crowds, in which high status is accorded to groups most developed in heterosexual structure. The

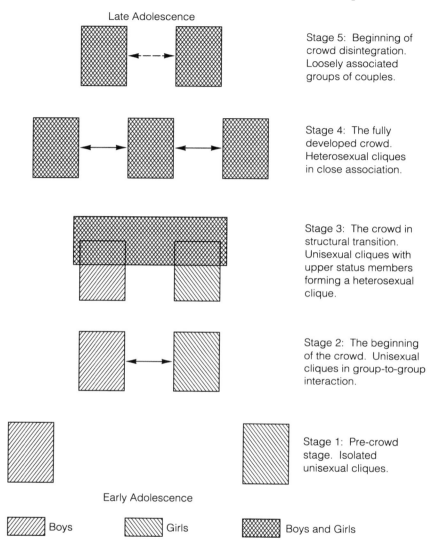

Late Adolescence

Stage 5: Beginning of crowd disintegration. Loosely associated groups of couples.

Stage 4: The fully developed crowd. Heterosexual cliques in close association.

Stage 3: The crowd in structural transition. Unisexual cliques with upper status members forming a heterosexual clique.

Stage 2: The beginning of the crowd. Unisexual cliques in group-to-group interaction.

Stage 1: Pre-crowd stage. Isolated unisexual cliques.

Early Adolescence

Boys   Girls   Boys and Girls

Figure 13.2. Stages of group development in adolescence (Reprinted by permission from D. C. Dunphy, "The social structure of urban adolescent peer groups," *Sociometry* 26 [1963], 230–46.)

course of the individual's social development appears to be strongly influenced by his position within this structure. (1963, p. 235–37)

Dunphy reports that in Sydney, Australia, where his study was carried out, about 70 percent of the boys and 80 percent of the girls at ages 14 and 15 belonged to peer groups similar to the types he has described. He sees these groups as extending the socialization process begun in the family, including the differences between instrumental and expressive lines of behavior, the movement to more complex systems of relationships, and the personality development inherent in this movement.

Dunphy's description of the makeup of adolescent peer groups is very complete and is most useful for understanding the social structure of peer groups. It has been the basis for a great deal of subsequent research. A good deal of work has looked at the difference between clique members and nonmembers (for example, Eder, 1985; Fine, 1980). Another role has been introduced, that of a liaison (Burt, 1982; Rogers and Kincaid, 1982). The idea of the liaison role is that individuals may not be solely members of single crowds and cliques but may have many relations to various groups. In a social structure with many liaison roles there would be more communication and more flexibility.

Studies have now shown that cliques differ in importance in different grades (Brown et al., 1986; Crockett et al., 1984; Hallinan, 1979). Fine and Eder's ethnographic studies put in question the thesis that cliques and their members increase throughout school. It might be that the feeling of concern about group membership grows well into high school but that the social structure itself is less stable, with more and different kinds of groupings.

Shrum and Cheek (1987) used data on 2,299 children, in grades 3 through 12, from a number of schools. They found that the number of children belonging to cliques increases through the sixth grade and then declines. The number classified as *liaisons* increases throughout.

Prior to the notion of "liaison," these individuals would have been classified as nonmembers of cliques and thought of as isolates, persons who do not belong. The liaison role is by no means a negative one, and may allow greater movement and activity within and among the cliques and crowds of a school than clique membership allows. As has been the case with other ideas we have followed in this text through 30 or 40 years of research, we are unsure if these current findings are the result of new ideas and research methods or if the situation under study has changed. Were peer social structures more rigid and better defined, with more and tighter group membership 25 years ago? Or are we now able to discern subtleties in social structures because we have better conceptual and methodological approaches for studying them? It is very difficult to tell.

Nevertheless, these current research descriptions of the social structure of schools picture the traditional social groupings but with great permeability. From junior high school on, it would appear that adolescents can be members of particular cliques or have liaison roles and still be quite involved within the social structure of the high school. Liaisons might have more friends than members of cliques, but by definition their friends will be from among a number of groups. In some ways this pattern appears similar to Dunphy's crowd stage, and also a logical development en route to associations with and membership in adult groups. Shrum and Cheek refer to this as a "degrouping process."

FRIENDS

The smallest, closest, and most intimate peer group to which an adolescent belongs is his friendship group, which in fact may be purely a one-to-one, dyadic, friendship group. In this section, as the movement from family to community is viewed, the recurring issues are "What can I do?", "How many ways can I be?" or "What can I be?", and "How can I find this out?" Put differently, the issues are the development of self in the process of growth into a larger community and how social facilitators enable and encourage this growth. Cliques and crowds and their interrelationship just described operate as facilitators, and the liaison role and degrouping process illustrate the movement of the individual into the larger community on his or her own. A crucial facilitator is friendship.

Friends are people who will like you anyway. They will like you regardless of your success or failure, of your victories or losses, of your social finesse or social faux pas.

> Friendship engages, discharges, cultivates, and transforms the most acute passions of the adolescent, and so allows the youngster to confront and master them. Because it carries so much of the burden of adolescent growth, friendship acquires at this time a pertinence and intensity it has never had before nor (in many cases) will ever have again. (Douvan and Adelson, 1966, p. 174)

The cognitive developments of adolescence allow perspective taking and thus the ability to share and empathize (Tesch, 1983), and increase the capacity for awareness and comparison of feelings (Paris and Lindauer, 1982). A great deal of variability in the quality of adolescents' friendships has been noted between the sexes (Hunter and Youniss, 1982; Johnson and Aries,

1983) and between individual adolescents on the basis of personality (Coie and Dodge, 1983) and social skills (Gottman, 1983). Moreover, earlier, we discussed at length the variability in cognitive development among adolescents and the understandings of friendship that evolve as part of social cognition.

So often in therapy one sees adults who in the process of adolescence have missed the close and open communication of a friendship. They have missed a learning that is essential to growing into a healthy, functioning adult. They do not know that other people are concerned about small and everyday occurrences, and therefore they either overlook much of what happens in their day-to-day lives or worry excessively that they are different and are the only ones to worry in this manner. I once saw a client who was acutely embarrassed when, on entering the office, he had difficulty taking off his overshoes. When I remarked that this kind of difficulty bugged me also, he was amazed. He said, "I didn't know you should even think about these things."

In adolescence, the satisfaction and also the crucial importance of a friendship is in being able to share, to reveal one's feelings and thoughts about everything, from the most mundane to the most important events and considerations in one's life. "My parents make me mad when . . . ," "Would he/she like me if I . . . ," "I don't know if I can . . . ," "Do you think I should . . . ," "Do you ever feel . . . ," "Do you ever think . . . ," etc., etc., etc. The questions, the concerns, the intimacies are endless. In the process of helping each other, each adolescent helps himself. As friends, "they explain themselves to each other, and in so doing, each explains himself to himself" (Osterrieth, 1969, p. 19).

The adolescent wants and needs friends, as does everyone. The friends he chooses will most likely share common interests and personal and social characteristics, and although some of these may be complementary rather than similar (Byrne and Griffith, 1966), in general the friendship will be built more on similarity of characteristics than on differences (Douvan and Gold, 1966). But in the process of demanding that he make his own friends, the function of the friendship comes second to learning to make friendships themselves. Since "the adolescent insists upon choosing his own friends, he often makes mistakes . . . the friendship is broken, and the adolescent is then disillusioned" (Hurlock, 1967, p. 130). With age and experience, obviously, most adolescents become more critical and successful in their choice of friends.

There are sex differences in adolescent friendship patterns. Generally, girls' friendships are more frequent, deeper, and more dependent than are those of boys, and girls' friendships are more intimate and provoke more upset when they appear to be faltering (Douvan and Adelson, 1966). The nature of girls' friendships would appear to be more expressive in much the same way that the nature of girls' roles in peer groups is more expressive. Boys, on the other hand, tend to stress, relatively more, the results of their friendship, as in having a companion with whom one gets along while participating in activities of common interest (Douvan and Adelson, 1966). Again this seems to show the instrumental perspective of boys in friendships, as we have previously seen in social roles. The sex difference in perspective on sexual matters may influence the quality of same-sex friendship. Boys are more likely to see sex as a motive relatively specific and independent of love, whereas girls are more likely to integrate the sexual and love aspects of heterosexual relationships (Bardwick, 1971).

Douvan and Adelson (1966) characterize the changes in function, quality, and content of friendship through adolescence as proceeding from more superficial friendship in early adolescence to the intense sharing of middle adolescence and then a more realistic, both interdependent and independent, relationship in later adolescence. This movement may be seen as relating to the development of formal operations and the tremendous experimenting with possibilities that characterize middle adolescence. The early adolescent's more superficial friendship is based on concrete activities, sharing things rather than thoughts, sharing time and the doing of favors. The friendship of middle adolescents is characterized more by the trying on of roles, styles, and feelings and the testing of the limits of personal abilities and of friends' and society's endurance and tolerance—a movement into the area of hypothesis testing—"What ways can I be?" By late adolescence the individual has come to better define himself and therefore does not need the continuous support of a friend for all and sundry feelings and behaviors. Therefore, the friendship can be built with greater emphasis on the friend's personality and talents, on what the friend brings to the relationship, and on a greater degree of tolerance for individual differences (Douvan and Gold, 1966).

Rogers (1972b) says that the intimate friendships of adolescence serve the following purposes: (1) they permit an opportunity for exploration and extension of the self that kinship intimacy does not; (2) they help in establishing an identity that the person feels confident with; (3) they serve to relieve guilt, provide reassurance, and establish controls; and (4) they provide a transition to heterosexuality and a heterosexual adult sex-role identity. These purposes, and in fact this entire discussion of friendships in adolescence, point to the transitional character of the extreme, intense, adolescent friendship and the socialization function of adolescent friendship to bring the adolescent into adulthood, where he may have friendship, yet be "himself" in a great variety of other social roles.

Conger (1973) speaks of the emphasis by contemporary adolescents, both early and late adolescents, on the need for more true friendship and love in a world that is generally viewed as impersonal, competitive, and constantly changing. He cites a 1971 Harris survey in which 9 out of 10 adolescents expressed agreement about the importance of more friendship and love between people. Conger feels that the reason for this emphasis may be, first, the difficulty adolescents have in the current social climate with developing open, honest, warm relationships, even with peers, and second, that despite their concern for this type of relationship, many adolescents have difficulty in practicing what they preach, or at least what they desire. A third reason that he gives has to do with the meaning and definition of close and meaningful friendship according to the subjective requirements of today's adolescents.

These requirements may be more demanding and more stringent than those of adolescents, or for that matter adults, in earlier generations. Wolf (1974), in a discussion of why Reich's *Greening of America* was not the answer to the problems of our young, speaks to this question. Adolescents began to feel that the essential ingredients of proper friendships and relationships were as follows:

> The only true connection with others was . . . the "I-thou" relationship, in which one authentic self and another meet without hiding anything. This relationship one should have with every other man, not only friend with friend, or lover with lover, but businessman with clerk, and passenger to conductor, and student to janitor. Everything must be fully human. (p. 19)

Wolf explains why this demand for authenticity in relationships goes unmet:

> The I-thou relationship is very hard. Our young were mistaken when they thought it could be maintained all the time, that one could be utterly open and available to every other human being. It is possible only to pretend to speak openly for hour after hour, to listen openly hour after hour, to treat every person as if he were your beloved, or as if he were your self. Buber has told us that one inevitably moves in and out of I-thou relationships. And so one goes back into the world of I-it. We cannot always treat the janitor as if he were our friend; we must learn how to treat the janitor as if he were the janitor. (p. 20)

Development into a stage of realistic friendship in late adolescence, as explained by Douvan and Adelson, is often, it would seem today, not reached by many adolescents who require friendships of the type and level described by Conger and by Wolf. Even in early adolescence, the benefits postulated by Sullivan (1963) for chumship, such as abating loneliness, are not necessarily met (Yarcheski and Mahon, 1984). It seems that we can ask a great deal, and adolescents expect a great deal, in friendship, but an adolescent can ask no more of friendship than a friendship can provide and still remain himself. A 15-year-old girl wrote:

> A friend is a person who you can:
> 1—trust
> 2—put a burden upon
> 3—share happiness
> 4—share sadness
> 5—depend upon
> 6—love
>
> I've really never experienced the feeling of having a friend whose personality made all of the above possible. I thought I had such a friend once, but it turned out that just like all other people I know, he was an acquaintance. I hope someday I'll find a real friend I'll want to feel close to. (Bravler and Jacobs, p. 56)

CONFORMITY

In friendships, cliques, crowds, and sets, adolescents have been seen to choose and more than likely be with people who are more like themselves than different from themselves. A solid degree of veracity in the statement "birds of a feather flock together" is acknowledged by almost everyone. The similarity in adolescents' friends, cliques, and crowd members has been seen to occur in a broad spectrum of demographic variables, such as socioeconomic status, ethnicity, etc. Attitude similarity as a determinant of attraction would appear to underlie many of the similarities in friendship patterns. Much research has shown that degree of attitude similarity relates to degree of attraction and that proportion of similar attitudes relates almost linearly to attraction—i.e., the more attitudes we agree on, the more we are attracted (Baron et al., 1974, p. 41). This relationship has been seen to hold for people of all ages and across nations.

It makes very good sense within this framework to see adolescents who have the opportunity to make clear and unencumbered choices of friends and associates, albeit somewhat limited in distance, to associate with people who are similar to them. What then appears to be conformity behavior within the peer groups could be, and no doubt to some degree is, a function of the similarities in attitudes that promoted the development of attraction and establishment of the peer group. However, conformity in adolescents is even greater than these factors might indicate. A number of social-pressure experiments, in which adolescent subjects were influenced in some subtle manner to see whether they would change behavior or attitudes to go along with, to conform to, the other people in the experiment, give support to a long-held notion "that a rigid, 'slavish' type of conformity characterizes early adolescence and diminishes in the later adolescent years" (Landsbaum and Willis, 1971, p. 334). The explanation for this finding is most generally based on socialization theory.

> With the onset of pubescence, the child becomes acutely aware of his social peers and relies on them for many of his external behavior patterns. . . . Therefore, the child at the pubescent stage displays much uncertainty with his own judgment and mirrors the behavior of his peers. By the postadolescent and the early adult stages, the individual has learned that there are both situations which call for conformity and those which call for individual action. (Costanzo and Shaw, 1966, p. 974)

In a study with subjects ranging in age from 5 to 19 years, Collins and Thomas (1972) found that the degree of conformity to peer pressure, "the degree of yielding increased from the early childhood to the middle childhood group, decreased in the preadolescent group, then increased to a maximum in the adolescent group before decreasing in the later adolescent group" (p. 85). The increase in yielding or conformity to peer pressure in middle childhood is explained as a result of the child's learning about social pressure. The spurt in yielding in adolescence is said to result from an increase in peer-group power. The adolescent conforms, yields, because he "is ready to rely on his social peers or yield to their pressure" (p. 85).

The adolescent is more likely to conform in areas such as fashion, haircut, and manners, those areas in which the adolescent might consider his peer group has more expertise than his parents, and we can see that conformity or yielding to peer pressure could increase as an individual moves into new areas where he is not sure of his stance. Both of these socialization factors could account for much of the increase in the conformity in adolescence.

However, the additional influences of moral development and cognitive development as related thereto may contribute to conformity behavior in adolescence. It seems safe to say that in the process of developing from concrete to formal operations, and until such time as formal operations are established, an adolescent may be less sure of himself in terms of his rationale for decision making than he would be either formally in concrete operations or formally in formal operations. So too, in developing through the moral-developmental stages of Kohlberg, the movement, particularly in the last three stages, is from clear-cut, more precise, acknowledgment of the forces influencing judgments to more complex and involved judgmental processes. Fodor (1971) discusses this, showing that on Kohlberg's moral judgment scale,

> stages three and four, for example, imply a degree of submissiveness to the social influence of others, whether they be peers or authority figures. The greater preponderance of principled moral reasoning (stages five and six), therefore, the less susceptible should one be to various forms of social influences. (p. 122)

Fodor found that "subjects who successfully resisted attempts by the interviewer to induce them to reverse their moral decisions were found to be more advanced in moral development as measured by the Kohlberg interview" (p. 124). It would appear that moral and cognitive development in adolescence may account for some of the rise, the spiking effect, in conformity behavior in early to middle adolescence. One might also wonder whether the differences in cognitive development and moral development between the lower and upper-middle socioeconomic status groups might account for the greater homogeneity found among upper socioeconomic groups in comparison to lower socioeconomic groups.

The Deviancies in Context

To this point this text has dealt with "normal" adolescence and adolescents. At least the intention has been to refer to and speak about those developments in adolescence which are, and those adolescents who are, more mainstream, more usual, thought to be normative and hence normal. We have seen, obliquely referred to at many places in the text, the problems of thinking of much of adolescent development and behavior as normative, as normal:

1. There is such great variability in development during adolescence that "normal" levels and "normal" timings of developments are very broad. You will remember, as examples, the approximately six-year "normal" range for the onset of puberty, or the large disparity in moral judgment level among adolescents of any one age and across all adolescent ages.

2. The "normal" life situations of adolescents are also so varied that determining what is normal is difficult if not impossible. For instance, the differences found between adolescents of the various socioeconomic statuses and races are real differences but do not make one status or racial group's life situation normal in opposition to the others. Or, across subgroups, with the substantial percentage of adolescents living with one parent, we cannot say that it is not normal to be living in a one-parent family, even if it might be said that the two-parent home is normative or normal in the sense of ideal.

In one way or another, the discussions in this text have attempted to take into consideration these diversities under a general aegis of normal adolescence and normal adolescents.

In this chapter the discussion will turn to abnormal or deviant behavior of adolescents, or abnormal, deviant adolescents. Funnily enough, similar qualifications apply to both the abnormal and the normal. Feelings of deviancy exist among adolescents within normal ranges and situations. Behaviors labeled as deviant or delinquent, such as alcohol and drug use, may be usual, done by a majority of adolescents in some groups or the majority of adolescent subgroups. Should something done by a large majority of adolescents be considered an abnormal behavior? Maybe in terms of societal standards, historical standards, and traditional social labeling, a usual behavior at one historical time or among particular subgroups at one time may be deviant and abnormal. So too, a behavior or set of behaviors that is detrimental to health and well-being, even if participated in by large numbers in a society at a time in history, may be labeled abnormal or deviant. In the remaining sections of this book, abnormal and deviant behaviors and the adolescents labeled as deviant because they involve themselves with, or exhibit, these behaviors will be covered.

Another set of questions should be looked at when we are considering deviant behaviors in adolescence and/or deviant adolescents. These questions have to do with whether the behaviors, the deviancies, arise in some way because of, or related to, the developments and period called adolescence; whether the deviancies have to do with being an adolescent in this society; and/or whether these behaviors are usual in the society as a whole and termed deviant throughout the society or termed deviant only when exhibited by adolescents.

These questions may be somewhat confusing but may be important for understanding and analyzing deviance in adolescence. Therefore they are stated somewhat differently in the following. For some or all deviancies:

1. Are there normal developments, such as physical, cognitive, and social developments, that make adolescents vulnerable to the deviancy, or that may make it easier or reasonable that some adolescents come to behave in this deviant manner because of their developmental level?
2. Are there aspects of the adolescent role that make it easier for, or possibly even necessary for, at least some adolescents to behave in ways that the greater (or older) society deems deviant?
3. Are there behaviors that are termed deviant only, or mainly, when exhibited by adolescents, that are not seen as equally deviant or deviant at all when exhibited by adults?

These questions will underlie much of the discussion of adolescent deviancies that follows. To the extent that we can see how normal developments and customs of adolescence and roles that adolescents occupy influence their tendencies to become deviant, we will better understand adolescence. To the extent that we can see how the deviancies in society are made available to or foisted on adolescents, we will better understand deviancy. And to the extent that we can merge these understandings, we will better understand adolescent deviancy.

JUVENILE DELINQUENCY

"Juvenile delinquency is defined as illegal behavior committed by a minor" (Shaw, 1983, p. 880). This simple definition is probably the only simple thing about juvenile delinquency. If delinquency is illegal behavior by a minor, everybody, with only the rarest of exceptions, can be found to have been a juvenile delinquent. Before you were 21, or by now, if you are not yet 21, did you ever go to a bar and have an alcoholic drink, use a fake ID or lie about your age, not attend or leave school without permission, gamble for money? According to the foregoing definition, these were acts of juvenile delinquency.

Did you ever steal anything? Talking about this subject in classes for many years in many places, I have always asked, "Did you during your adolescence ever steal anything?" Almost everyone almost everywhere has raised his or her hand to respond yes, not proudly, not defiantly, but in acknowledgment that sometime during adolescence they took something that did not belong to them. Researches in high schools have shown that 90 percent to 100 percent of the students will report that they have engaged in one or more delinquent acts, with boys reporting a higher incidence than girls (Hindelang, 1971; Kratcoski and Kratcoski, 1975). Some of the people in the class have been very surprised that others did as they had done. They had held their transgression as a deep secret.

Then I tell of the time in sixth or seventh grade when I went into the local 5-and-10 to steal a yo-yo, just as all my friends had. But I didn't need a yo-yo. So I attempted to steal a paper packet of yo-yo strings, two for a nickel. Having looked in all directions, I grabbed at a packet and pushed it into my jacket pocket. To my horror, the packets were stapled together and I left the store hurriedly with sixteen packets of yo-yo strings in my pocket. After racing around the corner, I calculated my theft at 80 cents before tax, generously distributed the strings to my friends, walked away with four packs left and threw them out before getting home. Knowing about the statute of limitations, I do not quake when I think about this conscious act of "delinquency," but almost 40 years later, I can recall exactly what happened and how I felt then. I was never discovered and never accused, but I certainly felt that I had been delinquent.

Because they are never discovered, accused, and convicted, many adolescents who have broken the law are never labeled delinquent. Until a juvenile has been apprehended by the authorities, the official label of delinquent is not applied. Therefore many people have engaged in delinquent behavior who have never been termed delinquent.

At the most basic level, delinquent behavior may be said to fall into two categories: acts, of whatever type, that constitute criminal behavior for adults as well as juveniles, and acts that are not deemed criminal if performed by adults but are deemed criminal if performed by juveniles. Acts that are criminal for adolescents but not for adults are called *status offenses*—one's age status makes them offenses. Frequent examples of status offenses include skipping school without permission, running away from home, defying parents' authority, patronizing a saloon or dram shop where intoxicating liquor is sold, wandering streets at night while not on lawful business, and use of intoxicating liquor (Vedder and Somerville, 1975).

The official figures on the frequency of status offenses are, at best, a gross underestimate of the actual frequency of the acts. Yet Haskell and Yablonsky (1982) determined that status offenses account for approximately 25 percent of juvenile court cases.

For example, FBI figures for 1983 show 112,000 juvenile runaway arrests, whereas estimates in the literature range from a half million to over a million runaways annually. In my town, when a youngster is picked up as a runaway, he or she is brought to the juvenile detention facility and held briefly until a parent arrives. Discussions at that time, and in other circumstances, determine whether the child will be arrested. The police officer responsible, full time, for dealing with runaways is clearly more interested in placing kids safely back at home, with whatever help might be needed and available, than in arrests. A substantial number of other status offenses and even criminal offenses, when committed by first-time, nonhabitual offenders, are dealt with by the police in ways that avoid formal arrest and thereby escape inclusion in the arrest statistics.

A substantial percentage, 30 percent or more, of arrests nationally for suspicion, violation of liquor laws, and vandalism are of persons age 18 and under. These figures undoubtedly do not represent the actual behavior of juveniles, for many reasons, and the importance of the discrepancy is questionable, given that the largest discrepancies probably occur in the status offense data.

The first reason that arrests do not represent actual numbers of crimes is the same for juveniles as for adults—only a small fraction of lawbreakers are apprehended.

Secondly, and particularly for status offenses, many law officers, with or without their department's blessing, are reluctant to, or unenthusiastic about, charging juveniles.

There are a number of reasons for the slippage in juvenile delinquency statistics that have to do with the nature of the data themselves. Legally, juvenile delinquency records are not, or should not, be carried forward to be used or available for criminal cases against adults. Therefore, juvenile records have often not been accessible or have been destroyed. Record keeping has not been a forte of many police departments, with the juvenile records seemingly even less important than other records. Thus prior to computer records, at least, it was difficult to put much faith in juvenile delinquency statistics. That record keeping is undoubtedly improving.

The total number of arrests of juveniles annually is the gross figure people refer to when they speak about juvenile delinquency's going up or down, increasing or decreasing. It makes sense for us to want to know the magnitude of this problem and possibly the effectiveness of programs aimed at preventing or discouraging it. Unfortunately, the total arrests figure does not convey all of the information we might want.

Over the past decade and more, crime rates, arrest numbers, have been rising, if not dramatically then steadily. Juvenile delinquency figures have not been. From 1975 to 1983, arrests of suspects under age 18 dropped from 25.9 percent of the total arrests to 16.8 percent. The drop in the actual number of juvenile arrests is not as dramatic as the percentage drop, but it still comes to a quarter of a million fewer juveniles arrested.

So many factors are involved in these statistics that there is no simple answer to any question of why—why the large number of juvenile arrests to begin with, why the recent decline, and so on. Suffice it to say that these questions are, and will remain, important because a subsample of the juveniles arrested are repeat offenders, ones we might call "truly delinquent," and they are likely to continue a pattern of criminal behavior when adult (Faretra, 1981; Loeber, 1982). So an equally complex question is also relevant: Who are the delinquents?

TYPES OF DELINQUENTS

Within the general framework of this text, the most useful and understandable way to categorize types of delinquents takes into account the individual psychology of the adolescent and his or her familial and social situation. This approach does not, however, account directly for the biological explanation of criminality that should be mentioned. It has been shown that slower development of the brain may result in neurophysical dysfunction and delinquent behavior (Voorhees, 1981); that the autonomic nervous system of criminals may be slower in recovering from stimulation and therefore criminals may be slower in changing their behavior (Mednick and Christiansen, 1977); that some criminals have a chromosomal abnormality, an extra Y chromosome in the male, the XYY combination, that may lead to greater aggressiveness and criminality (Polani, 1970); and that other organic causes, such as chemical imbalances or what Adler would have called organ inferiorities, such as visual or neurological impairments, may lead to delinquent behavior (Sheppard, 1974).

The biological explanation does not, it is viewed here, present the reasons for the types of delinquent behavior, but, rather, with the possible exception of chromosomal abnormality, it presents us with a variety of biological and physiological bases for persons' feeling themselves to be different and/or feeling that they must act differently, which may be seen as reasons for choosing delinquent behavior and also being accepted in some delinquent groups. The three types of delinquency in the most accepted classification system are socialized delinquency, neurotic or sociopersonalogical delinquency, and characterological delinquency.

Socialized delinquency refers to delinquent behavior in a subcultural environment in which this kind of antisocial behavior is condoned. In such environments, many people, individually or in concert, are involved in illegal activities, and many of these people are seen as successful and of higher status because of their involvement in these activities. In fact, people who go along with this antisocial code may be well adjusted to their environment, whereas those who do not may be alienated from those around them and, for adolescents, may not be part of a social group that is respected by peers (Friedman, Mann, and Friedman, 1975).

From the previous paragraph you might have concluded that socialized delinquency is limited to low-income and poverty neighborhoods, which is not the case. Reread the previous paragraph and think about that portion of most groups who have some involvement with antisocial behavior, or think about the deviant group in most high schools with the same involvement. Adolescents seem to have good antennae for picking out those groups in their environment and also for spotting hypocrisy among their peers. Thus those who see the antisocial ones in their community as important, major, and respected figures may be drawn to them and their ways, whereas those who see the antisocial ones as a minority who are disrespected and alienated may be drawn to them as an alternative to the straight, middle-class ways that they see as hypocritical or unaccepting of them.

The point is that socialized delinquents may appear in all segments of society. As much as 70 percent of urban youth crime is estimated to be committed by groups of socialized delinquents (Miller, 1980). The "guys" in the middle class may be the "gang" in the lower class, and in both the potential for criminal behavior may be increased, although more in the latter group.

Generally, boys, and gangs members are usually boys (Bowker, Gross, and Klein, 1980), become associated with a group for the group itself, for membership and belonging, for status and association, rather than as a mechanism for participating in criminal behavior. The criminal behavior may be a plus for them because it is endorsed in their community, but it is probably not the reason for their association. However, their eventual participation in criminal behavior as a member of the gang is not a moral issue for them, the behavior gets its meaning from the group. Thus if their group does it, it is OK, no matter what the public, parents, or "pigs" say.

As members of a community, often a lower social class, a poverty neighborhood, or a subculture such as a high school subgroup, that condones antisocial behavior, adolescents who feel a part of that group are socialized into its ways—therefore, socialized delinquency.

Neurotic (or sociopersonalogical) delinquency refers to delinquent behavior that is an expression of the personal needs, concerns, and difficulties of the adolescent and that is therefore a symptom of these underlying problems (Dollinger, 1983). This is not to say that the delinquent behavior itself may not become a problem for the adolescent or that the adolescent may not have problems if he or she is classified as delinquent. Rather, this category of delinquency points to the reason for some delinquent behavior, and that reason is personal problems which the adolescent expresses through delinquent behavior. Delinquent behavior may be unusual for these adolescents. They probably do not have a history of getting in trouble with the law. Rather, it is as if the adolescent at this time of his life tries delinquent behavior as a means of getting attention, being noticed, for what he may see as positive reasons or negative reasons.

For the unnoticed or overlooked adolescent, getting attention may seem like a positive aim in itself. In such cases, the means for getting attention is secondary. Without some clear response from others that he or she is noticed, the adolescent may feel totally apart from others. There is a classic story in Adlerian psychology circles that speaks to this issue:

> Parents of a high school freshman are called into the school because their boy is getting in trouble. They are informed of the variety of his transgres-

sions and told that everyone in the school knows that their son is the worst troublemaker ever to enroll there.

The parents are shocked and amazed. They tell the high school authorities that this is a complete turnaround for their son. There must be something wrong with the high school or the friends he has made in the high school. They tell them to call his previous school to see what kind of a kid he really is. At his last school he was a model student. He got extremely good grades, was well liked, participated in extracurricular activities, and, in fact, everyone in the school knew that their son was the best kid ever to enroll there.

Our tendency in this matter, as in many others, is to search the person's environment for a cause of the change in behavior, as if the change is caused without regard to the person. In an Adlerian, teleological, goal-directed analysis, we look for the individual's goals, the individual's intentions, to see how they have changed or remained the same as circumstances change.

Thus the tendency is to do as the parents did in this story, look for what made their son change. However, if we credit people, even young people, with having greater control over their behavior and lives, we can look for what the boy wanted in the situations by looking at what he got. Looked at this way, the boy did not change his goals and intentions. Looked at this way, we see that the boy's goal was not to be the best kid or the worst kid in each school. The boy's goal was to be the best-known kid in each school — and at this he succeeded.

If a youngster does not feel that he or she can fit in, find a place, belong, in a positive social way, he or she may choose a negative way. This may seem neurotic, if the emphasis is on the individual's unrealistic sense of inferiority, or it may seem merely a logical outcome from a sociopersonalogic viewpoint, but the outcome the adolescent seeks is a feeling of his or her place in society.

In some instances, adolescents feel they have problems with which they are unable to deal and for which they are also unable to get help. This neurotic dilemma may seem untenable for the adolescent, something he can't get out of. The logic of this situation, again, is for the adolescent to draw attention to himself. However, the adolescent's aim is not merely to find a place but to have others see that he or she is in trouble and needs help.

Referring to our example again, if the boy had not shown a consistent propensity to stand out, but had been, say, average, a spate of antisocial behavior might well be thought of as a call for help. Oftimes adolescents show this type of behavior when they have been dislodged from their accustomed social place by a move, by a change of school, or, more dramatically, by a change of family status through death or divorce (Chiles, Miller, and Cox, 1980).

Characterological delinquency refers to delinquent behavior that is an outgrowth of the adolescent's personality itself and the nature of that personality, which is distinctive for its lack of, or diminished, conscience and sense of connectedness with others. This type of personality has been referred to as psychopathic, sociopathic, or antisocial personality disorder.

Characterological delinquency, then, is quite different from the other two types of delinquency in that it is not so much based on the adolescent's current sociocultural environment or the adolescent's hopes for or demands from others. Characterological delinquency is *asocial* or *antisocial*, whereas the other types of delinquency are *social*.

It is quite difficult to understand the characterological delinquent, the psychopathic personality, because such individuals do not have the same feelings about others and situations that most people have. However, they have usually noticed how other people behave in relation to each other and in social situations, and they usually behave, or try to behave, as others seem to do. Therefore much of the time it is difficult, if not impossible, to discern whether someone is psychopathic.

Yet, no matter how proficient a psychopath is at imitating others' behavior, he or she does not identify with others and does not feel the same way that others do. The feelings of others, the wishes of others, the rights and privileges of belonging to a group and to society, are noticed by the characterological delinquent but are considered irrelevant, except as they seem useful to the delinquent's wishes and purposes. Thus the characterological delinquent may be a part of a group or not, as and when he wishes. He may be with you or against you as it suits him. And the characterological delinquent may feel he is different from others, and usually that the others are weak or sappy, or he may feel that the others are like him. But seldom do characterological delinquents think there is anything the matter with themselves, which makes them very difficult to work with and change in educational or clinical settings.

The psychodynamics of these three types of delinquents, and of the individuals within these groups, may be very different, but their delinquent behavior is likely to lead to similar types of trouble for them (Hoffman, 1984).

Because one factor is so seldom referred to as contributing to delinquency and is so often a major factor in delinquent acts, it is important to point it out. Namely, it must be recalled that many deviant acts are fun — hedonistic, adventureful, playful, fun. Sometimes these acts are carried out for this purpose and in this spirit. "Vandalism could be partially explained this way, as could some instances of pre-marital and extra-marital sex, homosexuality (or bisexuality), drug use (or experimentation), drunkenness, shoplifting, auto theft," *joy* riding, "gambling, fist fights, reckless driving, profanity and prostitution, at least from the client's point of view—to mention a few" (Reimer, 1981, p. 39).

Although many of these acts in themselves or in certain circumstances are criminal, and for adolescents delinquent, they may not be carried out for criminal purposes in the same sense that robbing a bank might usually be. On the other hand, some small percentage of people who rob banks do it as much for the fun, for the excitement and adventure, as for the profit.

For adolescents, some unknown portion of delinquent behavior is carried out "just for the fun of it." These behaviors when carried out by gangs will be seen as socialized delinquency. When individuals who have strong needs for, personality propensities toward, excitement, thrills, and risk taking act on those needs, their behaviors will be seen as neurotic delinquency. And when individuals without regard for others and the rules do things "for kicks," their behaviors will be seen as characterological delinquency. The reasoning behind these labels may be valid, but the reasoning behind the delinquent acts may be no more than "fun."

CAUSES OF DELINQUENCY

The huge social and behavioral science literature on delinquency and delinquents cuts the pie every which way with a single underlying intent—to find *the* cause and *the* cure for delinquency.

> In the first half of this century, criminologists voiced a good deal of optimism regarding the search for the causes of crime and delinquency. Further, they exhibited a good deal of enthusiasm for correctional interventions based upon scientific knowledge. However, although criminological knowledge had grown impressively in the past two or three decades, criminologists have produced many specific findings and conditional propositions but few unequivocal scientific generalizations. (Gibbons, 1986, p. 186)

The two main questions posed in the introduction to this chapter are another way of organizing the material with a similar intent, but certainly not the same intent, because the basic assumption (or the primary conclusion) herein differs from the historical goal in this field. The questions being asked here are: Are there normal developments of adolescence that influence some people's becoming delinquent? And are there aspects of being adolescent that open the way to, or seem to lead, some people into delinquency?

You may have noticed in this text that we seldom (I hope never) have said that *X* causes people to do *Y*. A *causal* model has not been used because, as we have shown many times, the most social and behavioral science data can establish is weak relationships, or *soft determinisms.* That means that we can say that under such and such conditions, some or many people will probably do *Y*, but we cannot say that *X* causes *Y*, absolutely or at all.

In the case of delinquency, the long efforts to find a single cause demonstrate that there is no single cause. There are many conditions and circumstances that may lead some adolescents to do illegal acts; there are many conditions and circumstances in which it is unlikely that many adolescents will become delinquent; but there are no general conditions or circumstances that eliminate all possibilities of an adolescent's becoming delinquent and there are no conditions or circumstances that will lead every adolescent to illegal acts. Some adolescents will be delinquent in the best of circumstances and conditions—those that no research would predict would produce delinquency. Some adolescents will not be delinquent under the worst circumstances and conditions—those that research would predict would produce delinquency.

People make up their own minds. They behave as they do because of who they think they are, because of their personalities, in the world they understand as they understand it, with the purpose of fitting in, having their place in society, as they believe they can. Therefore the questions asked in this chapter have to do with developments in adolescence and circumstances of adolescents that some might understand, or misunderstand, in ways that lead them to act illegally, and because this is an important factor, lead them to be labeled delinquent, to get caught.

DEVELOPMENT, CIRCUMSTANCE, AND DELINQUENCY

Hirschi and Hindelag reviewed the literature on IQ and delinquency and concluded that "the assertion that IQ affects the likelihood of delinquent behavior through its effect on school performance is consistent with the available data. The corollary descriptive assertion that delinquents have lower IQs than nondelinquents is firmly established" (1977, p. 584).

For many kids, the question of scholastic problems and delinquency is a matter of "which came first." For some, their problems in school lead to truancy, which in itself is a violation of the law, and their out-of-school activities lead to more delinquent behavior. For others, their delinquent behaviors lead to school difficulties. To the extent that the adolescent is less able academically, there is greater likelihood of difficulty in school, etc. In some instances, this may be because the youngster gets in with others who are in school difficulty and delinquent activities, whereas in others, the youngster may be turned off and act out because he or she feels rejected by the school, or feels hurt that he or she is not successful when trying in school, and on and on. There are many reasons why a kid who has trouble in school may turn against schooling. Hirschi and Hindelag's conclusion makes sense when we consider the importance of school in keeping kids in line and providing a path to being productive citizens.

The relationship between intellectual and cognitive abilities and moral-developmental level has been detailed earlier in this text. As the relationship between intellectual ability and delinquency has been established, one would predict a relationship between moral-developmental level and delinquency for logical reasons and because of the relationship between moral-developmental level and IQ. This relationship has been found. Hudgins and Prentice (1973) found that delinquents and their mothers were at lower moral judgment stages than nondelinquents and their mothers. Comparing nondelinquents and incarcerated delinquents, Emler, Heather, and Winton (1978) found moral reasoning level significantly higher among the nondelinquents. From studies of this type, a "developmental lag" was posited for delinquents. Hains' results (1981) indicated that delinquents are deficient in moral reasoning and logical cognitive ability, and he suggested that delinquents have a "structural developmental lag" in comparison to nondelinquents. Hains did not find differences in self-concept or role-taking skills.

Delinquents run the gamut in level of self-esteem, from those with very low self-esteem, who feel there is no proper path for them, who follow wherever they are led, or who give up, to those with higher self-esteem, who fail to see or accept the discrepancy between what they are doing and how they see themselves and who do not accept responsibility for their behavior (Mitchell and Dodder, 1983; Zieman and Benson, 1983). No level of self-esteem or personality type has been directly associated with delinquency. But the adolescents who are more likely to run into trouble with the law are hostile, destructive, highly assertive, ambivalent toward or defiant of authority, and lacking self-control and impulse control (Curtis, Feczko, and Marohn, 1979; Eisikovits and Sagi, 1982; Serok and Blum, 1982; Stefanko, 1984). These traits may be associated with events, experiences, and practices in their growing up, or they may not be. They may relate to biological factors in some delinquents, but they may not in others. They all cohere, in some way, with the personality of the delinquent, which does not seem to show any greater change in adolescence than that of nondelinquents. Adolescents would appear to enter adolescence with their personalities intact and amenable to events, experiences, and situations that assist them in movement toward or away from delinquent situations and behavior.

Even if we cannot find a direct link between particular family types, parenting styles, and the personalities of the parents and the children, we have seen that children develop their personalities in their families and in relation to their families. Family disturbance and disruption are consistently more likely among adolescents who are delinquent (Haskell and Yablonsky, 1982), even if there is no direct causal link, as Glueck and Glueck (1968) suggested. Many reasons for this association suggest themselves. Children who come to see themselves without a secure place in the family may look elsewhere for attention and a sense of importance, and may be willing and anxious to be part of a gang to feel belonging. A family disruption in adolescence may prompt the same kind of efforts as well as a call for help, via a call from the juvenile authorities, when the adolescent feels shunted aside and overlooked in the midst of the parents' hassles. I have seen cases where, in fact, this tactic worked, where the adolescent in trouble with the law became the focus of all members of a disrupted family to improve the situation for the adolescent and thereby improve the family situation. This is not a tactic that I would prescribe, but the adolescent bent on belonging to and maintaining his family can use this tactic for a positive outcome.

Divorce and family disruption are endemic in our society, prevalent at all levels and in all regions. If at one time family disruption and single-parent families were more usual in lower social-class groups, and if these groups had higher juvenile delinquency rates, this is no longer the case. We may be more aware of certain kinds of delinquency that we associate with lower socioeconomic groups, but the current rates of delinquency do not show that association to be dominant.

"Accumulated data suggest that for the past four decades there has been a . . . decline in association between social class and crime/delinquency, with contemporary (those done since 1970) self-report and official statistics studies finding essentially no relationship between class and crime/delinquency" (Tittle, Villemez, and Smith, 1978, p. 654). Delinquency that is part of the subculture is evident, in particular ways, in all subcultures, whether socioeconomic or ethnic. Delinquency that is personalogical is also evident at all levels of society. Any and all of the developments that occur in adolescence may provoke an adolescent to experiment in or take up delinquent acts in an attempt to find a place, as the adolescent's personality and situation warrant. Adolescence itself, as a time of new groups, places, and opportunities, opens the door for adolescents so disposed to take advantage of the opportunity, it may be said, of becoming delinquent.

DRUG AND ALCOHOL USE AND ABUSE

REASONS AND PATTERNS OF DRUG USE

In a classic paper, "Becoming a Marijuana User," Howard S. Becker showed that marijuana use for pleasure occurs when an individual learns to use the drug to produce a "real effect," learns to recognize the effects as drug use — "to get high," and learns to enjoy the feeling. Becker's

> analysis of the genesis of marihuana use shows that the individuals who come in contact with a given object may respond to it at first in a great variety of ways. If a stable form of a new behavior toward the object is to emerge, a transformation of meanings must occur, in which the person develops a new conception of the nature of the object. . . . Persons who do not achieve the proper kind of conceptualization are unable to engage in the given behavior and turn off in the direction of some other relationship to the object or activity. (1953, p. 242)

In the following analysis of adolescent drug and alcohol use and abuse we will try to remember Becker's conclusions. As we do, we should see that adolescents will use or not use each and every drug according to its meaning for them at the time and that they will continue to use, and to abuse, the drug according to the meaning they eventually attach to the drug and its use.

For individuals, adolescents and adults, drug use may be classified into different patterns: experimental, social, medicinal, or addictive (Weiner, 1982). Experimental use is usually based on curiosity. The extreme of this pattern was startlingly brought to my attention one time when I saw a boy whose parents where very worried about his drug use. The 17-year-old boy and I talked for some time about drugs, and we were able to agree that he was not using, and did not intend to use, drugs frequently and consistently. We talked about the drugs he had tried and those he had not. Although he understood and agreed that some of the drugs he had not tried were exceptionally dangerous, he stated flat out that he probably would eventually try them all "just to see what it's like."

Most adolescents will encounter drugs at some social gatherings during their teen years. They may on those occasions "take drugs as a way of participating in a pleasureable group activity with peers" (Kimmel and Weiner, 1985, p. 496). If these occasions are infrequent, the use of drugs in this pattern, like the experimental pattern, does not necessarily signify a problem for the adolescent, remembering the hazards of even the single use of certain drugs.

Some adolescents, and adults, use drugs as they would medicine for the pleasure they get and/or for the relief they feel from tension, concern over problems, and stress. These people are much more likely to continue to use drugs, possibly with others and by themselves, for what they feel they personally are getting out of the drug use.

When medicinal drug use leads to habitual use — that is, regular use to keep feeling the drug's effects — the use is said to be addictive. These people are most likely to use drugs by themselves or with others on a regular basis, and if they stop taking the drugs, for whatever reason, they suffer withdrawal symptoms.

The difference in patterns of use and the type of drugs used define the difference between drug use and drug abuse. Alcohol and marijuana, the mild drugs, used infrequently in experimental or social patterns, cannot be considered drug abuse but merely drug use, unless one's perspective is heavily influenced by the legal or moral issues related to drugs. The medicinal pattern and the addictive pattern, to which the lighter patterns may lead, particularly when hard drugs are used, are more apt to define drug abuse.

It should come as no surprise to any reader that the "mild" drugs may be abused. The alcoholic is an abuser of a mild drug. There are high school students, as well as college students and adults, who go through every day stoned on marijuana. I think, in this regard, particularly of a 30-year-old woman I saw in therapy. She came in very upset, having "awakened" from 13 years smoking marijuana daily. The issues we had to work on in therapy, in addition to staying off drugs, had to do with establishing meaningful heterosexual relationships, choosing a career, finishing school, etc. — the issues she had not resolved in high school when she started abusing marijuana, when she turned on and never turned off.

FREQUENCY OF USE AND ABUSE

Drug use has not been constant in this country, and the rising rate through the 1960s and 1970s has, overall, been halted and mildly reversed in the 1980s. Nonetheless, drug use is a serious problem, and I would not want this section to imply otherwise. Drugs of all types are very available to adolescents who want them, and very near for those who do not.

To get a sense of the use and abuse of drugs, however, it is necessary to differentiate between the figures for those who have ever tried a drug, called incidence of drug use, and those who are using the drug at a particular time, called prevalence of drug use. According to a national sample of 1981 high school graduates, here are the percentages of high school graduates who have *never* used the following drugs: 99 percent never tried heroin, 88 percent never tried inhalants, 87 percent never tried hallucinogens, 83 percent never tried cocaine, 68 percent never tried stimulants, 40 percent never tried marijuana or hashish, and only 7 percent never tried alcohol (Johnston, Bachman, and O'Malley, 1981). We must bear in mind that these figures are for a sample of graduating high school seniors and therefore do not include the large number of dropouts and their incidence of drug use. Nonetheless, it is clear that some drugs had been tried by the majority of the sample and others by a minority or very few.

Drug use occurs more frequently in the final three years of high school, although for between one-fifth and one-third of the total number of students drug involvement began before the 10th grade. Looking then at prevalence of drug use in a national sample of adolescents ages 12 to 17, the figures for reported use of particular drugs in the 1982 month previous to the survey, Miller et al. (1983) found 27 percent had used alcohol, 12 percent had used marijuana, 3 percent had used stimulants, 2 percent had used cocaine, and 1 percent had used hallucinogens.

Because some percentage of these students were probably experimental or social users, and maybe one-time users, these prevalence figures give us a clearer picture of the somewhat lower level of abuse of certain drugs than publicity and our fear of drugs might have led us to believe. Yet, again, the caution holds — some of the users and abusers are going to die, or their lives are going to be severely distorted and damaged as a direct result of their drug use.

WHY USE AND ABUSE?

The meanings that drugs have for adolescents influence whether they try them or not and whether they continue to use them or not. Because drug use is thought to be a sin, some adolescents will not sin by using drugs. Because drug is illegal, some adolescents will not break the law by using drugs. Because drug use is vigorously discouraged by some parents, some adolescents will not try drugs for this reason and some will try drugs precisely for this reason.

The meanings of drug use should be associated with the meanings of other behaviors, and thus we would expect associations between the behaviors. For example, there is a substantial literature attesting to the relationship between family factors and drug use and abuse. Drug abusers are more likely to come from broken homes, have difficult parental relations, and experience less positive communication, less cooperation, and less freedom to express opinions in the home (Gantman, 1978; Kandel et al., 1978). The family relationships of adolescent drug abusers is reminiscent of the relationships of delinquents with their families and of adolescents with psychological problems, psychopathologies.

Many studies have found a link between substance abuse and delinquency (Blane, 1982; Gibbs, 1982; Simonds and Kashani, 1980), with no clear conclusion that one precedes or causes the other (Clayton, 1980; Kraus, 1981). A study by Farrow and French (1986) found that there is a "common perception among delinquent youth who are drug users that there is a discrete association" (p. 958). These adolescent drug abusers believe that their delinquent behavior is associated with their drug use, and Farrow and French conclude that their study "reinforces the notion that drug use, abuse, and delinquent behavior are part of a spectrum of sociopathic development" (p. 958).

Hundleby et al. (1982) found general delinquency and school misbehavior positively correlated with drug use. They also found drug use positively correlated with sexual behavior and social behavior, but negatively correlated with studying/reading, school achievement, and domestic (intrafamily) behavior.

Bry, McKeon, and Pandina hypothesized that "extent of drug use is an increasing function of the number of diverse etiological variables instead of any particular set of them" (1982, p. 274), and found support for the hypothesis. This is a multiple-risk-factor study. These types of studies have begun to show that it is the number of risk factors, the number of things that an individual has to cope with, that are associated with depression, heart disease, mental illness, etc., rather than a particular factor or an ordered set of factors. Newcomb, Maddahian, and Bentler (1986) looked at ten risk factors in relation to drug use among 10th through 12th graders and found those with three or less risk factors less likely to be heavy drug users, those with five or more risk factors more likely, and those with seven or more risk factors over nine times as likely to be heavy hard drug users than the rest of the sample. The ten risk factors in this study were (1) poor academic achievement, (2) lack of religiosity, (3) early alcohol use, (4) poor self-esteem, (5) psychopathology, (6) poor relationships with parents, (7) deviance, lack of social conformity, (8) sensation seeking, (9) perception of drug use, and (10) perception of adult drug use.

The finding of these studies, "that extent of drug use is a function of the number of risk factors" (Bry, McKeon, and Pandina, 1982, p. 277), increases our confidence in the notions that no single cause for drug abuse, or delinquency for that matter, exists, and, that the number of risks, the number of situations, events, and circumstances, increases the possibilities of deviancies—delinquency, drugs, pathology—that may appear in concert.

Two recent studies remind us of the importance of personality in drug use. Labouvie and McGee (1986) speak of risk factors of personality in relation to drug use, such as high levels of autonomy, exhibition, and impulsivity and low levels of achievement and harm avoidance. They see that drug use may satisfy these overt personality needs, may allow expression of covert personality needs, and may be perceived as assisting the adolescent in coping with the disfunctionality of these needs. Stein, Newcomb, and Bentler (1987), in a longitudinal study into young adulthood, found that changes in drug use could be predicted by personality factors, which speaks to the just mentioned possible ways that drug use seems satisfying to the adolescent's personality.

Throughout, this text has referred to adolescents' experimenting in and with new situations. We have spoken about the fit of their behavior with their personality and the misfit that comes from ignorance of the situation itself and being without experience in the situation. Transition to new schools has been used as a good, and standard, example of a new situation entered with limited or no information. A fascinating study by Douglas Reid, Martinson, and Weaver investigated drug use among eighth graders who had entered their middle school at different grades—fifth, sixth, or seventh. They found that "eighth grade students beginning middle school in the fifth and sixth grade had more favorable attitudes about drug use, had more drug using peers, and sensed that more of their friends approved of drug use than did students beginning middle school in the seventh grade," and concluded that "the school's organization does not cause maladjustment or drug use, however, it is contributory. Contributory in the sense that earlier or later transitions into middle school result in earlier or later exposure to drug using peers. It is the earlier or later exposure to drug using peers which has the most influence on these students' psychosocial adjustment and drug use" (1986, p. 229).

Adolescents do not know how to behave in many new situations and come to know how to behave, are socialized, in the situation itself. This study points to that phenomenon and suggests the possibility that with greater information and maturity adolescents moving into situations where they could be socialized into drug use may be less influenced by peers in this direction.

A general conclusion regarding the reasons for drug use and abuse necessarily glosses over the specifics that might apply for a particular group or individual. Nonetheless, the conclusions of Kovach and Glickman seem to cohere with the discussion presented herein. Their "results seemed to confirm suggestions in the literature that drug use has become a normal, predictable form of behavior that accompanies adolescent development. Psychopathological factors were found to be important in cases of severe drug-using behavior" (1986, p. 61). That is to say, at this time, drugs, especially the mild drugs, are readily available to adolescents and, as the figures show, a majority to almost all adolescents at least try these drugs. Some adolescents, because of the specific place they are, their personality, the availability of stronger drugs at that time, and the current myths, rumors, and comments about these drugs, may try stronger drugs as if their use had the same meaning as the use of alcohol or marijuana. The continued and regular use of both mild drugs and stronger drugs probably indicates medicinal and/or addictive use; a psychopathological, strong personological, basis for use; and an unhealthy, risky, environmental basis for their use.

PSYCHOPATHOLOGY

Psychological disorders are grossly categorized according to the three central domains of human functioning — affect, thought, and behavior. The disorders of behavior in adolescence, called conduct disorders, cause considerable concern among adults. The adolescent conduct disorders, which we have covered earlier in this chapter, focus on delinquency and antisocial personality. Disorders of thought and feeling are the psychopathologies to be addressed in this section. The disorders can, and have been, classified and labeled in many ways. Here, the simplest classifications will be used. Our issues do not have to do so much with the specificity of the disorders, as would be the case in a text on the psychopathologies, as with developmental aspects, the general issues of pathology in the developmental time of adolescence.

A review by Rutter (1980) of epidemiological surveys in Britain shows 10 to 15 percent of adolescents ages 14 to 15 with psychiatric disorders, and the figure would rise as high as 21 percent if it represented those suffering from disorders that were not noticed by teachers or parents. Psychiatric disorders increase in prevalence during adolescence, as compared to childhood, and may reach a level as high as in mid-adulthood. The disorders that increase in prevalence during adolescence are suicide and suicide attempts, alcohol and drug abuse, schizophrenia, anorexia nervosa, and depression. In effect, of the adolescents with psychiatric conditions, 40 percent had emotional disorders, 40 percent had conduct disorders, slightly under 20 percent had both antisocial and emotional disorders, and a very few were psychotic. Of hospitalized adolescents, approximately 15 percent of those under age 15 and 25 percent of those over age 15 were diagnosed as psychotic. Girls have more emotional disorders than boys in early adolescence, with higher percentages of neurosis and suicide attempts.

In texts on adolescence and treatises on psychopathology in adolescence, this is the customary point at which to list and describe the most frequent types of pathologies in adolescence: schizophrenic disorders (schizophrenia), affective disorders (mainly depressions), anxiety disorders (often phobias), and eating disorders (more often mentioned — anorexia nervosa and bulimia, less often mentioned — obesity). There is now an enormous amount of material on the possible causes of these disorders, in general if not specifically in adolescence. The technical, diagnostic descriptions of the disorders describe the symptoms, though they do not convey the tremendous range and variety of manifestations of the disorders.

To refrain from adding to the seemingly massive number of references in this text, which I have so far been unable to avoid (though I have tried), and to involve the reader while allowing a more relaxed pace, I will omit lists and descriptions of pathologies and instead present a somewhat speculative essay on why a psychological disturbance might seem useful to an adolescent, or, the function of adolescent psychopathology.

Until recently, mental health professionals were often unsure if certain disturbances in adolescence were the same as those disturbances in adulthood. Today, in most instances, the belief is that the disturbances are basically the same, although symptoms may be somewhat different.

It is often quite difficult to detect the onset of a disturbance in adolescence because the behavior in the mild or early stages of the disorder may not be that different from some aspects of "typical" adolescent behavior in terms of highs and lows, frequency and magnitude of swings of emotion, and extremes of conduct.

Lastly in this regard, children often exhibit behaviors that could be understood as early signs of a disorder if their behavior were being read diagnostically. However, parents are not usually able, and do not usually attempt, to understand their children's behavior from this viewpoint. Teachers too, in general, accept a full range of children's behavior and do not suspect an underlying problem until it is quite extreme. Teachers seldom have the training, much less the time, to analyze and evaluate each child's behavior for its short- or long-term meanings. When adults who are not mental health professionals deal with youngsters and observe them, they interpret their behavior according to their understanding of kids themselves.

Children fantasize, go off to "their own worlds," and so on, but these kinds of behaviors diminish, are put in their place, in creative activities, and are unobtrusive by late childhood and adolescence. For some youngsters more than others, it is easier to come to the fantastical, illogical, unexpected, peculiar, and made up. For some, this kind of thinking continues, probably submerged so that others who have told them not to do so or have ridiculed them for it do not know that they are still thinking this way. In adolescence, and adulthood, people who think more and more in these ways, and apply this kind of thinking to their own life situations, may not be socially active or effective. They may behave inappropriately as they react to situations they understand within the context of their fantasy life and not as others interpret the situations. An imaginary companion may be healthy at age 4 but not at age 14 or 24. You may not be made to participate in kindergarten because "creatures from another planet" scared you, but in high school you will not be able to participate, or wanted as a participant, if you give the same reason.

A "sad" child will get a lot of coaxing. It is very hard to refuse big eyes looking up at you out of a sad little face. Parents, teachers, and playmates dance tentatively around kids who change moods quickly: "Sometimes he's so nice and sometimes he's so mean." Children learn early and easily that being in certain moods will probably lead to certain outcomes from others. When adolescents are very sad, a lot of their behavior conveys a different message: "I can't. I won't. I don't want to." Others read that message and, maybe after a bit of coaxing, leave them alone, which is likely to make them more sad and less able and willing to participate. Adolescents who turn hot and cold at will or whim draw others to them and involve themselves with others at some times and put others off at other times—usually when they are not getting their own way.

Stage fright is probably the best known instance of being scared of doing something. At the simplest level, it is a recognition that we have to be "up" for the performance, and at that level, it is the basic function of anxiety to energize us and get us "up" for the task at hand. We probably all have had twinges of it. Stage fright resembles phobias and other anxiety disorders in the way we function when we feel it and the way we use the feelings. Basically, stage fright works in two general ways. Either (1) we are so scared of going on stage that we don't, or (2) we "overcome" the fright and go on stage anyway. In the first case, we avoid what we are scared of and may never approach it again. We may also use the same feelings to avoid other things—being on teams or in contests or any situation where we might have to perform individually under scrutiny. We may even turn our efforts from the issue of performance to the issue of overcoming the bad feelings, in which case we have successfully avoided all that we wanted and provided a controllable sideshow that we alone are involved in and know about. In the second case, we hedge our bets, we "make a mountain out of molehill," we exaggerate the task. In this way we cannot fail. If we do poorly, we have our fright as an excuse, and if we do well, we can think of how superbly we would have done had we not had our fright.

We coax and coddle and pamper the scared child. We pity the scared adolescent or adult. There are things to be cautious of and things to be scared of, and our feelings of caution and fright keep us aware of the very real danger of these things. But excessive, uncontrolled fear of something, as in phobias, not only keeps us aware of dangers, even imagined and unrealistic dangers, but also allows us to be involved in our own feelings and not in other things around us.

Parents can spend inordinate amounts of time preparing food for and spoon-feeding a skinny child. Parents can enjoy the look of the fat child and the satisfaction he or she gets from eating and overeating. However, the very thin or very fat adolescent will not receive the same kind of social reinforcement that was received in childhood, although he or she still might look for it. Such youngsters will not receive the positive interest in their weight and appearance that they did as children, but they may receive the same degree of attention. They may give themselves that same degree of attention if others do not give it to them. They may see their thinness as a means to beauty and their obesity as way of being larger than others and larger than life.

All of these somewhat unusual descriptions of schizophrenic, affective, anxiety, and eating disorders illustrate something basic to human living — that it is social and its meanings are social. What we call "normal" behavior in adolescence is normal not only because it is normative, usual, but also because it is understandable to others, adolescents and/or adults, as social behavior. What we call "abnormal" is so both because it is not usual and because it does not make sense to others as a way of getting on and getting ahead.

The dynamics of these disorders in adolescence may not be different from those in adulthood. Some people may be biologically or genetically more disposed to developing one disorder or another, and this predisposition may lead to earlier or later onset. Yet the way in which the pathologies function is the same. The purposes, social purposes, and thus the outcomes, social outcomes, are similar. They are not exactly the same because the life situations of adolescents are different from the life situations of adults, and, presumably, adults have a better idea of what their lives are about. We think that adults understand their social roles and responsibilities better than adolescents do, and as we have seen, adolescent roles and responsibilities can be very unclear. Logically, this helps us to understand why some adolescents seem to become disturbed over what adults might see as very minor circumstances, and why they often become disturbed so very dramatically and quickly.

Let us review, as examples, a couple of the major points made earlier in this book and see how they relate to this view of adolescent psychopathology. A first, overriding point has to do with the issue of belonging, development of personality, and consistency. The consistency of personality was stressed earlier, and can be briefly explained as the continual attempt to fit into the human group in the ways first learned in the family. As an adolescent meets new developmental tasks, his or her personality may not be appropriate for success. Put another way, the ways that an adolescent has created to fit into his or her family may not work in adolescent society or with adolescent tasks. Some adolescents may be able to adjust their ways of moving toward their goals to accommodate the demands of living as an adolescent. However, some adolescents may not be able to adjust and they, in essence, try harder at their old ways — they continue to try to belong in the ways they felt worked at home. They work hard and keep trying these old, ineffective ways. They fantasize more and develop their own world, which seems better than the one they can't break into as an adolescent. They give up and sit around sadly waiting for the help and nurturance that should still be there. They develop new and more frightening fears to fight and beat when it looks as if they can't win elsewhere. They eat too little or too much to look a way that will make them loved the way they used to be.

Physical changes and their timing, as we have seen, can be stressful for adolescents. They can be particularly difficult if the child has placed undue emphasis on size or shape as an essential of self-concept and personality. For example, I saw a 14-year-old boy who was said to have an antisocial personality. He poked and prodded, annoyed and fought, frustrated and just plain "bugged" his schoolmates and teachers. At home, according to his widowed mother, he was as helpful and kind as he could be. This was a boy who lost his father when he was very young and became, for his mother and in his own mind, the man of the house. As a late developer, and a small boy at that, he was losing his sense of being "the man" and only knew aggressiveness as a way of maintaining that image of himself. With a little understanding of what he was after and some strategies for being "an OK fellow" as he was, he was able to find an acceptable place among his peers in high school. Without that intervention, he might have continued on to extremes of antisocial behavior that would have justified the initial diagnosis.

With so many unknowns facing the adolescent, it is no wonder that many are unsure of how to belong in groups and situations that they do not understand. For some, the development of formal operations is an exciting and interesting new blessing, experience, or challenge. But for others, the opening up of possibilities and hypotheses about themselves and the world around them also opens up many new possible ways to be inferior, to mess up, to not belong. For them, this aspect of cognitive development can be extremely frightening and depressing. They may be very confused. Without the personality basis for adapting, and the confidence to do so, they can appear and become schizophrenic as they delve into old fantastic strategies and develop new ones. Sometimes a minor but early intervention can inhibit this development.

SUICIDE

> The rise in adolescent suicide has been so dramatic since the 1960s, it can no longer be ignored. In the United States in 1957, the adolescent suicide rate was 4.0 per 100,000 people; 10.9 per 100,000 people in 1974; and 12.2 per 100,000 in 1975. . . . In the most recent information available, Calvin Frederick, chief psychologist at the Veteran's Administration Medical Center, Brentwood, California, stated that five teenagers in the United States commit suicide daily. (Ray and Johnson, 1983, p. 131)

As dramatic as the rise in adolescent suicide has been, the rise in suicide attempts has been astonishing. Population-wide estimates of the ratio of attempts at suicide to completions of suicide ran at 8:1 for many years and crept up to 50:1. Current estimates for the younger population are 200:1 for persons ages 15 to 24 (Angle, O'Brien, and McIntire, 1983), and 312:1 for persons ages 15 to 18 (Curran, 1984). These data illustrate both the magnitude of the suicide and attempted suicide behavior in adolescence and the relative preponderance of attempts at suicide among adolescents as compared with adults.

Curran comprehensively summarizes the multiple influences conjectured as responsible for the increase in suicide behavior:

> We have before us an impressively dangerous formula for self-destruction among our young. There exists in combination, a highly stressful, fast-paced society, which our more troubled young feel both compelled to enter and at times hopelessly alienated from, an increasingly prolonged and complex adolescence, a proliferation of the means and acceptability of non-mastery, avoidant and self-destructive methods of coping with challenge and stress, the diminished ability of the nuclear family to bear up under the strain and provide necessary support to their young, reduced fear of suicide among the young, increasing modeling of suicidal behavior and subsequent familiarity with it. (1987, p. 11)

There is considerable research and informed speculation about the combined effects of the stresses of society and adolescence itself with the negative coping strategies of drugs, alcohol, and other forms of acting out on suicide behavior. The most prominent background characteristic of adolescent suicide behavior is family disruption and alienation. Everything from loss of parent by death, divorce, separation, or extended absence to geographic mobility of the family to poor intrafamily communication and excessive expectations and punishments have been shown to relate to adolescent suicide behavior.

The situation, at this time in this country, could be said to be, for many adolescents, depressing. And that is precisely what many adolescents become—depressed. Depression is the most commonly felt emotion of suicidal people.

We can sit here objectively and run off a list of positive and constructive things that people can do to end their depression. However, we have to remember that depressed people often feel that there is nothing they can do, and because they are depressed, they have great difficulty in coming up with options. As we have seen, adolescents are learning to play many roles and become adept at either not showing that they feel or showing ways of feeling that are beyond what they feel or exaggerated for their situation. Depressed adolescents may do this also. Thus, it is often difficult to assess the degree to which an adolescent is depressed because he or she is unwilling to express it. Unfortunately, adolescents, particularly formally operational adolescents, speculate on possibilities and, as we have noted earlier, tend to think of outlandish and dramatic scenarios. Suicide certainly fits that level of possibility.

Unfortunately also, suicide, while always a potential option for the depressed, has been well publicized as an adolescent phenomenon. Every adolescent suicide becomes well known in the local community, if not nationwide. The awareness of suicide as an option, and an option that brings a great deal of attention, whether successful or not, provides a model for the forlorn, foresaken, and depressed adolescent. Gould and Shaffer "examined suicides in the (New York) tri-state area in the weeks surrounding broadcast of four movies on suicide in 1984 and 1985. In three of the four cases, teenage suicide rates rose in the two weeks after the broadcasts" (*Columbia*, November 1986, p. 19).

The widely accepted clinical judgment that suicide attempts and suicide threats are often "calls for help," the huge proportion of attempts to completions, and the modeling effect of other suicides and media coverage all reinforce the notion, which has been constantly reiterated in this text, that human behavior is social and that suicide behavior is social also.

A review of the changes in behavior to be noticed for identifying a suicidal adolescent is useful in itself, and also for illustrating the social nature of the changes. Although not all suicidal adolescents exhibit these behaviors, many show changes in personal appearance and interpersonal social behavior, changes in concentration and judgment with shifts in quality of schoolwork, preoccupation with death, guilt, shame, and sometimes fantasies, delusions, and hallucinations. Relationships and friendships often are terminated, and suicidal statements and final arrangements are made. Often these behaviors start with or soon after a life crisis or the loss of a person, place, or thing due to death, moving, retirement, etc.

CONCLUSION

Suicide behavior is seen as pathological or the result of pathology. The causes, as such, run the full gamut of influences on behavior. We can posit, in some cases, biochemical bases for depression or drug-induced depression. In some cases, an individual's pathology appears based primarily on personality problems created or determined solely by the individual or in the context of faulty family structure or family life. The import of these causes may be affected by the developments, length, and strain of adolescence. So too, they may all be affected by greater, or larger, social structure, factors that could convey meanings of importance to the adolescent about his or her belonging — personal, local factors such as standards for achievement, size of school, and relative material well-being, and macro factors such as nuclear threat, the international economy, and even good and evil in the world. Khan's "experience with suicidal adolescents has indicated that a suicide attempt is a symptom, albeit a very serious one, occurring in a heterogeneous population of adolescents with different premorbid personalities and different intrapsychic conflicts. Regarding suicidal adolescents as a single group with a unitary underlying psychopathology is unproductive" (1987, p. 92).

"There is a reluctance in clinicians to diagnose mental disturbances in adolescents even when clear diagnostic criteria are present" (Stein et al., 1982, p. 301). This section has attempted to present a view of the complexity of psychopathologies in adolescence, as well as a view that places the pathologies in the personal-social world of the individual adolescent.

To conclude a text on adolescence with the deviancies, psychopathology, and suicide may seem to incorrectly summarize adolescence. To begin a text on adolescence with these topics would be even more inappropriate because the deviancies can only be understood in the framework of the normal. The normal in adolescence, the psychological and self and identity developments and the life and developmental tasks, as we have seen and clearly determined, are relatively easy to deal with, to cope with, to go through successfully, and even enjoyably, on the way to young adulthood. This text has, I hope, provided you with information and a framework to better understand the particular way each adolescent makes it, or not.

REFERENCES

Achenbach, T., and Zigler, E. Social competence and self-image disparity in psychiatric and nonpsychiatric patients. *Journal of Abnormal and Social Psychology*, 1963, 67, 197–205.

Adam, J. Sequential strategies and the separation of age, cohort, and time-of-measurement contributions to developmental data. *Psychological Bulletin*, 1978, 85(6), 1309–1316.

Adams, J. F. Adolescents' identification of personal and national problems. *Adolescence*, 1966, 1, 240–250.

Adelson, J. Adolescence and the generalization gap. *Psychology Today*, 1979, 12 (9).

Adler, A. *What life should mean to you*. London: Allen and Unwin, 1932.

Allen, G., and Martin, C. G. *Intimacy*. Chicago: Cowles Book Co., 1971.

Allport, G. W. *Personality: A psychological interpretation*. New York: Holt, 1937.

Allport, G. W. *Becoming*. New Haven: Yale University Press, 1955.

Allport, G. W. *Pattern and growth in personality*. New York: Holt, 1961.

Allport, G. W. Crises in normal personality development. *Teachers College Record*, 1964, 66, 235–241.

Almquist, E. M., and Angrist, S. S. Career salience and atypicality of occupational choice among college women. *Journal of Marriage and the Family*, 1970, 32(2), 242–248.

Ambron, S. R. *Child development*. San Francisco: Rinehart Press, 1975.

Anderson, J. *The psychology of development and personal adjustment*. New York: Holt, 1949.

Anderson, J. E. Prediction of adjustment over time. In I. Iscoe and H. A. Stevenson (eds.), *Personality development in children*. Austin: University of Texas Press, 1960.

Angle, C., O'Brien, T., and McIntire, M. Adolescent self-poisoning: A nine-year follow-up. *Developmental and Behavioral Pediatrics*, 1983, 4, 2, 83–87.

Ansbacher, H. L., and Ansbacher, R. R. (eds.) *The individual psychology of Alfred*

Adler: A systematic presentation in selections from his writings. New York: Basic Books, 1956.

Ansbacher, H. L., and Ansbacher, R. R. *Superiority and social interest: Alfred Adler*. Evanston, IL: Northwestern University Press, 1964.

Arbus, D. *Diane Arbus*. Millerstown, NY: Aperture Books, 1972.

Aries, P. *Centuries of childhood*. New York: Knopf, 1962.

Arlin, P. K. Cognitive development in adulthood: A fifth stage? *Developmental Psychology*, 1975, 11(5), 602–606.

Armour, R. *A diabolical dictionary of education*. New York: McGraw-Hill, 1969.

Arnold, R. A. The achievement of boys and girls taught by men and women teachers. *Elementary School Journal*, 1968, 68, 367–371.

Auden, W. H. *Epistle to a godson and other poems*. New York: Random House, 1972.

Ault, R. L. *Children's cognitive development* (2nd ed.). New York: Oxford University Press, 1983.

Ausubel, D. P. *Theory and problems of adolescent development*. New York: Grune and Stratton, 1954.

Ausubel, D. P. *Educational psychology: A cognitive view*. New York: Holt, 1968.

Ausubel, D., and Ausubel, P. Cognitive development in adolescence. *Review of Educational Research*, 1966, 36(4), 403–413.

Bachman, J. G., Johnston, L. D., and O'Malley, P. M. *Monitoring the future: Questionnaire responses from the nation's high school seniors, 1980*. Ann Arbor: Institute for Social Research, University of Michigan, 1981.

Bakan, D. Adolescence in America: From idea to social fact. In C. J. Gaurdo (ed.), *The adolescent as individual*. New York: Harper and Row, 1975.

Baltes, P. B., and Nesselroade, J. R. Cultural change and adolescent personality development: An application of longitudinal sequences. *Developmental Psychology*, 1972, 7(3), 244–256.

Bamber, J. H. Adolescent marginality — A further study. *Genetic Psychology Monographs*, 1973, 33, 3–21.

Bandura, A., and Walters, R. H. *Social learning and personality development*. New York: Holt, 1963.

Bardwick, J. M. *Psychology of women*. New York: Harper and Row, 1971.

Barker, R. G. *The definition of ecology and psychology: Concepts and method for an ecobehavioral science*. Stanford, CA.: Stanford University Press, 1968.

Barnes, M. E., and Farrier, S. C. A longitudinal study of the self-concept of low income youth. *Adolescence*, 1985, 77, 199–205.

Baron, R. A., Byrne, D., and Griffith, W. *Social psychology: Understanding human interaction*. Boston: Allyn and Bacon, 1974.

Baruch, G. K. Maternal influence upon college women's attitude toward women and work. *Developmental Psychology*, 1972, 6, 32–37.

Becker, H. S. Becoming a marihuana user. *The American Journal of Sociology*, 1953, 59, 235–242.

Bell, A. P. Role modeling of fathers in adolescence and young adulthood. *Journal of Counseling Psychology*, 1969, 16, 30–35.

Bell, R. R., and Chaskes, J. B. Premarital sexual experience among coeds, 1958 and 1968. *Journal of Marriage and the Family*, 1970, 32, 81–84.

Bem, D. J., and Allen, A. On predicting some of the people some of the time: The search for cross-situational consistencies in behavior. *Psychological Review*, 1974, 81, 506–520.

Bem, S. L. The measurement of psychological androgyny. *Journal of Consulting and Clinical Psychology*, 1974, 42, 155–162.

Bem, S. L. Sex role and adaptability: One consequence of psychological androgeny. *Journal of Personality and Social Psychology*, 1975, 31(4), 634–643.

Bender, L. Childhood schizophrenia. *Psychiatric Quarterly*, 1953, 27, 663–679.

Benedict, R. *Patterns of culture*. New York: New American Library, 1934.

Berger, B. M. On the youthfulness of youth culture. *Social Research*. 1963, 30, 319–342.

Bhatnagar, K. P. Academic achievement as a function of one's self-concepts and ego functions. *Education and Psychology Review*, 1966, 6(4), 178–182.

Bidwell, C. E., and Kasarda, J. D. School district organization and student achievement. *American Sociological Review*, 1975, 40, 55–70.

Bieliauskas, V. J. A new look at "masculine protest." *Journal of Individual Psychology*, 1974, 30, 92–97.

Billy, J. O. G., and Udry, J. R. The influence of male and female best friends on adolescent sexual behavior. *Adolescence*, 1985, 77, 21–32.

Blane, H. T. Problem drinking in delinquent and non-delinquent males. *American Journal of Drug and Alcohol Abuse*, 1982, 9(2), 221–232.

Blau, P. M., et al. Occupational choice: A conceptual framework. *Industrial Labor Relations Review*, 1956, 9, 531–543.

Bloch, H. A., and Niederhoffer, A. *The gang: A study in adolescent behavior*. New York: Philosophical Library, 1958.

Blocher, D. H., and Schutz, R. A. Relationships among self-description, occupational stereotypes, and vocational preferences. *Journal of Counseling Psychology*, 1961, 8, 314–317.

Block, J. H. Conceptions of sex role: Cross-cultural and longitudinal perspectives. *American Psychologist*, 1973, 28, 512–526.

Block, J. H., Haan, N., and Smith, M. B. Activism and apathy in contemporary adolescents. In J. F. Adams (ed.), *Understanding adolescence*. Boston: Allyn and Bacon, 1973.

Blos, P. *On adolescence: A psychoanalytic interpretation*. New York: Free Press, 1962.

Blos, P. The second individuation process of adolescence. In P. Blos, *The adolescent passage: Developmental issues*. New York: International University Press, 1979.

Bohrnstedt, G. W., and Felson, R. B. Explaining the relations among children's actual and perceived performances and self-esteem: A comparison of several causal models. *Journal of Personality and Social Psychology*, 1983, 45, 43–56.

Borow, H. Career development in adolescence. In J. F. Adams (ed.), *Understanding adolescence*. Boston: Allyn and Bacon, 1973.

Bowker, L. H., Gross, H. S., and Klein, M. W. Female participation in delinquent gang activities. *Adolescence*, 1980, 60, 509–519.

Bradway, K. P., and Thompson, C. W. Intelligence at adulthood: A twenty-five year follow-up. *Journal of Educational Psychology* 1962, 53, 1–14.

Bralver, E., and Jacobs, L., Jr. *Teen-agers inside out*. New York: Washington Square Press, 1974.

Brittain, C. V. Adolescent choices and parent-peer cross-pressures. *American Sociological Review*, 1967, 28(3), 385–391.

Brittain, C. V. A comparison of rural and urban adolescents with respect to peer vs. parent compliance. *Adolescence*, 1969, 4(13), 57–68.

Broderick, C. Social heterosexual development among urban Negroes and whites. *Journal of Marriage and the Family*, 1965, 27, 200–203.

Brookover, W. B., Erikson, E. L., and Johnson, L. M. Self-concept of ability and school achievement. Vol. III. *Relationship of self-concept to achievement in high school*. U. S. Office of Education, Cooperative Research Project No. 2831. East Lansing: Office of Research and Publications, Michigan State University, 1967.

Brophy, J. Teacher influences on student achievement. *American Psychologist*, 1986, 41(10), 1069–1077.

Brown, B. B., et al. The importance of peer group ("crowd") affiliation in adolescence. *Journal of Adolescence*, 1986, 9, 73–96.

Bry, B. H., McKeon, P., and Pandina, R. J. Extent of drug use as a function of number of risk factors. *Journal of Abnormal Psychology*, 1982, 91(4), 273–279.

Buck-Morss, S. Socioeconomic bias in Piaget's theory. In A. R. Buss (ed.), *Psychology in a social context*. New York: Irvington Publishers, 1979.

Burke, J. P., Ellison, G. C., and Hunt, J. P. Measuring academic self-concept in children: A comparison of two scales. *Psychology in the Schools*, 1985, 22, 260–264.

Burt, R. *Toward a structural theory of action*. New York: Academic Press, 1982.

Buxton, C. E. *Adolescents in school*. New Haven: Yale Univeristy Press, 1973.

Byrne, D., and Griffith, W. A developmental investigation of the law of attraction. *Journal of Personality and Social Psychology*, 1966, 4, 699–703.

Cameron, P. The generation gap: Beliefs about sexuality and self-reported sexuality. *Developmental Psychology*, 1970, 3, 272. (a)

Cameron, P. The generation gap: Which generation is believed powerful versus generational members' self-appraisals of power. *Developmental Psychology*, 1970, 3, 403–404. (b)

Cannon, K. L., and Long, R. Premarital sexual behavior in the sixties. *Journal of Marriage and the Family*, 1971, 33, 36–49.

Carlin, L. O. Vocational decisions and high school experiences. *Vocational Guidance Quarterly*, 1960, 8, 168–170.

Carter, D. B., and Patterson, C. J. Sex roles as social conventions: The development of children's conceptions of sex-role stereotypes. *Developmental Psychology*, 1982, 18(6), 812–824.

Carter, T. P. The negative self-concepts of Mexican-American students. *School and Society*, 1968, 96, 217–219.

Cartwright, D. Lewinian theory as a contemporary systematic framework. In S. Koch (ed.), *Psychology: A study of a science* (vol. 2). New York: McGraw-Hill, 1959.

Carver, C. S., and Ganellen, R. J. Depression and components of self-punitiveness: High standards, self-criticism, and overgeneralization. *Journal of Abnormal Psychology*, 1983, 92(3), 330–337.

Case, D., and Collinson, J. M. The development of formal thinking in verbal comprehension. *British Journal of Educational Psychology*, 1962, 32, 103–111.

Chabassol, D. J., and Thomas, D. C. Sex and age differences in problems and interests of adolescents. *Journal of Experimental Education*, 1969, 38, 16–23.

Charters, W. W., Jr. The social background of teaching. In N. L. Gage (ed.), *Handbook of research on teaching*. Chicago: Rand McNally, 1963.

Cherry, N. Components of occupational interest. *British Journal of Educational Psychology*, 1974, 44, 22–30.

Chiam, H. Change in self-concept during adolescence. *Adolescence*, 1987, 85, 69–76.

Chiles, J. A., Miller, M. L., and Cox, G. B. Depression in an adolescent delinquent population. *Archives of General Psychiatry*, 1980, 37, 1179–1184.

Chilman, C. S. *Adolescent sexuality in a changing American society* (2nd ed.). New York: Wiley, 1983.

Christensen, H. T., and Gregg, C. F. Changing sex norms in America and Scandinavia. *Journal of Marriage and the Family*, 1970, 32, 616–627.

Clark, K. *Another part of the wood: A self-portrait*. New York: Harper and Row, 1974.

Clayton, R. R. The delinquency and drug use relationship among adolescents: A critical review. *National Institute on Drug Abuse Research Monograph Series*, 1980, 38, 82–103.

Cloutier, R., and Goldschmid, M. L. Individual differences in the development of formal reasoning. *Child Development*, 1976, 47, 1097–1102.

Coelho, G. V., Silber, E., and Hamburg, D. A. Use of the student TAT to assess coping behavior in hospitalized, normal and exceptionally competent college freshmen. *Perceptual and Motor Skills*, 1961, 14, 355–366.

Cofer, C. N., and Appley, M. H. *Motivation: Theory and research*. New York: Wiley, 1964.

Coie, J. D., and Dodge, K. A. Continuities and changes in children's social status: A five-year longitudinal study. *Merrill-Palmer Quarterly*, 1983, 29, 261–282.

Colby, A., Kohlberg, L., Gibbs, J., and Lieberman, M. A longitudinal study of moral judgment. *Monographs of the Society for Research in Child Development*, 1983, 48 (4, Serial #200).

Coleman, J. C. *Relationships in adolescence*. London: Routledge & Kegan Paul, 1974.

Coleman, J. C. Current contradictions in adolescent theory. *Journal of Youth and Adolescence*, 1978, 7, 1–11.

Coleman, J. S. *The adolescent society*. New York: Free Press, 1961.

Coleman, J. S. How do the young become adults? *Review of Educational Research*, 1972, 42(4), 431–440.

Coleman, J. S., et al. *Equality of educational opportunity*. U.S. Department of Health, Education and Welfare, 1966.

Collins, J. K., and Thomas, N. T. Age and susceptibility to same sex peer pressure. *British Journal of Educational Psychology*, 1972, 42, 83–85.

Committee on Adolescence, Group for the Advancement of Psychiatry. *Normal adolescence: Its dynamics and impact*. New York: Schribner's, 1968.

Conant, J. B. *The comprehensive high school: A second report to interested citizens*. New York: McGraw-Hill, 1967.

Conger, A., Peng, S., and Dunteman, G. National longitudinal study of the high school class of 1972: Group profiles on self-esteem, locus of control, and life goals. Unpublished manuscript, 1977.

Conger, J. J. *Adolescence and youth: Psychological development in a changing world*. New York: Harper and Row, 1973.

Cooley, C. H. *Human nature and the social order*. New York: Scribner's, 1902.

Cooper, C. R. and Ayers-Lopez, N. Family and peer systems in early adolescence: New models of the role of relationships in development. *Journal of Early Adolescence*, 1985, 5(1), 9–21.

Cooper, C. R., Grotevant, H. D., and Condon, S. M. Individuality and connectedness in the family as a context for adolescent identity formation and role taking skill. In H. D. Grotevant and C. R. Cooper (eds.), *New directions for child development: Adolescent development in the family*. San Francisco: Jossey-Bass, 1983.

Costanzo, P. R., and Shaw, M. E. Conformity as a function of age level. *Child Development*, 1966, 37, 967–975.

Crane, A. R. The development of moral values in children. *British Journal of Educational Psychology*, 1958, 28, 201–208.

Crites, J. O. Parental identification in relation to vocational interest development. *Journal of Educational Psychology*, 1962, 53, 262–270.

Crites, J. O. *Vocational psychology*. New York: McGraw-Hill, 1969.

Crockett, L., et al. Perceptions of the peer group and friendship in early adolescence. *Journal of Early Adolescence*, 1984, 4, 155–181.

Cropper, D. A., Meck, D. S., and Ash, M. J. The relation between formal operations and a possible fifth stage of cognitive development. *Developmental Psychology*, 1977, 13, 517–518.

Curran, D. K. Peer attitudes toward attempted suicide in mid-adolescents. Unpublished doctoral dissertation. Boston College, Chestnut Hill, MA, 1984.

Curran, D. K. *Adolescent suicide behavior.* Washington, DC: Hemisphere Publishing Corp., 1987.

Curry, J. F., and Hock, R. A. Sex differences in sex role ideals in early adolescence. *Adolescence*, 1981, 16(64), 779–789.

Curry, R. L. The effect of socioeconomic status on the scholastic achievement of sixth grade children. *British Journal of Educational Psychology*, 1962, 32, 46–49.

Curtis, G., Feczko, M. D., and Marohn, R. C. Rorschach differences in normal and delinquent white male adolescents: A discriminant function analysis. *Journal of Youth and Adolescence*, 1979, 8, 379–392.

D'Augelli, J. F., and D'Augelli, A. R. Moral reasoning and premarital sexual behavior: Towards reasoning about relationships. *Journal of Social Issues*, 1977, 33(2), 46–66.

Damon, A., Damon, S. T., Reed, R. B., and Valadian, I. Age at menarche of mothers and daughters, with a note on accuracy of recall. *Human Biology*, 1969, 41, 161–175.

Davis, K. E. Sex on the campus: Is there a revolution? *Medical Aspects of Human Sexuality*, Winter 1970.

Dickstein, E. B. Biological and cognitive bases of moral functioning. *Human Development*, 1979, 22, 37–39.

Dollinger, S. J. Childhood neuroses. In C. E. Walker and M. C. Roberts (eds.), *Handbook of clinical child psychology.* New York: Wiley, 1983.

Dornbusch, S. M., Carlsmith, J. M., Gross, R. T., Martin, J. A., Jennings, D., Rosenberg, A., and Duke, P. Sexual development, age, and dating: A comparison of biological and social influences upon one set of behaviors. *Child Development*, 1981, 52, 179–185.

Douglas Reid, L., Martinson, O. B., and Weaver, L. C. The effect of earlier and later transition into middle school on students' psychosocial adjustment and drug use. *Journal of Drug Education*, 1986, 16(3), 221–232.

Douvan, E., and Adelson, J. *The adolescent experience.* New York: Wiley, 1966.

Douvan, E., and Gold, M. Modal patterns in American adolescence. In L. W. Hoffman and M. L. Hoffman (eds.), *Review of child development research* (vol. 2). New York: Russell Sage Foundation, 1966.

Dreikurs, R. *Fundamentals of Adlerian psychology.* Chicago: Alfred Adler Institute, 1953.

Dreikurs, R. The scientific revolution. *Humanist*, Jan/Feb 1966, 1–6.

Dreikurs, R., and Mosak, H. H. The tasks of life I. Adler's three tasks. *The Individual Psychologist*, 1966, 4(1), 18–22.

Dreikurs, R., and Mosak, H. H. The tasks of life II. The fourth life task. *The individual Psychologist*, 1967, 4(2), 51–55.

Dreyer, P. H. Sex, sex roles, and marriage among youth in the 1970s. In R. J. Havighurst and P. H. Dreyer (eds.), *Youth: The 74th Yearbook of the National Society for the Study of Education.* Chicago: University of Chicago Press, 1975.

Dreyer, P. H. Sexuality during adolescence. In B. B. Wolman (ed.), *Handbook of developmental psychology*. Englewood Cliffs, NJ: Prentice-Hall, 1982.

Dudek, S., Lester, E., Goldberg, J., and Dyer, G. Relationship of Piaget measures to standard intelligence and motor scales. *Perceptual and Motor Skills*, 1969, 28, 351–362.

Dunphy, D. C. The social structure of urban adolescent peer groups. *Sociometry*, 1963, 26(2), 230–246.

Eder, D. The cycle of popularity: Interpersonal relations among female adolescents. *Sociology of Education*, 1985, 58, 154–165.

Ehrman, W. *Premarital dating behavior*. New York: Henry Holt & Co., 1962.

Ehrmann, W. Marital and nonmarital sexual behavior. In H. T. Christensen (ed.), *Handbook of marriage and the family*. Chicago: Rand McNally, 1964.

Eisenberg, L. The autistic child in adolescence. *American Journal of Psychiatry*, 1956, 112, 607–612.

Eiskoits, Z., and Sagi, A. Moral development and discipline encounter in delinquent and nondelinquent adolescents. *Journal of Youth and Adolescence*, 1982, 11, 217–230.

Eitzen, D. S. Athletics in the status system of male adolescents: A replication of Coleman's The adolescent society. *Adolescence*, 1975, 38(10), 265–276.

Elkind, D. Quantity concepts in junior and senior high school students. In R. Grinder (ed.), *Studies in adolescence*. New York: Macmillan, 1963.

Elkind, D. Adolescent cognitive development. In J. F. Adams (ed.), *Understanding adolescents*. Boston: Allyn and Bacon, 1968.

Elkind, D. Egocentrism in adolescence. In R. E. Grinder (ed.), *Studies in adolescence*. New York: Macmillan, 1969.

Elkind, D. *A sympathetic understanding of the child six to sixteen*. Boston: Allyn and Bacon, 1971.

Elkind, D. Understanding the young adolescent. *Adolescence*, 1978, 13, 127–134.

Elkin, F., and Westley, W. A. The myth of adolescent culture. *American Sociological Review*, 1955, 20.

Ellis, L. J., and Bentler, P. M. Traditional sex-determined role standards and sex stereotypes. *Journal of Personality and Social Psychology*, 1973, 25(1), 28–34.

Emler, N. P., Heather, N., and Winton, M. Delinquency and the development of moral reasoning. *British Journal of Social and Clinical Psychology*, 1978, 17, 325–331.

Englander, M. E. A psychological analysis of vocational choice: Teaching. *Journal of Counseling Psychology*, 1960, 7, 257–264.

Enright, R. D., Lapsley, D. K., and Shukla, D. G. Adolescent egocentrism in early and late adolescence. *Adolescence*, 1979, 14, 687–695.

Epstein, S. The self-concept revisited. *American Psychologist* 1973, 28, 404–416.

Erikson, E. H. Identity and the life cycle. *Psychological Issues*, 1959, 1(1).

Erikson, E. H. *Childhood and society*. New York: Norton, 1963.

Erikson, E. H. *Identity, youth and crisis*. New York: Norton, 1968.

Ernsberger, D. J. Intrinsic-extrinsic religious identification and level of moral development. Unpublished doctoral dissertation, University of Texas at Austin, December 1976.

Fakouri, M. E. Cognitive development in adulthood: A fifth stage? A critique. *Developmental Psychology*, 1976, 12, 472.

Faretra, G. A profile of aggression from adolescence to adulthood: An 18-year follow-up of psychiatrically disturbed and violent adolescents. *American Journal of Orthopsychiatry*, 1981, 51, 439–453.

Farrow, J. A., and French, J. The drug abuse–delinquency connection revisted. *Adolescence*, 1986, 21(84), 951–960.

Fasick, F. A. Parents, peers, youth culture and autonomy in adolescence. *Adolescence*, 1984, 19(73), 143–157.

Faust, M. S. Developmental maturity as a determinant in prestige of adolescent girls. *Child Development*, 1960, 31, 173–184.

Feldman, D., and Markwalder, W. Systematic scoring of ranked distractions for the assessment of Piagetian reasoning levels. *Educational and Psychological Measurement*, 1971, 31, 346–362.

Felson, R. B. Ambiguity and bias in the self-concept. *Social Psychology Quarterly*, 1981, 44, 64–69.

Fenichel, O. *The psychoanalytic theory of neurosis*. New York: Norton, 1945.

Fine, G. A. The natural history of preadolescent male friendship groups. In H. Foot, A. Chapman, and J. Smith (eds.), *Friendship and social relations in children*. New York: Wiley, 1980.

Flavell, J. H. On cognitive development. *Child Development*, 1982, 53, 1–10.

Fleege, U. H. *Self-revelation of the adolescent boy*. Milwaukee: Bruce, 1945.

Fodor, E. M. Resistance to social influence among adolescents as a function of level of moral development. *Journal of Social Psychology*, 1971, 85, 121–126.

Francoeur, R. T. *Becoming a sexual person*. New York: Wiley, 1982.

Freud, A. Adolescence as a developmental disturbance. In G. Caplan and S. Lebovici (eds.) *Adolescence: Psychosocial perspectives*. NY: Basic Books, 1969.

Freud, S. *New introductory lectures on psychoanalysis*. Translated by W. J. H. Sprott. New York: Norton, 1933.

Freud, S. *A general introduction to psychoanalysis*. Translated by Joan Riviere. New York: Permabooks, 1953.

Freundlich, D., and Kohlberg, L. Moral judgment in youthful offenders (mimeo). Howard University, 1971.

Friedman, C. J., Mann, F., and Friedman, A. S. A profile of juvenile street gang members. *Adolescence*, 1975, 10(40), 563–607.

Frisk, M., et al. Psychological problems in adolescents showing advanced or delayed physical maturation. *Adolescence*, 1966, 1(2), 126–140.

Furnham, A. Youth unemployment: A review of the literature. *Journal of Adolescence*, 1985, 8, 109–124.

Gallagher, J. McC. Cognitive development and learning in the adolescent. In J. F. Adams (ed.), *Understanding adolescence*. Boston: Allyn and Bacon, 1973.

Gantman, C. A. Family interaction patterns among families with normal, disturbed, and drug-abusing adolescents. *Journal of Youth and Adolescence*, 1978, 7, 429–440.

Gardner, R., and Moriarty, A. *Personality development at preadolescence*. Seattle: University of Washington Press, 1968.

Gessel, A. L., Ilg, F. L., and Ames, L. B. *Youth: The years from ten to sixteen*. NY: Harper & Row, 1956.

Getzels, J. W., and Jackson, P. W. The teacher's personality and characteristics. In N. L. Gage (ed.), *Handbook of research on teaching*. Chicago: Rand McNally, 1963.

Gibbons, D. C. Juvenile delinquency: Can social science find a cure? *Crime and Delinquency*, 1986, 32(2), 186–204.

Gibbs, J. T. Psychosocial factors related to substance abuse among delinquent females: Implications for prevention and treatment. *American Journal of Orthopsychiatry*, 1982, 52(2), 261–271.

Gilberg, A. L. Adolescence: The interface of neurophysiology and cultural determinants. *The American Journal of Psychoanalysis*, 1978, 38, 87–90.

Gillespie, J. W., and Allport, G. *Youth's outlook on the future*. Garden City, NY: Doubleday, 1955.

Ginsburg, H., and Opper, S. *Piaget's theory of intellectual development*. Englewood Cliffs, NJ: Prentice-Hall, 1969.

Ginsburg, S. D., and Orlofsky, J. L. Ego identity status, ego development, and locus of control in college women. *Journal of Youth and Adolescence*, 1981, 19, 297–307.

Ginzberg, E. Toward a theory of occupation choice: A restatement. *Vocational Guidance Quarterly*, 1972, 20, 169–176.

Ginzberg, E., Ginsburg, S. W., Axelrad, S., and Herma, J. L. *Occupational choice: An approach to a general theory*. New York: Columbia University Press, 1951.

Glass, D. C. Theories of consistency and the study of personality. In E. F. Borgatta and W. W. Lambert (eds.), *Handbook of personality theory and research*. Chicago: Rand McNally, 1968.

Glueck, S., and Glueck, E. *Unraveling juvenile delinquency*. Cambridge, MA: Harvard University Press, 1950.

Glueck, S., and Glueck, E. *Delinquents and nondelinquents in perspective*. Cambridge, MA: Harvard University Press, 1968.

Goethals, G. W., and Klos, D. S. *Experiencing youth: First-person accounts*. Boston: Little, Brown, 1970.

Goldburgh, S. J. *The experience of adolescence*. Cambridge, MA: Schenkman, 1965.

Goodman, N. The adolescent's reference set. Paper presented at the annual meeting of the American Sociological Association, 1965.

Goodman, N. Adolescent norms and behavior: Organization and conformity. *Merrill-Palmer Quarterly*, 1969, 15, 199–211.

Goodnow, J. A test of milieu effects with some of Piaget's tasks. *Psychological Monographs*, 1962, 72(36, Whole No. 555).

Gottlieb, D., and Ramsey, C. *The American adolescent*. Homewood, IL: Dorsey Press, 1964.

Gottman, J. M. How children become friends. *Monographs of the Society for Research in Child Development*, 1983, 48 (3, Serial #201).

Grannis, J. C. Going beyond labels: The significance of social class and ethnicity for education. *Equal Opportunity Review*, Teachers College, Columbia University, July 1975.

Grant, C. A., and Sleeter, C. E. Race, class, and gender in education research: An argument for integrative analysis. *Review of Educational Research*, 1986, 56(2), 195–211.

Gray, D. F., and Gair, E. L. The congruency of adolescent self-perceptions with those of parents and best friends. *Adolescence*, 1974, 9, 299–303.

Greenfield, P. Oral and written language: The consequences for cognitive development in Africa and the United States. Paper presented at the annual meeting of the American Educational Research Association, Chicago, February 1968.

Grotevant, H. D., Thorbeck, W., and Meyer, M. An extension of Marcia's identity status interview into the interpersonal domain. *Journal of Youth and Adolescence*, 1982, 11, 33–47.

Gump, P. V. *Big schools, small schools*. Moravia, NY: Chronicle Guidance Publications, 1966.

Guttmann, J., Ziv, A., and Green, D. Developmental trends of the relativistic-realistic dimension of moral judgment in adolescence. *Psychological Reports*, 1978, 42, 1279–1284.

Haan, N., Smith, M., and Block, J. Moral reasoning and young adults: Political-social behavior, family background, and personality correlates. *Journal of Personality and Social Psychology*, 1968, 10(3), 183–201.

Hafner, J. L., Fakouri, M. E., and Etzler, D. R. Early recollections of individuals preparing for careers in chemical, electrical, and mechanical engineering. *Individual Psychology* 1986, 42, 3, 360–366.

Hains, A. A. Variables in social cognitive development: Moral judgment, role-taking, cognitive processes, and self-concept in delinquents and nondelinquents. *Journal of Adolescence*, 1981, 4(1), 65–74.

Hall, C. S., and Lindzey, G. *Theories of personality*. New York: Wiley, 1957.

Hall, G. S. *Adolescence*. 2 vols. New York: Appleton-Century-Crofts, 1916.

Haller, A. O., and Miller, I. W. The occupational aspiration scale: Theory, structure and correlates. *Tech. Bulletin 288*, Agricultural Experimentation Station, Michigan State University, 1963.

Hallinan, M. Structural effects on children's friendships and cliques. *Social Psychology*, 1979, 42, 43–54.

Hamachek, D. E. Toward more effective teaching. In D. E. Hamachek (ed.), *Human dynamics in psychology and education*. Boston: Allyn and Bacon, 1972.

Hamilton, S. F. The secondary school in the ecology of adolescent development. In E. W. Gordon (ed.), *Review of research in education*. Washington, DC: A.E.R.A., 1984.

Hanson, S. L., Myers, D. E., and Ginsburg, A. L. The roles of responsibility and knowledge in reducing teenage out-of-wedlock childbearing. *Journal of Marriage and the Family*, 1987, 49, 241–256.

Hare, B. R. Self-perception and academic achievement: Variations in a desegregated setting. *American Journal of Psychiatry*, 1980, 137(6), 683–689.

Harmon, L. W. The childhood and adolescent career plans of college women. *Journal of Vocational Behavior*, 1971, 1(1), 45–56.

Harrison, D. E., Bennett, W. H., and Globe, G. H. Sexual permissiveness: White and black high school students. *Journal of Marriage and the Family*, 1969, 31, 783–787.

Harrison, G. I. Relationships between home background, school success, and adolescent attitudes. *Merrill-Palmer Quarterly*, 1968, 14, 331–344.

Haskell, M. R., and Yablonsky, L. *Juvenile delinquency* (3rd ed.). Boston: Houghton-Mifflin, 1982.

Havighurst, R. J. *The public schools of Chicago*. Chicago: Board of Education of the City of Chicago, 1964.

Havighurst, R. J. Unrealized potentials of adolescents. *National Association of Secondary School Principals Bulletin*, 1966, 50, 75–96.

Havighurst, R. J. *Developmental tasks and education*. New York: McKay, 1972.

Havighurst, R. J., and Dreyer, P. H. *The national study of American Indian education*. Minneapolis: Center for Urban and Regional Affairs, University of Minnesota, 1971.

Havighurst, R. J., and Dreyer, P. H. Youth and cultural pluralism. In R. J. Havighurst and P. H. Dreyer (eds.), *Youth*. 74th Yearbook NSSE. Chicago: University of Chicago Press, 1975.

Havighurst, R. J., and Neugarten, B. L. *Society and education* (3rd ed.). Boston: Allyn and Bacon, 1967.

Hawley, P. What women think men think: Does it affect their career choice? *Journal of Counseling Psychology*, 1971, 18(3), 193–199.

Hayakawa, S. I. *Language and thought in action*. New York: Harcourt, 1964.

Heath, R. W., and Nielson, M. A. The research basis for performance-based teacher education. *Review of Educational Research*, 1974, 44(4), 463–484.

Herold, E. S. A dating adjustment scale for college students. *Adolescence*, 1973, 8, 53–60.

Herold, E. S. Variables influencing the dating adjustment of university students. *Journal of Youth and Adolescence*, 1979, 8, 73–79.

Herrnstein, R. IQ. *Atlantic*, 1971, 43–64.

Higgens-Trenk, A., and Gaite, A. Elusiveness of formal operational thought in adolescents. *Proceedings of the 79th Annual Convention of the American Psychological Association*, 1971.

Hindelag, M. J. Age, sex, and the versatility of delinquency involvements. *Social Problems*, 1971, 18, 522–535.

Hirschi, T., and Hindelag, M. J. Intelligence and delinquency: A revisionist review. *American Sociology Review*, 1977, 22, 571–587.

Hoebel, E. A. *The Cheyennes: Indians of the Great Plains*. New York: Holt, 1960.

Hoelter, J. W. The relationship between specific and global evaluations of self: A comparison of several models. *Social Psychology Quarterly*, 1986, 49, 129–141.

Hoffman, V. J. The relationship of psychology to delinquency: A comprehensive approach. *Adolescence*, 1984, 19(74), 55–61.

Holden, G. S. Scholastic aptitude and the relative persistence of vocational choice. *Personnel and Guidance Journal*, 1961, 40, 36–41.

Holland, J. L. A personality inventory employing occupational titles. *Journal of Applied Psychology*, 1958, 42, 336–342.

Holland, J. L. Major programs of research on vocation behavior. In H. Borow (ed.), *Man in a world at work*. Boston: Houghton Mifflin, 1964.

Holland, J. L. *The psychology of vocational choice*. Waltham, MA: Blaisdell, 1966.

Holland, M. Relationships between vocational development and self-concept in sixth grade students. *The Journal of Vocational Behavior*, 1981, 18, 228–236.

Hollingshead, A. B. *Elmstown's youth*. New York: Wiley, 1949.

Holtzman, W. H., Diaz-Guerrero, R., Swartz, J. D., and Lara Tapia, L. Cross-cultural longitudinal research in child development. In J. P. Hill (ed.), *Minnesota symposia on child psychology* (vol. 2). Minneapolis: University of Minnesota Press, 1968.

Hotaling, G. T., Atwell, S. G., and Linsky, A. S. Adolescent life changes and illness: A comparison of three models. *Journal of Youth and Adolescence*, 1978, 7(4), 393–403.

Hudgins, W., and Prentice, N. Moral judgment in delinquent and nondelinquent adolescents and their mothers. *Journal of Abnormal Psychology*, 1973, 82(1), 145–152.

Hundleby, J. D., et al. Adolescent drug use and other behaviors. *Journal of Child Psychology and Psychiatry*, 1982, 23(1), 61–68.

Hunt, J. McV. *Intelligence and experience*. New York: Ronald Press, 1961.

Hunter, F. T., and Youniss, J. Changes in functions of three relations during adolescence. *Developmental Psychology*, 1982, 18, 806–811.

Hurlock, E. B. *Child development*. New York: McGraw-Hill, 1964.

Hurlock, E. B. *Adolescent development*. New York: McGraw-Hill, 1967.

Hurlock, E. B. *Developmental psychology*. New York: McGraw-Hill, 1975.

Husbands, C. T. Some social and psychological consequences of the American dating system. *Adolescence*, 1970, 5(20), 451–462.

Illich, I. *Deschooling society*. New York: Harper and Row, 1971.

Inhelder, B., and Piaget, J. *The growth of logical thinking from childhood to adolescence*. New York: Basic Books, 1958.

Jackson, P. W., and Getzels, J. W. Psychological health and classroom functioning: A study of dissatisfaction with school among adolescents. *Journal of Educational Psychology*, 1959, 50, 295–300.

Jackson, P. W., and Lahaderne, H. M. Scholastic success and attitude toward school in a population of sixth graders. *Journal of Educational Psychology*, 1967, 58, 15–18.

Jackson, S. The growth of logical thinking in normal and subnormal children. *British Journal of Educational Psychology*, 1965, 35, 255–258.

James, W. *Psychology: The briefer course*. New York: Holt, 1910.

Jennings, J. Children, sugar and premature sexuality. *Prevention*, October 1975, 178–184.

Jessor, S. L., and Jessor, R. Maternal ideology and adolescent problem behavior. *Developmental Psychology*, 1974, 10, 246–254.

Jessor, S. L., and Jessor, R. Transition from virginity to nonvirginity among youth: A social-psychological study over time. *Developmental Psychology*, 1975, 11(4), 473–484.

Johnson, E. G. The impact of high school teachers on the educational plans of college freshmen. Testing and Counseling Service Report No. 32 (mimeo). Orono: University of Maine, 1967.

Johnson, F. L., and Aries, E. J. Conversational patterns among same-sex pairs of late adolescent close friends. *Journal of Genetic Psychology*, 1983, 142, 225–238.

Johnston, L. D., and Bachman, J. G. The functions of educational institutions in adolescent development. In J. F. Adams (ed.), *Understanding adolescents*. Boston: Allyn and Bacon, 1973.

Johnston, L. D., Bachman, J. G., and O'Malley, P. M. *Student drug use in America: 1975–1981*. Rockville, MD: National Institute on Drug Abuse, 1981.

Jones, M. C. The later careers of boys who were early- or late-maturing. *Child Development*, 1957, 28, 113–128.

Jones, M. C. Psychological correlates of somatic development. *Child Development*, 1965, 36, 899–911.

Jones, M. C., and Bayley, N. Physical maturing among boys as related to behavior. *Journal of Educational Psychology*, 1950, 41, 129–148.

Jones, M. C., and Mussen, P. H. Self-conceptions, motivations and interpersonal attitudes of early- and late-maturing girls. *Child Development*, 1958, 29, 491–501.

Jordan, W. D. Searching for adulthood in America. In E. H. Erikson (ed.), *Adulthood*. New York: Norton, 1978.

Jurich, A. P., and Jurich, J. A. The effect of cognitive moral development upon the selection of premarital sexual standards. *Journal of Marriage and the Family*, November 1974, 736–741.

Kaats, G. R., and Davis, K. E. The dynamics of sexual behavior of college students. *Journal of Marriage and the Family* 1970, 32, 390–399.

Kagan, J., and Moss, H. *Birth to maturity*. New York: Wiley, 1962.

Kahl, J. A. *The American class structure*. New York: Holt, 1957.

Kandel, D. B., et al. Antecedents of adolescent initiation into stages of drug use: A developmental analysis. *Journal of Youth and Adolescence*, 1978, 7, 13–40.

Kanter, J. F., and Zelnik, M. Sexual experience of young unmarried women in the United States. *Family Planning Perspectives*, 1972, 4, 9–18.

Katz, P., and Zigler, E. Self-image disparity: A developmental approach. *Journal of Personality and Social Psychology*, 1967, 5, 186–195.

Keasey, C. B. Implicators of cognitive development for moral reasoning. In D. J. DePalma and J. M. Foley (eds.), *Moral development: Current theory and research*. Hillsdale, NJ: Lawrence Erlbaum Associates, 1975.

Keniston, K. Student activism, moral development, and morality. *American Journal of Orthopsychiatry*, 1970, 40, 577–592.

Keniston, K. Prologue: Youth as a stage of life. In R. J. Havighurst and P. H. Dreyer (eds.), *Youth*. 74th Yearbook NSSE. Chicago: University of Chicago Press, 1975.

Kennedy, W. A. *Child psychology*. Englewood Cliffs, NJ: Prentice-Hall, 1975.

Kerpelman, L. C. Student activism and ideology in higher education institutions. Final Report, Project No. 8A-028, Washington, DC: Bureau of Research, U.S. Office of Education, March 1970.

Kessen, W. The American child and other cultural inventions. *American Psychologist*, 1979, 34(10), 815–820.

Khan, A. U., Heterogeneity of suicidal adolescents. *Journal of the American Academy of Child and Adolescent Psychiatry*, 1987, 26, 1, 92–96.

Kiell, N. *The universal experience of adolescence*. New York: International Universities Press, 1964.

Kimmel, D. C., and Weiner, I. B. *Adolescence: A developmental transition*. Hillsdale, NJ: Lawrence Erlbaum and Associates, 1985.

Kinsey, A. C., Pomeroy, W. B., and Martin, C. E. *Sexual behavior in the human female*. Philadelphia: Saunders, 1953.

Kirkwood, J. *There must be a pony*. New York: Avon Books, 1960.

Klausmeier, H. J., and Goodwin, W. *Learning and human abilities*. New York: Harper and Row, 1966.

Kleiber, D. A., and Manaster, G. J. Youth's outlook on the future: A past-present comparison. *Journal of Youth and Adolescence*. 1972, 1(3), 223–232.

Kleinfeld, J. The relative importance of teachers and parents in the formation of Negro and white students' academic self-concept. *Journal of Educational Research*, 1972, 65(5), 211–212.

Knox, R. A. Study finds no norms in girls coming of age. *Boston Evening Globe*, March 26, 1976.

Kohlberg, L. The development of modes of moral thinking and choice in the years ten to sixteen. Unpublished doctoral dissertation, University of Chicago, 1958.

Kohlberg, L. Development of moral character and ideology. In M. L. Hoffman (ed.), *Review of child development research* (vol. 1). New York: Russell Sage Foundation, 1964.

Kohlberg, L. Stage and sequence: The cognitive developmental approach to socialization. In D. A. Goslin (ed.), *Handbook of socialization theory and practice*. Chicago: Rand McNally, 1969.

Kohlberg, L. Continuities and discontinuities in childhood and adult moral development revisited. In *Collected papers on moral development and moral education* (mimeo), 1973.

Kohlberg, L. *Essays on moral development: The psychology of moral development* (vol. 2). New York: Harper and Row, 1984.

Kohlberg, L., and Gilligan, C. *The adolescent as a philosopher: The discovery of the self in a postconventional world.* Daedalus, Fall 1971, 1051–1086.

Kohlberg, L., and Turiel, E. *Recent research in moral development.* New York: Russell Sage Foundation, 1971.

Konopka, G. Adolescent girls: A two-year study. *Center for Youth Development and Research Quarterly Focus.* University of Minnesota, Fall 1975.

Kovach, J. A., and Glickman, N. W. Levels and psychosocial correlates of adolescent drug use. *Journal of Youth and Adolescence*, 1986, 15(1), 61–68.

Kramer, R. Moral development in young adulthood. Unpublished doctoral dissertation, University of Chicago, 1968.

Kratcoski, P. C., and Kratcoski, J. E. Changing patterns in the delinquent activities of boys and girls: A self-reported delinquency analysis. *Adolescence*, 1975, 10, 83–95.

Krau, E., The crystallization of work values in adolescence: A sociocultural approach. *Journal of Vocational Behavior*, 1987, 30, 103–123.

Kraus, J. Juvenile drug abuse and delinquency: Some differential associations. *British Journal of Psychiatry*, 1981, 139, 422–430.

Krebs, R. L. Moral judgment and ego controls as determinants of resistance to cheating. Unpublished manuscript, 1971.

Krogman, W. M. A handbook of the measurement and interpretation of height and weight in the growing child. *Monograph for Social Research on Child Development*, 1943, 13(3), (Whole No. 48).

Kuhlen, R. G. *The psychology of adolescent development.* New York: Harper and Row, 1952.

Kuhn, D., Langer, J., Kohlberg, L., and Haan, N. The development of formal operations in logical and moral judgment. Unpublished manuscript, 1971.

Kuhn, D., Langer, J., Kohlberg, L., and Haan, N. S. The development of formal operations in logical and moral judgment. *Genetic Psychology Monographs*, 1977, 95, 97–188.

Labouvie, E. W., and McGee, C. R. Relation of personality to alcohol and drug use in adolescence. *Journal of Consulting and Clinical Psychology*, 1986, 54(3), 289–293.

Lahaderne, H. M. Attitudinal and intellectual correlates of attention: A study of four sixth-grade classrooms. *Journal of Educational Psychology*, 1968, 59, 320–324.

Lameke, L. The impact of sex-role orientation on self-esteem in early adolescence. *Child Development*, 1982, 53(6), 1530–1535.

Landis, P. H. *Adolescence and youth.* New York: McGraw-Hill, 1945.

Landsbaum, J. B., and Willis, R. H. Conformity in early and late adolescence. *Developmental Psychology*, 1971, 4(3), 334–337.

Larson, L. E. An examination of the salience hierarchy during adolescence: The influence of the family. *Adolescence*, 1974, 9(34), 317–332.

Lavin, D. E. *The prediction of academic performance.* New York: Russell Sage Foundation, 1965.

Lay, R., and Wakstein, J. Race, academic achievement and self-concept of ability. *Research in Higher Education*, 1985, 22(1), 43–64.

Leadbetter, B. J., and Dione, J. P. The adolescent's use of formal operational thinking in solving problems related to identity formation. *Adolescence*, 1981, 16, 111–121.

Lecky, P. *Self-consistency: A theory of personality.* New York: Island Press, 1945.

Lecky, P. *Self-consistency.* New York: Island Press, 1951.

Leming, J. S. Moral reasoning, sense of control, and social-political activism among adolescents. *Adolescence*, 1974, 9, 507–528.

Lerner, R. M. Adolescent development: Scientific study in the 1980s. *Youth and Society*, 1981, 12(3), 251–275.

Lerner, R. M., and Knapp, J. R. Actual and perceived intrafamilial attitudes of late adolescents and their parents. *Journal of Youth and Adolescence*, 1975, 4, 17–36.

Levine, C., Kohlberg, L., and Hewer, A. The current formulation of Kohlberg's theory and a response to critics. *Human Development*, 1985, 28, 94–100.

Lewin, K. *Principles of topological psychology.* New York: McGraw-Hill, 1936.

Lewin, K. Field theory and experiment in social psychology: Concepts and methods. *American Journal of Sociology*, 1939, 44, 868–897.

Lewin, K. *Field theory in social science.* New York: Harper and Row, 1951.

Lidz, T. The adolescent and his family. In G. Caplan and S. Lebovici (eds.), *Adolescence: Psychosocial perspectives.* New York: Basic Books, 1969.

Livson, N., and Peskin, H. Perspectives on adolescence from longitudinal research. In J. Adelson (ed.), *Handbook of adolescent psychology.* New York: Wiley, 1980.

Loeber, R. The stability of antisocial and delinquent child behavior: A review. *Child Development*, 1982, 53, 1431–1446.

Lovell, K. A follow-up study of Inhelder and Piaget's The Growth of Logical Thinking. *British Journal of Psychology*, 1961, 52, 143–153.

Lovell, K. Some problems associated with formal thought and its assessment. In D. R. Green et al. (eds.), *Measurement and Piaget.* New York: McGraw-Hill, 1971.

Lovell, K., and Butterworth, I. Abilities underlying the understanding of proportionality. *Mathematics Teaching*, 1966, 37, 5–9.

Lovell, K., and Shields, J. Some aspects of the study of the gifted child. *British Journal of Educational Psychology*, 1967, 37, 201–208.

Luckey, E., and Nass, G. A. A comparison of sexual attitudes and behavior in an international sample. *Journal of Marriage and the Family*, May 1969, 364–379.

Lueptow, L. B. Social change and sex-role change in adolescent orientations toward life, work, and achievement: 1964–1975. *Social Psychology Quarterly*, 1980, 43(1), 48–59.

Lunneborg, P. W. Role model influencers of nontraditional women. *Journal of Vocational Behavior*, 1982, 20, 276–281.

MacFarlane, J., Allen, L., and Honzik, M. *A developmental study of the behavior problems of normal children between 21 months and 14 years.* Berkeley: University of California Press, 1954.

McCandless, B. R. *Adolescents: Behavior and development.* Hinsdale, IL: Dryden Press, 1970.

McCord, W., McCord, J., and Zola, I. Origins of crime: *A new evaluation of the Cambridge-Somerville youth study.* New York: Columbia University Press, 1959.

Maccoby, E. E., and Jacklin, C. N. *The psychology of sex differences.* Stanford, CA: Stanford University Press, 1974.

Maddi, S. *Personality theories: A comparative analysis.* Homewood, IL: Dorsey Press, 1980.

Malina, R. M. Adolescent changes in size, build, composition and performance. *Human Biology*, 1974, 46, 117–131.

Malina, R. M. Secular changes in size and maturity: Causes and effects. In A. F. Roche (ed.), Secular trends in human growth, maturation, and development. *Monographs of the Society for Research in Child Development*, 1979, 44 (3–4, Serial #179).

Mallet-Joris, F. *The paper house.* New York: Farrar, Straus, and Giroux, 1971.

Manaster, G. J. Coping styles, sense of competence, and achievement. Unpublished doctoral dissertation, University of Chicago, 1969.

Manaster, G. J. Coping style, sense of competence, and achievement. Paper presented at the annual meeting of the American Educational Research Association Meeting, 1972.

Manaster, G. J., Ahuja, S. J., and Pannu, P. S. Occupational aspirations and expectations of adolescents in India. *Journal of Psychological Research*, 1976, 20.

Manaster, G. J., and Ahumada, R. Adolescent occupational aspirations and expectations in Puerto Rico and Mexico. *Revista Internamericana de Psicologia*, 1970, 4, 81–94.

Manaster, G. J., and Corsini, R. J. *Individual psychology: Theory and practice.* Itasca, IL: F. E. Peacock Publishers, 1982.

Manaster, G. J., Friedman, S. T., and Larson, P. Pre-med students' survivability and specialization. *Psychological Reports*, 1976, 39, 35–45.

Manaster, G. J., Greer, D. L., and Kleiber, D. A. Youth's outlook on the future, III: A second past-present comparison. *Youth and Society*, 1985, 17(1), 97–112.

Manaster, G. J., and Havighurst, R. J. *Cross-national research: Social-psychological methods and problems.* Boston: Houghton-Mifflin, 1972.

Manaster, G. J., and King, M. R. Mexican-American group cohesiveness and academic achievement. *Urban Education*, October 1972, 235–240.

Manaster, G. J., and King, M. Early recollections of male homosexuals. *Journal of Individual Psychology*, 1973, 29, 26–33.

Manaster, G. J., and Perryman, T. B. Early recollection and occupational choice. *Journal of Individual Psychology*, 1974, 30, 232–237.

Manaster, G. J., Saddler, C. D., and Wukasch, L. The ideal self and cognitive development in adolescence. *Adolescence*, 1977, 7(48), 547–558.

Marcia, J. E. Development and validation of ego identity status. *Journal of Personality and Social Psychology*, 1966, 3, 551–558.

Marcia, J. E. Identity in adolescence. In J. Adelson (ed.), *Handbook of adolescent psychology*. New York: Wiley, 1980.

Marlowe, H. A., Jr. Social intelligence: Evidence for multidimensionality and construct independence. *Journal of Educational Psychology*, 1986, 78, 1, 52–58.

Marsh, H. W., and Shavelson, R. Self-concept: Its multifaceted, hierarchical structure. *Educational Psychology*, 1985, 20(3), 107–123.

Martineau, P. Adulthood in the adolescent perspective. *Adolescence*, 1966, 1(3), 272–280.

Mayle, P. *What's happening to me?* Secaucus, NJ: Lyle Stuart, 1975.

Mead, M. *Growing up in New Guinea*. New York: New American Library, 1935.

Mednick, S. S., and Christiansen, K. O. *Biosocial bases of criminal behavior*. New York: Gardner Press, 1977.

Meisels, M., and Canter, F. M. A note on the generation gap. *Adolescence*, 1971, 6, 523–530.

Meilman, P. W. Cross-sectional age changes in ego identity status during adolescence. *Developmental Psychology*, 1979, 15, 230–231.

Merelman, R. M. Role and personality among adolescent political activitists. *Youth and Society*, 1985, 17(1), 37–68.

Miller D. C. and Form, W. *Industrial sociology*. NY: Harper & Row, 1951.

Miller, G. W. Factors in school achievement and social class. *Journal of Educational Psychology*, 1970, 61, 260–269.

Miller, J. D., et al. *National survey on drug abuse: Main findings, 1982*. Rockville, MD: National Institute on Drug Abuse, 1983.

Miller, K. A., Kohn, M. L., and Schooler, C. Educational self-direction and the cognitive functioning of students. *Social Forces*, 1985, 63, 923–944.

Miller, K. A., Kohn, M. L., and Schooler, C. Educational self-direction and personality. *American Sociological Review*, 1986, 51, 372–390.

Miller, P. Y., and Simon, W. The development of sexuality in adolescence. In J. Adelson (ed.), *Handbook of adolescent psychology*. New York: Wiley, 1980.

Miller, W. B. Gangs, groups and serious youth crime. In D. Shichor and D. H. Kelly (eds.), *Critical issues in juvenile delinquency*. Lexington, MA: D. C. Heath, 1980.

Mirande, A. M. Reference group theory and adolescent sexual behavior. *Journal of Marriage and the Family*, 1968, 30, 572–577.

Mischel, W. Sex-typing and socialization. In P. H. Mussen (ed.), *Carmichael's manual of child psychology*. New York: Wiley, 1970.

Mitchell, J., and Dodder, R. A. Types of neutralization and types of delinquency. *Journal of Youth and Adolescence*, 1983, 12, 307–318.

Money, J., and Clopper, R. R., Jr. Psychosocial and psychosexual aspects of errors of pubertal onset and development. *Human Biology*, 1974, 46, 173–181.

Monge, R. H. Developmental trends in factors of adolescent self-concept. *Developmental Psychology*, 1973, 8(3), 382–393.

Morgan, J. C. Adolescent problems and the Mooney problem check list. *Adolescence*, 1969, 4, 111–126.

Morris, H. Aggressive behavior disorders of childhood. *American Journal of Psychiatry*, 1956, 112, 991–996.

Morrison, R. L. Self-concept implementation in occupational choices. *Journal of Counseling Psychology*, 1962, 9, 255–260.

Moss, J. J., Apolonio, F., and Jensen, M. The premarital dyad during the sixties. *Journal of Marriage and the Family*. 1971, 33, 1–10.

Mowsesian, R. *Golden goals, rusted realities: Work and aging in America*. Far Hills, NJ: New Horizon Press, 1986.

Mullener, N., and Laird, J. D. Some developmental changes in the organization of self-evaluations. *Developmental Psychology*, 1971, 5(2), 233–236.

Munns, M. Is there really a generation gap? *Adolescence*, 1971, 6, 197–206.

Munns, M. The values of adolescents compared with parents and peers. *Adolescence*, 1972, 7, 519–524.

Murphy, J. M., and Gilligan, C. Moral development in late adolescence and adulthood: A critique and reconstruction of Kohlberg's theory. *Human Development*, 1980, 23, 77–104.

Murphy, L. B. *The widening world of childhood: Paths toward mastery*. New York: Basic Books, 1962.

Mussen, P. H., and Bouterline-Young, H. Relationship between rate of physical maturing and personality among boys of Italian descent. *Vita Humana*, 1964, 7, 186–200.

Mussen, P. H., Conger, J. J., and Kagan, J. *Child development and personality*. New York: Harper and Row, 1969.

Mussen, P. H., and Jones, M. C. Self-conceptions, motivations and interpersonal attitudes of late- and early-maturing boys. *Child Development*, 1957, 28, 243–256.

Muuss, R. E. *Theories of adolescence*. New York: Random House, 1968.

Muuss, R. E. Social cognition: Robert Selman's theory of role taking. *Adolescence*, 1982, 17(67), 499–525.

National Center for Educational Statistics. *High school and beyond: A capsule description of high school students*. Washington, DC: U.S. Government Printing Office, 1981.

Neilson, P. Shirley's babies after fifteen years. *Journal of Genetic Psychology*, 1948, 73, 175–186.

Neimark, E. D. Intellectual development during adolescence. In F. D. Horowitz (ed.) *Review of child development research*. Vol. 4, Chicago: University of Chicago Press, 1975.

Nelson, G. The relationship between dimensions of classroom and family environments and the self-concept, satisfaction and achievement of grade 7 and 8 students. *Journal of Community Psychology*, 1984, 12, 276–287.

Nesselroade, J. R., and Baltes, P. B. Adolescent personality development and historical change: 1970–1972. *Monographs of the Society for Research in Child Development*, 1974, 39, 1.

Neufield, I. Application of individual psychological concepts in psychosomatic medicine. *Journal of Individual Psychology*, 1955, 11, 104–117.

Newcomb, M.C., Maddahian, E., and Bentler, P.M. Risk factors for drug use among adolescents: Concurrent and longitudinal analyses. *American Journal of Public Health*, 1986, 76(5), 525–531.

Nichols, R. C. Nature and nurture in adolescence. In J. F. Adams (ed.), *Understanding adolescents*. Boston: Allyn and Bacon, 1973.

Nottlelmann, E. D. Competence and self-esteem during transition from childhood to adolescence. *Developmental Psychology*, 1987, 23(3), 441–450.

Nowicki, S., and Segal, W. Perceived parental characteristics, locus of control orientation, and behavioral correlates of locus of control. *Developmental Psychology*, 1974, 10, 33–37.

Offer, D. Studies of normal adolescents. *Adolescence*, 1966/1967, 1(4), 305–320.

Offer, D. *The psychological world of the teenager*. New York: Basic Books, 1969.

Offer, D., and Offer, J. A longitudinal study of normal adolescent boys. *American Journal of Psychiatry*, 1970, 126, 917–924.

O'Malley, P., and Bachman, J. Self-esteem and education: Sex and cohort comparisons among high school seniors. *Journal of Personality and Social Psychology*, 1979, 37(7), 1153–1179.

Oppenheimer, E. A. The relationship between certain self-constructs and occupational preferences. *Journal of Counseling Psychology*, 1966, 13, 191–197.

Oshman, H., and Manosevitz, M. The impact of the identity crisis on the adjustment of late adolescent males. *Journal of Youth and Adolescence*, 1974, 3(3), 207–216.

Osipow, S. H. *Theories of career development*. New York: Appleton-Century-Crofts, 1968.

Osipow, S. H. *Theories of career development* (3rd ed.). Englewood Cliffs, NJ: Prentice-Hall, 1983.

Osipow, S. H., Ashby, J. D., and Wall, H. W. Personality types and vocational choice: A test of Holland's theory. *Personnel and Guidance Journal*, 1966, 45, 37–42.

Osterrieth, P. A. Adolescence: Some psychological aspects. In G. Caplan and S. Lebovici (eds.), *Adolescence: Psychology perspectives*. New York: Basic Books, 1969.

Packard, V. *The sexual wilderness*. New York: Pocket Books, 1970.

Page, R. A. Longitudinal evidence for the sequentiality of Kohlberg's stages of moral judgment in adolescent males. *Journal of Genetic Psychology*, 1981, 139, 3–9.

Paris, S. G., and Lindauer, B. K. The development of cognitive skills during childhood. In B. B. Wolman (ed.), *Handbook of developmental psychology*. Englewood Cliffs, NJ: Prentice-Hall, 1982.

Parsons, F. *Choosing a vocation*. Boston: Houghton Mifflin, 1909.

Parsons, T., and Bales, R. F. Family, socialization and interaction process. Glencoe, IL: *The Free Press*, 1955.

Patterson, F. The purpose and trend of the conference. In W. C. Kvaraceus et al. (eds.), *Negro self-concept: Implications for school and citizenship*. New York: McGraw-Hill, 1965.

Pearson, H. *G.B.S.: A full-length portrait*. New York: Harper and Row, 1942.

Peck, R. F., et al. *Coping styles and achievement: A cross-national study of school children* (vol. 5). Final Report, HEW, Contract OE-85–063, 1973.

Peck, R. F., and Galliani, C. Intelligence, ethnicity, and social roles in adolescent society. *Sociometry*, 1962, 25(1), 64–72.

Peck, R. F., and Havighurst, R. J. *The psychology of character development*. New York: Wiley, 1960.

Peel, E. A. *The pupil's thinking*. London: Oldbourne, 1960.

Peel, E. A. Intellectual growth during adolescence. In R. E. Grinder (ed.), *Studies in adolescence*. New York: Macmillan, 1963.

Peel, E. A. Predilection for generalising and abstracting. *British Journal of Educational Psychology*, 1975, 45, 177–188.

Perrone, P. A. Factors influencing high school seniors' occupational preferences. *Personnel and Guidance Journal*, 1964, 42, 976–980.

Pesch, H. G. Sex variations of eighth-grade students on Piagetian task performance. *Journal of Genetic Psychology* 1984, 146(1), 141–142.

Peskin, H. Pubertal onset and ego functioning. *Journal of Abnormal Psychology*, 1967, 72(1), 1–15.

Pestrak, V. A., and Martin, D. Cognitive development and aspects of adolescent sexuality. *Adolescence*, 1985, 20(80), 981–987.

Peters, J. F. Adolescents as socialization agents to parents. *Adolescence*, 1985, 20(80), 921–933.

Petersen, A. C. Can puberty come any earlier? *Psychology Today*, 1979, 12(9).

Petersen, A. C. Those gangly years. *Psychology Today*, September 1987, 28–34.

Petroni, F. A. Adolescent liberalism: The myth of a generation gap. *Adolescence*, 1972, 7(26), 221–232.

Phelps, H. R., and Horrocks, J. E. Factors influencing informal groups of adolescents. *Child Development*, 1958, 29, 69–86.

Phye, G. D. and Sola, J. L. Stability of expressive and instrumental traits in an adolescent female population. *Journal of Genetic Psychology*, 1984, 145, 2, 178–184.

Piaget, J. *The psychology of intelligence*. New York: Harcourt, 1947.

Piaget, J. Three lectures. *Bulletin of the Menninger Clinic*, 1962, 26, 120–145.

Piaget, J. Intellectual evaluation from adolescence to adulthood. *Human Development*, 1972, 15, 1–12.

Piaget, J., and Inhelder, B. *The psychology of the child.* New York: Basic Books, 1969.

Polani, P. Chromosome phenotypes—sex chromosomes. In F. C. Fraser and V. A. McKuisick (eds.), *Congenital malformations.* New York: Excerpta Medica, 1970.

Ponzo, Z., and Strowig, R. W. Relations among self-role identity and selected intellectual and non-intellectual factors for high school freshmen and seniors. *Journal of Educational Research,* 1973, 67(3), 137–141.

Poole, M. E., and Cooney, G. H. Careers: Adolescent awareness and exploration of possibilities for self. *Journal of Vocational Behavior,* 1985, 26, 251–263.

Porter, J. K. Predicting the vocational plans of high school senior boys. *Personnel and Guidance Journal,* 1954, 33, 215–218.

Powell, G. J., and Fuller, M. Self-concept and school desegregation. *American Journal of Orthopsychiatry,* 1970, 40, 303–304.

Proefrock, D. W. Adolescence: Social fact and psychological concept. *Adolescence,* 1981, 16(64), 851–858.

Purkey, W. W. *Self-concept and school achievement.* Englewood Cliffs, NJ: Prentice-Hall, 1970.

Ramsey, C. V. Sex information of younger boys. *American Journal of Orthopsychiatry,* 1943, 13, 347–352.

Raphael, D., and Xerlowski, H. G. Identity status in high school students: Critique and a revised paradigm. *Journal of Youth and Adolescence,* 1980, 9, 383–389.

Ray, L. Y., and Johnson, N. Adolescent suicide. *Personnel and Guidance Journal,* 1983, 62, 3, 131–134.

Reimer, J. W. Deviance as fun. *Adolescence,* 1981, 16(61), 39–43.

Reiss, I. L. *Premarital sexual standards in America.* New York: Free Press, 1960.

Reiss, I. L. The sexual renaissance: A summary and analysis. *Journal of Social Issues,* 1966, 22, 123–137.

Reiss, I. L. *The social context of premarital sexual permissiveness.* New York: Holt, 1967.

Reiss, I. L. Premarital sexual standards. In C. B. Broderick and J. Bernard (eds.), *The individual, sex, and society.* Baltimore: Johns Hopkins Press, 1969.

Reister, A. E., and Zucker, R. A. Adolescent social structure and drinking behavior. *Personnel and Guidance Journal,* 1968, 46, 304–312.

Rest, J. Morality. In P. Mussen (ed.), *Carmichael's manual of child psychology* (vol. 4). New York: Wiley, 1983.

Rest, J. R., Davison, M. L., and Robbins, S. Age trends in judging moral issues: A review of cross-national, longitudinal and sequential studies of the Defining Issues Test. *Child Development,* 1978, 49, 263–279.

Rice, F. P. *The adolescent: Development, relationships and culture.* Boston: Allyn and Bacon, 1975.

Richman, C. L., Clark, M. L., and Brown, K. P. General and specific self-esteem in late adolescent students: Race × gender × SES effects. *Adolescence,* 1985, 20(70), 555–566.

Roche, A. F. Secular trends in human growth, maturation, and development. *Monographs of the Society for Research in Child Development*, 1979, 44 (3–4, Serial #179).

Roche, J. P. Premarital sex: Attitudes and behavior by dating stage. *Adolescence*, 1986, 21(81), 107–121.

Roe, A. *The psychology of occupations*. New York: Wiley, 1956.

Roe, A. Early determinants of vocational choice. *Journal of Counseling Psychology*, 1957, 4, 212–217.

Roe, A., and Siegelman, M. The origins of interest. *APGA Inquiry Studies, No. 1*. Washington, DC: American Personnel and Guidance Association, 1964.

Roff, M., and Sells, S. B. Relations between intelligence and sociometric status in groups differing in sex and socio-economic background. *Psychological Reports*, 1965, 28, 511–516.

Rogers, C. R. *Client-centered therapy*. New York: Houghton Mifflin, 1951.

Rogers, D. *The psychology of adolescence*. New York: Appleton-Century-Crofts, 1972.

Rogers, E., and Kincaid, J. *Communications networks: Towards a new paradigm for research*. New York: Free Press, 1982.

Rosenberg, M. *Society and the adolescent self-image*. Princeton, NJ: Princeton University Press, 1965.

Rosenkrantz, P., et al. Sex-role stereotypes and self-concepts in college students. *Journal of Consulting and Clinical Psychology*, 1968, 32(3), 287–295.

Rosenshine, B. and Furst, N. Research on teacher performance criteria. In B. O. Smith (ed.) *Research in teacher education: A symposium*. Englewood Cliffs, N.J.: Prentice-Hall, 1971.

Rousseau, J. J. *Emile*. Translated from the 1762 3dition by B. Foxley. New York: E. P. Dutton, 1911.

Royce, J. E. Does person or self imply dualism? *American Psychologist*, October 1973, 883–886.

Rutter, M. *Changing youth in a changing society*. Cambridge, MA: Harvard University Press, 1980.

Saltzstein, L., Diamond, R. M., and Belensky, M. Moral judgment level and conformity behavior. *Developmental Psychology*, 1972, 7, 327–336.

Salzman, L. Adolescence: Epoch or disease? *Adolescence* 1973, 8, 247–256.

Savin-Williams, R. C., and Demo, D. H. Developmental change and stability in adolescent self-concept. *Developmental Psychology*, 1984, 20, 6, 1100.

Scarr, S., and Weinberg, R. A. The influence of "family background" on intellectual attainment. *American Sociological Review*, 1978, 43, 674–692.

Schaie, K. W. A general model for the study of developmental problems. *Psychological Bulletin*, 1965, 64, 92–107.

Schill, W. J., McCartin, R., and Meyer, K. Youth employment: Its relationship to academic and family variables. *Journal of Vocational Behavior*, 1985, 26, 155–163.

Schoeppe, A., and Havighurst, R. J. A validation of development and adjustment hypotheses of adolescence. *Journal of Educational Psychology*, 1952, 43, 339–353.

Schulz, B., et al. Explaining premarital sexual intercourse among college students: A causal model. *Social Forces*, 1977, 56, 148–164.

Schulz, D. D. *The changing family*. Englewood Cliffs, NJ: Prentice-Hall, 1972.

Schutz, R. A., and Blocher, D. H. Self-satisfaction and level of occupational choice. *Personnel and Guidance Journal*, 1961, 39, 595–598.

Scottish Council for Research in Education. *Social implications of the 1947 Scottish mental survey*. London: University Press, 1953.

Segal, S. J. A psychoanalytic analysis of personality factors in vocational choice. *Journal of Counseling Psychology*, 1961, 8, 202–210.

Segal, S. J., and Szabo, R. Identification in two vocations: Accountants and creative writers. *Personnel and Guidance Journal*. 1964, 43, 252–255.

Seidman, J. *The adolescent*. New York: Dryden Press, 1953.

Selman, R. L. Toward a structural analysis of developing interpersonal relations concepts: Research with normal and disturbed preadolescent boys. In A. D. Pick (ed.), *Minnesota Symposia on Child Psychology* (vol. 10). Minneapolis: University of Minnesota Press, 1976.

Selman, R. L. A structural-developmental model of social cognition: Implications for intervention research. *Counseling Psychologist*, 1977, 6, 3–6.

Selman, R. L. *The growth of interpersonal understanding: Development and clinical analysis*. New York: Academic Press, 1980.

Serok, S., and Blum, A. Rule-violating behavior of delinquent and nondelinquent youth in games. *Adolescence*, 1982, 17, 457–464.

Seward, G. H., and Williamson, R. C. A cross-national study of adolescent professional goals. *Human Development*, 1969, 12, 248–254.

Seward, G. H., and Williamson, R. C. (eds.). *Sex roles in changing society*. New York: Random House, 1970.

Shainberg, D. It really blew my mind: A study of adolescent cognition. *Adolescence*, 1970, 5, 17–36.

Shavelson, R., Hubner, J. J., and Stanton, G. C. Validation of construct interpretations. *Review of Educational Research*, 1976, 46, 407–441.

Shaw, W. J. Delinquency and criminal behavior. In C. E. Walker and M. C. Roberts (eds.), *Handbook of clinical child psychology*. New York: Wiley, 1983.

Shayer, M. Has Piaget's construct of formal operational thinking any utility? *British Journal of Educational Psychology*, 1979, 49, 265–276.

Sherif, C. W. Adolescence: Motivational, attitudinal and personality factors. *Review of Educational Research*, 1966, 36(4), 437–449.

Sherif, M., and Sherif, C. W. *Reference groups*. New York: Harper and Row, 1964.

Sherif, M., and Sherif, C. W. (eds.), *Problems of youth*. Chicago: Aldine, 1965.

Sheppard, B. J. Making the case for behavior as an expression of physiological condition. In B. L. Kratoville (ed.), *Youth in trouble*. San Rafael, CA: Academic Therapy Publications, 1974.

Shibutani, T. *Society and personality*. Englewood Cliffs, NJ: Prentice-Hall, 1961.

Shrum, W., and Cheek, N. H., Jr. Social structure during the school years: Onset of the degrouping process. *American Sociology Review*, 1987, 52, 218–223.

Sieg, A. Why adolescence occurs. *Adolescence*, 1971, 23(6), 337–348.

Silberman, C. E. *Crisis in the classroom*. New York: Random House, 1970.

Simmons, R. G. Blacks and high self-esteem: A puzzle. *Social Psychology*, 1978, 4(1), 54–57.

Simmons, R., Brown, L., Bush, D., and Blyth, D. Self-esteem and achievement of black and white adolescents. *Social Problems*, 1978, 26(1), 86–96.

Simmons, R. G., and Rosenberg, F. Sex, sex roles and self-image. *Journal of Youth and Adolescence*, 1975, 4(3), 229–258.

Simmons, R. G., Rosenberg, F., and Rosenberg, M. Disturbance in the self-image at adolescence. *American Sociological Review*, 1973, 38(5), 553–568.

Simon, W., and Gagnon, J. H. Selected aspects of adult socialization. Unpublished paper, 1967.

Simon, W., and Gagnon, J. H. (eds.). *The sexual scene*. Chicago: Trans-Action Books, 1970.

Simonds, J. F., and Kashani, J. Specific drug use and violence in delinquent boys. *American Journal of Drug and Alcohol Abuse*, 1980, 7(3–4), 305–322.

Simpson, R. L. Parental influence, anticipatory socialization, and social mobility. *American Sociological Review*, 1962, 27, 517–522.

Skipper, J. K., Jr., and Nass, G. Dating behavior: A framework for analysis and an illustration. *Journal of Marriage and the Family*, 1966, 30, 412–420.

Smith, T. E. Some bases for parental influence upon late adolescents: An application of a social power model. *Adolescence*, 1970, 5, 323–338.

Snarey, J. Reply. *Psychology Today*, August 1987, 5.

Snygg, D., and Combs, A. W. *Individual behavior*. New York: Harper and Row, 1949.

Soares, A. T., and Soares, L. M. Self-perceptions of culturally disadvantaged children. *American Educational Research Journal*, 1969, 6, 31–49.

Soares, A. T., and Soares, L. M. Critique of Soares' and Soares' "Self-perceptions of culturally disadvantaged children" — A reply. *American Educational Research Journal*, 1970, 7, 631–635.

Soares, A. T., and Soares, L. M. Comparative differences in the self-perceptions of disadvantaged and advantaged students. *Journal of School Psychology*, 1971, 9, 424–429.

Soares, L. M., and Soares, A. T. Self-concepts of disadvantaged and advantaged students. *Child Study Journal*, 1970/1971, 1, 69–73.

Song, I., and Hattie, J. Home environment, self-concept, and academic achievement: A causal modeling approach. *Journal of Educational Psychology*, 1984, 76, 6, 1269–1281.

Sorenson, R. C. *Adolescent sexuality in contemporary America: Personal values and sexual behavior, ages 13–19*. New York: World Publishing Co., 1973.

Spence, J. T. Comments on Baumrind's "Are androgenous individuals more effective persons and parents." *Child Development*, 1982, 53, 76–80.

Spence, J. T., and Helmreich, R. L. *Masculinity and femininity: Their psychological dimensions, correlates, and antecedents.* Austin: University of Texas Press, 1978.

Spencer, C. P. Selective secondary education, social class and the development of adolescent subcultures. *British Journal of Educational Psychology*, 1972, 42(1), 1–12.

Staton, T. F. *Dynamics of adolescent adjustment.* New York: Macmillan, 1963.

Stefanko, M. Trends in adolescent research: A review of articles published in *Adolescence*, 1976–1981. *Adolescence*, 1984, 19, 1–14.

Stein, B. A., Elliott, K. C., and McKeough, M. J. Trends in adolescent psychopathology. *Canadian Journal of Psychiatry*, 1982, 27, 301–306.

Stein, J. A., Newcomb, M. D., and Bentler, P. M. Personality and drug use: Reciprocal effects across four years. *Personality and Individual Differences*, 1987, 8(3), 419–430.

Steinberg, L. Bound to bicker. *Psychology Today*, September 1987, 36–39.

Steinberg, L., et al. Effects of working on adolescent development. *Developmental Psychology*, 1982, 18, 385–395.

Steinberg, L., and Silverberg, S. B. The vicissitudes of autonomy in early adolescence. *Child Development*, 1986, 57, 841–851.

Steinmann, A. A study of the concept of the feminine role of 51 middle-class American families. *Genetic Psychology Monographs*, 1963, 67, 275–352.

Stendler, C. B. (ed.). *Readings in child behavior and development.* New York: Harcourt, 1964.

Stephens, B., and McLaughlin, J. Analysis of performance by normals and retardates on Piagetian reasoning assessments as a function of verbal ability. *Perceptual and Motor Skills*, 1971, 32, 868–870.

Stephens, W. B., Piaget, J., and Inhelder, B. Application of theory and diagnostic techniques to the area of mental retardation. *Education and Training of Mentally Retarded*, 1966, 1, 75–87.

Stephenson, R. M. Occupational aspirations and plans of 443 ninth graders. *Journal of Educational Research*, 1955, 49, 27–35.

Sternglass, E. J., and Bell, S. Fallout and SAT scores: Evidence for cognitive damage during infancy. *Phi Delta Kappan*, 1983, 64, 539–545.

Stockard, J., Lang, D., and Wood, J. W. Academic merit, status variables, and students' grades. *Journal of Research and Development in Education*, 1985, 18(2), 12–20.

Stockin, B. G. A test of Holland's occupational level formulation. *Personnel and Guidance Journal*, 1964, 42, 599–602.

Stone, C. A., and Day, M. C. Competence and performance models and the characterization of formal operational skill. *Human Development*, 1980, 23, 323–353.

Stone, L. J., and Church, J. *Childhood and adolescence* (2nd ed.). New York: Random House, 1968.

Stubbins, J. The relationship between level of vocational aspiration and certain personal data: A study of some traits and influences bearing on the prestige level of vocational choice. *Genetic Psychology Monographs*, 1950, 41, 327–408.

Sullivan, E. V. A study of Kohlberg's structural theory of moral development: A critique of liberal social science ideology. *Human Development*, 1971, 20, 352–376.

Sullivan, H. S. *The interpersonal theory of psychiatry*. New York: W. W. Norton, 1953.

Super, D. E. Vocational adjustment: Implementing a self-concept. *Occupations*, 1951, 30, 88–92.

Super, D. E. *The psychology of careers*. New York: Harper and Row, 1957.

Super, D. E. Computers in support of vocational development and counseling. In H. Borow (ed.), *Career guidance for a new age*. Boston: Houghton Mifflin, 1973.

Super, D. E., et al. *Vocational development: A framework for research*. New York: Bureau of Publications, Teachers College, Columbia University, 1957.

Super, D. E., et al. *Career development: Self-concept theory*. Princeton, NJ: College Entrance Examination Board, 1963.

Super, D. E., and Bachrach, P. B. *Scientific careers and vocational development theory*. New York: Bureau of Publications, Teachers College, Columbia University, 1957.

Super, D. E., and Crites, J. O. *Appraising vocational fitness* (rev. ed.). New York: Harper and Row, 1962.

Swift, D. F. Family environment and 11 + success: Some basic predictors. *British Journal of Educational Psychology*, 1967, 37, 10–21.

Tanner, J. M. *Education and physical growth*. London: University of London Press, 1961.

Tanner, J. M. Human growth and constitution. In G. A. Harrison, J. S. Weiner, J. M. Tanner, and N. A. Barnicot (eds.), *Human biology: An introduction to human evolution, variation and growth*. Oxford: Clarendon Press, 1964.

Tanner, J. M. The trend towards earlier physical maturation. Working paper, 1965.

Tanner, J. M. Sequence, tempo, and individual variation in the growth and development of boys and girls aged twelve to sixteen. *Daedalus*, 1971, 100(Fall), 907–930.

Taylor, P. H. Children's evaluations of the characteristics of the good teacher. *British Journal of Educational Psychology*, 1962, 32, 258–266.

Terman, L. M., et al. *Genetic studies of genius I: Mental and physical traits of a thousand gifted children*. Stanford, CA: Stanford University Press, 1925.

Tesch, S. A. Review of friendship across the life span. *Human Development*, 1983, 26, 266–276.

Thomas, D. L., and Weigert, A. J. Socialization and adolescent conformity to significant others: A cross-national analysis. *American Sociological Review*, 1971, 36, 835–347.

Thomas, I. E. Family correlates of student political activism. *Developmental Psychology*, 1971, 4, 206–214.

Thomas, L. *The occupational structure and education.* Englewood Cliffs, NJ: Prentice-Hall, 1956.

Thornburg, H. D. Adolescence: A re-interpretation. *Adolescence,* 1970, 5, 463–484.

Thornton, A., and Freedman, D. Consistency of sex role attitudes of women, 1962–1977. Working Paper. Institute for Social Research, University of Michigan, 1980.

Thrasher, F. M. *The gang.* Chicago: University of Chicago Press, 1936.

Tittle, C. R., Villemez, W. J., and Smith, D. A. The myth of social class and criminality: An empirical assessment of the empirical evidence. *American Sociological Review,* 1978, 43, 643–656.

Tolman, E. Kurt Lewin: 1890–1947. *Psychological Record,* 1948, 55, 1–4.

Tomlinson-Keasey, C., and Keasey, C. B. The mediating role of cognitive development in moral judgment. *Child Development,* 1974, 45, 291–298.

Trowbridge, N. T. Self-concept of disadvantaged and advantaged children. Paper presented at the annual meeting of the American Educational Research Association, Minneapolis, March 1970 (a).

Trowbridge, N. T. Effects of socio-economic class on self-concept of children. *Psychology in the Schools,* 1970 (b), 7, 304–306.

Tseng, M. S. Social class, occupational aspiration and other variables. *Journal of Experimental Education,* 1971, 39, 88–92.

Tuddenham, R. The constancy of personality ratings over two decades. *Genetic Psychological Monographs,* 1959, 60, 3–29.

Turiel, E. Conflict and transition in adolescent moral development. *Child Development,* 1974, 45, 14–29.

Turiel, E. The development of social concepts: Mores, customs and conventions. In D. J. DePalma and J. M. Foley (eds), *Moral development: Current theory and research.* Hillsdale, NJ: Erlbaum, 1975.

Turiel, E. Distinct conceptual and developmental domains: Social conventions and morality. In C. B. Keasey (ed.), *Nebraska Symposium on Motivation* (vol. 25). Lincoln: University of Nebraska Press, 1978 (a).

Turiel, E. Social regulations and domains of social concepts. In W. Damon (ed.), *New directions for child development.* Vol. 1, *Social cognition.* San Francisco: Jossey-Bass, 1978 (b).

U'Ren, R. C. A perspective on self-esteem. *Comprehensive Psychiatry,* 1971, 12, 466–472.

Unger, R. K. Toward a redefinition of sex and gender. *American Psychologist.* 1979, 34 (11), 1085–1094.

University of Texas at Austin, Division of Extension. *Adult functional competency: A summary.* Austin: Adult Performance Level Project, March 1975.

U. S. Bureau of the Census. *School enrollment — social and economic characteristics of students: October 1981.* Current Population Reports, Series P-20, No. 373. Washington, DC: U. S. Government Printing Office.

U. S. Department of Labor. *School and work among youth during the 1970s.* Special

Labor Force Report 241. Washington, DC: Bureau of Labor Statistics, January 1981.

Vedder, C. B., and Somerville, D. B. *The delinquent girls* (2nd ed.). Springfield, IL: Charles C. Thomas, 1975.

Vener, A. M., and Stewart, C. S. Adolescent sexual behavior in America revisited: 1970-1973. *Journal of Marriage and the Family*. 1974, 36, 728-735.

Vener, A. M., Stewart, C. S., and Hager, D. L. The sexual behavior of adolescents in middle America: Generational and American-British comparisons. *Journal of Marriage and the Family*, 1972, 34, 696-705.

Vernon, P. Environmental handicaps and intellectual development: Part I. *British Journal of Educational Psychology*, 1965, 35, 9-20.

Voorhees, J. Neuropsychological differences between juvenile delinquents and functional adolescents: A preliminary study. *Adolescence*, 1981, 61, 57-66.

Wallace, J. R., Cunningham, T. F., and Del Monte, V. Change and stability in self-esteem between late childhood and early adolescence. *Journal of Early Adolescence*, 1984, 4(3), 253-257.

Wallach, M. A. Research in children's thinking. In *Child Psychology*, 62nd Yearbook, Part I. NSSE. University of Chicago, 1963.

Warner, W. L., Meeker, M. L., and Eells, K. *Social class in America*. NY: Harper Torchbooks, 1960.

Watson, E. H., and Lowrey, G. H. *Growth and development of children*. Chicago: Year Book Publishers, 1951.

Weed, S. E., and Olsen, J. A. Effects of family-planning programs on teenage pregnancy: Replication and extension. *Family Perspective*, 1982, 20(3), 173-195.

Weiner, A. S. Emotional problems of adolescence: A review of affective disorders and schizophrenia. In C. E. Walker and M. C. Roberts (eds.), *Handbook of Clinical Child Psychology*. New York: Wiley, 1983, 741-758.

Weiner, I. B. *Child and adolescent psychopathology*. New York: Wiley, 1982.

Weisbroth, S. P. Moral judgments, sex, and parental identification in adults. *Developmental Psychology*, 1970, 2, 396-402.

White, R. W. Sense of interpersonal competence. In R. W. White (ed.), *The study of lives*. New York: Atherton, 1964.

Wicker, A. W. Undermanning, performances, and students' subjective experiences in behavior settings of large and small high schools. *Journal of Personality and Social Psychology*, 1968, 10, 255-261.

Wilks, J. The relative importance of parents and friends in adolescent decision making. *Journal of Youth and Adolescence*, 1986, 15(4), 323-333.

Williams, J. E., Bennett, S. M., and Best, D. L. Awareness and expression of sex stereotypes in young children. *Developmental Psychology*, 1975, 11(5), 635-642.

Wilson, A. B. Residential segregation of social classes and aspirations of high school boys. *American Sociological Review*, 1959, 24, 836-845.

Wohlwill, J. F. Methodology and research strategy in the study of developmental change. In L. R. Goulet and P. B. Baltes (eds.), *Life-span developmental psychology*. New York: Academic Press, 1970.

Wolf, A. J. Consciousness four. *Yale Alumni Magazine*, November 1974, 19–21.

Wylie, R. C. Children's estimates of the schoolwork ability as a function of sex, race, and socioeconomic level. *Journal of Personality*, 1963, 31, 204–224.

Yamaguchi, K., and Kandel, D. Drug use and other determinants of premarital pregnancy and its outcome: A dynamic analysis of competing life events. *Journal of Marriage and the Family*, 1987, 49, 257–70.

Yarcheski, A., and Mahon, N. E. Chumship relationships, altruistic behavior and loneliness in early adolescence. *Adolescence*, 1984, 19(76), 913–924.

Yarrow, L., and Yarrow, M. Personality continuity and change in the family context. In P. Worchel and D. Byrne (eds.), *Personality change*. New York: Wiley, 1964.

Youmans, E. G. Occupational expectations of twelfth grade Michigan boys. *Journal of Experimental Education*, 1956, 24, 259–271.

Young, A. M. The difference a year makes in the nation's youth work force. *Monthly Labor Review*, 1979, 102, 34–38.

Youniss, J. *Parents and peers in social development: A Sullivan-Piaget perspective.* Chicago: University of Chicago Press, 1980.

Yudin, L. Formal thought in adolescence as a function of intelligence. In E. Evans (ed.), *Adolescents: Readings in behavior and development*. Hinsdale, IL: Dryden Press, 1970.

Zarb, J. M. Non-academic predictors of successful academic achievement in a normal adolescent sample. *Adolescence*, 1981, 16(64), 891–900.

Zieman, G. L., and Benson, G. P. Delinquency: The role of self-esteem and social values. *Journal of Youth and Adolescence*, 1983, 12, 489–500.

Zirkel, P. A., and Moses, E. G. Self-concept and ethnic group membership among public school students. *American Educational Research Journal*, 1971, 8, 253–265.

NAME INDEX

SUBJECT INDEX

THE BOOK'S MANUFACTURE

Adolescent Development was typeset at
Stanton Publication Services, Inc.,
Minneapolis, Minnesota.
The typefaces are Garamond 49 for text
and display; Helvetica for tables and figures.
Printing and binding were done by
Arcata Graphics, Kingsport, Tennessee.
Cover design and internal design
were done by John B. Goetz,
Design & Production Services Co., Chicago.